Practical WebObjects

CHARLES HILL AND SACHA MALLAIS

APress Media, LLC

Practical WebObjects

Originally published by Apress in 2004
MyCopy version of the original edition 2004

DOI 10.1007/978-1-4302-0751-1

Lead Editor: Steve Anglin
Technical Reviewers: Shehryar Khan and Gary Teter

Project Manager: Tracy Brown Collins
Copy Edit Manager: Nicole LeClerc
Copy Editor: Suzanne Goraj
Production Manager: Kari Brooks
Production Editor: Ellie Fountain
Interior Book Designer: Diana Van Winkle, Van Winkle Design Group
Compositor: Diana Van Winkle, Van Winkle Design Group
Proofreader: Gregory Teague
Indexer: Michael Brinkman
Artist: Diana Van Winkle, Van Winkle Design Group
Cover Designer: Kurt Krames
Manufacturing Manager: Tom Debolski

To my parents Lorne and Rachel and to my wife Laksanavadee,
for their love and support.
—Chuck

To my family and friends for their love and support, to my colleagues
for their good work and expertise, and to the entire WebObjects community
for helping keep WebObjects alive and ticking.
—Sacha

Contents at a Glance

Contents

About the Authors

SACHA MALLAIS has been the president of Global Village Consulting, Inc. since it was founded in 1995. He has been using WebObjects since 1998 and Java since 1999. He received his education from the University of British Columbia, where he primarily studied database design and networking. He lives in British Columbia, where the constant rain gives him a ready-made excuse for playing on his computer instead of going outside.

CHUCK HILL was raised in Manitoba where he learned programming in the days of punched cards. He attended Brandon University, majoring in both Mathematics and Computer Science with a minor in Physics to fill his idle hours. Upon graduation, realizing that a career in COBOL beckoned, he set off to tour the world. After wandering through Africa, India, and Central America, he ended up living in Thailand and Taiwan for almost seven years. He now makes his home in the Canadian Wet Coast city of Vancouver, where Global Village Consulting employs him. On those rare occasions when he is not sitting in front of a computer, he collects and restores old tools and tries to fit in the occasional bit of woodworking.

About the Technical Reviewers

SHEHRYAR KHAN is a Senior Architect at Ubermind Inc. He's been doing WebObjects development since the days of WebObjects 2.0, and did EOF/AppKit-based client server application development before that. Shehryar has successfully led teams of WebObjects developers on large projects for the U.S. government and the financial and telecommunications industries.

GARY TETER is the architect and lead developer of WireHose Server, the leading personalization and smart metadata framework for WebObjects. Formerly CEO and CTO of Bulldog Beach Interactive, he is now focused on refining WireHose and creating other technologies to make the world a better place.

About the Authors

Writing a book is hard work. We've read that many times in the front of other books and we now know it to be true. It's certainly not a job for one or even two people. Writing a book is a collective effort requiring the professional skills of many people. This book would not have been written without the support and assistance of these people.

We will start by thanking Lucas Rockwell of UC Berkeley, who first suggested to Apress that they might want to publish a book on WebObjects. Lucas went on to name names of likely authors, and we were tapped to write the book.

Although their names do not appear on the cover, two additional authors had a hand in three chapters of the book. We would like to thank our two collaborators for sharing their unique WebObjects knowledge and experience with our readers and with us.

Dov Rosenberg (dov.rosenberg@conviveon.com, `http://www.conviveon.com`) wrote chapters 10 and 11 on J2EE and XML. Dov is the president of Conviveon Corporation, an Orlando, Florida–based company. Conviveon sells a WebObjects-based enterprise content management tool called SiteConnect Server, which heavily leverages WebObjects/EOF, XML, and JSP Servlet technology. He also helped design and develop the American Automobile Association's web site, one of the largest non-Apple WebObjects applications on the Internet. Since he discovered WebObjects/Java in 1997 he can't bring himself to suffer lesser technologies. He is married to Cindy (his very understanding wife of nearly 20 years) and has two teenagers, Andrew and Molly.

Pierre Frisch (Pierre@sPearWay.com) wrote Chapter 8 on localization and internationalization. Pierre, an Apple developer since the beginning of Apple's developer program, founded sPearWay Limited (`http://www.spearway.com`) in 1992 to offer comprehensive solutions to serve businesses. He developed the first commercial WebObjects application for luggage lockers in 1997, localized in 37 languages. The most recent sPearWay product is sPearCat, a stand-alone, easy-to-use, multilingual Web catalogue-building tool.

Special thanks are due to our two technical reviewers, Gary Teter and Shehryar Khan. Gary Teter is the genius behind the WebObjects-based WireHose platform (`http://www.wirehose.com`) for building web applications. WireHose can personalize access to any kind of enterprise object; it's a next-generation portal and smart metadata API that's light years ahead of anything offered by Sun, IBM, or BEA. Gary's knowledge of WebObjects is enviable. Shehryar Khan is a senior architect at Übermind (`http://www.ubermind.com/`), a WebObjects and J2EE consulting house. If you are looking for WebObjects training, Übermind offers an excellent WebObjects course. Shehryar was tireless in his suggestions of ways to improve the text. His knowledge of J2EE technologies brought a more informed view to comparisons of those technologies.

Shehryar and Gary's WebObjects expertise benefited the accuracy and quality of this book considerably. Any remaining mistakes are ours alone (and probably due to our not listening to them). Gentlemen, we thank you.

The wonderful people at Apress made writing this book as pleasurable as possible. Tracy Brown Collins worked hard to keep us on some semblance of a schedule despite our best attempts to keep writing forever. If it wasn't for Tracy, we'd probably still be typing and editing.

Thanks to our editor Steve Anglin for supporting our many, many changes as we tried to make the best book we could. Thanks also to Suzanne Goraj, Ellie Fountain, Beth Christmas, and all the unsung heroes who toiled away in the background.

Thanks to Leon Salvail, CEO of Global Village Consulting, for supporting our efforts in writing this book. We also thank Josephine Garcia and Andrew "Muskie" McKay for helping us better understand some of the difficulties in mastering WebObjects.

Chuck would like to thank Jeff Martirano for helping him to truly appreciate the Eclipse IDE, and Sacha would like to thank Steven K. Besler for introducing him to WebObjects in the first place.

Finally, we would like to thank our family and friends for tolerating our absences and preoccupation while writing this book. We promise that we won't do it again!

CHAPTER 1

Making Your Code Better

By the work one knows the workman.

—Jean de La Fontaine

Better a little which is well done, than a great deal imperfectly.

—Plato

In this chapter, we are going to try to explain some of the things that we, as programmers, do to make our own lives easier. We will try to avoid prescribing a particular practice as something you must do; however, we will make a case for several tools and techniques that should help to make your code better.

Eclipse and WOLips/WOProject

This section will describe the Eclipse platform and one of its plug-ins, WOLips (pronounced "woe lips"), which integrates some of the WebObjects tools and concepts with Eclipse. You will learn about using Eclipse and WOLips/WOProject when developing WebObjects apps.

What Is Eclipse?

Eclipse, as we will use it in this book, is an open source, cross-platform IDE. It was originally initiated by IBM, but is now supported by a consortium of other companies, including Borland, Rational Software, Red Hat, Oracle, and others. Eclipse is open source software; the project web page is located at `http://www.eclipse.org/`.

In reality, though, Eclipse is much more than an IDE. It is a platform, as the Eclipse documentation says, "for anything, and for nothing in particular" ("Eclipse Platform Technical Overview," page 2). Eclipse by itself doesn't actually do anything: it is just a set of hooks that Eclipse plug-ins can extend to provide services to users. The standard distribution betrays its focus, though. It includes all of the tools you would expect from a modern IDE for writing Java apps:

- Source editor with syntax highlighting
- Code completion
- Code templates

- Comprehensive searching facility
- Full-featured Java debugger
- Java package explorer and outline view of Java classes
- Javadoc generation
- JUnit test creation and test running
- Incremental compilation
- Refactoring tools
- Configurable key bindings (Emacs bindings built-in)
- Built-in revision control and integration with CVS (others available via plug-ins)
- Update Manager

Eclipse itself is written entirely in Java so can be run on many different platforms, including Mac OS X and Windows (see Figure 1-1).

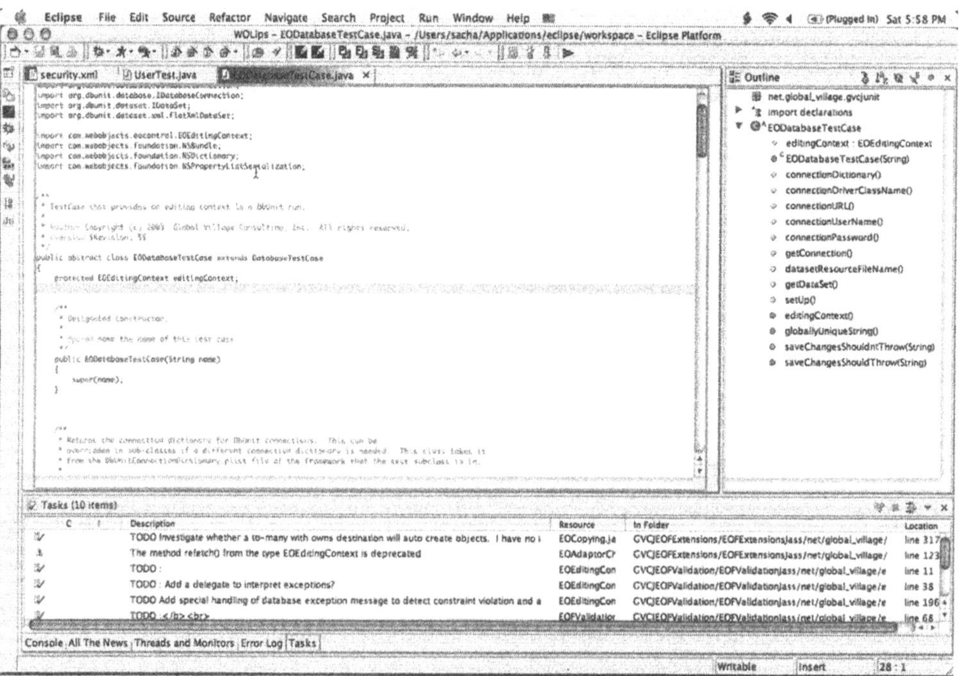

Figure 1-1. *Develop on Mac or Windows.*

What Is WOLips/WOProject?

WOLips is an Eclipse plug-in that brings WebObjects development to Eclipse. Specifically, WOLips maintains the PB.project file (note that this is the older "ProjectBuilderWO" project format and not the newer "ProjectBuilder" format), which allows the other WebObjects tools, such as EOModeler and WOBuilder, to interact with your Eclipse projects in much the same ways as they did with your PB projects.

WOProject is a set of Ant scripts that can be used to build WebObjects framework and application bundles with Ant alone, which WOLips can use to provide build services in Eclipse. WOLips and WOProject are also open source projects, and although not as mature as Eclipse, they do their job very well and are being actively supported and extended.

WOProject was initially developed by Andrei Adamchik with help from Emily Bache and others. Ulrich Koester was the originator of WOLips. The WOLips/WOProject home page can be found at `http://www.objectstyle.org/woproject/`.

■ NOTE Ant is a Java-based build tool, like `make` in purpose but with less nasty build files. Ant uses XML-based configuration files and is extended with Java classes. Yes, Ant is a cross-platform `make` replacement that the rest of us can understand. Part of the Apache Project, Ant can be found at `http://ant.apache.org/`.

Why Use Eclipse and WOLips/WOProject?

Eclipse and WOLips/WOProject require some additional setup and administration to use, so are not always an obvious choice. Add to this the fact that all of the bugs you knew and loved in PB or PBWO are now gone and replaced by other, completely different bugs, and you may not be so keen on working in Eclipse. Don't fret; we have found Eclipse to be well worth the effort, but if you decide you don't want to switch, you will still get lots out of this book. We are going to use Eclipse- and WOLips-format projects in the book to prod people to actually sit down and look at them, but doing so is not required.

You would be most likely to use Eclipse if you were working on Windows, or in an environment with both Mac and Windows (and perhaps other) machines. Several years ago, Apple released a cross-platform (Windows and Mac only) version of their ProjectBuilder IDE. Many users began developing on Windows machines, but in recent years Apple began releasing new versions of ProjectBuilder for Mac only (called PBX, and later, Xcode), and their Windows-compatible version (now called ProjectBuilderWO or PBWO to differentiate it from the newer PBX) languished. Now that PBWO has been end-of-life'd by Apple, Windows users have no Apple alternative for developing in WebObjects; perhaps worse, developing in a mixed environment is now a nightmare, since Windows and Mac users cannot share projects and must create and maintain them separately. With Eclipse, Windows and Mac are once more able to develop WebObjects software together.

PLUG-INS FOR ECLIPSE

Check out all the great plug-ins you can get for Eclipse at `http://www.eclipse.org/community/plugins.html`. Here are some of our favorites:

- **Jass for Eclipse** (`http://www.global-village.net/jass4eclipse`): Integrates Jass (see our discussions about Jass later in the chapter) into Eclipse
- **WOProject/WOLips** (`http://www.objectstyle.org/woproject`): Is strongly suggested for WebObjects development
- **Call Hierarchy** (`http://eclipse-tools.sourceforge.net/call-hierarchy/index.html`): Details what methods call or are called by a given method
- **Tab Navigator** (`http://www.zclipse.org/projects/tabnavigator/`): Along with a gazillion other keyboard enhancements, allows the Tab key to indent Java code to the correct place
- **Eclipse Spell Checker Plug-in** (`http://www.bdaum.de/eclipse/`): Provides spell checking for Java code and property files
- **All The News** (`http://negrej.free.fr/allthenews/index.html`): Satisfies that info addiction

Issues with Eclipse

Eclipse has some stability issues, though no more so than PBX or PBWO. In addition, on OS X, navigating around in Eclipse is a bit sluggish (Eclipse 3 reportedly fixes this problem, and is more stable than even the Apple tools; the final release is due out sometime late 2004). Finally, running applications and unit tests requires some manual setup of classpaths due to the idiosyncrasies of WebObjects. Other than that, though, both Eclipse and WOLips/WOProject are very good, and, in the authors' opinion, well worth the effort.

Pros and Cons

Here we have listed some of the benefits and drawbacks of using Eclipse/WOLips over PB or PBWO. Keep in mind that the Eclipse and WOLips/WOProject teams are actively maintaining and improving these projects, so the situation may have changed by the time you read this.

Pros

Using Eclipse/WOLips will get you this:

- Fully functional Windows development (in particular, a real Java debugger).
- Cross-platform development.
- An open source project with lots of developers working on the Eclipse platform itself as well as on many, many plug-ins. DIYers rejoice!
- Cross-platform development!

- Buckets of productivity tools: templates, perspectives, tool tips, code completion, and others, many of which are not available at any price for PB or PBWO.
- Did we mention cross-platform development?

Cons

But using Eclipse/WOLips has some downsides, too:

- Sluggish user interface on OS X. This is reportedly being worked on for version 3.
- Java files must be placed in a directory structure matching the package structure. This is not the case with either PB or PBWO, so converting existing projects can be a bit of a hassle, especially if you are using a source code control system (and you are, aren't you?) that loses file history when you move files around.
- Less than perfect control of resources. Some resources are not automatically copied into the Resources directory, requiring manual changes to the build file.
- The occasional need for manual classpath setup when running your application (or JUnit tests).
- Some minor stability issues. Version 3 is reported to be very stable.

So, if you want cross-platform WebObjects development and can stand the inevitable foibles of open source software, then you should use Eclipse. If you want a real development environment and you are not on OS X, then you should use Eclipse. Otherwise, stick with PB or PBWO. We have used Eclipse/WOLips for all of the projects in this book as an incentive for you to take Eclipse for a spin.

Automated Unit Testing

How often have you wondered what effect a code change would have on the rest of a system? Ever wanted a code example using a certain method? Or maybe you have just wished you could release a piece of code to your local pointy-haired manager with confidence. With automated unit testing, you can do all these things and more.

The Case for Automated Unit Testing

Automated unit testing is an investment in your future sanity. For a small up-front cost, you help insulate yourself from the biggest bugbear of software development: change. Inevitably, either during the development of a system or during the maintenance of a system, you will be faced with change. Often, the *developer* will be the driving force behind a change: a good developer will refine the design of a system as a more complete understanding of the requirements is gained. Refactoring without automated tests is an exercise in faith: are you sure that your new design will actually work the same as the previous one? Of course, good object-oriented design helps to localize changes that may otherwise ripple throughout the entire system, but even with the best designs, changes often have unanticipated side effects. Automated unit testing helps to mitigate the risks of change.

If that were the only benefit to automated unit testing, it would be worth it. But, as you may have guessed, there's more: unit tests act as usage examples of your code. In other words, unit tests are documentation! Additionally, tests that are run on a regular basis are guaranteed to be in sync with the code they test. This is the best kind of documentation. You needn't worry whether a test shows the current semantics of a method or whether something has changed since they were written: you just run the test.

Finally, automated unit testing gives you confidence in your code. When your manager asks you if your code is ready for release, you can answer with confidence, "It passed all the tests." If you were diligent in writing your tests, you can release your code, knowing that it has actually been "used" in your testing code. And if, despite your best efforts, your code still does have a bug in it, you can later add a test to test that bug to ensure that it never crops up again. Bugs squashed stay squashed.

CAUTION It should be noted that unit testing is not a panacea. It takes discipline to write good test code, code that doesn't directly contribute to "making it go." Managers and clients often don't want to pay for this "extra" time, and it won't make your code bug-free, either: automated unit tests are no substitute for a black-box, independent test cycle. However, if you make the effort to create good tests they *will* pay off in the long run.

JUnit: Java Unit Testing

JUnit is the *de facto* standard package for automated unit testing in Java. It is a set of simple classes that aid in creating, running, and displaying the results of a test run. JUnit is described in detail on the JUnit homepage (`http://www.junit.org/`). JUnit also has several extensions written for it: DbUnit (testing with a database, described further on), JUnitPerf (performance testing), and many others (see `http://www.junit.org/news/extension/index.htm`).

Writing JUnit Tests

The JUnit documentation is very good, but here is just a taste for developers who have not yet had the pleasure of using JUnit. If you are familiar with JUnit, you can skip this section.

The normal way to create tests in JUnit is to subclass `junit.framework.TestCase`. This class allows you to group tests that use similar features of your code (these features are called the fixtures of the test case). Listing 1-1 is an example `TestCase` that tests `java.lang.String`.

Listing 1-1. *A Simple, Partial Test Case for* `java.lang.String`

```
public class StringTest extends TestCase {
    protected String testString;

    public StringTest(String name) {
        super(name);
    }
```

```
    /**
     * Sets up the fixtures.  Called before each test method.
     */
    public void setUp() throws java.lang.Exception {
        super.setUp();
        testString = "This is a test";
    }

    /**
     * Test the replace() method.
     */
    public void testReplace() {
        testString = testString.replace('t', 'T');  // NB: Change testString
        assertTrue(testString.endsWith("TesT"));
    }

    /**
     * Test charAt(). Even though testString was changed in testReplace(),
     * it will be reset by setUp().
     */
    public void testCharAt() {
        assertEquals('T', testString.charAt(0));
        assertEquals('t', testString.charAt(13));
    }
}
```

Of course, this example is pretty trivial, but you can see the basic ideas of JUnit tests:

- Test fixtures are set up before each test in `setUp()` and are torn down after each test in `tearDown()` (this test case doesn't have one, since `testString` will be automatically garbage collected).
- Tests use `assertTrue()`, `assertEquals()`, and others to actually test the code.
- Test class names are prefixed or suffixed with "Test." This allows JUnit (and Eclipse) to determine which classes to examine for tests.
- Test methods are named with a "test" prefix. This allows JUnit (and Eclipse) to automatically identify methods that are tests. You can add helper methods as long as they don't start with "test."
- The constructor is required, but not very useful: just call `super`.

Once you have several test cases, you will probably want to run groups of them all at once, for which JUnit provides the `junit.framework.TestSuite` class. Test suites are subclasses of `junit.framework.TestSuite` that run sets of test cases. You can use them to group logically related test cases and to provide common initialization code for the tests, as shown in Listing 1-2.

Listing 1-2. *A Test Suite*

```
public class AllTestsSuite extends TestSuite {
    public static Test suite() {
        return new AllTestsSuite();
    }

    public AllTestsSuite () {
        super();

        // put global (cross-test case) initialization code here
        // For example, you may want to set connection dictionaries here

        // now add all the tests we want to this suite
        addTest(new TestSuite(StringTest.class));
        addTest(new TestSuite(ClassTest.class));
    }
}
```

Since `TestSuite` implements the `Test` interface, a test suite is run just like any other test.

Using JUnit with WebObjects

You can use JUnit with WebObjects as you would any other tool (see the JUnit documentation): if you don't have Eclipse, you can run the tests manually from the command line, or you can set up a `make` target if you are using PBWO. Also available is WOUnitTest (`http://wounittest.sourceforge.net/`), a framework that allows you to run your tests in the context of a WebObjects application.

JUnit and Eclipse

Using JUnit with Eclipse is remarkably easy. The fine folks who developed Eclipse saw fit to include JUnit with the default distribution, so you don't even need to download any additional software. With WebObjects and the current release of WOLips, however, you will need to do some manual setup of the classpath in order to run tests that use WebObjects resources (see Figure 1-2).

If the bundle you are testing does not have any resources, your test run can use the classpath that JUnit sets up for you. However, most will have resources, which requires that you include on the classpath the framework that was built by WOLips. Depending on whether you are using WOLips' incremental builder or its Ant builder (see the WOLips site for an explanation of the difference), you will have to include either the framework's Java directory (in the Resources directory) or the framework's Jar file (found inside the Java directory) or framework directory (if there is no Jar file). These can be added to the run configuration's classpath using the Advanced button.

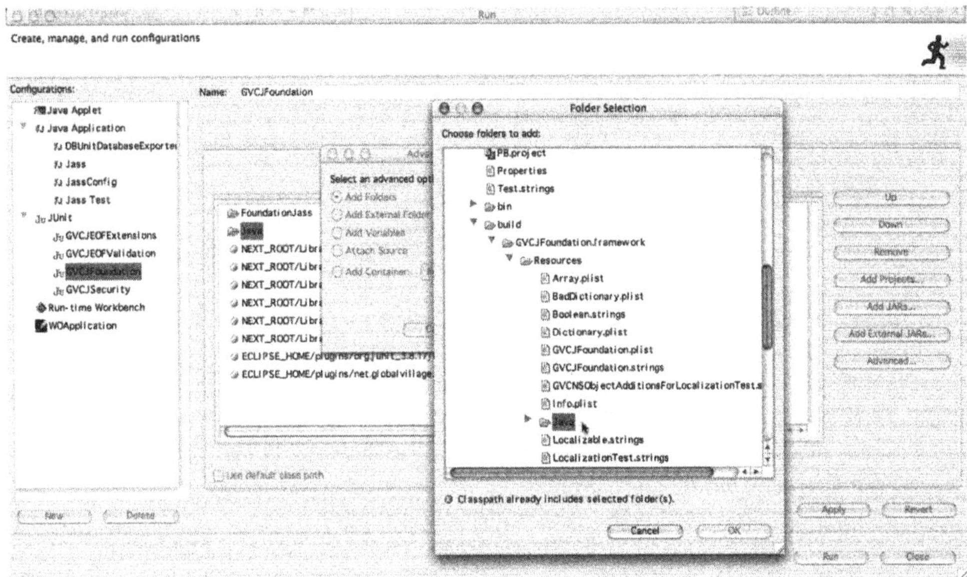

Figure 1-2. *Set up a test run's classpath in Eclipse.*

JUnit and EOF: DbUnit

The Enterprise Objects frameworks (EOF) is, at least in our opinion, the powerhouse of WebObjects development. It allows you to work with objects rather than with SQL and think in terms of the problem you are solving rather than the technology you are using. Unit testing would be of limited use if it couldn't accommodate testing methods backed by EOF. While JUnit doesn't have any specific facilities for testing with a database, DbUnit (`http://dbunit.sourceforge.net/`) is an extension to JUnit that adds the ability to set up a set of database tables to a known state before a test starts.

One of the problems when testing WebObjects applications is getting your data in a consistent state so that you can get consistent results. DbUnit is a tool to help with that exact problem. With DbUnit, you define sets of data in XML files, which are used to populate your database before a test. It also handles clearing the data before and after the test.

Using DbUnit

Using DbUnit is virtually identical to using JUnit, the difference being setting up the database before each test in DbUnit. Normally, you will just subclass `DatabaseTestCase` (part of the DbUnit package), override the `getConnection()` and `getDataSet()` methods, and use it as if it were a JUnit test case (Listing 1-3).

Listing 1-3. *Simple DbUnit-Supported TestCase*

```
public class DatabaseTest extends DatabaseTestCase {
    protected Privilege privilegeOne;

    public DatabaseTest(String name) {
        super(name);
    }

    /**
     * Return a new connection to the database.
     */
    protected IDatabaseConnection getConnection() throws Exception {
        // First, make sure the driver is loaded into the JVM
        Class driverClass = Class.forName("jdbc.FrontBase.FBJDriver ");
        // Get a JDBC connection
        Connection jdbcConnection = DriverManager.getConnection(
                "jdbc:FrontBase://hostName/databaseName ", "user", "password");
        // Make a DBUnit connection out of the JDBC connection
        return new DatabaseConnection(jdbcConnection);
    }

    /**
     * Return the dataset to initialize the database with.
     */
    protected IDataSet getDataSet() throws Exception {
        NSBundle bundle = NSBundle.bundleForClass(getClass());
        String dataPath =
            resourcePathForLocalizedResourceNamed("dataset.xml", null);
        byte[] dataBytes = bundle.bytesForResourcePath(dataPath);
        String dataString = new String(dataBytes);
        return new FlatXmlDataSet(new StringReader(dataString));
    }


    // An example test
    public void testUserExists() {
        assertTrue(User.userExists("Name One", new EOEditingContext()));
    }
}
```

Some of you are probably a little worried that this test class uses non-EOF technology. Well, you're right: it uses DbUnit and JDBC directly in addition to EOF. But don't worry; EOF won't get confused or anything. We use DbUnit and JDBC to set up and tear down the database, but EOF should be used for everything else, as you would expect.

Unless you need more control of the setup/teardown procedure, that's all you'll ever need to know. From here, you just write tests like any other JUnit test. You may want to define an abstract superclass for all of your tests so that the connection creation is localized (and/or you could put the connection string into a configuration file). In our own projects, we have created a DatabaseTestCase subclass that sets up an editing context, loads the connection URL from a configuration file, and has some other utility methods.

DbUnit XML Datafiles

DbUnit XML datafiles come in two flavors, one that uses a generic Document Type Definition (DTD) and one that uses a custom DTD that represents your schema. See Listing 1-4 for an example of the former.

Listing 1-4. *DbUnit XML Datafile Using the Generic DTD*

```
<?xml version='1.0' encoding='UTF-8'?>
<dataset>
  <USER CAN_CHANGE_PASSWORD='N' IS_ACCOUNT_DISABLED='N'
    MUST_CHANGE_PASSWORD='N' PASSWORD='password' USER_ID='1'
    USER_NAME='Name One'/>
  <USER CAN_CHANGE_PASSWORD='N' IS_ACCOUNT_DISABLED='N'
    MUST_CHANGE_PASSWORD='N' PASSWORD='password' USER_ID='2'
    USER_NAME='Name Two'/>
  <PRIVILEGE NAME='Privilege Five' PRIVILEGE_ID='5'/>
  <PRIVILEGE NAME='Test Privilege' PRIVILEGE_ID='6'/>
  <USER_PRIVILEGE PRIVILEGE_ID='6' USER_ID='1'/>
</dataset>
```

As you can see, this defines two rows on the USER table, with attributes CAN_CHANGE_PASSWORD, IS_ACCOUNT_DISABLED, and so on, two more rows on the PRIVILEGE table, and another row on the USER_PRIVILEGE table. DbUnit uses this file both for insertion and for deletion. It inserts the rows in the order they occur in the file, and deletes them in the reverse order (so be sure that your file is set up so as not to cause referential integrity violations when deleting).

■ **NOTE** Since DbUnit uses the table and column names found in the database, not the entity and attribute names found in the EO model, you have to be careful when making changes to your model.

Design by Contract

Design by Contract (DBC), a trademark of Eiffel Software, is one of the exciting new developments in software engineering. First introduced by Bertrand Meyer, it has received a lot of attention from others in recent years due to its power at making better code.

The traditional alternative to DBC is defensive programming. This entails manual checking of parameters and return values. Despite being used for many years, most programmers know that defensive programming doesn't work, and, often, the result is no error checking at all! Where it is used, it is applied unevenly, because programmers don't know what the error conditions actually are. It is often overused: checking results of methods "just in case," leading to more code than necessary, and increasing the likelihood of bugs. Finally, this error-checking code remains in the final application, since there is no easy way to remove it once you are sure that the program works.

The standard exception mechanism, used in Java and many other languages, is also insufficient, since it also does not formally specify what can go wrong. Programmers have to rely on Javadoc comments to determine when an exception can be raised. In addition, many programmers don't know when an exception should actually be raised, leading to exceptions that act as return values or status messages.

What is needed is a formal way of specifying both what a method requires before it can run correctly and what the method ensures that it will do (not only not throwing exceptions, but also taking actions that are correct with respect to the business logic). In other words: a contract.

What Are Contracts?

DBC is a method of specifying "contracts" on your code that specify valid entry and exit states for every method. The simplest way to look at contracts is as code-level gatekeepers for your methods (and for the class itself—more on that later). A contract specifies the conditions under which it is valid to call a method (called *preconditions*) and the state that a method will leave our system in (called *postconditions*). In our code, for example, we often specify that arguments to a method must not be `null`. Listing 1-5 shows what a method with contracts might look like.

Listing 1-5. *A Method with Contracts*

```
/**
 * This method changes the user's password and removes the flag to ask the user
 * to change their password.
 *
 * @param newPassword the password to replace the existing one
 */
public void changePasswordTo(String newPassword) {
    /** require
    [valid_newPassword] newPassword != null;
    [new_password_is_different] ! newPassword.equals(password()); **/
    setPassword(newPassword);
    setMustChangePassword(new Boolean(false));
    /** ensure
    [password_is_changed] newPassword.equals(password());
    [doesnt_need_to_change_pswd] ! mustChangePassword().booleanValue(); **/
}
```

■ **NOTE** There is no standard syntax for the contracts in Java. As with most other situations where there is no standard, people just make up their own. We are using the Jass-style contracts here (see the list of Design by Contract packages at the end of this section for more information on Jass and other DBC implementations), but, though the syntax may change, the concept is the same.

The two specially formatted comments at the top and bottom of the body of the method are the contracts for the method. The precondition (at the top) says that this method requires that the newPassword parameter is non-null and that the new password must not equal the existing password. The postcondition (at the bottom) asserts that the password is actually changed (which is the definition of the method, more or less); as a side effect, this method also ensures that the user no longer needs to change their password. You can see that this method refuses to handle null passwords or new passwords that are the same as the old password. Satisfying the precondition is the responsibility of the calling code, which has more information on whether these conditions are possible and what to do if they occur. This method's job is just to change the password and reset the flag, nothing more and nothing less. A method cannot validly call this method without first satisfying the precondition, and this method cannot exit (unless it throws an exception) without first satisfying the postcondition.

Listing 1-6 is a slightly more complex example that (we hope) shows some of the power of this method.

Listing 1-6. *A Method Specified by Its Contract*

```
/**
 * Returns all users.
 *
 * @param ec the editing context to fetch into
 */
public static NSArray allUsers(EOEditingContext ec) {
    /** require [valid_ec] ec != null; **/

    // fetch the users into the editing context

    /** ensure
    [valid_result] Result != null;
    [result_contains_users] (forall i : {0 .. Result.count() - 1} #
        Result.objectAtIndex(i) instanceof User); **/
}
```

Notice that we do not even need to see the implementation of the method. The contract says it all: if we give this method a valid editing context, we will get a non-null array full of User objects (of course, not all of the semantics of the method are preserved in the postcondition: how do you write a contract that ensures that *all* the users were returned?). The last postcondition just asserts that the returned array will only contain User objects, which can be useful in a language (such as Java) that does not have genericity.

It may be a concern to some readers that this method as yet has no implementation, but has probably about as much code as the implementation will have! In fact, there are cases where we have to essentially write the method twice: once in the body of the method and once again in the contracts—witness Listing 1-5, where we have two lines of implementation and four lines of contracts. We will discuss the reasons to use DBC in "Why Contract Your Code."

The Class Invariant

The invariant is a contract that applies to the entire class. It asserts that objects of the class will be in a given state at all times. Here is an example:

```
/** invariant [has_password] password != null; **/
```

This asserts that the object's password instance variable will always be non-`null` (after the constructor has been executed). You can think of an invariant as a precondition/postcondition on every method, meaning that this line of code will be executed before and after every method call on the class. The only exception to this is that it does not have to hold while control is in the context of the class. So if a class has a method, A, that calls another method, B, on the same class, then the class invariant gets checked at the beginning and end of A.

NOTE You might be asking, "So how does all this Design by Contract stuff actually work in Java?" The answer depends on which implementation you are using, but in Jass (like others), there is a separate compiler that precompiles the code, transforming your specially-formatted contracts-cum-comments into code. Other implementations allow you to write Java code directly as contracts. Most implementations (including Jass) will allow you to turn your contracts on and off, thus freeing your code from the performance hit of all this extra error checking in a production system, while maintaining the semantics captured by your contracts during testing.

DBC and Unit Testing

DBC and unit testing are complementary technologies. DBC tests the system at runtime, ensuring that the actual state of each object is consistent. Unit testing verifies that certain input provides certain output, and is not done during normal operation of an application.

An obvious question that we have had is: should one test the contracts? In other words, should the tests attempt to invoke methods with invalid parameters? In general, we have found the answer to be "No." This is because those tests are usually redundant, and we all want to avoid writing useless code. Sometimes, though, a particularly complex contract on a method might warrant a few tests, just to make sure that you've actually got it right, and to make sure that someone doesn't come along later and change it.

What Design by Contract Is Not

Design by Contract is not an input-checking tool. Contracts are inviolate assertions about the state of the system. It is a programming error when one is violated, and since you can't be sure that a given input method (the user, for example) will always give valid input, you can't use contracts to check input.

Also, since contracts can be turned off in the production version, the functionality of the program should not rely on contracts being there. If your program is bug-free, contracts in the code are redundant, like error checking.

More on Design by Contract

We have tried to give a basic outline of the Design by Contract method, but there is a lot more to know. If you are interested, you should read Bertrand Meyer's excellent book *Object Oriented-Software Construction*, 2nd edition (Prentice Hall PTR, 2000).

Why Contract Your Code?

Usually, we want to reduce the amount of code we write. This, in fact, has been one of the guiding philosophies of language design for the past several decades, and one of the benefits of object-oriented design and programming: less code means fewer bugs, less to know, and more functionality that developers can implement. However, there are several reasons to use contracts in your code:

- Contracts are error checking.
- Contracts are documentation.
- Like unit tests, contracts ensure that changes to one part of the code don't break the rest of the code.

Contracts Are Error Checking

Or, more accurately, they alleviate the common problems with error checking. As described in the introduction on DBC, there are two common error-checking philosophies: check everything (defensive programming) and check nothing. The problems associated with checking nothing are obvious. However, checking everything is equally problematic: all that error-checking code can cause a serious performance hit. Contracts, on the other hand, are not part of the code and can be turned off for a system about to go into production. More importantly, it can be impossible to know what errors to check for. Some methods can't take `null` parameters, others can. Some always return a non-`null` result, others don't. Good Javadocs will aid the process, but are they up-to-date?

Contracts Are Documentation

You may have noticed in the preceding example that the Jass-style contracts look a lot like Javadoc comments. This is no coincidence. One of the greatest benefits of Design by Contract is that it automatically documents your code. And you can be sure that it is accurate documentation at all times. Just by looking at the generated Javadoc (which can be made to include the contracts), we can see exactly what the method needs to complete successfully and what the method will do—or rather, what states are required on entry to the method and are ensured on exit from the method (see Figure 1-3).

Method Detail

editingContext

`public com.webobjects.eocontrol.EOEditingContext editingContext()`

Return the editing context for use with this test case.

Returns:
the editing context for use with this test case

---

globallyUniqueString

`public java.lang.String globallyUniqueString()`

Generates a globally unique string.

Ensures:
valid_result: `Result!=null`

---

saveChangesShouldntThrow

`public void saveChangesShouldntThrow(java.lang.String message)`

Saves changes on `editingContext` and calls fail `fail(message)` if an exception is thrown.

Parameters:
`message` - the message to pass to `fail()`
Requires:
valid_param: `message!=null`

---

saveChangesShouldThrow

`public void saveChangesShouldThrow(java.lang.String message)`

Saves changes on `editingContext` and calls fail `fail(message)` if an exception is not thrown.

Parameters:
`message` - the message to pass to `fail()`
Requires:
valid_param: `message!=null`

Package Class Use Tree Deprecated Index Help
PREV CLASS NEXT CLASS FRAMES NO FRAMES
SUMMARY: NESTED | FIELD | CONSTR | METHOD DETAIL: FIELD | CONSTR | METHOD

Figure 1-3. *DBC Javadocs as generated by Jass*

Contracts Protect Against Change

Contracts check your program logic dynamically rather than with the static tests of unit testing. Contracts will find the unanticipated cases that arise when the program is being used, the cases that you did not think to write a unit test for. Any change can first be verified by running the unit tests; then you can run your application with the contracts enabled and verify that your change works in production.

Java and DBC

Unfortunately, the only language for which DBC is fully and completely implemented is Meyer's own Eiffel (see `http://www.eiffel.com/`). Fortunately, several packages for Java partially implement DBC. Here is a (nonexhaustive) list:

- **Jass** (`http://csd.informatik.uni-oldenburg.de/~jass/`): Open source (LGPL) DBC preprocessor. Has some bugs and architectural limitations, but overall a very good package. The people working on Jass also have some interesting experimental additions to Jass's DBC mechanism.
- **iContract** (`http://www.reliable-systems.com/tools/iContract/iContract.htm`): Although more mature than Jass, iContract is not open source and does not appear to be maintained any longer.
- **JMSAssert** (`http://www.mmsindia.com/JMSAssert.html`): Windows-only DBC.

We use Jass in our work because it has sufficient functionality for our purposes, and because it is open source software that is still being maintained by its original authors.

An overview of DBC support in Java can be found at `http://www.jot.fm/issues/issue_2002_08/article1/article1`.

Debugging Techniques: Logging in WebObjects

Our next section on making your code better deals with logging. While some people believe that logging just pollutes source code and decreases legibility, we believe that, used properly, logging can provide a big benefit. One of the ways that this is possible is by using logging in a noninvasive manner—using subclasses, notifications, and delegates to provide copious amounts of information without the log statements getting in the way of most of your code. Don't debate the matter! Put in the log statements to start with; you will be glad you did!

Using Subclasses

Perhaps the most powerful (or at least the most flexible) logging technique is subclassing. Subclassing gives you all the control of a debugger without having to actually step through the code. You can easily write to your log each time a certain method is called, allowing you to see where it is called from in various circumstances. For example, we once needed to find out when and how often `WOComponent`'s `awake()` and `sleep()` methods were called in the latest version of WebObjects. By simply overriding those methods, we were able to verify that they were only called once each at the beginning and end, respectively, of the request—response loop.

Of course, logging is most useful when it is left in place to provide information on your program on an ongoing basis. Some of the more useful things to override are

- **`dispatchRequest()`** on **`WOApplication`**: We will discuss this one shortly as an example of subclassing to provide log messages.

- **awake()** and **sleep()** on **WOComponent**, **WOSession**, and **WOApplication**: These are useful to determine when your components are actually being viewed.
- **takeValuesFromRequest()**, **invokeAction()**, and **appendToResponse()** on **WOComponent**, **WOSession**, and **WOApplication**: These are often-used methods for logging what is happening during the request—response loop.
- **saveChanges()**, **insertObject()**, **deleteObject()**, **lock()**, **unlock()**, and many others on **EOEditingContext**: One of the central objects in any EOF application, an EOEditingContext subclass can provide copious amounts of useful logging.

Overriding dispatchRequest()

The dispatchRequest method on WOApplication is one of the first methods called during the request—response (r—r) loop. Not surprisingly, it handles dispatching the request to the proper request handler. Overriding this method allows you to see what exactly is getting sent to your application, and what exactly is being sent back in the response. This might be useful if you are seeing unexpected session creation, if you are debugging cookie problems, to determine if result headers are set properly for downloads, and for identifying which requests result in large increases in memory consumption. Listing 1-7 is an example of dispatchRequest() using NSLog.

Listing 1-7. *Logging with* dispatchRequest()

```
public WOResponse dispatchRequest(WORequest request) {
    WOResponse result;
    if (properties().booleanPropertyForKey("DebugRequestResponseLoop")) {
        NSLog.debug.appendln("=========== Cycle Start for URI " + request.uri());
        NSLog.debug.appendln("Request's headers: " + request.headers());
        NSLog.debug.appendln("          cookies: " +
            request.headerForKey("cookie"));
        result = super.dispatchRequest(request);
        NSLog.debug.appendln("Response cookies " + result.cookies());
        NSLog.debug.appendln("Response headers: " + result.headers());
        NSLog.debug.appendln("===========  Cycle End  for URI " + request.uri());
    }
    else {
        result = super.dispatchRequest(request);
    }
    return result;
}
```

An important aspect of this is that it is not always on. Having log output is good only if you can see the information you want to. Having to scroll through 100 pages of text to find the line you want is no better than just stepping though the code. In the preceding snippet, we use a Boolean property from a configuration file to determine whether we want to write out the log.

TIP There are many ways of loading configuration information, from the now-deprecated infoDictionary to command line arguments to pure-Java Property files. You should make sure that you understand at least one way to do this and *use it*. Being able to change configuration options, such as logging, with minimal effort is well worth it.

Delegates

Delegates are objects that implement functionality delegated from another object. You can think of the delegation mechanism as having one class allow another class to make decisions for it. In WebObjects, the delegate can also decide to not decide (which is still a decision), and the delegating class will then make a default decision. Delegation is a way of using one class to customize the behavior of another class without the need for subclassing. Some delegate methods commonly used for logging are

- **`EOAdaptorChannel.Delegate`**: Used for logging fetched rows and other low-level SQL logging
- **`databaseContextShouldSelectObjects`** in **`EODatabaseContext.Delegate`**: Called before a `SELECT` operation
- **`databaseContextDidSelectObjects`** in **`EODatabaseContext.Delegate`**: Called after a `SELECT` operation
- **`EditingContextWillSaveChanges`** in **`EOEditingContext.Delegate`**: Called before a `saveChanges()`

See the "Snooping on EOF" section further on for an example of using delegates for logging.

Using Notifications

Notifications are broadcast messages sent by one object that can be received (caught) by many other objects. Catching select notifications is another powerful way to debug your application. There are many different notifications used throughout WebObjects, all of which can be used to determine what is going on behind the scenes. Listing 1-8 shows a simple class that can log arbitrary notification messages (these methods are also in the `EOFDebugAdditions` class in the PracticalUtilities framework).

Listing 1-8. *Class That Logs Arbitrary Notification Messages*

```
public class NotificationLogger {
    // So we don't get garbage collected
    private static Vector _loggers = new Vector();

    /**
     * Log messages from a specific notification.
     *
```

```
     * @param notificationName the name of the notification to log
     */
    public NotificationLogger(String notificationName) {
        super();
        /** require [valid_param] notificationName != null; **/

        NSNotificationCenter defaultCenter = NSNotificationCenter.defaultCenter();
        NSSelector notificationCallback = new NSSelector("notificationCallback",
            new Class[] {NSNotification.class});
        defaultCenter.addObserver(this,
            notificationCallback, notificationName, null);
        _logger.add(this);
    }

    /**
     * Log messages from all notifications. LOTS of messages!
     */
    public NotificationLogger() {
        super();

        NSNotificationCenter defaultCenter = NSNotificationCenter.defaultCenter();
        NSSelector notificationCallback = new NSSelector("notificationCallback",
            new Class[] {NSNotification.class});
        defaultCenter.addOmniscientObserver(this, notificationCallback);
        _logger.add(this);
    }

    public void notificationCallback(NSNotification notification) {
        /** require [valid_param] notification != null; **/

        // Only write to the log if the debug level is "detailed"
        if (NSLog.debugLoggingAllowedForLevel(NSLog.DebugLevelDetailed)) {
            NSLog.debug.appendln("Received notification " + notification.name() +
                " with object " + notification.object() + " and with userInfo: " +
                notification.userInfo());
            // Could also log a stack trace here if you want to know exactly
            // where the notification came from
        }
    }
}
```

Some of the more important notifications and their uses are

- **ClassDescriptionNeededForClassNotification** and **ClassDescriptionNeededForEntity-NameNotification** in **EOClassDescription**: Notification that an EOEntity needs a class description. Use this when you want to know when an EOEntity is getting used for the first time (at which point it posts this notification).

- **`ObjectsChangedInEditingContextNotification`** in **`EOEditingContext`**: Notification of a change to an EO in an editing context. Use this to find out when an EO changes.

- **`AdaptorContextBeginTransactionNotification`**, **`AdaptorContextCommitTransactionNotification`**, and **`AdaptorContextRollbackTransactionNotification`** in **`EOAdaptorContext`**: Useful to see where your transactions are starting and ending.

- **`ModelAddedNotification`** in **`EOModelGroup`**: One of the notifications that we sometimes use to find out exactly what models are being loaded.

You can use `NSLog`'s debug groups to provide a lot of this logging (see the following discussion). The notification mechanism allows you to fine-tune the output you want, and, obviously, allows you to act on the notification in other ways useful to your application.

NSLog and Other Logging Tools

`NSLog` is a class of WebObjects that allows you to control the log messages that WebObjects generates. The methods previously described for logging can all be enhanced or even replaced by using `NSLog`'s debug groups and debug levels.

Debug groups and debug levels are two ways of controlling what log messages are printed. These can be set on the command line, allowing you to see a lot of information without a recompile. If you are thinking of adding logging to your application, then a look at WebObjects' logging will give you an idea of what kinds of things are useful to log.

Debug levels control the granularity of log messages:

- **`DebugLevelOff`**: No log messages.

- **`DebugLevelCritical`**: Only the most important messages are logged. These log messages are not supposed to impact application performance much.

- **`DebugLevelInformational`**: More than Critical, less than Detailed.

- **`DebugLevelDetailed`**: All log messages.

Debug groups offer more fine-grained control of logging, allowing you to choose what part of WebObjects should give log messages. Here are some of the more interesting debug groups:

- **`DebugGroupModel`**: Logs dealing with the EOModel

- **`DebugGroupSQLGeneration`**: Certainly one of the most-used debug groups in an EOF application

- **`DebugGroupDeployment`**: For those inevitable deployment gotchas

- **`DebugGroupValidation`**: Logs validation of your EOs

You can also define your own debug groups, which will give you as much control over your own log messages as over WebObjects' own.

NSLog is a big step up from previous versions of WebObjects, which provided what amounted to println (and did not provide much logging of its own). You definitely need to be able to use NSLog and its debug levels and debug groups. There is a lot of information that you can get just by setting a couple of arguments to your application. However, NSLog still has some limitations, which other tools, such as log4j, address.

log4j

log4j (http://jakarta.apache.org/log4j/) is an open source logging tool that provides several benefits over NSLog: hierarchical loggers (or categories), appenders that can write to arbitrary places and do arbitrary things, and layouts that allow you to customize the format of log messages just by changing a configuration file. While not as obvious a choice as PBWO versus Eclipse (at least for us), log4j certainly merits a closer look, since it does offer some useful facilities.

log4j includes several concepts that are similar to the ones used by NSLog. Levels (or priorities) are basically the same as debug levels, and logger categories are analogous to debug groups. The major difference is that, with log4j, you can define a hierarchy of loggers (similarly to the way you define Java packages), which allows you to enable a whole set of log messages with one configuration option.

While NSLog and log4j both allow you to redirect the output of log messages to any file (including the standard out and standard error "files"), log4j takes this one step further with the concept of "appenders." Appenders are classes that control the output of your log messages. Instead of just writing to a file, you can do some interesting things with appenders:

- **RollingFileAppender** can limit the size of log files by backing up log files.
- **NTEventLogAppender** can write your log messages to the NT event log.
- **SMTPAppender** e-mails log messages.
- **JDBCAppender** writes log messages to a database.

The appender that your application uses can be configured without a recompile by just changing a configuration file. Listing 1-9 shows a class that redirects NSLog and/or System.out and System.err messages to log4j.

Listing 1-9. *Class to Redirect* NSLog *and/or* System.out *and* System.err *Messages to log4j*

```
final public class LogPrintStream extends PrintStream {
    protected Level level;
    protected String categoryName;

    public LogPrintStream(Level aLevel, String aCategoryName) {
        super(null);
        /** require
        [valid_level] aLevel != null;
        [valid_category] aCategoryName != null; **/
```

```
        level = aLevel;
        categoryName = aCategoryName;
    }

    public void println(String aValue) {
        logMessage( aValue + "\n");
    }

    public void print(String aValue) {
        logMessage( aValue );
    }

    protected void logMessage(String aValue) {
        if (aValue != null) {
            Logger logger = Logger.getInstance(categoryName);
            logger.log(level, aValue);
        }
    }

    /** invariant
    [has_level] level != null;
    [has_category] categoryName != null; **/
}
```

Listing 1-10 shows how to use the `LogPrintStream` class from Listing 1-9.

Listing 1-10. *Using the* `LogPrintStream`

```
LogPrintStream logPrintSteam = new LogPrintStream(myLevel, myCategory);
System.setOut(logPrintStream);
System.setErr(logPrintStream);
((NSLog.PrintStreamLogger)NSLog.out).setPrintStream(logPrintStream);
((NSLog.PrintStreamLogger)NSLog.debug).setPrintStream(logPrintStream);
((NSLog.PrintStreamLogger)NSLog.err).setPrintStream(logPrintStream);
```

Finally, layouts are patterns for the formatting of a log message. The `PatternLayout` class writes the message using a format pattern (similar to C's `printf`), again configurable from a file. With `NSLog` you are stuck with log messages that look like this:

```
[2003-06-21 18:29:05 PDT] <main> Important log message
```

You are able, with log4j, to mimic that format or to create your own. Some of the more interesting pattern characters can be found in Table 1-1.

Table 1-1. *Example log4j Pattern Characters*

Pattern Character	Use
L	Generates the line number from which the log message originated (slow!)
d	Generates the date and time of the log message
t	Generates the name of the thread that logged the message
m	Generates the text of the log message
r	Generates the number of milliseconds from the application's start to the point the message was logged
C	Generates the class name from which the log message originated (slow!)

We are not going to go into a detailed discussion of how to use log4j in your application. There are already lots of good articles on the subject, and there is no point in rehashing that material here as WebObjects introduces no significant differences. See `http://logging.apache.org/log4j/docs/documentation.html` for links to articles and documentation. For a quick, but limited, example of usage, take a look at the example application for Chapter 6.

NOTE The 1.4.1 JDK ships with a logging API that is functionally equivalent to log4j.

Snooping on EOF

In this section we will look more in depth at logging with EOF. The easiest, and most basic, information to get is a log of all the SQL that EOF generates. This is done by setting the appropriate logging levels and groups in `NSLog`. If you did not plan ahead and make SQL logging an item in your application's configuration (you did, didn't you?) you can turn it on from the command line with `-DEOAdaptorDebugEnabled=true`. The problem with doing it this way is that you turn it on everywhere. Often you only want to log what happens in a select section of code.

The `EOFDebugAdditions` class in the PracticalUtilities framework (part of the download for this book) has several convenience methods to make debugging easier. The `logSQL()` method, Listing 1-11, makes pinpoint SQL logging convenient.

Listing 1-11. *The* `logSQL()` *Method for Convenient Pinpoint SQL Logging*

```
/**
 * Turns EOAdaptor SQL logging on or off to aid in debugging.
 *
 * @param shouldLog <code>true</code> if SQL logging should be turned on,
 * <code>false</code> if it should be turned off.
 */
public static void logSQL(boolean shouldLog) {
    if (shouldLog) {
        NSLog.allowDebugLoggingForGroups(NSLog.DebugGroupSQLGeneration
                                         | NSLog.DebugGroupDatabaseAccess
                                         | NSLog.DebugGroupEnterpriseObjects);
```

```
    }
    else {
        NSLog.refuseDebugLoggingForGroups(NSLog.DebugGroupSQLGeneration
                                            | NSLog.DebugGroupDatabaseAccess
                                            | NSLog.DebugGroupEnterpriseObjects);
    }
}
```

Digging Deeper: Seeing the Fetched Data

Sometimes the SQL that EOF is sending is not enough; you might also need to see the data that it is getting back in response. While there is no convenient NSLog group for this, there is an EOAdaptor delegate method:

```
public void adaptorChannelDidFetchRow(EOAdaptorChannel, NSMutableDictionary);
```

The dictionary parameter contains the fetched values, and it is simple enough to log these values. The challenge here is to get to the EOAdaptorChannel instance in order to set the delegate. The layered architecture of the classes in EOAccess can be difficult to navigate your way through at first. It can feel as if you are following a endless "knee bone connected to the thigh bone connected to the hip bone" progression and end up wandering in circles. You may even start to wonder if there really is any path from A to B. Relax. It is not as convoluted as it seems at first. There are usually multiple ways of getting from A to B, the choice being dictated by convenience and what you have to start with. To get to an EOAdaptorChannel instance, all we need to know is the name of an EOModel. For a simple project with a single EOModel (or with multiple models sharing the same DB connection), it can be as simple as the code in Listing 1-12.

Listing 1-12. *Code Showing How to Get from an* EOModel *to the* EOAdaptorChannel

```
EOEditingContext ec = new EOEditingContext();
ec.lock();
try {
    EOObjectStoreCoordinator.defaultCoordinator().lock();
    try {
        EODatabaseContext dbContext =
            EOUtilities.databaseContextForModelNamed(ec, "ModelName");

        EODatabaseChannel dbChannel = dbContext.availableChannel();
        if ( dbChannel != null ) {
            dbChannel.adaptorChannel().setDelegate(this);
        }
    } finally {
        EOObjectStoreCoordinator.defaultCoordinator().unlock();
    }
} finally {
    ec.unlock();
}
```

What Listing 1-12 is saying is that an editing context is connected to a database context, which is connected to a database channel, which is connected to an adaptor channel—and that is where we wanted to end up. An editing context can be connected to more than one database context, and that is why the EOModel is needed: it defines which database context we want to talk to. Note that you need to lock both the editing context and the object store coordinator (see Chapter 3 for more information on locking).

For more complicated applications with multiple models and multiple database connections, the code gets a little more complex. Listing 1-13 shows how to handle this more complex situation.

Listing 1-13. *How to Get Adaptor Channels When Multiple Models and Database Connections Are Involved*

```
EOEditingContext ec = new EOEditingContext();
ec.lock();
try {
    EOObjectStoreCoordinator.defaultCoordinator().lock();
    try {
        NSArray modelNames = (NSArray)EOModelGroup.defaultGroup().models().
            valueForKey("name");
        Enumeration modelNameEnumerator = modelNames.objectEnumerator();
        while (modelNameEnumerator .hasMoreElements()) {
            String modelName = (String)modelNameEnumerator.nextElement();
            EODatabaseContext dbContext =
                EOUtilities.databaseContextForModelNamed(ec, modelName);

            Enumeration channelEnumerator =
                dbContext.registeredChannels().objectEnumerator();
            while (channelEnumerator.hasMoreElements()) {
                EODatabaseChannel dbChannel =
                    ((EODatabaseChannel)channelEnumerator.nextElement());
                if (dbChannel.adaptorChannel().delegate() == null) {
                    dbChannel.adaptorChannel().setDelegate(myDelegate);
                }
            }
        }
    } finally {
        EOObjectStoreCoordinator.defaultCoordinator().unlock();
    }
} finally {
    ec.unlock();
}
```

Unless you have manually created `EOModelGroups`, `EOModelGroup.defaultGroup()` will return a list of all of the models loaded into your application. Each of these might have its own database context, so we need to check each one. We also might get a reference to a database context having more than one channel. You should set this delegate early enough in the application's life that the chance of having multiple channels is slim, but we ought to check anyway. Finally, we check to see if the channel already has a delegate. If so, it is (probably) our delegate, which was set by a previous model.

You can even get EOF to print a stack trace when it fetches data. Although this is more useful for optimization, it also has uses for general debugging. Yes, it's another delegate method, this time on `EODatabaseContext`. The delegate method to use is:

```
public void databaseContextDidSelectObjects(EODatabaseContext dc,
                                            EOFetchSpecification fs,
                                            EODatabaseChannel channel)
```

As we have already seen how to get to a database context, we will leave using this delegate method as an exercise for the reader.

The Last Log Entry

As you have seen, logging can provide a lot of useful information. If you want to see the state of your application at a certain point, consider logging instead of stepping through with a debugger. If you do it right, the code will still be pretty, and the log messages can be turned off (or rather, since off should be the default, they can be turned on) with ease. A little forethought will allow groups of log messages to be turned on and off (with either `NSLog` or log4j), providing a quick way to examine a whole aspect of your application at once.

Creating Java Classes from EOModels

One of the annoyances with WebObjects "out of the box" is that when you change an EOModel and generate the Java files, you are stuck merging your hand-written code in with the generated code. No matter how you look at it, merging just isn't fun. Fortunately there is a much better way.

The Generation Gap Pattern

The basic idea behind this pattern is to have generated code placed in a class by itself. This class can be abstract, as it should never be instantiated directly. Hand-written code is then placed in a subclass. Thus, if you make changes in the model and need to regenerate the Java classes, you can do so without having to worry about merging your code in with the generated code. You can make model changes without having to give it a second thought. This is an implementation of the Generation Gap pattern, which you can read about at `http://www.research.ibm.com/designpatterns/pubs/gg.html`.

The Trusty EOGenerator

EOGenerator (`http://www.rubicode.com/Software/EOGenerator/`) is a template-driven code generator that implements the Generation Gap pattern for WebObjects. It generates two classes (from two different templates) for each entity in an EOModel. The first class is the class that would normally be generated from EOModeler, but with an underscore in front of the name. This is the superclass in the Generation Gap pattern. This superclass (see Listing 1-14) contains all of the enterprise object's accessors and mutators and anything else that can be automatically generated from the EOModel.

Listing 1-14. *The Superclass Generated from the EOModel*

```
package com.apress.practicalwo.practicalutilities.tests;

import com.webobjects.eocontrol.EOGenericRecord;
import com.webobjects.foundation.NSArray;
import com.webobjects.foundation.NSMutableArray;

/**
 * Created by eogenerator
 *
 * DO NOT EDIT.  Make changes to CooperatingEditingContextTestObject.java instead.
 *
 * @author author  Copyright (c) 2003
 */
public abstract class _CooperatingEditingContextTestObject extends EOGenericRecord
{

    public static final String NAMEDOBJECTS = "namedObjects";
    public static final String RELATEDOBJECT = "relatedObject";
    public static final String STRINGVALUE = "stringValue";

    public String stringValue()
    {
        return (String)storedValueForKey("stringValue");
    }

    public void setStringValue(String aValue)
    {
        takeStoredValueForKey(aValue, "stringValue");
    }
```

The second class generated is an empty subclass of the first. EOGenerator never touches this file after it is initially generated. The code that you write by hand goes in this subclass (see Listing 1-15). This does make your code slightly more difficult to read because it places your enterprise object's accessors/mutators in a superclass (unless you have a way of displaying inherited methods in your IDE, as Eclipse does). However, it will save you hours of grunt work merging changes. Besides, there is rarely a need to look at the generated methods.

EOGenerator was used to generate all of the enterprise objects in the code that accompanies this book. We have also included the templates we used as an example of what can be done easily. There is a lot more that can be done in the templates than these minimal examples show.

Listing 1-15. *The Subclass Containing Only Code That You Wrote*

```
import com.apress.practicalwo.practicalutilities.EOStateTransition;
import com.webobjects.eocontrol.EOEditingContext;
import com.webobjects.eocontrol.EOGlobalID;
import com.webobjects.foundation.NSLog;
import com.webobjects.foundation.NSTimestamp;

/**
 * EOEnterpriseObject specially configured to assist in testing the
 * CooperatingEditingContext.
 *
 * @author Chuck Hill and Sacha Mallais  Copyright (c) 2003
 */
public class CooperatingEditingContextTestObject
                extends _CooperatingEditingContextTestObject
implements EOStateTransition
{
    // Use ints so that we can tell if it was called more than once
    public int calledHasInserted = 0;
    public int calledWillDelete = 0;
    public int calledHasDeleted = 0;
    public int calledWillUpdate = 0;
    public int calledHasUpdated = 0;
    public EOGlobalID ourGlobalID;
    public EOEditingContext ourEC;

    public void hasInserted()
    {
        calledHasInserted++;
        if (NSLog.debugLoggingAllowedForLevel(NSLog.DebugLevelDetailed))
        {
            NSLog.out.appendln("Called hasInserted for " +
            editingContext().globalIDForObject(this) + " in " + editingContext());
        }
    }
```

Alternatives to EOGenerator

EOGenerator is the best-known tool that generates EOs, but it is not the only one. Others include eojenerator (`http://www.prnet.de/RegEx/eojenerator.tgz`), a pure-Java rewrite of EOGenerator, and WOGen (`http://www.objectstyle.org/woproject/ant/wogen.html`), an Ant task that is part of WOProject. We still use EOGenerator, mostly for historical reasons, but the alternatives are worth checking out.

Summary

The techniques and tools we have looked at in this chapter can be generically applied to almost any Java development effort. They are handy tools to have in your development tool box, sharpened and close at hand even if you are not using WebObjects. In the next two chapters we will be taking a closer look at the core of WebObjects, the Enterprise Objects Foundation (EOF), and examining specific things you can do to make your code better and your life easier.

CHAPTER 2

EO Modeling Techniques

Always design a thing by considering it in its next larger context—a chair in a room, a room in a house, a house in an environment, an environment in a city plan.

—Eliel Saarinen

This chapter deals with one of the central activities in most WebObjects applications: enterprise object (eo) modeling. We will discuss inheritance, considerations when forming relationships between objects, special attribute modeling, EO prototypes, and Eclipse issues with eo modeling.

Before you start into this and the next chapter, we strongly suggest that you review the WebObjects' documentation on Enterprise Objects (`http://developer.apple.com/documentation/WebObjects/Enterprise_Objects`) and Using EOModeler (`http://developer.apple.com/documentation/WebObjects/UsingEOModeler`). We are not going to repeat this documentation and assume that you are at least superficially familiar with it. We will limit ourselves to commenting on topics that are not covered in the documentation or are not adequately covered in the documentation.

Inheritance

In this section, we will discuss some of the details of inheritance implementation, how to use inheritance with EOF, and some of the common pitfalls associated with inheritance.

Inheritance Implementation Details

In theory, inheritance just works. You merely assign one entity to be the parent of another. In reality, though, you need to know some of the details of how it works, since when you model your entities, you will also be choosing a representation of your entities in the database. Using inheritance usually carries with it a performance hit, and this is even more the case when implementing inheritance in a relational database.

There are three types of inheritance implementations in EOF: single-table inheritance, vertical inheritance, and horizontal inheritance. Following are descriptions of each.

Single-Table Inheritance

One of the best performers, single-table inheritance is a common choice for representing your entities in a database. This option puts all of the attributes from both the superentity and the subentity into one table. Attributes that are inherited are not duplicated in the table; the subentity uses the same columns as the superentity (which makes sense, since they are actually the same!). One negative to this method is that you need to have a way of distinguishing the two different entities to EOF, which can sometimes result in a "type" attribute that has no other than this purpose.

Horizontal Inheritance

Horizontal inheritance puts a complete copy of each entity into a separate table, including all inherited attributes. This is a reasonably good performing option. The only situation in which it does worse than single-table inheritance is when you fetch on the superentity and ask it to get subentity objects as well (a "deep fetch"); then it has to scan two or more tables instead of one. Of course, the opposite is true as well: when looking for objects of a specific entity, vertical inheritance only has the rows in the one table to scan, whereas with single-table inheritance, EOF has to filter out results from other entities.

Vertical Inheritance

A rarely used option, vertical inheritance puts only the values that aren't common to both the superentity and the subentity into another table. In other words, the superentity's table contains all of the values common to both it and the subentity, while the subentity's table only contains those attributes that it introduces. You also have to have an attribute that designates which entity each row in the common table belongs to, the same as with single-table inheritance.

The problem with this option is that it has all of the negatives of both horizontal and single-table inheritance: not only do you have to filter out the subentities when doing a shallow fetch, but you also have to do two or more table lookups when doing a deep fetch. Vertical inheritance nicely normalizes your database, but at a performance cost that is usually too high.

Inheritance and Primary Keys

Each row in a relational database must have a unique primary key—unique, that is, within the table itself. Similarly, in EOF, each object must have a unique key, but with EOF, the key must be unique within its entire inheritance hierarchy. EOF accomplishes this by using the primary key generator (whatever that might be for the particular database platform you're using) for the topmost entity's table—that is, the table containing the entity that most directly inherits from `EOGenericRecord`.

Inheritance and the Overly Required Attribute

When using inheritance, there is one detail that you need to be aware of: in some circumstances, the SQL for required attribute columns can be generated incorrectly by EOF. This results in a table definition in which certain entities can never be inserted!

This problem only occurs with single-table inheritance where one entity, B, is a subentity of another entity, A (entity B subclasses entity A). If entity B introduces a required attribute, then EOModeler, when generating the table definition SQL, will incorrectly specify that attribute's column in the table to be not `null`. Because entity A doesn't define this attribute, any objects of entity A that get inserted will cause the new attribute to be set to `null`, which will cause a constraint violation in the database and cause the insert to fail. This also happens if entity B inherits an optional attribute from entity A and makes it a required attribute for entity B. If you run into this, the solution is simple: remove the constraint from the database. The only issue here is that this problem will be re-created each time you regenerate the database. Possible workarounds include copying the SQL to a file and maintaining it manually, and writing an SQL script that removes the spurious constraint. We have not found either solution to be entirely satisfactory, but if you are aware of the problem, you will likely not be burned too badly by it.

Inheritance and the Impossible Constraint

There is a similar problem with foreign key constraints and horizontal inheritance. It is caused by a mismatch between the relational and object technologies. This problem occurs when you have an inheritance hierarchy, entity B and its subentities C and D, and a relationship from a third entity A to entity B (see Figure 2-1). In Java any instance of B, C, or D will satisfy A's reference of type B. This is not so in a RDBMS (relational database management system); the relationship cannot be defined in the database as a foreign key constraint. This is because the constraint would point to B's table, and any objects of type C and D will be inserted into different tables and so will not satisfy the constraint. Fortunately EOModeler no longer generates the SQL to cause this problem, but you should be aware of it, as it can occur if you add inheritance to an existing schema. The only resolution to this problem is to remove the constraint from the database.

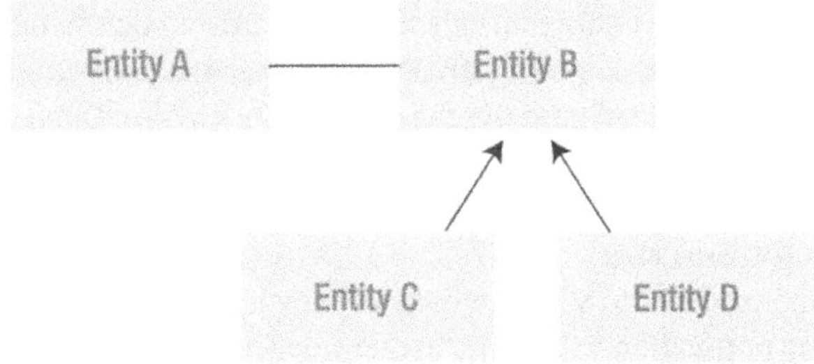

Figure 2-1. *Entity A related to superentity B with subentities C and D*

Inheritance and Multiple Models

EOModeler generally handles multiple models gracefully. Well, at least as gracefully as it handles anything else. With cross-model inheritance, however, things start to go awry. EOModeler does not directly support creating a subentity of an entity in a different model. It expects the subentity to be in the same model as the superentity. But don't despair—it can be done! Here is one way:

1. In the model with the superentity, select the entity for which you want to create a subentity, pull down the Properties menu, and choose Create Subclass. This will create a new entity in the same model (which is not where you want it).
2. Set the new entity's Name, Table Name, and Class.
3. Select the new entity in the source model and cut and paste it into the destination model. When you do this, the Parent and all of the relationship information will be lost.
4. Select the entity that you just pasted, open the Inspector, and set the Parent to the superentity. If the superentity is not available in the list, you will need to modify your project to include the framework containing the superentity's EOModel.
5. To fix the missing relationships, copy them from the superentity and paste them into the subentity. Sometimes EOModeler cannot do this in a single step (flattened relationships have this problem) and you may need to do it in several.
6. Check the consistency of the model to ensure that the subentity conforms to the parent entity. Inherited attributes and relationships are shown in italics, and you can use this to confirm that the inheritance is connected correctly.
7. You can now add any new attributes and relationships unique to the subentity.

Inheritance, Multiple Models, and SQL Generation

Generating the schema definition SQL from EOModeler requires some extra planning when cross-model inheritance is involved. The first step is to determine the dependency order of the frameworks. The tables for EOModels with the superentities should be created before the tables for EOModels with subentities—unless you are using single-table inheritance, in which case you should create the subentity's tables instead (and *not* the superentity's table). Open each of the EOModels in order of the dependencies and set the connection information. Then generate and execute the SQL. Don't generate the foreign key constraints if these cannot be enforced with the inheritance scheme you are using.

An alternate way to do this is to not execute the SQL, but instead copy it from the window and paste it into a script. This allows the population to be done in one step (running the script), which makes deployment much easier and reduces the chance of user error.

TIP We very rarely generate our database schema directly from EOModeler and instead use the SQL from EOModeler as the base for a script. There are several advantages to a hand-edited script: we can correct the SQL produced when inheritance is involved, we can selectively apply foreign key constraints when inheritance prevents their use, we can extend the SQL with performance indexes, we don't have to fumble with multiple models each time we want to generate the database, and we can easily run the script against different databases without needing to fiddle with the connection dictionary. Sure, it is a bit of work to keep in synch, but the benefits outweigh the cost. One day we will write an application or EOModeler bundle to read the EOModels and do all this for us, but until that day arrives we will be using scripts.

Relationships

In the following sections, we discuss some of the issues of modeling relationships.

Optimizing Relationships with Batch Faulting

Normally, EOF fires faults one at a time when the data for an object is required. Each such fault requires a round trip to the database to get the data. When you access many of the objects in a to-many relationship, such as when you are iterating through a to-many relationship, each related object fires off its own fault, requiring many round trips to the database. Batch faulting eliminates some of this overhead by allowing you to tell EOF to retrieve multiple objects' data at once.

You will most often want to use this when you have a relationship that you are going to access multiple objects through, as, for example, when calculating the total amount of an order by iterating through its order items. EOF allows you to specify the maximum number of objects returned by a single batch fault, which will keep performance reasonable when you have an order with 10,000 order items.

There are two ways to configure batch faulting:

- Set the maximum number of faults to batch in the relationship, using the Advanced Relationship Inspector. This is the most often used option, as it is quick and easy and allows you to have a different maximum batch fault size for each relationship (see Figure 2-2).

- Set the maximum number of faults to batch in the entity, using the Advanced Entity Inspector. This sets the maximum batch size for all relationships (except those that explicitly specify a different size).

Even a small maximum batch size can dramatically increase faulting performance. Resist the urge to set this to a ridiculously high value: a batch size of two cuts in half the per-row overhead of a round trip. Somewhere between 10 and 100 is probably best. If you set it higher, your users may experience noticeable lags when another user (perhaps needlessly) faults in 10,000 rows. It might also cause EOF to generate an SQL command longer than your database is prepared to deal with!

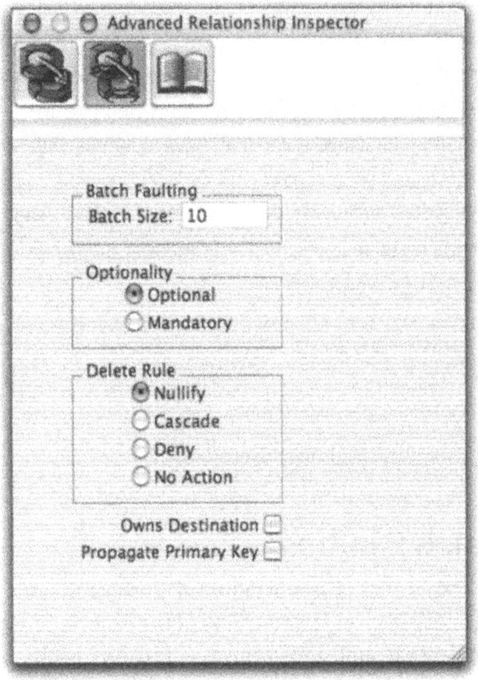

Figure 2-2. *Setting the maximum batch size for a relationship*

■ TIP You can manually batch fetch faults in code using the `EODatabaseContext` method `batchFetchRelationship()`. This is useful if you only want batch fetching behavior in specific situations. Be careful when using this method: it will force a fetch from the database even if the objects are already cached in the object store. Used incorrectly this can reduce, rather than increase, performance.

One-Sided Relationships

When a to-many relationship from an eo is first referenced, EOF creates faults for all of the related objects. In other words, if you have an Order entity and a related OrderItem entity, the first reference to `orderItems()`, even just asking for a count, causes EOF to create faults for all of its related `OrderItem` objects as placeholders for the real objects (which themselves will be faulted in as they are accessed). The mechanism works well under most circumstances, but when you have many, many related objects, the fault creation can take up an unacceptable amount of time.

You can find more details about the complex process of resolving faults for related objects at `http://developer.apple.com/documentation/WebObjects/Enterprise_Objects/Fetching/chapter_6_section_5.html`

Consider, for example, an Address entity with a relationship to a Country entity that indicated which country the address was in. Each Address would only have one Country, which would not cause a problem when the Address was faulted in. What would happen if Country had a back-pointing relationship to Address for all of the addresses in that country? When a

Country referenced `addresses()`, as would happen when assigning a Country to an Address using `addObjectToBothSidesOfRelationshipWithKey()`, a fault would be created for every Address that was in that Country. That could be very time consuming indeed.

The way to avoid this is to create a one-sided relationship between your Address and Country entities, pointing from Address to Country. EOF still maintains the relationship, as you would expect; the only difference is that if you ever wanted to get all Addresses in a Country, you would have to do it manually, through a fetch.

One-sided relationships are most often used with small "lookup" tables (sometimes called reference tables, code tables, and many other names besides), such as Country, which act as lists of acceptable values for an attribute in another entity.

Delete Rules and One-Sided Relationships

Since your delete rules are specified on relationships, a missing relationship means you don't have a delete rule for that relationship. This is usually not a problem, since you can manually provide any delete rule that you need in code. Here are the various delete rules and ways to provide the functionality manually:

- **No Action**: Need we say more? Be careful, though: it is rare that you actually want no action! You will leave dangling references unless you are careful.
- **Nullify**: Since the inverse relationship doesn't exist, there is nothing to nullify.
- **Cascade**: Specifies that deleting the current object will also delete all objects attached to this relationship. Manual intervention is the only way to provide this functionality. (Since you generally only do this manually if you're interested in higher performance, you might want to look at using `EOAdaptorChannel`'s `deleteRowsDescribedByQualifier` method.)
- **Deny**: Doesn't allow the delete if the related object or objects exist. Use `validateForDelete()` to make sure that the related object doesn't exist.

One-Sided Story

The final word on one-sided relationships is: use them with caution where performance is a concern. You don't need to use them for any other reason, and they make some things more difficult. We have found that so-called lookup tables make good candidates for modeling with one-sided relationships, since they often have many, many related objects that you rarely want faulted in.

AddObjectsToBothSidesOfRelationshipWithKey()

When dealing with two related objects, you often want to make or break the relation between them. The obvious way to do this is to use the mutators on each of the entities, as in the following:

```
EntityA a;  // Assume these entities exist
EntityB b;
a.setB(b);
b.setA(a);
```

Unfortunately, this works only if you actually have a relationship both from `EntityA` to `EntityB` and vice versa, from `EntityB` to `EntityA`. What many programmers do instead is use the `EOCustomObject` (defined in the `EORelationshipManipulation` interface) method `addObject-ToBothSidesOfRelationshipWithKey()`, which uses key-value coding to set both the forward-pointing relationship and the back-pointing relationship *if it exists*. The smart (or practical) programmer will use `addObjectToBothSidesOfRelationshipWithKey()` liberally.

■ NOTE Some programmers don't like the fact that you lose compile-time type checking when you use key-value coding methods, such as `addObjectToBothSidesOfRelationshipWithKey`. We think that the chance of using an incorrect type is much less than the chance of a relationship getting added or removed. Also, if you are an OO purist, you may not like key-value coding's ability to break encapsulation.

Attribute Value Types

EOF does a good job of handling the different attribute value types without much effort on your part. When you create an attribute on an entity, you assign it a type (one of the fundamental types provided with EOF or a custom type, discussed further on) and it just goes. There are, however, a few issues that you should be aware of.

Noninteger Numbers

Many applications have the need to work with noninteger data. An obvious example, and one that happens often, is money. How often has a client told you to round to the nearest dollar? Sounds like something out of a movie (that's *Superman II*, for the uninitiated). Applications that work with such values also tend to want those numbers to be precise.

The problem is that Java `floats` and `doubles` do not have arbitrary precision, and even some simple values, such as 1/2, cannot be represented exactly (0.5 is represented as approximately 0.4999...). Of course, anyone familiar with number theory will tell you that there are an infinite number of values that cannot be represented exactly as a decimal expansion or fraction (the square root of 2, for example). The problem is that, while not many applications need to represent the square root of 2 exactly, there are many, many cases when having an exact representation of 1/2 is desirable.

Enter the `BigDecimal`. EOF has the ability to use `BigDecimals` instead of `floats` or `doubles` for representing noninteger data, and that is a good thing. `BigDecimals` do have arbitrary precision, unlike `floats` or `doubles`, which makes them the default choice in our work.

Floats (or Doubles) vs. BigDecimals

So why is there a `float` type at all? Naturally, there is a trade-off: the `BigDecimal` type is much slower than either `floats` or `doubles`. Listing 2-1 shows a little test class that demonstrates the difference in speed. Running this code will give the following output (on a G4 1GHz running OS X):

```
Float test: 5
BigDecimal test: 241
```

Listing 2-1. *Class Demonstrating Speed Difference Between* BigDecimal *and* Float

```
import java.math.BigDecimal;
public class BigDecimalTest {
   public static void main(String[] args) {
        final int NUMBER_OF_TRIALS = 100000;
        float[] floats = new float[NUMBER_OF_TRIALS];
        BigDecimal[] bigDecimals = new BigDecimal[NUMBER_OF_TRIALS];

        for (int i = 0; i < NUMBER_OF_TRIALS; i++) {
            floats[i] = i + (float)0.5221414; // More sense to me than 0.5221414f
            bigDecimals[i] = new BigDecimal(i + "0.5221414");
        }

        long startFloat = System.currentTimeMillis();
        for (int i = 0; i < NUMBER_OF_TRIALS - 1; i++) {
            float junk = floats[i] * floats[i+1];
        }
        long endFloat = System.currentTimeMillis();
        System.out.println("Float test: " + (endFloat - startFloat));

        long startBD = System.currentTimeMillis();
        for (int i = 0; i < NUMBER_OF_TRIALS - 1; i++) {
            BigDecimal junk = bigDecimals[i].multiply(bigDecimals[i+1]);
        }
        long endBD = System.currentTimeMillis();
        System.out.println("BigDecimal test: " + (endBD - startBD));
   }
}
```

As you can see, floats are more than 40 times as fast, even in this simple test. Despite the difference in performance, though, we have found that working with BigDecimals is much preferable, and well worth the speed loss unless you are doing lots (millions!) of calculations and some rounding errors are acceptable to your client.

Another alternative is to store the floating-point values as long integers and divide them by a power of ten for display. This works well for money. For example, $127.33 can be stored in a long as 12,733 and then divided by 100 for display. This avoids the inaccuracy of floats and works OK if the number of decimal places can be fixed and the size of the numbers involved does not overflow long. In money terms that works out to be $92,233,720,368,547,758.07, probably more than enough for most of us not working with national debt projections. If you can live with these limitations, this should be even faster than using float and as accurate as BigDecimal (unless you start multiplying and dividing). It does require more effort on your part to manage and display. Multiplying and dividing need some special thought. We'll leave that as "an exercise for the reader."

VALUE CLASSES AND VALUE TYPES

The value class that you specify for an attribute does not always tell EOF all that it needs to know. In some cases you need to refine the definition with a value type. The value class is the class in your code that will handle the type's data. For example, numbers use the `java.lang.Number` value class, while strings use the `java.lang.String` value class. However, `java.lang.Number` is an abstract class. The value type refines this into the exact subclass of `Number` that you want to get. For example, an "i" value type specifies `java.lang.Integer` and "d" `java.lang.Double`. Selecting the Internal Data Type from the Attribute Inspector of EOModeler sets both properties depending on what you select. The first figure here shows setting your attribute to be a `Double`. The second figure shows setting your attribute to be an `Integer`. Note that only the value type changes.

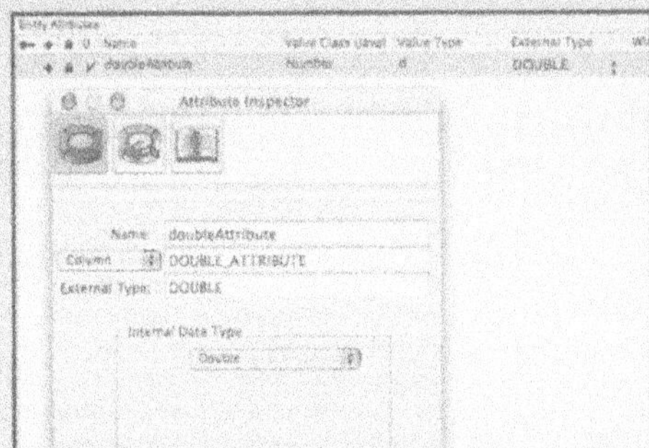

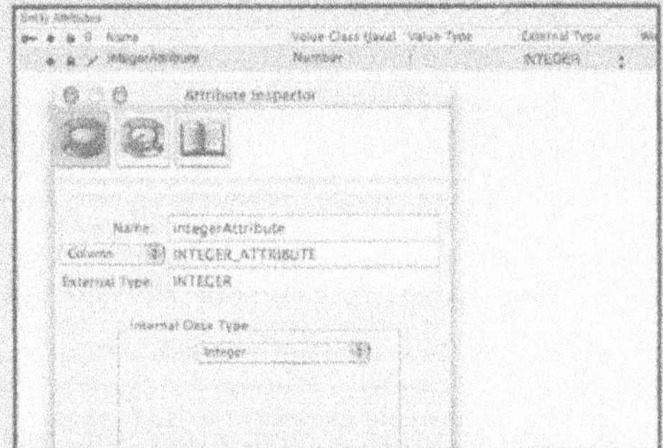

The value type can also control other aspects of JDBC adaptor-level communication and conversion between the values from the database and what your application uses. Strings, numbers, and timestamps can all be refined with a value type. Numbers require a value type, as there is no reasonable default. A value type is optional for strings and timestamps. The Apple documentation describes the value type values that are acceptable to EOModeler (see bottom of `http://developer.apple.com/documentation/WebObjects/UsingEOModeler/4WorkingWithAttributes/chapter_4_section_3.html`). Since they are used so often, we include the value types for numbers here (we tend to use "B"—`BigDecimal`—and "i"—`Integer`—most often):

- b: `java.lang.Byte`
- s: `java.lang.Short`
- i: (small "I") `java.lang.Integer`
- l: (small "L") `java.lang.Long`
- f: `java.lang.Float`
- d: `java.lang.Double`
- B: `java.math.BigDecimal`
- c: `java.lang.Boolean`

Custom Types

While the fundamental attribute types (`String`, `Integer`, etc.) provided by EOF are sufficient for basic applications, EOF provides a way to create custom attribute types (see Figure 2-3). You can probably get away without them, but this is a powerful technique that you are well advised to become familiar with. It allows you to create enterprise objects that are not bound by the basic types. For instance, you could have an `NSDictionary` or `NSArray` serialized into an attribute. A dictionary attribute can allow your objects to be extended without your having to create a completely new table in the database for them; you just add new attributes to the dictionary. (Of course, you won't be able to treat these "virtual" attributes as normal attributes—for example, you could not create a qualifier for them unless you do some extra work.)

CAUTION Since they are essentially serialized objects pushed into a database column, you will find it more difficult to use custom types with a non-WebObjects application.

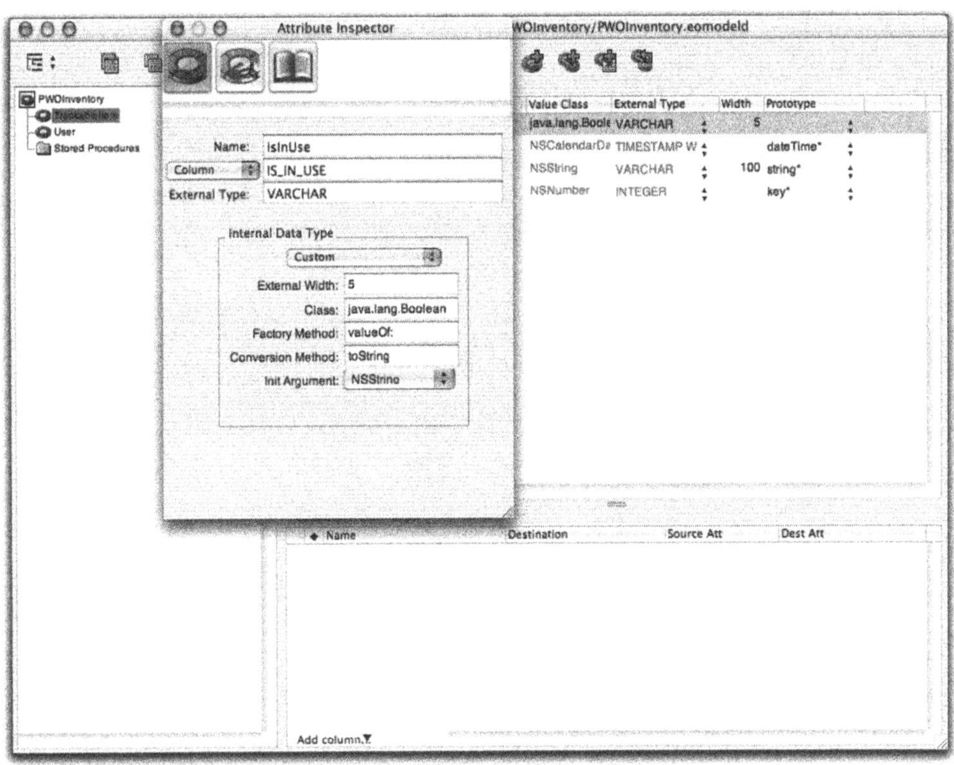

Figure 2-3. *Creating a custom attribute*

An EOF Boolean

For us, the most used custom type is the `Boolean`. EOF has no standard attribute value class for Boolean types. Something so obvious is not available in EOF? Perish the thought! Actually, WebObjects can hardly be faulted for this oversight: database vendors have been very inconsistent when it comes to the Boolean type (the SQL92 specification doesn't even specify a Boolean column type). At least, though, it gives us a great reason to use custom value types. There are several possible solutions to this, of course, and the one we used for the longest time was pretty simple: we created a class called, perhaps ambiguously, `Boolean`, and used it as a custom value type. Several other (and probably better) solutions can be found at `http://wodev.spearway.com/cgi-bin/WebObjects/WODev.woa/wa/Main?wikiPage=BooleanModeling`.

Our new favorite is to use `java.lang.Boolean` as the custom type on a string attribute with width of at least five. Then set the factory method to `valueOf:` and the conversion method to `toString` (see Figure 2-4). This will allow you to keep your Boolean attributes as real Java Booleans, while keeping your database data readable by humans (the values in the database will be the strings `true` or `false`), and you won't even have to create a new class!

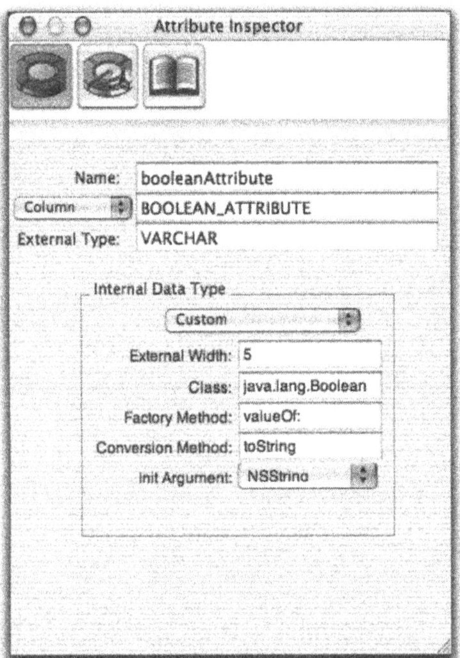

Figure 2-4. *A Boolean custom attribute*

Implementation Requirements for Custom Types

When creating custom attribute types, you need to ensure that the class of the attribute implements `clone()` and `isEqual()`. `clone()` is used when faulting an eo from the object store into an editing context and when faulting an eo from one editing context into another. `isEqual()` is used in EOF's optimistic locking mechanism to determine whether two attributes are different. A quick implementation note: immutable attributes can easily implement `clone()` just by returning `this` (think about it!).

USING NSARRAY AND NSDICTIONARY AS ATTRIBUTES

Since there is no static method to construct NSArray or NSDictionary from a string (the method, of course, must be static, since we are creating the object and have no instance), you would have to subclass those classes to use them as custom attributes in EOModeler. The following does the trick for a dictionary or array that holds string values:

```
public class MyDictionary extends NSDictionary {
    static public NSDictionary fromString(String dictionaryAsString) {
        /** require
        [non_null_param] dictionaryAsString != null; **/
        return (NSDictionary)NSPropertyListSerialization.
            propertyListFromString(dictionaryAsString);
        /** ensure
        [non_null_result] Result != null; **/
    }
}
```

Then set the custom attribute to have a class of MyDictionary and a factory method of fromString:. For a more complete implementation (one that can store nonstring values), see http://docs.info.apple.com/article.html?artnum=75173.

No Beach for You!

If you've never used custom attribute types, you probably haven't noticed that all of the fundamental attribute types (String, Integer, etc.) are immutable. This is by design. It is not an accident. This is one point of extreme importance that you must remember. Do not, on pain of spending a sunny long weekend at work debugging, use mutable objects (e.g., NSMutableDictionary, NSMutableArray) for attributes. We repeat, *do not use mutable objects for attributes.* Trust us, it was a nice weekend for the beach. EOF is not expecting attributes to be mutable and makes assumptions based on them not being mutable. Mutable attributes destroy its assumptions and havoc will rule your object store. If you need the attributes to act as if they were mutable, add cover methods like this:

```
public void addAppointment(String time, String reason) {
    super.willChange();
    NSMutableDictionary mutableAppointments = appointments().mutableClone();
    mutableAppointments.setObjectForKey(reason, time);
    setAppointments(mutableAppointments.immutableClone());
}
```

For the morbidly curious, here is why mutable attributes won't work. When EOF fetches in your eo, it initializes the eo with values from the snapshot. This is done by directly referencing the objects in the snapshot, not copying them. When you change a mutable attribute (e.g., add an object to an array) this change is not local to your eo but also updates the snapshot. This happens because both the eo and snapshot refer to the same object instance. When it is time to save the changes, EOF sees no difference between the value in your eo and the value in the snapshot and so does not update the external store (i.e., the database). The MutableAttributes example application (part of the code for this chapter) demonstrates the problem.

Handling LOB Data Efficiently

One of the things you should do when modeling your data is make sure that your EO model doesn't model things in such a way as to lead to resource contention. This is particularly important when dealing with Large OBjects, or LOBs, which can easily reach tens of megabytes or larger. If you start editing these, you can have multiple copies of a single LOB in various editing contexts and in the object store. Suddenly your 10MB MPEG gets duplicated five times and becomes 50MB. And this can stick around for a long time, depending on how long your object references and sessions last. Here are some guidelines for dealing with LOBs that will help you to avoid pulling out all your hair.

The biggest problem with modeling LOB data is memory usage. True, you also need to worry about how long transferring that data to the user takes (you might need to multithread your application) and about how long your database will be locked up when fetching your huge LOBs (in which case you might want to move the LOB onto the file system), but, from a modeling perspective, there is not much you can do but manage your memory consumption. What you must do is model your data in such a way as to make sure that your LOB data doesn't get fetched into your application unless absolutely necessary. One obvious way to do this is to break out the LOB data into a related entity with a one-to-one relationship to the entity that uses it. This allows you to avoid faulting in the LOB until you need it (see Figure 2-5).

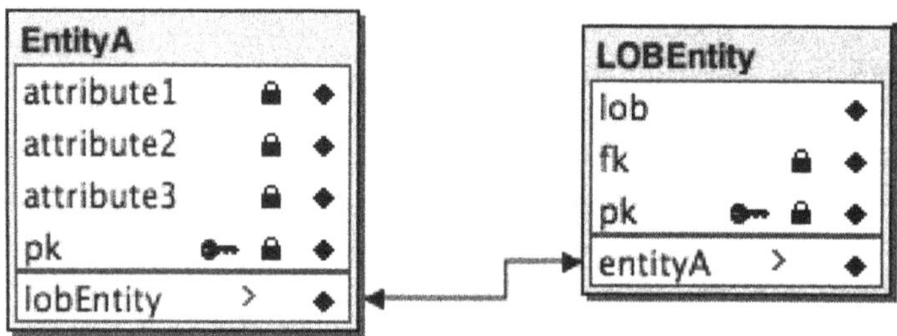

Figure 2-5. *Break out LOBs into separate entities.*

■ **CAUTION** As depicted in Figure 2-5, you should never use a LOB column for locking: your performance will take a huge hit, and with certain combinations of databases and data, it won't work at all.

Another common solution is to move the LOB data out of the database altogether, instead putting it on the file system. Then you never have to load the data until it is needed. This avoids a couple of problems—both memory management and resource contention on your database—but raises another: how do you keep the database and the files coordinated? You will need to delete the file when the row in the database is deleted, update it when the row is updated, and so on. What is really needed is a two-phase commit mechanism, which would allow us to cause an EOF `saveChanges()` to fail when operations on the file fail, but this doesn't exist in WebObjects so we need another solution. The "Seeing State Changes in the Object Graph" topic in Chapter 3 investigates a notification mechanism that comes close.

Prototypes

Prototypes are attribute templates. If you set an attribute's prototype, that attribute takes on all of the properties previously set up for the prototype. You can change any of the values of the prototyped attribute, in effect saying, "This property doesn't come from the prototype." EOModeler shows an asterisk beside the prototype name and displays the inherited and overridden properties in light and dark colors, respectively (see Figure 2-6). Any property that you don't change yourself comes from the prototype, and any changes to the prototype are reflected in attributes that you haven't changed. In a way it works similarly to subclassing, with the prototype being the superclass.

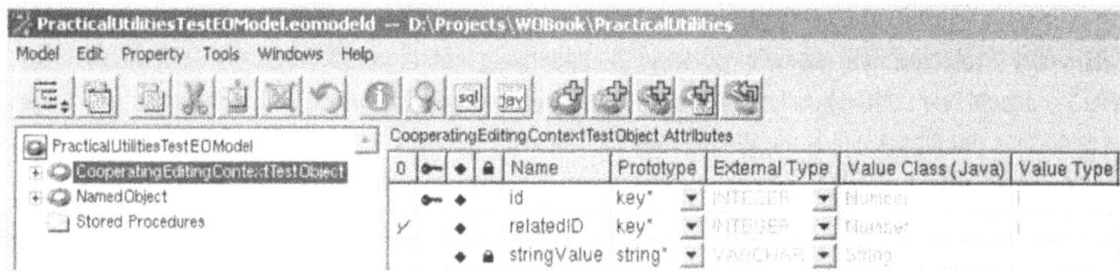

Figure 2-6. *Visual indication of customized prototypes and overridden properties (e.g., Name) compared to properties from the prototype (e.g., Value Class)*

TIP For anything other than the attribute name and column name properties, you are usually better off creating a new prototype than overriding the prototype's property. The reason is that if you later decide to change this custom setting across the application, you will have to examine each attribute rather than just changing a prototype. For example, rather than a string prototype whose length is overridden on each attribute, consider using a shortString, mediumString, and longString, or nameString, IdString, accountString, etc. Prototypes with more-specific names or with names relating to the domain are more powerful when making changes.

The use of prototypes is a powerful technique that allows you to make rapid implementation changes to your model with minimal effort. You'll be glad you used them when you find out that you have to make all of the names in an application 30 characters instead of 25 or when you discover that all of your `TIMESTAMP` fields should actually have been `TIMESTAMP WITH TIME ZONE`.

Prototypes are perhaps most useful when you decide to change databases. Why would you do that? Perhaps you have a client on Oracle who has grown tired of the licensing fees and wants to change to FrontBase. Then there is your other client with the application that you've just delivered running with FrontBase who is about to discover that his IT department will only deploy it with Microsoft's SQL Server. You are also about to get a new client who wants their applications to use DB2 as the database, something you don't have available. With other application development environments this could be a daunting task indeed, what with rewriting the vendor-specific SQL, handling all of the oddities of the database client library, and dealing with the inevitable data type differences. JDBC helps a lot by abstracting much of this, and EOF even more by taking care of all of the SQL generation for you. But there are still all of those attributes in all of those entities in your EOModels. Sigh. A programmer's lot is not an easy one.

Without prototypes, you would still have to go through each and every entity and change each and every attribute's external type (and perhaps other aspects of its definition). This is a tedious, boring process liable to leave you longing for a trip to the dentist or a month at your in-laws'. It is also an error-prone process, probably due to the mind-numbing boredom of it all. But with prototypes it becomes trivial. Once the prototypes for each database are set up, you can change back and forth on a whim.

■ **CAUTION** Prototypes will not help you avoid the underlying limitations of databases. They won't make Oracle 7.*x* accept two LONG columns in the same table and they won't help you with names that are longer than one of the databases will allow. We did mention that a programmer's lot is not an easy one, didn't we? The only way to avoid these is to be aware of them and construct your model to avoid them.

JDBC Prototypes (Old vs. New Prototypes)

Prototypes are defined by creating an entity named EO<EOAdaptor name>Prototypes. Attributes on this entity are used as prototypes in EOModels using that EOAdaptor. Any property you set on attributes in this special entity will be used to provide default values for other attributes that use that prototype.

■ **NOTE** There is another special entity called EOPrototypes, which defines prototypes that are applicable to all databases. Prototypes in this entity are overridden by prototypes in the EO<EOAdaptor name>Prototypes entity. The best way to use this feature is left as an exercise for the reader.

If you are a longtime WebObjects developer, or if you are just quick on the uptake, you will notice that the special entity's name will always be the same for every database, namely "EOJDBCPrototypes" (see Figure 2-7). Why is the name specified that way? Well, in the days when Objective-C ruled WebObjects, there was no single, standard adaptor that could be used with all databases. Your application would use a different EOAdaptor for each different database. The prototype definition mechanism made sense then, since you could have different sets of prototypes for each database—for example, EOOraclePrototypes, EOFrontBasePrototypes, and so on. As mentioned, this is one of the most obvious reasons to have prototypes in the first place, and this mechanism worked well with the old "one adaptor per database" way of doing things.

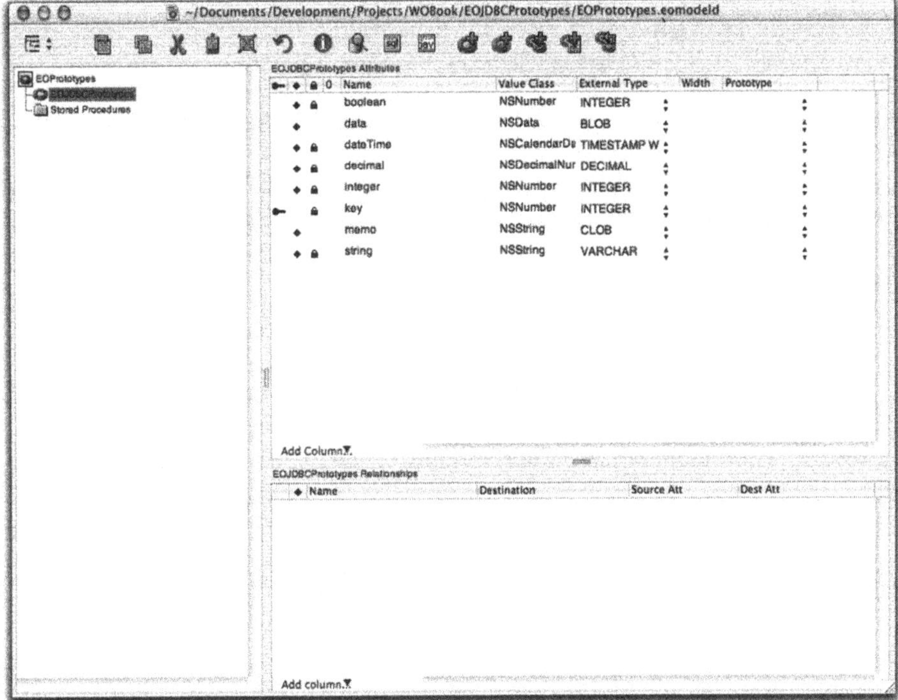

Figure 2-7. *The special prototypes entity*

The problem, of course, is that we no longer have one adaptor per database. In fact, we only have one adaptor ever: JDBC! So, are prototypes dead? Not by a long shot. They are worth it just for allowing you to change types and other properties across your entire model in one step. However, if you want to be able to support more than one database with a given application, you have a little more work to do.

Strategies for Managing Prototypes

The easiest way to work with prototypes is to do nothing out of the ordinary. If you have only a single application using the prototypes, you can simply put the EOJDBCPrototypes entity into one of the models that your application uses. If something ever does change, you can just make the changes there. If you don't have a compelling reason to do it differently, this is the way you should do it. It will save you time and sanity.

However, most of us have multiple frameworks and multiple WebObjects applications and the preceding solution is not going to be very useful for us. It is a good idea to have a standard set of prototypes, especially for applications that access the same data. If you share prototypes among a focused set of frameworks and applications, you can derive the most benefit by creating prototypes specific to the domain the application is for. If you want to share them among diverse frameworks and applications, you will need to choose prototypes that are more generic. Either way, we place the EOJDBCPrototypes entity in a model by itself and place that in a framework by itself. To use the prototypes, you just include the prototypes framework in your application or framework.

About now you are probably saying to yourself, "This is all well and good, but how do I conveniently change the prototypes for different databases?" Sadly, the answer to that is not so clear-cut, as it involves the EOModeler legacy application. While we can dynamically change the prototypes when our WebObjects application starts, EOModeler is not a Java application and is immune to anything we do in our code. It just looks for the EOJDBCPrototypes entity and takes what it finds. We have high hopes that Apple will rectify this situation in a future version of WebObjects, but that is going to require changes to EOModeler—something that does not happen very often! In the meantime it leaves us with a little more manual work.

Keeping Prototypes Segregated

A workable solution that we have used is to create one prototypes framework for each database that we need to use. We name these frameworks as the original prototype entities were named—EOOraclePrototypes, EOFrontBasePrototypes, etc. As described earlier, each of these frameworks contains only an EOModel, which contains the single entity EOJDBCPrototypes. When we want to switch databases, we simply remove one framework from the project and add another and rebuild (or change the classpath file if the application is built already). EOModeler thus sees the single EOJDBCPrototypes entity that it expects, and data browsing and SQL generation work as they always did. Life is good. Well, not for all of us. If you change back and forth frequently and don't often need to use EOModeler to browse data or generate SQL, this changing of frameworks and rebuilding (or playing with the classpath) can be a nuisance.

Changing Prototypes in Code

If ease of change is more important to you than ease of use in EOModeler, you can adjust the prototypes in code based on a configuration setting. Before we get into how to do this, we want to take a look at the costs. As we mentioned, EOModeler is not going to see any of this. It just wants its EOJDBCPrototypes. You are going to need to provide them in some form, if only to use when modeling the real entities. We have found that it works OK to have one EOModel (yep, all alone in a framework again) that contains not only the EOJDBCPrototypes entity but also an additional prototypes entity for each database that you will use (see Figure 2-8). We also give these the old style names (EOOraclePrototypes, EOFrontBasePrototypes, etc.) and take the database name from the JDBC URL—e.g., FrontBase from `jdbc:FrontBase://localhost/Test`. If we want to use EOModeler with a different database, we delete the existing EOJDBCPrototypes entity, copy and paste the prototypes entity for the database we want, and then rename the new entity to EOJDBCPrototypes.

You will also have to add to your project the plug-in framework for each database that you will use. Not every database requires a plug-in, and some are included with WebObjects (see the `com.webobjects.jdbcadaptor` package to find out which ones). Don't worry about having more than one plug-in framework in your project; EOF will choose the correct ones.

Now let's look at the code to change the prototypes on the fly. A prototype is really just an EOAttribute in disguise. Most of the work that we need to do has already been done in the `EOModelGroup`, `EOModel`, `EOEntity`, and `EOAttribute` classes. As complex as the discussion of prototypes was, we get off pretty much scot-free on the implementation, one of the beauties of the EOF and WebObjects frameworks. All we need to do is find the EOJDBCPrototypes entity, find the entity for the database we are interested in, and copy over the relevant properties. Finding an `EOEntity` is simple if you know its name. Either the `EOModelGroup` or its `EOModel` will handle this for you:

```
EOEntity anEntity = theModel.entityNamed("EOJDBCPrototypes");
EOEntity anEntity = EOModelGroup.defaultGroup().entityNamed("EOJDBCPrototypes");
```

Likewise, given the name of an EOAttribute, the EOEntity will locate it for you:

```
EOAttribute aPrototype = anEntity.attributeNamed("databaseKey");
```

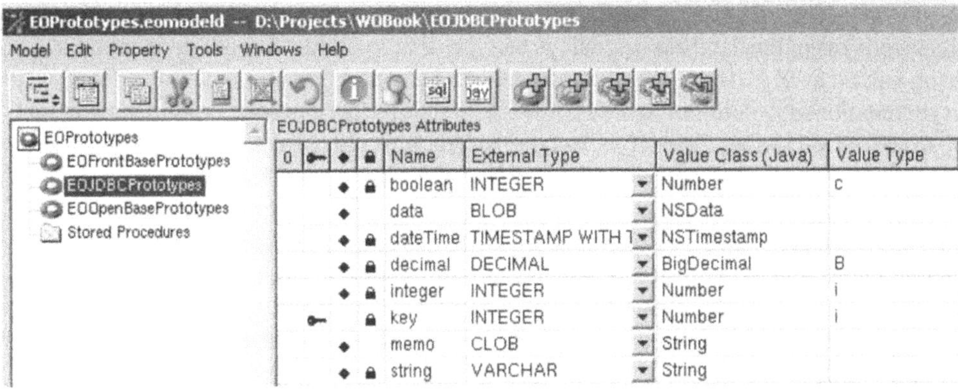

Figure 2-8. *The EOJDBCPrototypes and additional database-specific prototype entities*

■ TIP Most of the `somethingNamed()` methods will return null rather than raise an exception if they cannot find something with a matching name.

With that out of the way, it is trivial to make a loop to update the prototypes entity; see Listing 2-2.

Listing 2-2. *Updating the EOJDBCPrototypes Entity*

```
EOEntity jdbcPrototypesEntity = aModel.entityNamed("EOJDBCPrototypes");
EOEntity databasePrototypesEntity = aModel.entityNamed(dbPrototypesEntityName);
for (int i = 0; i < jdbcPrototypesEntity.attributes().count(); i++) {
    EOAttribute jdbcPrototype =
        (EOAttribute)jdbcPrototypesEntity.attributes().objectAtIndex(i);
    String prototypesName = (String)jdbcPrototype.name();
    EOAttribute dbPrototype =
        (EOAttribute)databasePrototypesEntity.attributeNamed(prototypesName);
    if (dbPrototype != null) {
        jdbcPrototype.setDefinition(dbPrototype.definition());
        jdbcPrototype.setExternalType(dbPrototype.externalType());
        jdbcPrototype.setPrecision(dbPrototype.precision());
        jdbcPrototype.setReadFormat(dbPrototype.readFormat());
        jdbcPrototype.setScale(dbPrototype.scale());
```

```
        jdbcPrototype.setUserInfo(dbPrototype.userInfo());
        jdbcPrototype.setValueType(dbPrototype.valueType());
        jdbcPrototype.setWidth(dbPrototype.width());
        jdbcPrototype.setWriteFormat(dbPrototype.writeFormat());
    }
}
```

The first thing to take note of here is the test for (dbPrototype != null). This implies that the database-specific prototypes entity is not required to override all of the definitions in EOJDBCPrototypes. This seems bad, as definitions not overridden could have cut-and-paste values from any of the database-specific prototypes entities. While this is a danger, there is a reason behind it. There is one more defect of the JDBC prototypes implementation that we've not yet mentioned: it does not handle connections to multiple database types. This worked fine in the old days when a model connecting to Oracle would use the EOOraclePrototypes and another model in the same application that connected to FrontBase would use the EOFrontBasePrototypes. What to do now that they all use the same prototypes entity? It's not pretty, but the only workable solution seems to be to give the prototypes for each connection different names. We don't mean oracleString and frontBaseString, though; that would defeat most of the purpose of prototypes. However, something like contractNumber (from the Oracle side) and customerNumber (from the FrontBase side) might be workable. So that is the reason why each database prototype entity is not required to define all of the prototypes. It is your responsibility to ensure that they are all defined by some combination of the database-specific prototypes.

The second thing to notice is the attributes that we copy. This is probably overkill; we just copy everything that seems like it might reasonably be needed. While there is even more that you could copy, in practice externalType() is the one you will be concerned with most of the time. Feel free to adjust this list to suit your needs.

Using the EOPrototypeSwitcher

The preceding code can be found in the updatePrototypes() method of the EOPrototypeSwitcher class in the PracticalUtilities framework. Each instance of this class handles switching a single set of database-specific prototypes. If you need more than one type of database, you will have to create more than one instance. The all-important method is the constructor:

```
public EOPrototypeSwitcher(String databaseType)
```

The databaseType parameter is used to form the name of the EOEntity from which the active prototypes should be taken: EO<databaseType>Prototypes. In the examples in this book, the databaseType parameter always reflects the type of the database. This is just convention, not a requirement. There is no reason why you could not name them EODevelopmentPrototypes, EODeploymentPrototypes, etc. However, the name of the database is more likely to be compatible with any fix that Apple might produce. You can update the prototypes in all of the models with this simple loop:

```
EOModelGroup defaultGroup = EOModelGroup.defaultGroup();
Enumeration modelEnumeration = defaultGroup.models().objectEnumerator();
while (modelEnumeration.hasMoreElements()) {
    prototypeSwitcher.updatePrototypes((EOModel) modelEnumeration.nextElement());
}
```

NOTE You can force all of the models in the application and all frameworks to be loaded by asking for the default model group, `EOModelGroup.defaultGroup()`. Otherwise they are loaded as needed.

It is even easier to switch prototypes using notifications. An `EOModelGroup` sends a `ModelAddedNotification` each time that it loads a model. The `EOPrototypeSwitcher` is set up to handle this notification for you. All you need to do is ask it to `listenForAddedModels()`. The implementation of the notification handler method is a single line of code:

```
updatePrototypes((EOModel) aNotification.object());
```

You can see the `EOPrototypeSwitcher` in action in the `EOTestSuite` class in the PracticalUtilities framework.

Aside: Using Notifications to Extend the Frameworks

Here we will take a little step back from prototypes and delve into WebObjects' notification mechanism.

The best-known method of extending functionality in the OO world is the use of subclassing. There are other ways; the EOF and WebObjects frameworks use two of them: delegation and notifications. Both were introduced in the first chapter in the context of debugging. Delegation is a little more obvious, and examples of its use appear in Chapter 3. We are going to take a closer look at notification as a mechanism for extending functionality. Be aware that there is no master list of the available notifications. Regrettably, the only way to know about them is to look through the documentation of the fields on each class.

It may not be readily apparent how being notified of something that some other code is doing can help you to extend the functionality of that other code. The class at the heart of this is `NSNotificationCenter`. Objects with a notification to send give it to the `NSNotificationCenter` for distribution. Objects wanting to receive a notification register with `NSNotificationCenter`. An important fact not clearly mentioned in the documentation is that `NSNotificationCenter` sends the notifications in the same thread that it receives them; in other words, notifications are sent synchronously. This is important as it means that all of the objects receiving the notification will have a chance to execute their code before the object that sent the notification continues. This is different from subclassing in that we are not replacing or extending a method (and may not even be aware of which method is sending the notification), but rather are changing the application's behavior when a predefined activity happens. Notification is not intended to replace default behavior, as with a delegate, nor can we know if any other objects have registered for the same notification and hence might be making other changes at the same point. If multiple objects are receiving the same notification, there is no way to predict the order in which the objects will receive it. On the other hand, notification does not suffer from the single-delegate restriction of the delegation scheme that the frameworks use, nor does it require you to replace framework classes with subclasses, something that is often not easy to accomplish. Each method of extending functionality has its own time and place, strengths and weaknesses. Being aware of each will help you in choosing the correct solution for a particular problem.

When you look at the documentation for NSNotificationCenter you will see references to NSSelector, which is a more flexible alternative to the Method class of Java's Reflection capabilities. Both represent a method and allow it to be invoked indirectly. With Method the method represented is tightly tied to the implementation in a particular class and its subclasses. Method, through Java's strong typing, guarantees the existence of the target method that it represents. NSSelector is not tied to any particular class or implementation and makes no such guarantee that the method exists. It does not even care if the method is static or an instance method! NSSelector frees your classes from having to inherit from a specific class or implement a specific interface in order to allow another class to call its methods with NSSelector. This is also why your delegate objects don't need to declare that they implement a specific delegation interface (which would force you to write *all* of the delegate methods—even if you never used them): objects that use delegates use NSSelectors internally to determine if the method is implemented before calling it.

NSNotificationCenter uses NSSelector so that the objects receiving the notifications can be of any class with no requirement for implementing a specific interface. The objects receiving notifications are called *observers*. To register your object as an observer for a specific notification, you need to tell the NSNotificationCenter which object is to receive the notification; give it an NSSelector identifying the method that will receive the notification; tell it the name of the notification to be received; and optionally provide a qualifying object if you only want to receive some of the notifications.

Here is an example registration:

```
NSSelector sessionCreatedSelector =
    new NSSelector("handleSessionCreatedNotification",
                   new Class[] { NSNotification.class } );
NSNotificationCenter.defaultCenter().
    addObserver(this,
                sessionCreatedSelector,
                WOSession.SessionDidCreateNotification,
                null);
```

The only choice you have when creating the NSSelector to handle a notification is the name of the method you want called: you can use anything you desire for this. The parameter, a single NSNotification object, is not open to negotiation. In this example the default notification center (usually the only one) is being instructed to inform this object when a SessionDidCreate notification is sent by calling the method

```
public void handleSessionCreatedNotification(NSNotification theNotification)
```

The null parameter at the end indicates that the notification is wanted regardless of which session is getting created.

Implementing methods that receive notifications, such as the preceding handleSessionCreatedNotification() method, is straightforward. You can ask the NSNotification for three things: the notification's name (from name()), the object associated with the notification (from object()), and the userInfo() dictionary of information specific to this notification. The name() will only be of interest if the same method is handling multiple notifications. The object() is what is most often needed. In the preceding example, it will be the session that was just created. The contents of the userInfo() dictionary are specific to a notification and often unused.

Here is an implementation of this method that just logs the ID of the newly created session:

```
public void handleSessionCreatedNotification(NSNotification theNotification) {
    /** require
        [valid_notification] theNotification != null;
        [is_session_created_notification]
        theNotification.name().equals(WOSession.SessionDidCreateNotification);
     **/

    Session createdSession = (Session) theNotification.object();
    NSLog.out.appendln("Created Session: " + createdSession);
}
```

One Last Consideration: The Connection Dictionary

We've purposely not mentioned this so far, but changing the prototypes is of no use if the connection dictionary points to the original database. Even if you are not using prototypes, the ability to change this programmatically is useful if you want to switch from using one copy of the data to another (e.g., from a copy on your local machine to one on the test server). If you can't do this in code, you would need to use EOModeler to change it.

Changing this is a lot easier than changing the prototypes. To connect to a database, EOF needs to know the name of the adaptor to use and the dictionary of connection information to provide. WebObjects comes with two adaptors, JDBC and JNDI. You can write your own, but we won't promise that this approach is easy or well documented. The adaptor name is used to form a framework name as Java<*adaptor name*>Adaptor—for example, JavaJDBCAdaptor. This is how EOF finds the code to load for the adaptor name. Of course, the adaptor framework has to be on the classpath, which is why you need to include it among the frameworks needed by your project even though you will rarely directly reference anything from it.

The dictionary of connection information is adaptor dependent. For the JDBC adaptor, it needs to have at least a key named `URL` associated with the complete JDBC URL for the database. If the URL does not include the user name and password, these can be included separately in the dictionary with the keys `username` and `password`. The connection dictionary can also include keys for the driver and plugin classes if the defaults used by EOF are not correct for your situation. Expressed in plist format, an example connection dictionary looks like this:

```
connectionDictionary = {
    URL = "jdbc:openbase://127.0.0.1/Test";
    username = tester;
    password = "";
    driver = "";
    plugin = "";
};
```

Unused keys can be omitted. In the preceding example, the keys `password`, `driver`, and `plugin` are not needed. Some databases—FrontBase, for example—can put all of the needed information in the URL:

```
connectionDictionary = {
    URL = "jdbc:FrontBase://localhost/Test/user=tester/upasswd=tester";
};
```

CAUTION When the appropriate logging is turned on, EOF will log the connection dictionary. If you put the password in the URL key, it will be sent in cleartext to your log file. However, if you use the password key, then EOF will mask the value.

Setting this information is conveniently easy:

```
EOModel aModel = EOModelGroup.defaultGroup().modelNamed("MyModel");
aModel.setConnectionDictionary(connectionDictionary);
aModel.setAdaptorName(adaptorName);
```

The difficult, inconvenient part is setting this at the proper time. If EOF has already connected to a database (with the connection information in the model) it can be nearly impossible to get it to disconnect and reconnect with the connection information that you want it to use. You need to set the connection information very early in your application's life, before any code does anything that might cause EOF to connect to the database. You've already seen that an EOModelGroup broadcasts a notification as soon as it loads a model. This seems like the ideal time to change the connection information; if the model was just loaded, it has not yet been used for a database connection.

The EOModelConnector class in the PracticalUtilities framework handles connecting models. As with the EOPrototypeSwitcher, this can be done manually or by listening for notifications. The EOTestSuite class has an example of using these classes together, though the EOModelConnector can be used by itself if you are not using prototypes.

Usage of EOModelConnector is very similar to the EOPrototypeSwitcher:

```
modelConnector = new EOModelConnector(connectionDictionary, NSArray.EmptyArray);
modelConnector.listenForAddedModels();
```

The first parameter is self-explanatory. The second parameter is a list of the names of models to ignore. You will use this if some models need different connection information, or if some of the models are only for unit testing and will not or should not be connected. This constructor assumes that the adaptor name is JDBC; if you need a different adaptor name, there is an alternate constructor. Models will only be connected if the model name is not in the ignored list and the adaptor name in the model matches that in the EOModelConnector.

CAUTION EOF shares a database connection among all models with the same connection information. However, in order for this to happen, the adaptor name and connection dictionary must pass an equals() test. Being equivalent is not good enough. If you are not using the EOModelConnector, be careful what you type in EOModeler.

Debugging JDBC Connection Problems

Sooner or later you are going to run into JDBC connection problems. Chances are, if you've been using WebObjects for more than a couple of hours, you've already run into them: you can see the database from EOModeler, the code compiles fine, the drivers are all there, but it just refuses to connect. We are going to look at some of the causes of these problems and introduce a class that places the burden of debugging back on the machine, where it belongs. After all, we have better things to do than wrestle with classpaths and extension directories, don't we?

Understanding the Source of the Problem

The first thing you need to do is understand some of the issues surrounding EOF and JDBC connections.

EOModeler Muddles

"EOModeler can see my database—why can't my application?" EOModeler is not a Java application; it is an Objective-C application. It is also rather old, and on Windows it uses JDK 1.1 and the JDBC 1.0 API due to the older Java Bridge (and if you don't know what that is, count yourself lucky!). WebObjects, and your application, uses JDK 1.3 (or newer) and the JDBC 2.0 API. On OS X, EOModeler uses a more modern JDK and the JDBC 2.0 API, so life is much easier there. The following discussion is mostly relevant to (i.e., concerned with troubles on) Windows.

EOModeler also takes its Java Runtime Environment (JRE) and classpath from a different location than your application. You can see the configuration used in the `JavaConfig.plist`, which is in `$NEXT_ROOT\Library\Java` on Windows and in `/System/Library/Java` on OS X. On Windows, the JDBC drivers that EOModeler is using are usually below that directory as individual class files (i.e., extracted from the Jar files). With few exceptions, these are not only different files from what your application will use, but include an entirely different driver as well.

The upshot of this is that EOModeler being able to connect to your database tells you nearly nothing about what will happen with your application. The only thing you can tell is that the JDBC URL and user information in the connection dictionary are correct. Conversely, if your application is working but EOModeler is not, the places to look are the `JavaConfig.plist` and the JDBC drivers below `$NEXT_ROOT\Apple\Library\Java` or `/System/Library/Java`.

■ NOTE FrontBase is an interesting anomaly in this division between JDBC 1.0 and 2.0. Those clever FrontBase developers have written their EOModeler plug-in so that it only uses the parts of the JDBC 2.0 API that are compatible with the JDBC 1.0 API. The result is that even if EOModeler is taking the driver from different files, it is still the same driver.

Plug-in Pickiness

As we discussed in the "Prototypes" section, every database uses the same adaptor now: the `JavaJDBCAdaptor`. While the abstraction of JDBC is all fine and good, the simple fact is that not all databases are the same. EOF recognizes this and accommodates it by allowing each connection to configure `com.webobjects.jdbcadaptor.JDBCAdaptor` with a plug-in. The plug-in is implemented as a subclass of `com.webobjects.jdbcadaptor.JDBCPlugIn` and functions like a delegate, providing database and JDBC driver-specific functionality. Unlike the delegates that the frameworks use, the plug-in object is mandatory. The `JDBCAdaptor` is happy to take a guess, based on the JDBC URL, as to the plug-in to use, or it can be specified explicitly in the connection dictionary. If you don't specify it and the `JDBCAdaptor` can't find anything that matches its guesses, it will default to using `com.webobjects.jdbcadaptor.JDBCPlugIn` directly.

The `com.webobjects.jdbcadaptor` package has plug-in classes for the databases that WebObjects officially supports. Other databases—FrontBase, for example—need plug-ins from an external source (often the database vendor). Still others work with the default `JDBCPlugIn`. If you do need a plug-in that is not part of WebObjects, it needs to be on the classpath for the application to run, but not to compile.

■ **NOTE** You can also define which plug-in to use by configuring the Properties file in the JavaJDBCAdaptor framework, or by calling the static method `setPlugInNameForSubprotocol()` on `JDBCPlugIn`. We've never had the need to do either.

Extension Exertions

The Java extension mechanism was added in JDK 1.2 as a convenient means of loading the noncore parts of the ever-expanding API. The aspect we are concerned with, installed extensions, is simply a directory where Jar files can be placed. Any Jar files in this directory are loaded when the Java Virtual Machine (JVM) initializes. This can be very convenient for standard, commonly used utility libraries, as it frees you from having to include them on the classpath. It is in fact a fine place to stick JDBC drivers.

But there is one small problem: *which* extension directory? On Windows and Solaris, there is one for each and every JVM installation, and you need to add the driver to the one under the JVM that is being used to launch your application. Unless the directory is being specified explicitly, it can be a little hard to figure out which one is getting used, especially with ProjectBuilderWO on Windows. Adding further aggravation to this is Windows' habit of accumulating increasing numbers of JRE installations, often of the exact same version, in different locations. It can be a trying task to locate the one getting used, or even just locating all of them.

You will notice that we have not mentioned OS X. Things are predictably different there. On OS X the main extensions directory is `/Library/Java/Extensions`. There is also a user-specific extensions directory at `~/Library/Java/Extensions`. Then there is the underdocumented `/System/Library/Java/Extensions` and the mysterious `/System/Library/Frameworks/JavaVM.framework/Versions/1.3.1/Home/lib/ext`, which is probably intended for JRE version–specific Jars. If you just stick with the standard `/Library/Java/Extensions` you should be able to avoid the problems that affect Windows with its plague of JRE installations.

WebObjects 5.2 introduced another extensions directory specific to WebObjects. The new `WOBootstrap` class uses this directory when launching an application. Any Jar files found in this directory are treated as if they appeared on the classpath and will be loaded with your application. While this was primarily done to avoid the very lame command-line length limit in Windows, it is also a convenient place to drop commonly used Jar files. In addition to being convenient, this can fix a lot of class loader–related problems, as the same class loader that is used for the WebObjects classes loads these extension Jars. The path for this directory is `$NEXT_ROOT/Local/Library/WebObjects/Extensions` on Windows and Solaris and `/Library/WebObjects/Extensions` on OS X. For the discussion that follows, we will consider anything in this directory to be "on the classpath."

■ **CAUTION** While it can be tempting to do so, don't place the plug-in class in one of the Java extensions directories. This is because of how Java looks through class loaders to find classes. A class can only see another class if it was loaded by its class loader, or by one of that class loader's parent class loaders. This means that classes in a class loader cannot see classes loaded by a child class loader. The class loader that loads the classes on the classpath (i.e., the classes from WebObjects and your application) is not the same class loader that loads the contents of the Java extensions directory. The practical result is that Java Extension classes cannot see classes on the classpath. What does this have to do with the plug-in? The parent class of a plug-in is `com.webobjects.jdbcadaptor.JDBCPlugIn`, which is loaded from the classpath and which therefore cannot be seen by the subclass in the Java extensions directory. The result of this is that the plug-in class cannot even be instantiated when loaded from the Java Extensions directory. The plug-in can be placed in the WebObjects extensions directory, as it shares a common class loader with the rest of the WebObjects application.

Finding and Fixing the Problem

If EOF produced clear and detailed error messages when problems with the JDBC connection arose, none of the previously mentioned problems would be particularly important. That, however, is not the case. Sometimes the messages are OK, but sometimes they are misleading, and sometimes they are just plain wrong. The error detection in the EOAccess level seems good, so the problem is likely in the plug-in implementation, or the meaningful exceptions are getting blindly caught at some higher level and rethrown as less meaningful ones. None of the exception messages offer much advice on what to do about fixing the problem or give any additional information that would help you to pinpoint it.

We are going to dive into the EOAccess classes and build up the connection layer by layer. We will look for failures along the way and indicate possible causes and resolutions. The end result will be a class we can pop into a malfunctioning application to get an analysis of the problem and suggested fixes.

In the Beginning There Was a JDBC Adaptor

The most basic step in the connection is to get an instance of the JDBCAdaptor. If we can't achieve that, nothing else is going to work. All we need to do is ask com.webobjects.eoaccess.EOAdaptor to create it for us by name:

```
JDBCAdaptor targetAdaptor = (JDBCAdaptor)EOAdaptor.adaptorWithName("JDBC");
```

Other than a misspelled JDBC, the only reason for this to fail would be that we've forgotten to include the JavaJDBCAdaptor framework in our project.

A Plug-in Is Born

The next step is to create a plug-in to configure the adaptor. The name of the plug-in class can be given directly in the connection dictionary, or the adaptor can infer it from the JDBC URL. We need to let the adaptor know the connection dictionary before asking it for the JDBCPlugIn:

```
targetAdaptor.setConnectionDictionary(aConnectionDictionary);
JDBCPlugIn targetPlugIn = targetAdaptor().plugIn();
```

Two bad things can happen here: the call to plugin() might throw an exception, or it might return an instance of com.webobjects.jdbcadaptor.JDBCPlugIn.

The only problematic exception that the plug-in creation might throw is NoClassDefFoundError. This exception won't be thrown for the plug-in class itself. If the plug-in class cannot be found, the adaptor assumes that there is no special plug-in and uses the JDBCPlugIn class. The exception will be thrown if the plug-in class needs the definition of another class that is not loaded. For example, the FrontBase plug-in needs the definition of FBJConnection from the FrontBase JDBC driver. This exception indicates a missing classpath entry or a Jar file missing from the extensions directory. You will have to look at which class the exception is thrown for in order to determine what is missing.

It is not an error by itself for plugin() to return an instance of com.webobjects.jdbcadaptor.JDBCPlugIn. Use of this superclass is allowed. However, JDBCPlugIn does not know the class of the JDBC driver to use and therefore requires the driver class to be defined in the connection dictionary under the key driver. We explicitly check if this key is needed and missing:

```
String driverClassName = (String)connectionDictionary
  .objectForKey(JDBCAdaptor.DriverKey);
if (targetPlugIn.getClass().equals(JDBCPlugIn.class) &&
    ((driverClassName == null) || (driverClassName.length() == 0)))
```

If this is true, one of five things is wrong:

- The JDBCPlugIn class is being used because the plug-in is missing from your classpath.
- The JDBCPlugIn class is being used because the connection dictionary has a misspelled plugin key.
- The JDBCPlugIn class is being used because the plug-in name specified under the plugin key is incorrect.

- The class name for the JDBC driver, under the key `driver`, is missing from the connection dictionary.
- The connection dictionary has a misspelled `driver` key.

The Driver, Please

Now we have a JDBC adaptor created and configured with a valid JDBC adaptor plug-in. The last thing we need to do before we attempt a live connection is to load the actual JDBC driver class. The `JDBCAdaptor` provides the `driverName()` based on information provided by the `JDBCPlugIn` subclass or the connection dictionary. All we need to verify is that we can load the class:

```
Class targetDriver = Class.forName(targetAdaptor.driverName());
```

If the class fails to load, it is missing either from the classpath or from the extensions directory.

Operator, Can You Connect Me?

The only things that now stand between us and a database connection are network problems and our own connection dictionary configuration mistakes. At this point there is little else to do or check, so we will jump directly to asking the adaptor to connect to the database to verify this last detail:

```
targetAdaptor().assertConnectionDictionaryIsValid();
```

As a variety of database-specific things can happen at this point, you will need to examine the exception message to determine what went wrong. It is not a WebObjects problem at this point. Things to check are:

- Is the database server name correct?
- Are you connected to the network?
- Can the database server be seen from the machine your application is running on?
- Is the database name correct?
- Is the user name (if any) correct?
- Is the user password (if any) correct?

The EOFJDBCConnectionAnalyzer Class

All of the logic and possible solutions to the preceding problem are found in the `EOFJDBCConnectionAnalyzer` class in the PracticalUtilities framework. No longer will you be held hostage to the complexity of making an EOF JDBC connection! Next time you have a connection problem, just include the framework and set this class to work:

```
new EOFJDBCConnectionAnalyzer("TheModel");
```

It can be created with a model, the name of a model, or just a connection dictionary. It will do its work and tell you what it finds out.

TIP The system properties can be a wealth of debugging information. `System.getProperties().getProperty("java.ext.dirs")` will return the Java extension directories in use. This can be particularly helpful on Windows when you are not sure which JRE is being used. Similarly, `System.getProperties().getProperty("java.class.path")` will return the actual classpath that the JVM is using, useful for checking your assumptions! Try printing all of the property names out to see what else you can find.

EO Modeling with Eclipse

EOModeler uses the PB.project file's `FRAMEWORKSEARCH` path to determine what frameworks to look in when resolving prototypes and relationships to entities in other models. The problem is that WOLips does not update the `FRAMEWORKSEARCH` path with the path to your frameworks in the Eclipse workspace. Instead, WOLips points the search path to the system library directory and the local library directory only. This means that you will need to do one of the following if you want to use prototypes in your projects (and you probably should; refer back to the "Prototypes" section), or if you have entity relationships that cross EOModels:

- Install the prototype or related model frameworks in one of those directories.
- Have all models (including the prototype model) in one project, since EOModeler automatically searches the current project.

Summary

You should seriously consider using eo inheritance on your next project if you have not already done so. Properly used, it is very effective at reducing complexity at a, usually, minor cost in performance. We feel the use of prototypes is almost mandatory. The initial cost is very low, they can speed your modeling, and the freedom to change that they provide is invaluable. Couple this with runtime switching of prototypes and connection dictionaries, and development against multiple servers and deployment configuration for multiple clients becomes trivial. And when you run into the inevitable JDBC connection problems, you now have a trusty debugging class to turn to. In the next chapter we will look at how to manipulate enterprise objects in code after you have modeled them.

CHAPTER 3

Managing the Object Graph

Every path but your own is the path of fate. Keep on your own track, then.

—Henry David Thoreau

One thing that separates the Enterprise Object frameworks (EOF) from many other object persistence mechanisms is that EOF maintains the relationships between Java enterprise objects, even when using inheritance. With EOF, there is no need to think in terms of rows in an SQL result set or to concern yourself with matching and setting primary and foreign keys. However, it does introduce the need to be aware of some object graph concepts and to follow some simple rules.

Understanding the Object Graph

The term *graph* comes from graph theory (no, nothing to do with pie charts) and refers to a set of nodes connected by vertices. In most cases we will be working with a disconnected graph—islands of connected objects that are not reachable from each other. You can visualize this graph as a network of objects; see Figure 3-1.

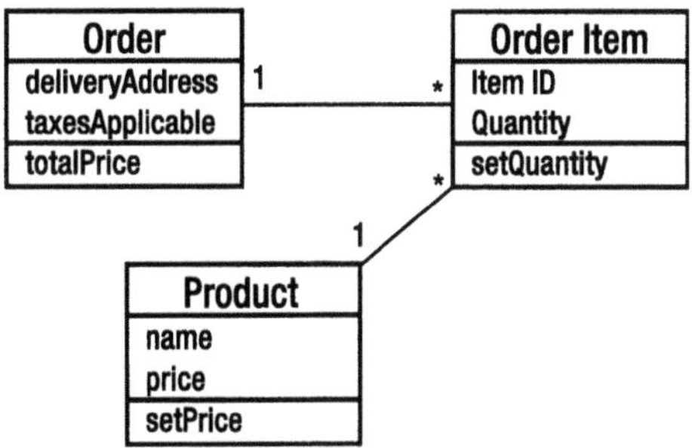

Figure 3-1. *Networks of objects in an object graph*

In EOF the nodes are your Java enterprise objects. The vertices are the references that one object holds to another (called relationships in EOF). It is the responsibility of EOF to maintain the consistency of this graph as you add and remove objects and make, break, and traverse relationships between them.

Viewing the Object Graph in Context

Understanding the `EOEditingContext`, and its relationship to the enterprise objects (a.k.a. eos, eo objects) that it manages, is crucial to success with EOF. What is an editing context anyway?

Before we answer that, let's take a step back and consider all of the enterprise objects that your application will be able to access at a point in time. In database terms, this is all of the rows that are in all of the tables in all of your databases at a point in time. We will call this the object space, the set of all objects that the application can access. Most instances of an application will not need to access all of the objects in the object space at one time. Most often, only a small subset will be in use. These "in use" objects are recorded in an object store in the application. An object store is an internally consistent view of a subset of the object space. We are using *object store* to collectively refer to a set of `EOObjectStore` objects (usually instances of `EODatabaseContext`) managed by a single `EOObjectStoreCoordinator`.

To recap, our application can potentially access all of the objects in the object space (all of the data in the databases). In practice, it is only using some of these objects and holds these in the object store. Since most processes in an application will need to use only a subset of the objects in the object store, we need to narrow this down further to get a useful working set of objects.

An editing context is a view of the object store that shows only this small working subset of objects. It acts as a sandbox in which you can view objects and make local changes to the object graph. You can, if you so decide, make these changes permanent and update the object store, which in turn updates the object space. Or you can discard your changes and it will be as if they never existed.

The primary responsibility of the editing context is to manage its enterprise objects to maintain an internally consistent view of that subset of the object store. Internally consistent means that

- Objects in that editing context only have references to other objects in the same editing context (ignoring, for now, the complications of the EOSharedEditingContext).
- The subset of the object graph that it contains appears the same regardless of which object you start navigating from.
- Objects not in the editing context are transparently brought into the editing context from the object store (and even the object space if necessary) when referenced.
- Changes in the object store are reflected in the editing context.

An editing context provides services for creating enterprise objects, relating enterprise objects, updating existing enterprise objects, and permanently deleting enterprise objects. If an enterprise object is changed in an editing context and the changes are saved, they are reflected in updates to the object space and the object store. All of the other editing contexts connected to that object store are also updated (or at least given the chance to update). EOF keeps the view of enterprise objects consistent across the editing contexts associated with an object store.

It is possible for a single application to be configured to have multiple object store coordinators, which results in the creation of multiple object stores. We won't stop here to go into why this might be done; see the online documentation `http://developer.apple.com/documentation/WebObjects/Enterprise_Objects/Geography/chapter_5_section_9.htm` for details. All you need to remember is that editing contexts in one object store will not reflect changes in another one. EOF handles this the same as it handles object stores in different application instances: it does not maintain consistency in this situation. Dealing with the inconsistencies that arise from this is one of the great challenges when working with EOF.

It is important to recognize the distinction between the objects in the object space and object store and enterprise objects as instances of Java classes in an `EOEditingContext`. Each object has a unique identity in the object space that is represented in Java as an `EOGlobalID`. An object has a less unique existence as a snapshot in an object store, as each application has its own object store and an application can have more than one, as discussed earlier. At the editing context level, objects are not very unique at all; see Figure 3-2. An object as a snapshot in the object store can (and often will) have representations as enterprise objects in many different editing contexts. Only a single copy of an enterprise object can be in any one editing context. EOF keeps track of all of these different copies and helps the editing context synchronize them through their `EOGlobalID`. The enterprise objects in an editing context are local copies of the objects in the object store. Changes can be made to them without affecting either the object store or the object space.

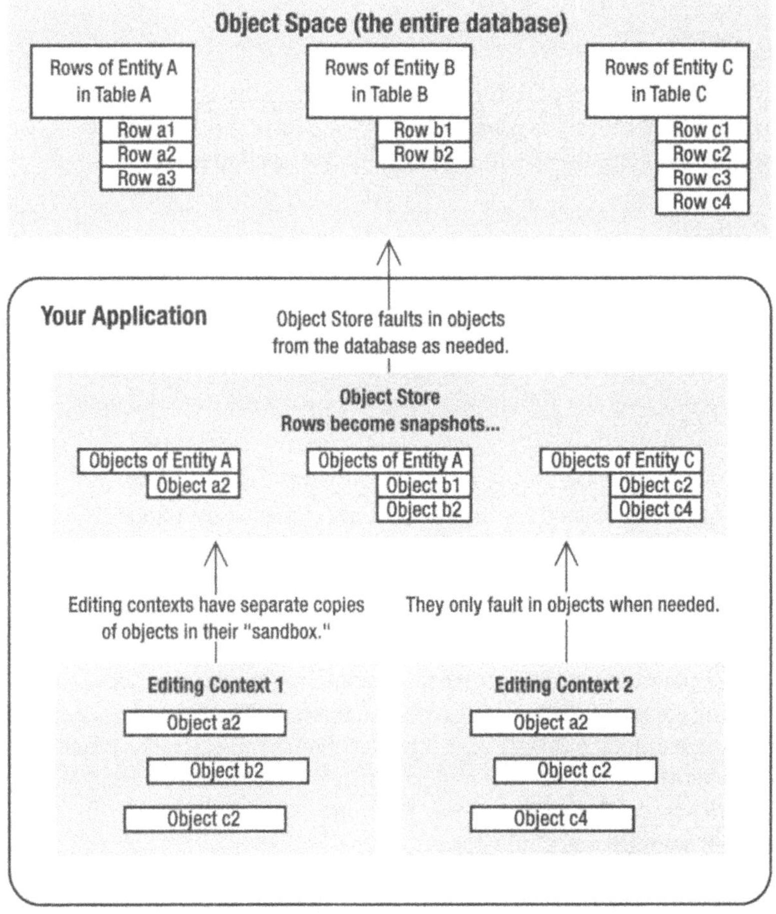

Figure 3-2. *An example object space*

Here there is an object space, with Entities A, B, and C and objects a1, a2, a3, b1, b2, c1, c2, c3, and c4. Note that the object store has snapshots for only a2, b1, b2, c2, and c4 in it. The two editing contexts each have a different subset of the object store in them, with copies of a2 and c2 appearing in both.

Understanding the Varieties of Editing Contexts

There are two fundamental types of editing context and several variations. This section briefly explains each of them.

The Ordinary Editing Context

One of the fundamental types, this is usually referred to as simply "an editing context" and is an ordinarily constructed instance of `com.webobjects.eocontrol.EOEditingContext`. Its parent `EOObjectStore` is usually an `EOObjectStoreCoordinator`. When this type of editing context saves, the changes update the object store, which updates the object space. You need to `lock()` and `unlock()` this type of editing context. This is a good, all-around utility sort of editing context.

The Peer Editing Context

Peer editing context is a term for ordinary editing contexts that share the same parent `EOObjectStore`. The parent `EOObjectStore` is usually an `EOObjectStoreCoordinator` but could be another editing context (see the "Child Editing Contexts" section further on).

The Default Editing Context

This is not really a variety of editing context, but rather a specially managed ordinary editing context provided as a convenience. The default editing context is created by `WOSession` and accessed by `session().defaultEditingContext()`. The Session takes care of calls to `lock()` and `unlock()`, freeing you from that chore. This editing context has a long life span and is best reserved for values needed over the lifetime of a session, such as the user's identity.

Child Editing Contexts

This variety of the ordinary editing context has another editing context as its parent. It is constructed by specifying the editing context that is to be the parent: `new EOEditingContext (parentEditingContext)`. When this type of editing context saves, the changes update the parent editing context but *not* the object store or object space. The parent editing context also needs to be saved in order for the changes to update the object store or object space (assuming that the parent's parent is an `EOObjectStoreCoordinator`). You need to `lock()` and `unlock()` this type of editing context, too; these calls are also forwarded to the parent, freeing you from the need to lock and unlock it as well. This is a good choice for wizardlike functionality and nested dialogs where the changes span multiple pages with a validation step on each page. While it is possible to nest editing contexts more than one level deep, doing so can get complex and confusing.

Nested Editing Contexts

This is another term for child editing context.

The Shared Editing Context

The other fundamental type, this is usually referred to as "the shared editing context" and is accessed by calling `EOSharedEditingContext.defaultSharedEditingContext()`. The shared editing context allows editing contexts (ordinary, nested, etc.) to share enterprise objects. The benefit is that fewer copies (one) of these objects are created and fewer trips to the database are made. The objects in a shared editing context are read only; changes to objects in a shared editing context are not permitted. Objects in a shared editing context are not allowed to have relationships to objects not in the shared editing context. There is no need to `lock()` and `unlock()` this type of editing context; EOF takes care of that for you. This is a good choice for objects that seldom change and have no relationships to other objects—e.g., lookup values.

Rules of Engagement

There are a few simple rules to follow when working with enterprise objects and editing contexts. If you do not follow them, sooner or later EOF will have its revenge!

Keep object relationships in the same editing context. This is the most important rule and the one you are most likely to break sooner or later. If you make a relationship (e.g., with `addObjectToBothSidesOfRelationshipWithKey()`) between an object in one editing context and a second object in another editing context, an exception will be thrown when either editing context is saved.

There is one exception to this rule. It does not apply when making unidirectional relationships to objects in an `EOSharedEditingContext`. Objects in a regular (not shared) editing context can have relationships to objects in a shared editing context. Objects in a shared editing context should not have relationships to objects in other editing contexts.

Most of the time you will get from one object to another by traversing relationships. This creates a copy of the related object in the same editing context. However, the time will come when you have an enterprise object in one editing context and you need to use it in another editing context. Despair not—it is easy to get it copied from one editing context to another. You can do it yourself by constructing a fault, but why go to so much work when `com.webobjects.eoaccess.EOUtilities` will do it for you? There are two relevant methods:

```
public static EOEnterpriseObject localInstanceOfObject(EOEditingContext ec,
                                                       EOEnterpriseObject object)
public static NSArray localInstancesOfObjects(EOEditingContext ec,
                                              NSArray objects)
```

They both work the same way, one for a single object and the other for an array. The `EOEditingContext` parameter is the editing context that you want to use the object in (that is, the one that it's not in now). The other parameter, `EOEnterpriseObject` or `NSArray`, is the object or objects in a foreign editing context that you want to use. For example:

```
EOEditingContext localEC = new EOEditingContext();
User userInSession = ((Session)session()).registeredUser();
User localUser = EOUtilities.localInstanceOfObject(localEC, userInSession);
```

Work with objects only in an editing context. Do not examine or modify an enterprise object that has not been inserted, fetched, or faulted into an editing context. Doing so will cause notifications to be broadcast when EOF is not prepared to handle them. The effects of this may not show up immediately but can cause later problems, such as changes not being written to the database. Debugging such problems can cause prematurely gray hair and loss of sanity. This rule is most commonly violated when values are set in the object's constructor. Although enterprise objects are Java objects, it is not appropriate to initialize default values in the constructor. Object initialization should be done in `awakeFromInsertion(EOEditingContext)`. Where you would normally use a constructor:

```
/**
 * Sets creationDate and sets type to default of ACCESS_GROUP_TYPE.
 */
public Group() {
    super();
    setCreationDate(Date.now());
    setType(ACCESS_GROUP_TYPE);
}
```

use `awakeFromInsertion` like this:

```
/**
 * Overridden to set default values. The default type() is ACCESS_GROUP_TYPE.
 * @param ec the EOEditingContext this object has been inserted into
 */
public void awakeFromInsertion(EOEditingContext ec) {
    // Call super first so that EOF can initialize the relationships
    super.awakeFromInsertion(ec);
    setCreationDate(Date.now());
    setType(ACCESS_GROUP_TYPE);
}
```

■ **NOTE** This is not quite as absolute as stated here. What you must never do is reference anything defined in the EOModel directly or indirectly nor call methods on classes in EOAccess or EOControl, as these may cause notifications to be sent or change EOF's internal state. If you declare your own nonpersistent instance variables (unrelated to anything in the EOModel), they can be initialized in the constructor. You can also call methods of classes that are not part of EOF. Be aware that the constructor is executed for each and every object of this class that is fetched or faulted in (even from another editing context). To avoid reducing performance, don't put anything time consuming in the constructor, and be careful when initializing your nonpersistent variables, as they will get reinitialized each time your object is faulted into a new editing context.

You might see code in other frameworks, and even in code generated by the Direct2Web framework, that violates this rule and gets away with it. Don't follow this practice. This is bad design and incorrect code, not to mention playing with fire. You have been warned!

TIP Objects don't disappear from your program when they are deleted from the object store. If you have variables referencing them, they will still point to the object after `saveChanges()` has been called. You should either ignore these or set them to `null`. To find out if an object has been deleted, check and see if it is in an editing context by comparing its editing context to `null`: `boolean wasDeleted = anObject.editingContext() == null;`.

Modify objects at appropriate times. EOF processes objects in phases: first the object's properties are changed; then the changes are validated; then, if valid, the changes are saved. It does not expect the phases to overlap. In particular, it does not expect properties to be modified while validation and saving are in progress. The effects of doing this are similar to those resulting from modifying properties in the constructor. It may appear to work without side effects, but you are setting the scene for disaster. You will usually be tempted to violate this in `validateForSave()` to do such things as set a modification date. Take careful note of the method name. It is `validateForSave()`, not `validateForSaveAndChangesSomeValues()`! There is no easy alternative to achieve this functionality. One possible method for dealing with this is examined in the next section.

Seeing State Changes in the Object Graph

A common need is to be able to take some action when something happens, or is about to happen, to an enterprise object. Some typical examples are deleting something from the file system after an object has been deleted and setting a modification date when any property of an object is modified. Unfortunately EOF has little to fill this need. `awakeFromInsertion()` can be used to handle actions driven by inserts. Setting a modification date could be done in the method `willChange()`, but that is not really what it is intended for and it gets called frequently. Setting the date could also be done in `validateForSave()` but, as previously discussed, you don't want to do that! For deletion there is nothing even remotely usable.

Before we get into how to accomplish this, let's take a quick look at the various transitions we might want to cause actions. There are three basic operations: insert, delete, and update. For each operation there are three points we will consider: immediately before an action happens, immediately after an action happens, and after the results of an action have been successfully saved. To make it easier, these points will be named *will*, *did*, and *has*.

Will Insert. This transition happens after a new object has been constructed, but before it is inserted into an editing context by calling `ec.insertObject(newObject)`. As you should never do anything to an enterprise object before it has been inserted into an editing context, this transition is not one we will bother with.

Did Insert. This transition happens after a new object has been inserted into an editing context by calling `ec.insertObject(newObject)`. The method `awakeFromInsertion()` is called on the object at this point, so there is no need to handle this transition either.

Has Inserted. This transition happens after a new object has been saved to the object store and object space. We want to handle this transition as there is no alternative. It could be used for saving external resources, such as writing a file to the file system.

Will Delete. This transition happens before an object is marked for deletion from an editing context by calling `ec.deleteObject(newObject)`. It can be used to cache values from relationships that will disappear after the deletion has been processed prior to saving. These values may be needed when handling Did Delete and Has Deleted.

Did Delete. This transition happens after all pending object deletions have been processed by the editing context in `processRecentChanges()`. At this point the deletion rules will have been applied. Relationships set to nullify will be `null`, and any objects that are the target of a cascade delete rule will have also been deleted. There is little need to interfere at this point and only incomplete information on which to base any actions. Also, as EOF is not expecting changes at this point in the save process, it is probably dangerous to make any changes to the object. For safety's sake, we won't handle this transition either.

Has Deleted. This transition happens after the deletion of an object has been saved to the object store and object space. At this point you should not refer to any properties or attributes, as this object is no longer in an editing context and references like this will call `willRead()` or `willChange()` on the object. EOF will not be expecting this. If you need any such values, you should make a copy of them in Will Delete and refer to the copies here. This transition is important for cleaning up resources related to the object, such as files in the file system.

Will Update. This transition happens just before an attribute or relationship is changed. This could be used to capture previous values, but there seems little point in that as these can be obtained from `editingContext().committedSnapshotForObject(this)`. It could also be used to set such things as the date last modified, but that would have to be carefully handled to avoid infinite recursion.

Did Update. This transition happens after attributes or relationships have been modified on an object and just before it is validated and saved to the object store and object space. This is a good place to record changed values for an audit trail and to set such things as the date last modified.

Has Updated. This transition happens after attributes or relationships have been modified on an object and saved to the object space. This transition is useful for saving resources related to the object, such as files in the file system.

Now we are left with the question of how to detect these transitions and how to handle them. As editing contexts are responsible for managing their objects, it seems reasonable to also have them handle detecting the transitions. The enterprise objects should best know how to handle their own transitions, so we will leave that responsibility with them. We will define an interface to allow the editing context to notify the enterprise objects of these transitions.

Introducing the EOStateTransition Interface

This interface has two responsibilities. The first is to identify which enterprise objects will be participating in our little notification scheme. The second is to codify the signatures of the methods that will be used to pass the notifications. Listing 3-1 shows the `EOStateTransition` interface; the code is in the PracticalUtilities framework.

Using an interface in this manner is the standard Java way of doing things. WebObjects often uses an alternative approach in which reflection is used to determine if a class implements a particular method. Some of the delegates implemented in the WebObjects frameworks use this approach; the `EOEditingContext` delegate is an example. This approach has the advantage of not requiring the code to explicitly implement an interface, inherit from a specific class, nor implement every method of an interface. We chose to do it the Java way as it was easier to implement and slightly faster.

Listing 3-1. *The* `EOStateTransition` *Interface*

```
/**
 * The interface used by the CooperatingEditingContext to determine which
 * Enterprise objects should receive notifications.
 */
public interface EOStateTransition
{
    /**
     * Called before deleteObject is invoked on super (EOEditingContext).
     * Make copies here of any values that you want to use in hasDeleted.
     */
    public void willDelete();

    /**
     * Called before saveChanges is invoked on super (EOEditingContext).
     * This would allow things such as setting the dateModified before
     * saving an EO.
     */
    public void willUpdate();

    /**
     * Called after a newly inserted object has been saved to the persistent
     * object store (a.k.a. database).  This can be used to save related,
     * non-EO, resources after the EO has been inserted.  This method should not
     * cause changes in the object graph as this may cause notifications to be
     * lost.
     */
    public void hasInserted();

    /**
     * Called after a deleted object has been removed from the persistent object
     * store.  This can be used to clean up related, non-EO resources after the
     * EO is deleted. This method should not cause changes in the object graph as
```

```
     * this may cause notifications to be lost.
     */
    public void hasDeleted();

    /**
     * Called after saveChanges is invoked on super (EOEditingContext).  This can
     * be used to save related, non-EO, resources after the EO has been updated.
     * This method should not cause changes in the object graph as this may cause
     * notifications to be lost.
     */
    public void hasUpdated();
```

To make our lives easier we've also created an `EOGenericRecord` subclass, `EOGenericStateTransitionRecord`, which implements the `EOStateTransition` interface with empty methods. This can be used as the superclass for enterprise objects instead of `EOGenericRecord`, which frees you from having to implement methods for notifications that you are not using. This class is particularly easy to use if you are using EOGenerator or a similar tool to generate Java files from the EOModel.

The CooperatingEditingContext

Now we get to the meat of the matter. We are going to need the cooperation of an `EOEditingContext` subclass, which we have cleverly named `CooperatingEditingContext`. This subclass is responsible for detecting these transitions and informing the enterprise objects that it is managing. In all other respects it functions as a standard `EOEditingContext`.

Recording the Object Graph Changes

An editing context maintains its own lists of objects undergoing changes: `updatedObjects()`, `insertedObjects()`, and `deletedObjects()`. However, we found that the contents of these sometimes changed in undesirable ways—for example, after calling `processRecentChanges()`. To avoid any possibility of problems, we implemented our own lists:

```
private NSMutableSet objectsToBeInserted = new NSMutableSet();
private NSMutableSet objectsToBeUpdated = new NSMutableSet();
private NSMutableSet objectsToBeDeleted = new NSMutableSet();
private NSMutableSet willBeDeletedObjects = new NSMutableSet();
```

We use sets to avoid sending the same notification twice (arrays can have duplicates, sets cannot) and make them private so that we can control what happens to them with contracts. Protected accessor methods are provided, and used exclusively in the implementation, so that subclasses can change how these lists are maintained with consistent results. Mutator (set) methods are not provided, as there was no apparent need for them.

TIP Private instance variables, protected accessor/mutator methods, and never referring to the instance variable outside of those methods is a pattern we use frequently in our code. We feel that private methods are a conceit of the designer. When you are creating a class you have no way of knowing how it will be used or extended. You know nothing of other developers' needs in the future. Private methods prevent other developers from doing what they know needs to be done. Trust them to be intelligent and use the knowledge they have in the future to do the responsible thing. While there are occasionally appropriate uses for private methods, we see them being overused in Java by developers who think they can see the future.

Handling Deletions

The place to catch object deletions is in the deleteObject() method. Here is what it looks like:

```
public void deleteObject(EOEnterpriseObject object) {
    /** require [valid_object] object != null;  **/
        if (objectGetsNotifications(object) &&
        ( ! willBeDeletedObjects().containsObject(object)))  {
        ((EOStateTransition) object).willDelete();
        willBeDeletedObjects().addObject(object);
    }
    objectsToBeDeleted().addObject(object);
    super.deleteObject(object);
    /** ensure
        [will_be_deleted_sent] ( ! objectGetsNotifications(object)) ||
                                willBeDeletedObjects().containsObject(object);
        [in_objectsToBeDeleted] objectsToBeDeleted.containsObject(object);  **/
}
```

The first thing we need to do is determine if this object wants to get notifications and if it has already been notified. It is unlikely that it has already been notified, but we can't rule that out and want to avoid duplicate messages so we check for this. If these conditions are met, we send the first deletion notification and record this so we don't send the notification again. As the lists are implemented as sets, we can just add the object to the list to be notified after save and then call super so that the deletion will be registered.

Handling Insertions

Similar to deletions, the place to catch object insertions is in the insertObject() method. There is nothing to do besides record the insertion for later:

```
public void insertObject(EOEnterpriseObject object) {
    /** require [valid_object] object != null;  **/
    objectsToBeInserted().addObject(object);
    super.insertObject(object);
    /** ensure [valid_state] objectsToBeUpdated().containsObject(object);  **/
}
```

We quickly discovered that this would not work for nested editing contexts. hasInserted gets called for the object in the nested editing context, but not on the parent. hasUpdated gets called on the object once it is in the parent, not at all what we want. We usually only want to perform a hasInserted action once the parent finishes saving the new object to the permanent object space. It turns out that when saving into the parent, editing context insertObject() is not called again. This was probably done to avoid a second call to awakeFromInsertion(). A quick look at the documentation for EOEditingContext suggested that an alternate method to use was insertObjectWithGlobalID(). This, however, did not work either. There was nothing else in the documentation, so the next stop was to open the Java Browsing perspective in Eclipse and take an in-depth look at the EOEditingContext API. The browser showed what appeared to be a related method, _insertObjectWithGlobalID(). Even though the access specified says that it is only protected, the leading underscore and lack of documentation suggests that Apple intends this to be internal, private API. Being left with no choice, we decided to ignore this conclusion and try it. Using this method has the desired effect and is the one we ended up using:

```
protected void _insertObjectWithGlobalID(EOEnterpriseObject object,
                                         EOGlobalID eoglobalid)  {
    /** require [valid_object] object != null;  **/
    objectsToBeInserted().addObject(object);
    super._insertObjectWithGlobalID(object, eoglobalid);
    /** ensure
    [in_objectsToBeInserted] objectsToBeInserted.containsObject(object); **/
}
```

TIP If you are using Eclipse, there are many alternatives for browsing the interface directly from a compiled class file. If you are not using Eclipse, WebObjects ships with the JavaBrowser, which should be sufficient for most of your interface browsing needs.

CAUTION Using private methods (basically anything not covered in the WebObjects' Javadocs) is not recommended unless you absolutely, really, really have to. Any minor release of WebObjects could change a private method so that it breaks your code. Good thing you've written some good unit tests, right?

Handling Updates

The editing context becomes aware of potential updates in objectWillChange(). As with insertions, there is nothing else that needs to be done:

```
public void objectWillChange(Object object)
{
    objectsToBeUpdated().addObject(object);
    super.objectWillChange(object);
}
```

There is one potential problem with detecting updates in this manner. objectWillChange() is called as a result of the enterprise object calling willChange() either directly or as a result of calling takeStoredValueForKey():

```
public void setId(Number aValue) {
    takeStoredValueForKey(aValue, "id");
}
```

The problem is that if the current value is the same as the new value, the object has not really changed, although the editing context thinks that it has. When the editing context is saved, EOF will realize that there has been no change and will not send an SQL update.

We can avoid calling willChange() and subsequently sending a notification in this situation by changing the enterprise object's mutator methods to check for a different value before changing it. For example:

```
public void setId(Number aValue) {
    if ( (aValue != id()) &&
         (aValue != null) &&
         ! aValue.equals(id()) ) {
        takeStoredValueForKey(aValue, "id");
    }
}
```

Another alternative is to allow willChange() to be called, but check that the object actually has changed values before sending the notification. The third alternative, and the one we will take, is to make this check optional and defer it until the willUpdate() method.

An eo can determine if any of its attributes have been changed with this test:

```
(changesFromSnapshot(
                 committedSnapshotForObject(this)).count() > 0))
```

committedSnapshotForObject() is an EOEditingContext method that returns a dictionary of the last fetched (or written) properties (attributes and relationships) of this object. changesFromSnapshot() is an EOEnterpriseObject method that returns a dictionary of the differences between the current values of the properties of the object and those in the passed dictionary. For our purposes, if the count() > 0 for the dictionary of differences, we know that at least one property has changed.

These methods are also useful to determine if a specific property has changed. For example, to determine if the password attribute of a User had been changed, we could make this test in a method of User:

```
changesFromSnapshot(editingContext().committedSnapshotForObject(this))
    .objectForKey("password") != null
```

If our eo should only process the willUpdate notification if there are actual changes, we write the willUpdate() method like this:

```
public void willUpdate() {
    if (changesFromSnapshot(
            editingContext().committedSnapshotForObject(this)).count() > 0) {
        // Process change here
    }
```

We prefer this approach, as it allows the object receiving the notification to decide if it cares whether it was really changed or not. In addition to being a better partitioning of responsibility, this allows one eo to cause another eo to receive the willUpdate() notification simply by sending it a willChange() message. This can be useful to defer updating of cached or summary values just prior to save. This can be a lot more efficient than having the eo recalculate them after every little change.

Processing a Save

Other than willDelete, all of the notifications are sent in the context of saveChanges():

```
public void saveChanges() {
    notifyWillUpdate();
    super.saveChanges();
    notifyHasDeleted();
    notifyHasInserted();
    notifyHasUpdated();
    resetLists();
}
```

There is nothing much to see here. Note that resetLists() is called at the end so that the editing context is ready for a new cycle of changes without duplicating messages. An important question to ask here is "What happens if super.saveChanges() raises an exception?" The only notification that will have been sent is willUpdate. You will see later on that this is written in such a way that objects will not be notified again if saveChanges() is called again. If revert() is called we are also safe, as all of the editing context's changes will be reversed and the lists cleared:

```
public void revert() {
    super.revert();
    resetLists();
}
```

Sending the "has" Notifications

We've already seen the willDelete notification being sent. The three notifications hasDeleted, hasInserted, and hasUpdated are all sent using the same basic pattern of iterating over the enterprise objects, checking if each should be notified, and sending the notification. Listing 3-2 shows the methods of sending these three similar notifications.

Listing 3-2. *Sending the* hasDeleted, hasInserted, *and* hasUpdated *Notifications*

```
/**
 * Sends the hasDeleted() notification to all the objects which have just been
 * removed from the persistent object store.
 */
protected void notifyHasDeleted() {
    Enumeration objectsToBeDeletedEnumerator =
        objectsToBeDeleted().objectEnumerator();
    while (objectsToBeDeletedEnumerator.hasMoreElements()) {
        Object deletedObject = objectsToBeDeletedEnumerator.nextElement();
        if (objectGetsNotifications((EOEnterpriseObject)deletedObject)) {
            ((EOStateTransition) deletedObject).hasDeleted();
        }
    }
}

/**
 * Sends the hasInserted() notification to all the new objects which have just
 * been saved to the persistent object store.
 */
protected void notifyHasInserted() {
    Enumeration objectsToBeInsertedEnumerator =
        objectsToBeInserted().objectEnumerator();
    while (objectsToBeInsertedEnumerator.hasMoreElements()) {
        Object insertedObject = objectsToBeInsertedEnumerator.nextElement();
        if (objectGetsNotifications((EOEnterpriseObject)insertedObject)) {
            ((EOStateTransition) insertedObject).hasInserted();
        }
    }
}

/**
 * Sends the hasUpdated() notification to all the updated objects which have just
 * been saved to the persistent object store.  Note that this is not sent to
 * objects which receive hasInserted or hasDeleted().
 */
public void notifyHasUpdated()
{
    // Don't send this notification to objects which have just been
    // inserted or deleted.
    NSMutableSet updatesOnly = objectsToBeUpdated().mutableClone();
    updatesOnly.subtractSet(objectsToBeDeleted());
    updatesOnly.subtractSet(objectsToBeInserted());

    Enumeration objectsToBeUpdatedEnumerator = updatesOnly.objectEnumerator();
    while (objectsToBeUpdatedEnumerator.hasMoreElements()) {
        Object updatedObject = objectsToBeUpdatedEnumerator.nextElement();
```

```
        if (objectGetsNotifications((EOEnterpriseObject)updatedObject)) {
            ((EOStateTransition) updatedObject).hasUpdated();
        }
    }
}
```

Sending the willUpdate Notification

The `willUpdate` notification is much more complex to handle. Sending this notification may result in newly updated objects that will also have to be notified. Because of this, the method is written to keep sending the notification until all affected objects have been notified. However, we also need to be careful to avoid notification cycles, which will result in an endless stream of notifications around and around the loop.

As an example, consider an `Order` and `OrderItem` scenario in which each maintains a `lastUpdatedDate`. In our business logic, an update to any item on the order is an update to the `Order` itself and forces recalculation of the order amounts as well. We could write the `willUpdate()` method for `OrderItem` like this:

```
public void willUpdate() {
    setLastUpdatedDate(new NSTimestamp());
    calculateExtendedPrice();
    order().willChange();
}
```

Take notice of the `order().willChange()` line. The `willUpdate()` method for `OrderItem` may result in an `Order` object that was not previously updated now being marked as updated.

The `Order` might need to recalculate for any number of reasons, so its `willUpdate()` method is simply

```
public void willUpdate() {
    setLastUpdatedDate(new NSTimestamp());
    recalculate();
}
```

It is important that the `willUpdate()` method for `Order` not update `OrderItem`, or a notification cycle will result as `OrderItem` changes `Order`, which changes `OrderItem`, which changes `Order`, and on and on.

The obvious way to avoid such cycles is to keep track of the objects already notified and not send the notification again. This will prevent cycles, to be sure, but it will also prevent the proper receipt of notifications. Consider the preceding `Order` and `OrderItem` in a scenario where both have been updated before `saveChanges()` is called. If `Order` is sent the `willUpdate` notification first, it will recalculate using the old `OrderItem` information. If we don't send the notification again after `OrderItem` calls `order().willChange()`, the `Order` will be saved with outdated information. Because of this we must allow the same notification to be sent multiple times to the same object.

The only cycle that we can exclude automatically is an object notifying itself. If we allowed that cycle, the `willUpdate()` methods we just discussed would cycle endlessly as setLastUpdatedDate() results in a call to willChange(), which puts the object back on the objectsToBeUpdated list. To avoid cycles caused by an object notifying itself, some modifications to the objectWillChange() method are needed. Listing 3-3 shows the final version.

All other cycles must be avoided by a combination of careful planning and the use of conditionals to prevent the willUpdate() method from needlessly updating other objects. Listing 3-4 shows how the willUpdate notification is sent in a loop until no new notifications result.

Listing 3-3. *The Final* objectWillChange *Method*

```
public void objectWillChange(Object object) {
    /** require [valid_object] object != null;  **/
    if (object != objectBeingNotified()) {
        objectsToBeUpdated().addObject(object);
        notifiedWillUpdateSet().removeObject(object);
    }
    super.objectWillChange(object);
    /** ensure
        [valid_state] (object == objectBeingNotified()) ||
                      (objectsToBeUpdated().containsObject(object) &&
                       ! notifiedWillUpdateSet().containsObject(object));  **/
}
```

Listing 3-4. *The* notifyWillUpdate *Method*

```
protected void notifyWillUpdate() {
    NSSet unNotifiedObjectsToBeUpdated = new NSSet(objectsToBeUpdated());
    resetNotifiedWillUpdateSet();

    while (unNotifiedObjectsToBeUpdated.count() > 0) {
        Enumeration objectsToBeUpdatedEnumerator =
            unNotifiedObjectsToBeUpdated.objectEnumerator();
        while (objectsToBeUpdatedEnumerator.hasMoreElements()) {
            EOEnterpriseObject updatedObject =
                (EOEnterpriseObject)objectsToBeUpdatedEnumerator.nextElement();
            setObjectBeingNotified(updatedObject);
            if (objectGetsNotifications(updatedObject)) {
                ((EOStateTransition) updatedObject).willUpdate();
            }
            // Mark this object as notified, it may be removed from this set
            // by a later update.
            notifiedWillUpdateSet().addObject(updatedObject);
        }
        // Call process recent changes so that inserts and deletes are processed
        // This may result in more updated objects
        processRecentChanges();
```

```
            unNotifiedObjectsToBeUpdated = objectsToBeUpdated().setBySubtractingSet(
                notifiedWillUpdateSet());
        }
        // Reset to avoid interfering with willChange()
        resetNotifiedWillUpdateSet();
        setObjectBeingNotified(null);
    }
```

Working with Nesting Editing Contexts

You need to take special care when using `CooperatingEditingContext` as a nested editing context. It might not be appropriate to perform some actions (e.g., deleting a file) when the nested editing context saves, as this only affects the parent editing context and does not permanently save the changes to the object store or object space. It can be simpler to use a plain `EOEditingContext` for the nested editing context and `CooperatingEditingContext` for the parent. It has been written so that the notifications are nearly the same regardless of whether they were caused by changes in the parent or in the child. The only difference is that when inserting a new object, `willUpdate` is called in the nested but not the parent editing context. We don't expect this to be a serious problem.

How to Use CooperatingEditingContext

The full source for all of the classes discussed here is in the PracticalUtilities framework.

The `CooperatingEditingContext` can be used as the session's `defaultEditingContext()` by changing the `Session` constructors to do this:

```
public Session() {
    super();
    setDefaultEditingContext(new CooperatingEditingContext());
}
public Session(String sessionID) {
    super(sessionID);
    setDefaultEditingContext(new CooperatingEditingContext());
}
```

Debugging Object Graph Problems

In this section we will take a look at two common problems and how to detect and fix them. For general debugging of object graph problems, use the advanced EOF debugging techniques introduced in Chapter 1.

Finding and Preventing Cross-Editing Context Relationships

Making a relationship between two objects in different editing contexts is probably the most common mistake made, either through ignorance or inattention. We have probably all done it more than once. It is useful to recognize what happens when you do this so you can find and fix the problem quickly. The tricky thing about relationships across editing contexts is that everything appears fine until you try to save. When you call saveChanges(), the editing context will throw up an ugly exception that looks like this:

```
java.lang.IllegalStateException: Cannot obtain globalId for an object which is
registered in an other than the databaseContext's active editingContext, object:
{values = {stringValue = "default"; relatedObject = "null"; id = ; etc.,
this = "<com.apress.practicalwo.practicalutilities.tests.
    CooperatingEditingContextTestObject etc
databaseContext: com.webobjects.eoaccess.EODatabaseContext@57aa53,
object's editingContext: com.webobjects.eocontrol.EOEditingContext@70c0d3,
databaseContext's active editingContext:
    com.webobjects.eocontrol.EOEditingContext@4cc588
```

You can see the whole exception and stack trace by running the DebuggingObjectGraph example application from this chapter. A bit of explanation of this message is probably in order. "`Cannot obtain globalId for an object which is registered in an other than the databaseContext's active editingContext`" means "Hey! I can't find this object in the editing context that I am saving!" The active `EOEditingContext` of an `EODatabaseContext` is the editing context that has the `EOObjectStoreCoordinator` locked (more on locking later) in order to fetch, save, etc. A database context can only perform these operations for one editing context at a time to preserve data integrity. The next part, where it says `object: {values =` and `this =`, is indicating the properties and class of the object that is in the wrong editing context. This should be useful in determining which object is in the wrong editing context. The rest of it just indicates the database context and the two editing contexts involved. This is only useful if you are also logging out the editing contexts so that you can tell which is which.

Using DBC to Prevent Cross-Editing Context Relationships

Design by Contract (DBC) can help you avoid ever having to fight this error again. Just change the templates that your enterprise object classes are generated from to have a contract in their relationship set methods that automatically detects this error. The contracts shown in Listing 3-5 assume that both objects are already in an editing context. A null pointer exception will be raised if they aren't, but you shouldn't be working with objects that are not in an editing context anyway!

Listing 3-5. *Using DBC to Avoid Cross-Editing Context Relationships*

```
// Set to-many relationship
public void setChildGroups(NSMutableArray newValues)  {
    /** require [same_ec] (forall i : {0 .. newValues.count() - 1} #
            ((EOEnterpriseObject)newValues.objectAtIndex(i)).editingContext() ==
                editingContext());  **/

    takeStoredValueForKey(aValue, "childGroups");
}

// Add to to-many relationship
public void addToChildGroups(com.gvcsitemaker.core.Group object) {
```

```
    /** require [same_ec]
        object.editingContext() instanceof EOSharedEditingContext ||
        object.editingContext() == editingContext();
     **/

    NSMutableArray array = (NSMutableArray)childGroups();
    willChange();
    array.addObject(object);
}

// Set to-one relationship
public void setFooter(com.gvcsitemaker.core.Footer aValue) {
    /** require [same_ec]
        (aValue == null) ||
        ((aValue.editingContext() instanceof EOSharedEditingContext) ||
        (aValue.editingContext() == editingContext()) );
     **/

    takeStoredValueForKey(aValue, "footer");
}
```

Defeating Referential Integrity Problems

Referential integrity refers to rules that govern how objects (or rows in a database) can be related. The most common rule is to require two objects to be related (a foreign key constraint at the database level) in order to be valid—for example, a rule could state that an item on an order is only valid if the order exists. In other words, order items are not allowed to exist independently of an order.

EOF does a pretty good job of maintaining such integrity within its object store (though with some poor modeling and a dab of sloppy coding, you can give it fits). However, EOF has no control over what happens in the database. People typing SQL or other processes can easily make a mess in the database behind EOF's back. If proper foreign key constraints are used in the database, problems can be avoided. The trouble is that proper foreign key constraints can't be (or aren't!) always used. For example, vertical inheritance and database foreign key constraints don't mix well, as the related object (destination row) may be in one of several tables. This is just an unavoidable mismatch between relational and object technology. Another common reason that foreign key constraints are not used is that EOF does not always order its operations in a way that allows these constraints to be enforced. This problem can be avoided if the database only enforces these when it commits by creating the constraints as `DEFERRABLE INITIALLY DEFERRED`. However, not all databases support this, and dropping the foreign key constraints is an easy, albeit nasty, solution.

Where lack of relational integrity can really cause you problems with EOF is in to-one relationships. When EOF tries to fetch the related object and can't find it, EOF does not, as one might expect, raise an exception. Instead it creates a dummy object of the correct class with all `null` values. While this is sometimes convenient, it is also unfortunate, as the problem is not immediately obvious. It usually lurks about and shows up later when you try to use one of the attributes and get a `NullPointerException`. Referential integrity problems are not what you usually think of when you see an exception like that.

Logging Referential Integrity Problems

It would be nice to know when this happens so that we can do something about it—for example, raise an exception or log it to be repaired. Thanks to EOF's use of delegates, we can indeed do this. The key method we will use is on EODatabaseContext's delegate:

```
public boolean databaseContextFailedToFetchObject(EODatabaseContext context,
                                                  Object object,
                                                  EOGlobalID globalID)
```

While it is theoretically possible to use this method to fix the referential integrity problem by creating values for object on the fly and registering a snapshot, we have never seen any case where that's a reasonable thing to attempt. So instead, we settle for making the failure a little less silent. Credit for the original idea goes to Kelly Hawk (see http://www.omnigroup.com/mailman/archive/eof/2000-December/001578.html). The code in Listing 3-6 is found in the EOFAdditions class in the PracticalUtilities framework.

Listing 3-6. *The* databaseContextFailedToFetchObject *Method*

```
/**
 * Delegate on EODatabaseContext that gets called when a to-one fault cannot
 * find its corresponding data in the database. The object is a cleared fault.
 * An exception is thrown to bring attention to this problem.
 */
public boolean databaseContextFailedToFetchObject(EODatabaseContext context,
                                                  Object object,
                                                  EOGlobalID globalID) {
    EOEditingContext ec = ((EOEnterpriseObject) object).editingContext();

    // We need to refault the object before raising, otherwise, if the caller
    // traps the exception, it will be a successful lookup the next time a fault
    // with the same global id fires.  NOTE: refaulting in a sharedEditingContext
    // is illegal, so we specifically check for that special case.
    if (! (ec instanceof EOSharedEditingContext)) {
        context.refaultObject((EOEnterpriseObject) object, globalID, ec);
    }

    String failureMessage = "Failed to fetch " + object.getClass() +
        " with globalID " + globalID;
    RuntimeException integrityException = new RuntimeException(failureMessage);

    // When thrown during one of the R-R loop phases (or due to Key-Value
    // coding?), the integrityException gets swallowed.  This seems to happen
    // often. To accommodate this, the exception should be written to an error
    // log that is checked so that it is not lost.
    NSLog.err.appendln(failureMessage);

    throw integrityException;
}
```

The comment at the end is important. We've seen many cases where the exception is never seen at the handleException method of Application, yet appears in the log. This is probably caused by some code in the frameworks that swallows all exceptions. Because of this, you should record the problem in a permanent log of severe errors so that someone will see it and fix the problem.

Using this delegate method is quite easy as EODatabaseContext provides a handy concept of a default delegate. The default delegate will be used for all database contexts unless they specifically set a different delegate. The easiest way to use this is to add this line to your Application constructor (EOFDebugAdditions can be found in the PracticalUtilities framework):

```
EODatabaseContext.setDefaultDelegate(new EOFDebugAdditions ());
```

The only permanent way of dealing with this error is to fix the invalid reference. The problem is finding which object and relationship the invalid reference comes from. It might be possible to do this programmatically by examining the model and fetching objects with a relationship to the entity for this object to find which object has the invalid reference. This would require a complex examination of the EOModels and is beyond the scope of our discussion. In the end, you often have to resort to SQL and your knowledge of the model to find the offending relationship.

Detecting Referential Integrity Problems

In some situations it might be preferable to detect these dummy snapshots and do something other than raising an exception or logging the problem. One option would be to find the invalid references programmatically and nullify them. Such dummy enterprise objects are easily detected by checking to see if an enterprise object has a snapshot. As these dummy objects do not really exist, they have no snapshot. Listing 3-7 shows how to detect them.

Listing 3-7. *Method to Detect Dummy Enterprise Objects*

```
/**
 * EOF resolves faults for objects that don't exist in the database to a dummy
 * object with empty attributes.  This method detects whether the parameter
 * is such a dummy object.
 * @param anObject the eo to test.  The eo's editing context must be
 * locked before entry
 * @return returns true if <code>anObject</code> is a dummy object
 * with empty attributes, <code>false</code> otherwise
 */
public static boolean isDummyFaultEO(EOEnterpriseObject anObject) {
    boolean isDummyFaultEO = false;

    // This method will fail if the object is still a fault.  We fire the fault
    // so that the correct result is returned.
    if (anObject.isFault()) {
        anObject.willRead();
    }

    EOEditingContext ec = anObject.editingContext();
```

```
    EOGlobalID globalID = ec.globalIDForObject(anObject);

    // NB: objects with temporary globalIDs legitimately have no DB snapshots,
    // since these are by definition not yet saved to the database.
    if (globalID != null && ! globalID.isTemporary()) {
        // Find the EODatabaseContext instance associated with anObject, or
        // null if no databaseContext association can be found.
        EOObjectStoreCoordinator rootStore =
            (EOObjectStoreCoordinator)ec.rootObjectStore();
        EODatabaseContext dbContext =
            (EODatabaseContext)rootStore.objectStoreForObject(anObject);
        dbContext.lock();
        try {
            isDummyFaultEO = dbContext.snapshotForGlobalID(globalID) == null;
        }
        finally {
            dbContext.unlock();
        }
    }

    return isDummyFaultEO;
}
```

Be aware that this method is incompatible with the database context delegate. When this method calls `willRead()` on the object, that delegate method will detect the failure to fetch and raise an exception. You must choose one method or the other.

If you find a dummy object, you must nullify references to it before attempting to save objects related to the dummy object. Calling `ec.forgetObject()` on the dummy object is not sufficient. If you don't nullify references to it, an assortment of snapshot exceptions will be thrown.

Locking, Concurrency, and EOF

Whether or not locking is really required has been a topic of some contention on the discussion lists. The documentation clearly states that you must lock, always. However, many people have years of experience with large applications that neither lock nor have apparent problems. Others have had difficulty in finding a way of properly locking that does not cause more deadlocks than it avoids. If an application does not access enterprise objects in threads (such as with the WOLongResponse page) or dispatch requests concurrently, there is no concurrency and thus no need to lock, right?

Wrong. There is no such thing as a single-threaded Java application. If nothing else, finalization runs in its own thread and WebObjects applications add a thread to handle session timeouts. Sure, these might not do much with EOF and the chances of a concurrent action are low, but do you really want an application that probably runs correctly most of the time? We often wonder when people report strange, hard-to-reproduce problems if not locking is the root cause. In case it is not clear, our advice is simple: lock.

What Needs to Be Locked?

Now that we have that out of the way, what do we lock? The individual enterprise objects themselves do not support locking. That's a good thing, or this would get complicated indeed. The effective locking of enterprise objects is accomplished by locking the editing context that manages them. EOF assumes that only the thread that has a lock on the editing context will touch them and does not enjoy having this assumption tested. The frameworks take care of locking the session's default editing context and all `EOSharedEditingContexts`. You should not lock an `EOSharedEditingContext` in your code. If the default and shared editing contexts are the only editing contexts you ever use, you don't have to do anything at all to lock correctly, unless you access the lower-level objects of EOF (described further on). However, those editing contexts alone are not going to suffice for most applications. You are responsible for locking and unlocking the editing contexts that you create, all of them.

■ **CAUTION** Be careful reading the documentation on concurrency and locking where it says, "Child or nested EOEditingContexts use their parent's lock." This is referring to them sharing the same lock object. It does *not* mean that you don't need to lock child editing contexts if their parent is locked. Locking the parent editing context does nothing to lock the children. The shared lock object simply prevents different threads from locking the parent and child or from locking two different children of the same parent. However, locking the child editing context does indeed lock the parent! See the NestedLockTest component in this chapter's application for some code demonstrating this.

The locking protocol for objects in the EOAccess layer has also changed in WebObjects 5.2. The gory details can be found in the "What's New in WebObjects 5.2" document on the WebObjects site. As of version 5.2 you must lock the associated `EOObjectStoreCoordinator` before directly accessing objects in the EOAccess layer that do not have `lock()` and `unlock()` methods. Unless your application creates more, there will be only a single `EOObjectStoreCoordinator` in your application. Locking this locks all of the `EODatabaseContexts` that it controls and all of the other related objects below it in the EOF stack.

How to Lock Correctly

Locking is handled with `NSRecursiveLock` objects. These locks allow a single thread to acquire a single lock multiple times without deadlocking. This frees the code using the lock from having to worry about whether it is locked already or not. The `NSRecursiveLock` keeps track of the number of times it has been locked and unlocked (actually the number of locks with no corresponding unlock). As long as there have been more locks than unlocks, it remains locked. When the number of locks and unlocks are equal, it is unlocked and released to other threads. When using an `NSRecursiveLock`, it is important to ensure that the calls to lock and unlock are balanced so that the lock eventually gets released.

There are two considerations with locking. The first is to ensure that you have locked early enough that there is no access without a lock. Failing to do this can result in other threads modifying objects at the same time you are. The second is to ensure that you unlock what you lock. Failure to do this correctly will quickly result in an unresponsive, deadlocked application.

Locking the Java Way

The Java solution to the first consideration is to lock an object as soon as you create it or obtain a reference to it. The Java solution to the second consideration is to use a try-finally block to ensure that it gets unlocked. For example:

```
EOEditingContext myEC = new EOEditingContext();
try {
    myEC.lock();
    // work with locked editing context here
}
finally {
    myEC.unlock();
    myEC.dispose();
}
```

CAUTION The EOF documentation says that allowing a locked editing context to be garbage collected is an acceptable way of discarding the lock. While this is true for peer editing contexts, it is not true for child editing contexts. Allowing a locked child editing context to be garbage collected will leave an outstanding lock on the parent. If the parent is the default editing context, the session will deadlock on the next request. We feel that allowing locked editing contexts to be garbage collected is a practice to be avoided.

Needless to say, WebObjects is complicated enough that this nice, clean solution is not going to get us very far. The application for this chapter has a lot of log messages tracing editing context locking and the request—response loop for Component Actions and Direct Actions with sessions. These will help to illustrate the problems to be overcome.

The fundamental problem has to do with the longevity of editing contexts. Unlike the preceding example, they usually live over several cycles of the request—response loop. Each request for a particular session may be handled by a different worker thread. If we just create the editing context and leave it locked, the next request for that session will block unless it just happens to get handled by the same worker thread.

The Complexity of Locking

That leaves us with the need to lock early in the request—response loop, before anything in an editing context gets touched, and unlock late in the loop, after which nothing in the editing context gets touched. A brief look at the request—response loop (http://developer.apple.com/documentation/WebObjects/Web_Applications/UserInput/chapter_5_section_2.html) suggests that the awake() and sleep() methods are good candidates. But which awake and sleep: WOApplication, WOSession, or WOComponent? We can rule out the WOApplication's awake() and sleep(), as it knows nothing about the editing contexts in a WOSession or WOComponent. Other than the default editing context, WOSession and WOComponent know nothing about editing contexts either, but perhaps they can learn.

Are both the WOSession and WOComponent awake() and sleep() equally good places to lock? Let's take a closer look at them. Run the application from this chapter and click the *Test EC Locking and Component Actions* link. Listing 3-8 shows the resulting console output.

Listing 3-8. *The Order of Calls to* awake() *and* sleep()

```
WorkerThread1 Application awake
WorkerThread1 Session zFsbPkDYnbCB8IhEP1stDg awake
WorkerThread1 creating new LockingTestPage1
WorkerThread1 LockingTestPage1 awake
WorkerThread1 LockingTestPage1 appendToResponse
WorkerThread1 LockingTestPage1 sleep
WorkerThread1 Session zFsbPkDYnbCB8IhEP1stDg sleep
WorkerThread1 Application sleep
```

From this, it appears that the WOSession and WOComponent methods could be equally useful. However, if you create and use an editing context in the WOComponent's constructor, you will still need to take care of manually locking and unlocking it, as this happens before awake().

What happens if two requests come for the same session at the same time? This could happen if a user double-clicks a link. The links between pages in the example application have a pause built in so that we can test this. Click twice on the *Go to page 2* link. Listing 3-9 shows what happens.

Listing 3-9. *The Order of Calls to* awake() *and* sleep() *for Concurrent Requests*

```
WorkerThread2 Dispatch request
    /cgi-bin/WebObjects/DebuggingObjectGraph.woa/wo/zFsbPkDYnbCB8IhEP1stDg/1.1
WorkerThread2 Application awake
WorkerThread2 Session zFsbPkDYnbCB8IhEP1stDg awake
WorkerThread2 LockingTestPage1 awake
WorkerThread2 LockingTestPage1 invokeAction
WorkerThread2 creating new LockingTestPage2
WorkerThread2 LockingTestPage2 awake

WorkerThread3 Dispatch request
    /cgi-bin/WebObjects/DebuggingObjectGraph.woa/wo/zFsbPkDYnbCB8IhEP1stDg/1.1
WorkerThread3 Application awake
WorkerThread2 LockingTestPage2 appendToResponse
WorkerThread2 LockingTestPage1 sleep
WorkerThread2 LockingTestPage2 sleep
WorkerThread2 Session zFsbPkDYnbCB8IhEP1stDg sleep
WorkerThread2 Application sleep
WorkerThread3 Session zFsbPkDYnbCB8IhEP1stDg awake
WorkerThread3 LockingTestPage1 awake
WorkerThread3 LockingTestPage2 awake
WorkerThread3 LockingTestPage2 appendToResponse
WorkerThread3 LockingTestPage1 sleep
```

```
WorkerThread3 LockingTestPage2 sleep
WorkerThread3 Session zFsbPkDYnbCB8IhEP1stDg sleep
WorkerThread3 Application sleep
```

There are a number of interesting things happening here. First, notice that when the second request arrives, worker thread 2 is still processing `invokeAction()` from the previous request. The second request is dispatched in another thread, worker thread 3. WebObjects uses worker threads that are not busy with other requests (and creates new ones as necessary) to handle dispatching requests that come in while other requests are processing. Once the first request has been responded to, the corresponding worker thread will be freed up to process another request.

See how worker thread 3 blocks after the `WOApplication` `awake()`even though the application is dispatching requests concurrently. It actually blocks trying to check out the session. See the documentation for the `checkOutSessionWithID()` method of `WOSessionStore` for details on this. WebObjects prevents two requests for the same session from executing concurrently. This makes locking easier, as we don't need to worry about concurrent requests for the same session. That could be a nightmare indeed! We can see that once worker thread 2 puts the `WOApplication` to sleep, worker thread 3 starts running again.

The Impact of Direct Actions on Locking

The `WOSession` and `WOComponent` `awake()` and `sleep()` methods seem fairly equivalent so far. What happens if we add Direct Actions into the mix? Go back to the main page and click the *Test EC Locking and Direct Actions* link. Listing 3-10 shows what happens in this situation.

Listing 3-10. *The Order of Calls to* `awake()` *and* `sleep()` *for Direct Actions Not Referencing the Session*

```
WorkerThread0 Dispatch request /cgi-bin/WebObjects/Chap3App.woa/wa/page1?
    wosid=eAEl0Q0DMpCMOigbuVVtT0
WorkerThread0 Application awake
WorkerThread0 Starting direct action page1
WorkerThread0 creating new com.apress.practicalwo.chap3app.DALockingTest1
WorkerThread0 com.apress.practicalwo.chap3app.DALockingTest1 awake
WorkerThread0 Ending direct action page1
WorkerThread0 com.apress.practicalwo.chap3app.DALockingTest1 appendToResponse
WorkerThread0 com.apress.practicalwo.chap3app.DALockingTest1 sleep
WorkerThread0 Application sleep
```

Wait a minute! We can see that there is a session, the ID is right there on the URL. Where are the calls to `WOSession`'s `awake()` and `sleep()` methods? The answer is that unless you actually reference `session()`, it will not be woken up and put to sleep in a Direct Action even if it already exists.

What happens if `session()` is referenced by a Direct Action? In this case, the session gets awoken when it is first referenced and put back to sleep at the regular place. To see this happen, click on the *Go to page 2* link. Listing 3-11 shows the interesting sequence of events.

Listing 3-11. *The Order of Calls to* awake() *and* sleep() *for Direct Actions Referencing the Session*

```
WorkerThread1 Dispatch request /cgi-bin/WebObjects/Chap3App.woa/wa/page2?
    wosid=eAEl0QODMpCMOigbuVVtTO
WorkerThread1 Application awake
WorkerThread1 Starting direct action page2
WorkerThread1 creating new com.apress.practicalwo.chap3app.DALockingTest2
WorkerThread1 com.apress.practicalwo.chap3app.DALockingTest2 awake
WorkerThread1 Ending direct action page2
WorkerThread1 com.apress.practicalwo.chap3app.DALockingTest2 appendToResponse
WorkerThread1 Session eAEl0QODMpCMOigbuVVtTO awake
WorkerThread1 com.apress.practicalwo.chap3app.DALockingTest2 sleep
WorkerThread1 Session eAEl0QODMpCMOigbuVVtTO sleep
WorkerThread1 Application sleep
```

Things are getting mixed up here! Now the session is awoken after appendToResponse() is called on the WOComponent that will be returned. This is not a rule, just an indication of where the session was first referred. If you are using sessions with Direct Actions, you can make the calling of awake() on session() consistent by calling existingSession() in performAction() before doing anything else:

```
public WOActionResults performActionNamed(String anActionName) {
    existingSession();
    return super.performActionNamed(anActionName);
}
```

If a session already exists it will be awoken, otherwise nothing will happen.

If you are not using sessions with Direct Actions, you will have to use the WOComponent awake() and sleep() to handle locking the editing context. Don't try any variations on this:

```
public WOActionResults page1Action() {
    EOEditingContext ec = new EOEditingContext();
    ec.lock();
    try {
        DALockingTest1 result = pageWithName("DALockingTest1");
        result.setEditingContextToUse(ec);
    }
    finally {
        ec.unlock();
        ec.dispose();
    }
    return result;
}
```

While that might look OK at first, it isn't. The editing context will be unlocked and disposed of when the method ends, long before generateResponse() is called on the result page. Nothing good will come of that.

Towards a Locking Practice

Where does that leave us? For applications that only use Component Actions, either the WOSession or WOComponent awake() and sleep() methods seem usable. For applications that use Direct Actions with sessions, we need to take an extra step to use the WOSession awake() and sleep() methods. Obviously, for applications that use only sessionless Direct Actions, the WOSession awake() and sleep() methods are of no use, but locking could be handled in the DirectAction class. It is time to take a look at how we might use either one to manage locking.

As WOSession already manages locking for the default editing context, it seems reasonable that it might also be made to handle locking of all editing contexts. While this will add more locking and unlocking to the request—response loop, locking should be lightweight and so not a significant concern.

The session will be responsible for creating or registering all editing contexts and locking and unlocking them. When a session is awoken it will lock all of the registered editing contexts. This will ensure that they are locked before any WOComponent code is executed. When it is put to sleep, it will unlock all of the editing contexts it knows about. The session will need to keep tabs on these editing contexts with a weak reference; otherwise they won't get garbage collected until the session terminates, and this could consume a lot of extra memory needlessly. What if an editing context that the session has locked gets garbage collected? That would be a problem for nested editing contexts (see the "Debugging Locking Problems" section later in this chapter), as a lock will be left on the parent. To accommodate this, the session will create a temporary strong reference during the request—response loop to ensure that everything gets unlocked.

You will be happy to know that this has already been implemented for you. Jonathan Rochkind's excellent MultiECLockManager is freely available from http://wocode.com/WOCode/Files/MultiECLockManager.java.

Locking at the WOComponent level is a lot more complex. Consider page construction. If the editing context is created and used in the constructor, it will need to be locked and unlocked there so that it is unlocked when it is locked in awake(). Otherwise the lock() in awake() will be the second lock and the single unlock() in sleep() will leave it locked.

What if the page does not create its own editing context and instead takes it from an enterprise object passed into the page? Calling methods on the component will happen after awake(), so awake() will have no chance to lock the editing context. The set method will have to lock it so that it will be locked when sleep() goes to unlock it. Alternatively, we could assume that the editing context is locked when we get it and will remain locked. Thus we could set a flag in the constructor and have sleep() skip the unlock() call if this flag was set. This gets even more complicated if two or more enterprise objects are passed into the page. The component has no control over which order the set ... methods are called in, so which one locks the editing context? To make matters even more confusing, sleep() will not be called on a component unless it generates its response. So code like

```
public WOComponent saveChanges() {
    editingContext.saveChanges();
    PageB resultPage = pageWithName("PageB");
    resultPage.setTemplate(pageWithName("PageA"));
    return resultPage;
}
```

will result in unbalanced calls to awake() and sleep() for PageA unless PageB calls appendToResponse() or generateResponse() on it during this request—response loop.

In the end, there is no one right answer. We hope you were not expecting a silver bullet! Properly managed, both ways will work. Improperly handled, both can result in access without locks or deadlock due to unreleased locks. Where possible, we recommend handling the locking in Session with MultiECLockManager. This is easier than any alternative, and the reusable implementation can be shared among applications. For sessionless Direct Actions and special situations, you will have to resort to locking in the component's awake() and sleep(). You really have to look at the design of your application and decide how to approach it, and keep a careful watch out for any places an extra call to lock() or unlock() might happen. User threads and WOLongResponsePages will need to create their own editing contexts and manage their own locks to avoid conflicts with the request—response loop.

■ **TIP** Regardless of how you handle locking, try—finally blocks should be used where there is even the remotest chance of an exception preventing unlock from being called. This definitely includes any calls to the superclass implementation.

Locking Other EO Objects

Locking objects in the EOAccess layer is considerably easier. If your application is using only the default object store coordinator, you can lock it directly:

```
EOObjectStoreCoordinator.DefaultCoordinator().lock();
```

If you are creating more object store coordinators, you can ask an editing context for the coordinator that it is using:

```
ec.rootObjectStore().lock();
```

These locks replace the individual locks that were needed previously, such as

```
ec.lock().
EODatabaseContext dbContext =
    EOUtilities.databaseContextForModelNamed(ec, "MyModel");
dbContext.lock();
```

This now becomes

```
ec.lock();
EOObjectStoreCoordinator.defaultCoordinator().lock();
EODatabaseContext dbContext =
    EOUtilities.databaseContextForModelNamed(ec, "MyModel");
```

■ **NOTE** If objects in the EOAccess layer implement `NSLocking`, you can lock them directly instead of using the `EOObjectStoreCoordinator`. There is no functional difference. We prefer the consistency of always locking the `EOObjectStoreCoordinator`.

Debugging Locking Problems

Locking is so critically important that the Enterprise Object frameworks have built in debugging code to detect access without locking. To turn this on requires only a single line:

```
NSLog.allowDebugLoggingForGroups(NSLog.DebugGroupMultithreading);
```

Listing 3-12 shows the resulting application log message if you access something without a lock.

Listing 3-12. *Example Access with No Lock Warning*

```
 [2003-06-19 22:10:11 PDT] <WorkerThread0> *** EOEditingContext:
    access with no lock: recordObject()!
[2003-06-19 22:10:11 PDT] <WorkerThread0> java.lang.Exception:
    This is not a real exception, just a stack trace of the location of
    the missing lock:
at com.webobjects.eocontrol.EOEditingContext
    ._EOAssertSafeMultiThreadedAccess(EOEditingContext.java:5033)
at com.webobjects.eocontrol.EOEditingContext
    .recordObject(EOEditingContext.java:1364)
at com.webobjects.eocontrol.EOEditingContext
    ._insertObjectWithGlobalID(EOEditingContext.java:2764)
at com.webobjects.eocontrol.EOEditingContext
    .insertObjectWithGlobalID(EOEditingContext.java:2791)
at com.webobjects.eocontrol.EOEditingContext
    .insertObject(EOEditingContext.java:2812)
at RelationshipsAcrossECs
    .saveChanges(RelationshipsAcrossECs.java:28)
etc.
```

You will need to follow the trace back until you get to your code, then try to figure out what did not get locked and why.

■ **NOTE** The "access with no lock" warning is not always right. The first time a `EODatabaseContext` connects to a database, an "access with no lock" warning is output from the `EODatabaseContext` constructor. This message can be safely ignored.

Debugging a Deadlocked Application

The opposite problem, not unlocking what you have locked, is much more difficult to debug. You only find out about it when some other thread tries to grab the lock and blocks. This might happen far away from the code that failed to unlock something. A good place to start debugging this is to get a thread dump (which includes a back trace of each thread) from the running application. At least then you will know where the deadlock is occurring.

Getting a thread dump is conveniently different on each platform. For the Unix variants, send a `QUIT` signal to the process by using `kill -QUIT <process id>` or `kill -3 <process id>` to the process. You can also do this by pressing `Ctrl+\` in the same shell you started the process from (if, in fact, you used a shell to start the app). For Windows, the key sequence is `Ctrl+Break`, but this only works in the same shell you used to start the app. If the application in question is running under JavaMonitor on a Unix variant, chances are that your precious dump is going straight to `/dev/null`. To change this, you will have to edit the script that starts `wotaskd` in `$NEXT_ROOT/System/Library/WebObjects/JavaApplications/wotaskd.woa/Contents/Resources/SpawnOfWotaskd.sh`. Change the line that reads

```
$@ 1>/dev/null 2>&1 &
```

to read

```
$@ 1>>[path to stdout log] 2>>[path to stderr log] &
```

where `[path to stdout log]` and `[path to stderr log]` are replaced by paths to valid files. Your thread dump will appear in the stderr log. See `http://www.omnigroup.com/mailman/archive/webobjects-dev/2003-February/031194.html` for more information. If you are running on Windows, you cannot get a thread dump for an application launched with JavaMonitor. You will need to launch your application from the command line.

For more information on stack traces and thread dumps, see `http://developer.java.sun.com/developer/technicalArticles/Programming/Stacktrace/`.

TIP An even more powerful way of doing this is to enable remote debugging when launching the application and attach to it with a debugger when it deadlocks.

The problem with thread dumps and stack traces is that they tell you the location of the effect of the problem, not the location of the cause of the problem. Most deadlocks are caused by locks that you have taken but not released. A small proportion are caused by bugs in EOF but, thankfully, these are becoming rare. The stack trace of a blocked thread only shows where the deadlock occurs. It would be much more useful to see where in the code the outstanding locks were taken rather than where they caused a problem.

Jonathan Rentzsch came up with the inspired idea of having an editing context subclass track the stack traces where locks were taken out. This became the `LockErrorScreamerEditingContext`, which can be found on the WODev site and in the PracticalUtilities framework. Anthony Ingraldi extended this to handle the multiple locks by a single thread allowed by `NSRecursiveLock`. They have kindly allowed us to reproduce their work here.

Use of the LockErrorScreamerEditingContext is very simple. You just use it as you would a regular EOEditingContext; the API is the same.

```
EOEditingContext parent = new LockErrorScreamerEditingContext();
EOEditingContext child = new LockErrorScreamerEditingContext(parent);
```

As many deadlocks are associated with the session's defaultEditingContext() you will probably want to replace that with a LockErrorScreamerEditingContext as well. This needs to be done in the session constructor. WOSession has two constructors, so you will need to do it twice:

```
public Session() {
    super();
    setDefaultEditingContext(new LockErrorScreamerEditingContext());
}

public Session(String sessionID) {
    super(sessionID);
    setDefaultEditingContext(new LockErrorScreamerEditingContext());
}
```

Once you have done this, all you need to do is run your application and wait for the error messages to appear in the log. The error traces should quickly point you to the offending bit of code.

The application for this chapter contains a page that you can use to see what these messages look like and to experiment with producing them and seeing the result of deadlock. Start the application and click the *Test LockErrorScreamerEditingContext* link. On the next page are links to make unbalanced locks and unlocks, and to refresh the page.

As long as you don't make concurrent requests, each will probably be processed by the same worker thread and thus avoid deadlocking no matter how much bad locking you do. The *Refresh with delay* link will help you get more threads in on the action. Click on the *Refresh with delay* link and then, while that worker thread is busy working, click the *Lock without unlock* or *Unlock without lock* link. These requests will go to other worker threads. This will allow you to experiment with the result of different threads trying to take or release locks. Listing 3-13 shows a partial trace from an attempt to lock the editing context when it is already locked by another thread.

Listing 3-13. *Example* LockErrorScreamerEditingContext *Message*

```
[2003-06-22 13:13:47 PDT] <WorkerThread1> !!! Attempting to lock editing context
  from WorkerThread1 that was previously locked in WorkerThread0
[2003-06-22 13:13:47 PDT] <WorkerThread1> !!! Current stack trace:
java.lang.Throwable
at com.apress.practicalwo.practicalutilities.LockErrorScreamerEditingContext.
    _trace(LockErrorScreamerEditingContext.java:152)
at com.apress.practicalwo.practicalutilities.LockErrorScreamerEditingContext.
    lock(LockErrorScreamerEditingContext.java:85)
at LockErrorScreamerEditingContextTester.
    lock(LockErrorScreamerEditingContextTester.java:24)
etc.
```

```
[2003-06-22 13:13:47 PDT] <WorkerThread1> !!! Stack trace for most recent lock:
java.lang.Throwable
at com.apress.practicalwo.practicalutilities.LockErrorScreamerEditingContext.
    _trace(LockErrorScreamerEditingContext.java:152)
at com.apress.practicalwo.practicalutilities.LockErrorScreamerEditingContext.
    lock(LockErrorScreamerEditingContext.java:61)
at LockErrorScreamerEditingContextTester.
    lock(LockErrorScreamerEditingContextTester.java:24)
```

The first trace shows where worker thread 1 deadlocked on the lock held by worker thread 0. The second trace shows the most recent lock taken by worker thread 0, which is clearly where the problem originated. Once the application deadlocks you will need to restart it, or at least start a new session. If the application is not dispatching requests concurrently, you will have no choice but to restart the application.

Managing Object Freshness

One of the great things about EOF is that it caches the object graph and keeps it updated instead of constantly making slow trips to the database. This is also one of the weaknesses of EOF, for it is not omniscient. It does not know when something else changes some of the objects that it has cached. Objects can get changed without EOF's knowledge by low-level calls to EOAccess in the same application or by some other process (e.g., another instance of the same application, another application, or some other non-EOF/WO process).

For some applications this will not matter. Slightly stale data is acceptable, or users work with a personal set of data and are unaffected by changes that others make. However, most of us will occasionally need to prod EOF to check and see if there have been changes since it last checked the database. As with many things EOF, there is more than one way to do this and no single right answer.

■ **CAUTION** Managing object freshness is about data presentation, not avoiding concurrency issues when updating. Regardless of what you do to present users with fresh data, if data is being edited you will have to handle optimistic locking failures.

Fetching Fresh Objects

The easiest way to get fresh data is with an `EOFetchSpecification` that is set to refresh the objects that it fetches:

```
EOFetchSpecification fetchSpec = new EOFetchSpecification();
fetchSpec.setEntityName("Invoice");
etc.
fetchSpec.setRefreshesRefetchedObjects(true);
editingContext().objectsWithFetchSpecification(fetchSpec);
```

This refreshes the data in the objects that are fetched. It does not refresh related objects; that only happens if they are also fetched. Fetching related objects is easy to accomplish by specifying the path to the related objects:

```
fetchSpec.setPrefetchingRelationshipKeyPaths(new NSArray("someRelationship"));
```

Using Snapshot Timestamps to Ensure Fresh Data

Each snapshot in the object store is associated with a timestamp that indicates exactly when it was fetched. Editing contexts have some control over the age of data that they will accept. An editing context's `fetchTimestamp()` is used to request that it receive data fetched on or after the timestamp.

It is important to note that not only is this just a *request*, but it is only considered when an object is *first* fetched or faulted into the editing context. It is very important to pay attention to the latter point. Once an object is in an editing context, changing this timestamp will not make the editing context refresh the object's data. The enterprise object needs to be refetched or refaulted for this to happen.

By default, editing contexts ask that the data have been fetched within the last hour. In most situations, that is not nearly fresh enough. Even in the case where each user's data is segregated, a user will expect to see fresh data when they log in. This is particularly important when running multiple instances. If a user logs into one instance, makes changes, then logs out and into another instance, they are going to expect to see their changes.

The data freshness that an editing context asks for can be set application-wide by using the `EOEditingContext` static method `setDefaultFetchTimestampLag()`. The default is expressed as a lag in milliseconds from when the editing context is created. To ask for objects to be created from data that was fetched no earlier than two seconds before the editing context was created, add this to the `Application` constructor:

```
EOEditingContext.setDefaultFetchTimestampLag(2000);
```

■ **NOTE** This lag is in milliseconds, *not* seconds. Don't confuse it with things like the `sessionTimeOut()`, which are expressed in seconds.

Individual editing contexts can override the default by specifying the absolute time (not a lag, as the default uses) that is the earliest they will accept data from. This is set by passing the timestamp to `setFetchTimestamp()`. This can be set as often as you wish during the lifetime of the editing context. However, it will only affect subsequent fetches and faulting.

■ **TIP** Nested editing contexts use their parent's `fetchTimestamp()`.

It is possible to use this timestamp to freshen objects already in the editing context. The trick is to set it and then turn the objects that you want fresh data for back into faults. New in WebObjects 5.2 is the not very well documented `refreshObject()` and `refreshAllObjects()`. Presumably these have the same freshening effect as `refaultObject()` and `refaultAllObject()` but without any of the side effects that the documentation warns of. Be aware that if you have a lot of objects in the editing context, calling `refreshAllObjects()` can result in a lot of work for EOF fetching the fresh data. Two simple lines will get you fresh data for all of the objects in an editing context:

```
ec.setFetchTimestamp(System.currentTimeMillis());
ec.refreshAllObjects();
```

You can try these out in the sample application with this chapter. Start the application and click the *Test Refreshing Objects* link.

CAUTION While `invalidateObjectsWithGlobalIDs()` and `invalidateAllObjects()` can be used to get fresh data, they are rather heavy in their effect. It is best to leave these alone unless you know something about the object graph that EOF doesn't—for example, if you have been using direct SQL to alter data.

Refreshing and Relationships

The refreshing methods just described are limited in that they only refresh the attributes and the to-one relationships (in other words, the data directly in the row). They do not refresh to-many relationships to show changes in objects that are in the relationship. This means that if objects are added to the relationship in another object store (or anything else updating the database), your code will not see them as being related. Conversely, if objects are removed from the relationship in another object store, they will still appear in the relationship.

Refreshing to-many relationships is unfortunately expensive and laborious, a shortcoming of EOF. One solution is to invalidate the objects that you need to refresh to-many relationships for. While this works, it can be expensive in terms of processing and have unintended side effects if the invalidated objects had unsaved changes. There is another option that we are a little reluctant to recommend. While it works, we have not used it enough to be fully confident that there are no unpleasant side effects when edits are in progress.

This method of refreshing to-many relationships works by setting the snapshot for the to-many relationship to `null`. It only works for one object and one relationship at a time. The implementation is slightly convoluted, as we need to get down to the `EODatabase` level. An example implementation can be found in the application for this chapter, in the RefreshingObjects component's method `refreshToManyRelationship(EOEnterpriseObject, String)`. Here is the gist of the code that refreshes `relationshipName` on `sourceObject`:

```
sourceEditingContext = sourceObject.editingContext();
EOEntity sourceObjectEntity = EOUtilities
    .entityForObject(sourceEditingContext, sourceObject);
EOModel sourceObjectModel = sourceObjectEntity.model();
EOGlobalID sourceGlobalID = sourceEditingContext.globalIDForObject(sourceObject);
```

```
EODatabaseContext dbContext = EODatabaseContext
    .registeredDatabaseContextForModel(sourceObjectModel,
                                       sourceEditingContext);
EODatabase database = dbContext.database();
database.recordSnapshotForSourceGlobalID(null, sourceGlobalID, relationshipName);
```

Freshening Data Through Distributed Change Notifications

We will briefly mention one final option for getting fresh data, the ChangeNotificationFramework. This framework was originally written in Objective-C by David Neumann of Apple. It watches the changes made in one application and sends notifications of the changes to the other applications. While great for maintaining object freshness, it does result in a lot of interprocess communication and might be overkill for many applications. There are two Java ports of this framework. One is hosted by Gary Teter at `http://www.wirehose.com/download/`. The other one is Java Message Service (JMS)–based. It is part of the ever-growing Project WONDER, `http://wonder.sourceforge.net/`.

Summary

This chapter discussed the basics of working with EOF to manage the object graph. Some of the code and concepts behind this can be difficult to master, and you may find yourself returning to this material and the WebObjects documentation again. If you want to delve deeper into this topic, the WebObjects documentation and the Javadocs for the packages `com.webobjects.eoaccess` and `com.webobjects.eocontrol` will get you started.

We introduced the `EOStateTransition` interface and `CooperatingEditingContext` as a way to allow enterprise objects to participate in their insert/update/delete changes. These provide some very useful functionality that is missing from EOF and will help to make your code more robust and easier to understand.

Two common difficulties with managing the object graph are forming relationships that cross editing contexts and dealing with referential integrity problems. We demonstrated how to generate code to automate detection of any attempt to form a relationship that crosses editing contexts. Referential integrity problems can't be prevented, only dealt with. Code to log such problems was shown, as well as code to detect the fake enterprise objects that EOF generates when relationships go bad.

Locking of enterprise objects is critical in Java, even more so if you are dispatching requests concurrently. We hope to have convinced you of the importance of doing this and doing it correctly. You should have enough information now either to confidently use something like the `MultiECLockManager` or to roll your own solution. While this won't make your application safe for multithreading by itself, it is an important step in the process.

EOF has its share of warts. Managing object freshness is certainly one of them. We've explored the roots of the problem and the mechanisms inside and outside of EOF that can be used to address this shortcoming.

CHAPTER 4

Authentication and Security

Let those who desire a secure homeland conquer it.

—José Martí

What, me worry?

—Alfred E. Neumann

It is unlikely that you will get very far in the world of WebObjects applications before running into the need to authenticate users, usually through some sort of login system. Even for a publicly available site, you might have a section only for registered users and will probably have a section that is only for the site administrators.

We are going to focus on what you can do in your code and not look at deployment, server, or web server security topics. These are vast topics indeed. (For a brief overview of issues related to those subjects, see `http://wodev.spearway.com/cgi-bin/WebObjects/WODev.woa/wa/Main?wikiPage=WebObjectsSecurity`.)

Beginning with the Basics

We will start with a quick look at the authentication and encryption of information exchanged with the Hypertext Transfer Protocol (HTTP).

The Technical Details of Secure HTTP

You don't want to use HTTP when sending sensitive information such as passwords and credit card numbers between the user's machine and your application. Plain HTTP uses unencrypted cleartext for the transmission, making it easy to intercept and gain access to that information. Sensitive information should be encrypted before being transmitted over public networks. The standard form of security through encryption for a web application is the Secure Sockets Layer (SSL) protocol. This protocol, originally developed by Netscape, provides communications privacy. The protocol permits a secure (authenticated and encrypted) channel of communication between applications that prevents eavesdropping, tampering, and message forgery.

The SSL protocol has two layers, one above the other. The SSL Record Protocol is the lower level and is itself layered on top of a reliable transport protocol, generally Transmission Control Protocol (TCP). The SSL Record Protocol encapsulates the second, higher-level protocol. There are several higher-level protocols, but the one relevant to web applications is HTTP.

The use of the HTTP protocol with security provided by the SSL Record Protocol is referred to as Secure HTTP (HTTPS). It is indicated in URLs by the use of `https://` instead of `http://`. Most browsers indicate the presence of HTTPS through the use of a lock (or related) icon.

While the authentication and encryption services of SSL are admirable, don't rush off and make your entire application use HTTPS if it does not need it. SSL makes heavy use of CPU-intensive cryptographic operations. You won't see any slowdown in your code while the web server performs the cryptographic operations, but it does take a toll on the machine. For efficiency's sake you should try to limit the use of HTTPS to the pages that actually need it.

■NOTE Transport Layer Security (TLS) is the successor to SSL. While TLS protocol adoption is spreading, SSL is still the term commonly used when referring to these technologies. Our use of SSL is intended to encompass both SSL and TLS.

Practical Use of HTTPS

The important result of using HTTPS is that the browser will encrypt the request before sending it to the server and the web server will encrypt the result before returning it to the client. The former is important if a form is submitting sensitive information (e.g., a password or a credit card number). The latter is important if the information returned is sensitive. It is not possible to send a secure request and get an insecure (unencrypted) response, nor to send an insecure request and get a secure response. You must make a secure request to receive a secure response.

Using HTTPS with WOHyperlink

To securely receive sensitive information, the browser needs to make an HTTPS request of the server. This is done by using a hyperlink that starts with `https: <a href="https://… ">`. This is easier said than done, as by default WebObjects uses partial URLs that are relative to the domain name:

```
<a href="/cgi-bin/WebObjects/Chap4App.woa/3/wo/4sdesm7DbjStYtZK8xoXF0/0.1">
```

There is an apparently easy solution to this. `WOHyperlink` has a `secure` binding for just this purpose (see Figure 4-1). Bind it to `true` and WebObjects will generate full HTTPS URLs. Bind it to `false` to generate full HTTP URLs, and leave it unbound to generate the WebObjects default of partial URLs.

■TIP WebObjects does not like to use `localhost` for the `cgiAdaptorURL()` that it uses when generating some URLs. However, the URLs that `WOContext` generates sometimes do use this (it appears that `WOContext` takes it from the headers, as we demonstrate further on). This flip-flopping domain can cause problems with HTTPS connections. You can fool WebObjects into using `localhost` for the `cgiAdaptorURL()` if you capitalize it: `-DWOAdaptorURL=http://LocalHost/cgi-bin/WebObjects`. Alternatively, you can use the loopback IP address: 127.0.0.1: `-DWOAdaptorURL=http://127.0.0.1/cgi-bin/WebObjects`.

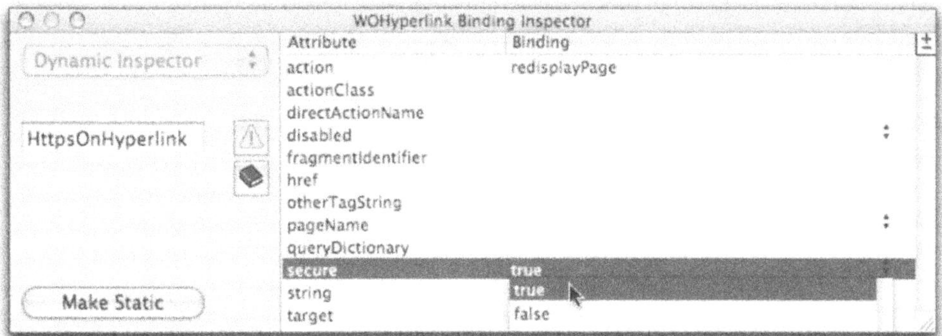

Figure 4-1. *The secure binding on* `WOHyperlink`

However (and you've probably guessed this), it does not work quite so smoothly. There is a defect in WebObjects' URL generation that shows up when a request is made via HTTPS and a `WOHyperlink` in the returned response has a secure binding of `false`. In this situation, the URL is generated incorrectly as

```
<a href="http://www.domain.com:443/cgi-bin/WebObjects/Chap4App.woa/3/wo/etc.">
```

This URL specifies HTTP as the protocol, but uses the standard HTTPS port number 443. Clicking this link results in an error from the web server.

Happily, there is a way to extend WebObjects to work around this problem. This URL is generated by the `WOContext` method `completeURLWithRequestHandlerKey()`. There are a number of ways to fix this, but explicitly specifying the port to use is probably the shortest:

```
public String completeURLWithRequestHandlerKey(String requestHandlerKey,
                                               String requestHandlerPath,
                                               String queryString,
                                               boolean isSecure,
                                               int somePort) {
    return super.completeURLWithRequestHandlerKey(requestHandlerKey,
             requestHandlerPath, queryString, isSecure, isSecure ? 443 : 80);
}
```

This method can also be useful if you need to use something other than the standard 80 and 443 for the HTTP and HTTPS ports.

A subclass of one of the framework classes won't do much good unless WebObjects can be convinced to use it instead of its own version. There is no consistent way to achieve this substitution; the method used depends on the class being replaced. The designers of the frameworks anticipated some of the cases in which classes would need to be replaced and made accommodations for such replacement. Replacing classes where this was not anticipated can be much more involved. Thus class replacement ranges from very easy (WebObjects automatically uses a subclass of `WOSession`) to very difficult (in the case of some classes in the `EOAccess` and `EOControl` packages).

In the case of WOContext, all that is needed to have WebObjects use your custom subclass is to override one method in your Application class:

```
/**
 * Returns the complete class name of the WOContext subclass to
 * use in place of WOContext.
 */
public String contextClassName() {
    return "com.apress.practicalwo.chap4app.SecureContext";
}
```

With that done, we now have a fully working dynamic URL to move the user's session into and out of HTTPS.

You can see all of this in action on the SecureLinks page of the example application for this chapter. This page demonstrates a link to switch to HTTPS, a link to switch to HTTP, a link to toggle between HTTP and HTTPS, as well a plain old WOHyperlink for comparison. The *Test WOHyperlink and HTTPS* link on the main page will take you there.

■ TIP There is no built-in way to determine if a request was made via HTTP or HTTPS. It can be difficult to determine, as there is no standard header to indicate this. Apache, for example, adds a special header, while in other cases you have to look at the port the request came to the web server on and make assumptions based on that. Complicating this is the needless inconsistency among the various adaptors for WebObjects in naming this information. The isSecure() method from the WORequestAdditions class in the Practical-Utilities framework attempts to figure this out for you. You might need to extend this for your particular situation.

Using HTTPS with WOForm

The easiest way to use HTTPS with a WOForm is to use a secure WOHyperlink to display the page containing the form. When this fits into your page design, it is the way to go. While a secure form on an insecure page can submit the form contents to an HTTPS URL, many users of web apps aren't familiar with how HTTPS works. They will expect the page that the form is on to also be secured with HTTPS, not realizing that encrypting a blank form has little security value. However, having the entire page secure is not always an option—for example, in the case of a small login form on a larger home page. There is no secure binding on a WOForm, unfortunately, so we will need to work a bit harder for this one.

WOForm offers us the option of submitting to a Component Action, to a Direct Action, or to some other URL that we specify. Without a secure binding there is little we can do to influence the generation of the Component or Direct Action URLs. We could try subclassing WOForm, but then we are faced with making WebObjects use our subclass. While we can easily do that using a WOCustomObject, it won't look and work like WOForm in WOBuilder. We think that is too high a price to pay for a secure URL. Instead we will take the responsibility for URL generation away from WOForm and give it to the page by using the href binding of WOForm (see Figure 4-2).

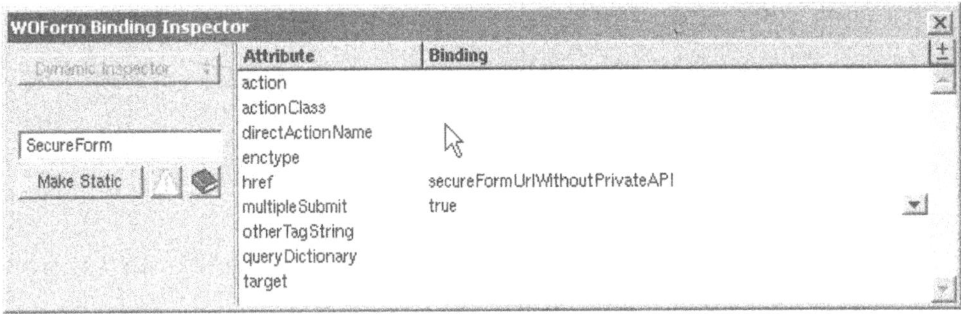

Figure 4-2. *Using* `href` *binding instead of* `action` *binding with* `WOForm`

Now we are left with the task of generating the URL that the form will submit to. Being lazy, we'd prefer that the frameworks do as much of the work for this as possible. Unfortunately, there is no documented support for HTTPS, leaving us with hacks, dirty tricks, and hard work as implementation choices.

Here is one possible implementation using the dirty trick of accessing private API. Long-time WebObjects developers will recognize it as a modernization of an earlier solution using Objective-C categories.

■ **NOTE** We (like all people who value their sanity) recommend against using private API unless absolutely necessary.

```
public String secureFormUrlWithPrivateAPI () {
    context()._generateCompleteURLs();
    String secureFormUrl = context()._componentActionURL(true);
    context()._generateRelativeURLs();
    return secureFormUrl;
}
```

`WOContext` has the job of most of the URL generation in WebObjects. The `WOContext` methods `_generateCompleteURLs()` and `_generateRelativeURLs()` instruct it to generate full URLs starting with HTTP or HTTPS. The method `_componentActionURL(boolean)` functions as the documented `componentActionURL()`, but returns an HTTPS URL if the parameter is `true`. The underscore at the start of these methods indicates that they are to be treated as `private` even though they have `public` access. This solution is short and efficient—and may stop working with the next release of WebObjects.

A more robust solution will not use private API. It will also be more effort. The `WOContext` method `componentActionURL()` still does most of the work for us. We need only supply either HTTP or HTTPS and the domain name. The latter, however, is a bit tricky.

We will ignore the inevitable roadblocks for a moment and peek at the final code:

```
public String secureFormUrlWithoutPrivateAPI () {
    return "https://" +
        WORequestAdditions.hostName(context().request()) +
        context().componentActionURL();
}
```

There is not much to see, is there? All the mysterious work happens in `WORequestAdditions`, where it determines the `hostName()` (a.k.a. domain).

The problem of determining the name of the host that was used in the request is similar to that of determining if the request was made via HTTP or HTTPS. There is no standard for this or consistency across the WebObjects adaptors. Once again, we are left holding the bag.

The solution shown in Listing 4-1 is the same brute force approach: we keep looking until we find what we want. If you have only one hostname hitting your application, you could use one of the various types of settings files to set up a default hostname, but this is a more general solution.

Listing 4-1. *Determining the Hostname Used in a Request*

```
// Add more options here (e.g. for IIS, NSAPI, etc.), if necessary...
public static final NSArray HOST_NAME_KEYS = new NSArray(new Object[]
    {"x-webobjects-server-name", "server_name", "Host", "http_host"});

/**
 * Returns the host name (a.k.a. server name, domain name) used in
 * this request. The request headers are examined for the keys in
 * HOST_NAME_KEYS to determine the name.
 */
static public String hostName(WORequest request) {
    /** require [valid_param] request != null; **/
    String hostName = null;
    for (int i = 0; (hostName == null) && (i < HOST_NAME_KEYS.count()); i++) {
        hostName = request.headerForKey((String) HOST_NAME_KEYS.objectAtIndex(i));
    }
    return hostName;
    /** ensure [valid_result] Result != null; **/
}
```

With the HTTPS URL built, we are almost done. Using the `href` binding of `WOForm` instead of the `action` binding has a side effect that you need to be aware of. `WOForm` does not permit both the `href` and `action` bindings to be set, as it would not know which to use. When using `href` to submit to a secure URL, it is not possible to have a form action. Instead, the `action` binding of a `WOSubmit` button must be used to define the method to be invoked when the form is submitted. You can still have multiple submit buttons in a form; of course, you will need to set the `multipleSubmit` binding to `true` as usual.

The lack of an action binding on the form has a couple of consequences. They both stem from the lack of a default action method associated with form submission. If the user presses Enter and a submit button doesn't have the focus, no action method will be invoked. The normal request—response loop will be followed and no error will result, but no action method code will be run either. This means that Enter can't be used to log in. The user needs to click on a submit button. You might be able to work around this with some fancy JavaScript.

The lack of a default action method also means that you can't have a default action method that updates the page contents. JavaScript event handlers (for example, a this.form.submit(); return false; in the onchange event of a WOPopUpButton) can use this sort of method to update the display when the user makes a selection. Since there is no default form action, you have to move this functionality to the appendToResponse() method before calling super.appendToResponse().

You can see all of this in action on the SecureForms page of the example application for this chapter. This page demonstrates a form on an insecure page that submits to a secure URL and subsequently displays a secure page. It also has two submit buttons to demonstrate that multiple submits still work. The *Test WOForm and HTTPS* link on the main page will take you there.

NOTE As is often the case, there are other ways to accomplish this. You could create a custom WOComponentContent or you could sniff the form's element ID. We'll leave these as an exercise for the reader.

Authenticating Users

Now that we have a way of getting information securely to and from the user, we can start to look at how to authenticate and track a user. Authentication almost always consists of validating a user-provided identity and credential to verify that the user is who they say they are. These typically take the form of a user name and password, as few of us have retina scanners on our desk. Once authenticated, the user is tracked in the session.

Introducing the AbstractUser

We're going to be looking at several methods of user authentication in this chapter. To make things easier on ourselves, we'll define an abstract class, AbstractUser, that sets out the common information and the authentication protocols. We'll use EOF inheritance to create a subclass for each authentication method. This separation of authentication methods across subclasses can also be useful in the real world. Consider the situation where staff authenticates using an institutional login mechanism and clients authenticate using an application-controlled user ID and password stored in the database.

AbstractUser will hold all the common information and behavior. While simple, it is sufficient for basic needs. This model of a user (see Figure 4-3) has only two attributes: an internal, unique identifier (oid) and the user identity (userID). You will notice that there is no password. This is intentional, as not all authentication methods require our application to store the password. Real world examples will likely add some additional information. In the following discussion, we will use *password* for what the user provides when they attempt to log in and *credential* for the authoritative version that the password is validated against.

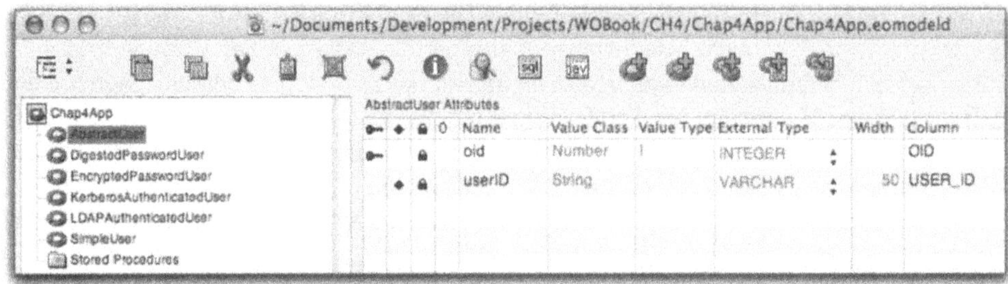

Figure 4-3. *The* `AbstractUser` *object*

The `AbstractUser` class shown in Listing 4-2 provides one concrete and two abstract methods to handle user authentication. The concrete method, `authenticatedUser()`, handles authentication for all subclasses.

Listing 4-2. *The* `AbstractUser` *Class*

```
/**
 * Attempts to locate a user identified by aUserID and authenticated with
 * aPassword. The user is returned if found, otherwise an exception is thrown.
 */
public static AbstractUser authenticatedUser(EOEditingContext ec,
                                             String aUserID,
                                             String aPassword)
    throws EOObjectNotAvailableException, EOUtilities.MoreThanOneException {

    /** require [valid_ec] ec != null;
                [valid_id] aUserID != null;
                [valid_credential] aPassword != null;   **/

    AbstractUser userWithIdentity =(AbstractUser) EOUtilities.
        objectMatchingKeyAndValue(ec, "AbstractUser", USERID, aUserID);

    if ( ! userWithIdentity.canAuthenticateWithPassword(aPassword)) {
        throw new EOObjectNotAvailableException("Failed to authenticate");
    }

    return userWithIdentity;

    /** ensure [valid_result] Result != null;  **/
}
```

There are three possible outcomes from calling this method: it was possible to authenticate the user; it was not possible to authenticate the user because the user ID or password was incorrect; or it was not possible to authenticate the user because there are multiple users with the same user ID. The latter should never happen and indicates a programming failure or problem with the data.

The user is fetched based solely on aUserID. This is done so that the password provided can be authenticated against the credential polymorphically. Each subclass of AbstractUser determines how it will perform authentication. authenticatedUser() relies on one of the abstract methods, canAuthenticateWithPassword(), to defer the unique aspects of authentication to the subclass:

```
/**
 * Return <code>true</code> if this user can be authenticated with password.
 */
public abstract boolean canAuthenticateWithPassword(String password);
```

The other abstract method is used to set the credential based on the password supplied:

```
/**
 * Sets authentication credential based on supplied password.
 */
public abstract void setPassword(String password);
```

For subclasses of AbstractUser where the password is not stored by the application, this can be implemented as an empty method.

EOF STRING CONSTANTS AND EOGENERATOR

The use of strings to identify methods representing attributes and relationships adds a lot of flexibility to EOF. It also adds a lot of fragility and delays identification of errors until runtime. The use of valueForKey(), addObjectToBothSidesOfRelationshipWithKey(), and similar methods litter your code with hard-coded strings. This is particularly a problem when you start renaming things in the EOModel. You then need to manually find each string and update it.

Rather than using hard-coded strings, you can use an EOGenerator template to automatically produce constants that can be used in their place. The call to EOUtilities.objectMatchingKeyAndValue() in the authenticatedUser method shows an example of using EOGenerator-created constants. USERID is a constant generated by EOGenerator in AbstractUser. When the model is changed, the constant names will get changed and the compiler will show an undeclared identifier error in each place that needs to be updated. As the references still need to be updated manually, this is not a complete cure. Using Eclipse's refactoring support to rename the constants before regenerating the code can eliminate much of the effort.

Introducing the SimpleUser

We will start with the simplest authentication case, which is a cleartext password stored in the database. To authenticate, we merely need to verify that the user's credential matches the password that the user enters:

```
/**
 * Return <code>true</code> if this user can be authenticated with password. This
 * is implemented by comparing the given password with the stored credential.
 */
public boolean canAuthenticateWithPassword(String password) {
    /** require [valid_password] password != null;  **/
    return password.equals(credential());
}
```

Setting the credential is even more trivial:

```
/**
 * Produces authentication credential from password.
 */
public void setPassword(String password) {
    /** require [valid_password] password != null;  **/
    setCredential(password);
    /** ensure [credential_set] credential() != null;
               [credential_equals_digest] credential().equals(password); **/
}
```

This code can be found in the SimpleUser class in the example application for this chapter. Before we look at other methods of authentication, we'll take a detour though logging in, logging out, and tracking the user after we've authenticated them.

Tracking the User After Authentication

WebObjects centralizes information about a user's session (interaction with the application) in a Session object. Session is a subclass of WOSession unique to each application. The exact definition of a user session can be a bit slippery, as it is possible for a single client (i.e., browser) to have more than one concurrent session and for two browsers to share the same session. We will just ignore those unusual situations and say simply that a session represents one visit by one user to one application. You can also handle user requests using only Direct Actions and avoid creating user sessions, but that is not relevant to the authentication topic at hand. We ignore Direct Actions in the following discussion.

When the application handles the first request from a user, it creates a Session object. When the application returns the response to the user, it stores the session (i.e., the Session object) for use with the next request from the same user. When the next request arrives, it contains a token (the Session ID) that identifies the previously stored session. Based on this token, the application restores the Session object for use when processing the new request. The Session object preserves the information needed to maintain continuity for the user. This is the logical place to track the authenticated user, as the user information will be restored with each new request.

Listing 4-3 shows a simple Session that handles user authentication, remembers the authenticated user, and can indicate if a user has been authenticated or not. You will notice that there is no setAuthenticatedUser() method. The only way to associate a user with a Session is to give it a user ID and an authenticating password. This separates the tasks of gathering the information for user authentication and actually authenticating the information and recording the user. It allows user authentication information to come from various sources and also simplifies what a login form will need to do.

Listing 4-3. *A* WOSession *Subclass Handling User Authentication*

```
public class Session extends WOSession {

    protected AbstractUser authenticatedUser;

    /**
     * Authenticates the user information provided and records the user
     * as the authenticatedUser().
     */
    public void authenticateUser(String userID, String password)
    {
        /** require [valid_user_id] userID != null;
                    [valid_ password] password!= null;   **/
        authenticatedUser = AbstractUser.authenticatedUser(defaultEditingContext(),
                                                           userID, password);
        /** ensure [has_authenticated_user] isUserAuthenticated();  **/
    }

    /**
     * Returns the authenticated user associated with this session or null if there
     * isn't one.
     */
    public AbstractUser authenticatedUser()
    {
        /** require [has_authenticatedUser] isUserAuthenticated();  **/
        return authenticatedUser;
        /** ensure [valid_result] Result != null;  **/
    }

    /**
     * Returns <code>true</code> if an authenticated user is associated with this
     * session.
     */
    public boolean isUserAuthenticated() {
        return authenticatedUser() != null;
    }
}
```

You can find this code in the Session class of the example application for this chapter. It is used for all types of user authentication in the chapter.

Producing a Login Form

There is nothing particularly complex about a login form. All that is needed is a form, two text boxes (one for the user ID and one for the password), a submit button, and some method of displaying login failure messages (see Figure 4-4).

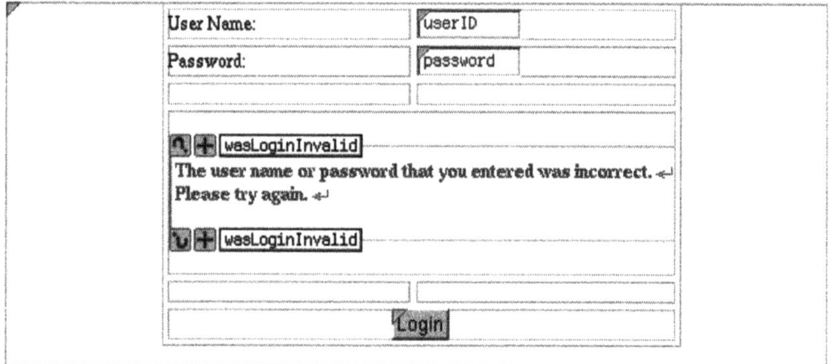

Figure 4-4. *A plain login form*

The SimpleLoginPage in the sample application demonstrates this in a functional, if not beautiful, login form. Processing the login, Listing 4-4, is nearly as straightforward as building the form.

Listing 4-4. *Processing User Login on the* SimpleLoginPage

```
/**
 * Attempts to validate the login information provided. Records the user in the
 * Session if successful. Redisplays this page with an error message if
 * not successful.
 */
public WOComponent login() {
    WOComponent nextPage = context().page();
    wasLoginInvalid = true;

    if ((userID != null) && (password != null)) {
        try {
            ((Session)session()).authenticateUser(userID, password);
            nextPage =  pageWithName("Main");
        }
        catch (EOObjectNotAvailableException e) {
            // Login was invalid, nothing else to do
        }
    }

    return nextPage;
}
```

The user ID and password entered are checked to ensure that they are not null, something we've chosen to disallow. If they are OK, the user is authenticated and recorded by the Session. Once that has been done, the page following login can be displayed. If an authentication failure exception is raised, or either of the data elements is missing, the login form is redisplayed with an error message.

If you try the code in Listing 4-4, you will notice that after logging in, the Main page is shown via HTTPS and the links on it make requests via HTTPS. This is not what we want to do, as there is nothing particularly secret on the main page. The login request (when the submit button is clicked) must be a secure request, but that then results in the Main page being shown securely. To display a page insecurely (via HTTP), the browser must make an insecure request. The only way to get back into insecure mode is to have the browser make another request after a successful login. The way to do this is to use a WORedirect, which is sent securely, to get the browser to request the main page via HTTP. To achieve this, replace nextPage = pageWithName("Main"); in the Listing 4-4 method with this:

```
String insecurePostLoginActionUrl = "http://" +
    WORequestAdditions.hostName(context().request()) +
    context().directActionURLForActionNamed("default", null);

nextPage =  pageWithName("WORedirect");
((WORedirect)nextPage).setUrl(insecurePostLoginActionUrl);
```

The WOContext method directActionURLForActionNamed() is the Direct Action counterpart to the Component Action method componentActionURL() that we briefly looked at earlier. Its job is to generate URLs to access Direct Actions. In this case we want the default action that displays the main page. The null second parameter indicates that there we have no parameters to pass to the direct action on the URL. We have to redirect to a Direct Action, as there is no way to redirect to the result of pageWithName(). The final, working version of this method is in the SimpleLoginPage class in this chapter's example application.

Handling Logout

Now that we have the user logged in (authenticated and recorded in the session), we are probably going to want some way of allowing them to log out. There are two tasks involved in this: discarding the user's session so that it cannot be used any more, and showing the user a page that does not require them to be authenticated. The former just requires us to call the terminate() method on the Session object. You might think that you can accomplish the latter by doing this:

```
public WOComponent logout() {
    WOComponent mainPage = pageWithName("Main");
    session().terminate();
    return mainPage;
}
```

However, that will usually not work. If the main page has a WOComponent with an action binding, it will be generated with a reference to the terminated session. The main page will also raise an exception in appendToResponse() if any references are made to things cleaned up in terminate(), such as the defaultEditingContext(). We need to avoid references to the terminated Session. Sending the user to a special logout page or redirecting them to the login page, the main page of your application, or another site entirely can accomplish the latter.

Here is a simple logout method that sends the user to the main (default) page of the application using a WORedirect with a Direct Action URL. The noWOSID dictionary is needed to prevent the URL from including the ID of the terminated Session object.

```
public static final NSDictionary noWOSID =
    new NSDictionary(Boolean.FALSE, "wosid");

public WOComponent logout() {
    session().terminate();
    WORedirect mainPage = (WORedirect) pageWithName("WORedirect");
    mainPage.setUrl(context().directActionURLForActionNamed("default",
        noWOSID)); // doesn't work for cookie-based session IDs

    return mainPage;
}
```

The code for authentication, logging in, and logging out can be found in the example application for this chapter. The *Login with SimpleLoginPage* link on the main page will take you to a login form to test this authentication mechanism. Some test users are automatically created. The userID/password pair chuck/foo belong to a SimpleUser.

■ TIP Be careful what you put on the page displayed after logout. It is best to avoid any WOComponent using an action binding (e.g., WOHyperlink) on this page. The use of an action binding will result in the creation of another session. This is not a security risk and does not prevent logout from succeeding, but it does waste memory.

Advanced Authentication Methods

In the previous section we demonstrated authentication by comparing a user-entered password with a cleartext version of the password stored in the database. In this section we will look at some more secure alternatives. Cleartext passwords are OK if you don't care much about security (that is, if the information protected is not really sensitive), or if your database and applications are on 100 percent secure servers and you trust everyone with access. For any other situations, you are going to want to choose a more secure method.

Obscuring the Password

A useful alternative to storing the password in cleartext is to obscure it using a hashing algorithm. A hashing algorithm processes an arbitrary piece of data and produces a fixed-size, condensed representation. Processing two pieces of identical data will yield the identical condensed representation. The transformation of the data into the condensed representation results in a loss of information that makes it impossible to determine the original data based only on the condensed representation. It is meaningless and can be stored openly.

For the purposes of authentication, we are interested in a particular class of hash algorithms: cryptographically secure hash algorithms. These special hash algorithms have the additional property of it being extremely unlikely that two different pieces of data will produce the same condensed representation. Thus, if the same condensed representation is computed for two different strings, we are all but guaranteed that the strings themselves are the same. The importance of this is that we only need to store the condensed representation of the password, not the password itself. There is no need to protect the condensed representation, as there is no path from it back to the original password.

The SHA and MD5 algorithms are two common examples of cryptographically secure hash algorithms. These two algorithms are commonly used in cryptography for their ability to not produce the same condensed representation for different inputs. In this context, the condensed representation is referred to as the Message Digest. You can find more information on these algorithms, and related topics, at `http://www.secure-hash-algorithm-md5-sha-1.co.uk/`.

The `MessageDigest` class in the `java.security` package (part of the JDK) provides implementations of cryptographically secure hash algorithms. We think the name of this class is somewhat confusing, as it *produces* a Message Digest; it is not the digest itself. JDK 1.3 comes with implementations for both SHA and MD5. You can generate a Message Digest from an input `String` like this:

```
MessageDigest md = MessageDigest.getInstance("SHA");
byte[] digest = md.digest(inputString.getBytes());
```

Either MD5 or SHA should be fine for most applications. SHA, which produces a longer digest, should be slightly more secure, but it is also correspondingly slower. You will probably never need to worry about either issue. If you are very paranoid, additional implementations and other algorithms are available from third parties. The Java Cryptography Extension (JCE) from Sun also has some more.

The `DigestedPasswordUser` in this chapter's example application is a subclass of `AbstractUser` that uses SHA to obscure the password.

We need to take special care when recording the credential. We need to digest (create a Message Digest from a piece of data) the cleartext password before saving it as the credential. It is not a good idea to do this in the `setCredential()` method. Doing so would open up the possibility of some of the WebObjects framework code effectively calling `setCredential(credential())` and thus redigesting the digest. That would render the credential useless. Instead, we use the `setPassword()` method introduced in `AbstractUser`. The job of this method for the `DigestedPasswordUser` subclass is to digest the cleartext password and set the secure credential:

```
/**
 * Uses messageDigest() to produce credential from password.
 */
public void setPassword(String password) {
    /** require [valid_password] password != null;  **/
    setCredential(digestedString(password));
    /** ensure [credential_set] credential() != null;
              [credential_is_digest] credential().equals(
             digestedString(password)); **/
}
```

The digestedString() method in Listing 4-5 is a convenience method that avoids a checked exception we are not concerned with. The bytes of the digest are encoded in Base64 to avoid the risk of them being garbled by encoding conversions when we store the binary data in a database.

Listing 4-5. *Creating an SHA Digest for a String*

```
/**
 * Processes <code>aString</code> through <code>messageDigest()</code> and
 * returns the result encoded in Base64.
 */
protected String digestedString(String aString) {
    /** require [aString_valid] aString != null; **/
    String digestedString;

    try {
        MessageDigest md = MessageDigest.getInstance("SHA");
        digestedString =  new sun.misc.BASE64Encoder().
            encode(md.digest(aString.getBytes()));    }
    catch (NoSuchAlgorithmException e) {
        throw new NSForwardException(e);
    }

    return digestedString;
    /** ensure [valid_result] Result != null;  **/
}
```

■ **TIP** NSForwardException can be useful if you catch a checked exception that you don't want to ignore, handle, or declare to be thrown by your method. It converts a checked exception into an unchecked RuntimeException. Another, more elegant alternative can be found at http://www.smotricz.com/kabutz/Issue033.html.

To authenticate the user's password, we need only compare a digest of what they entered with the stored digest of the original password:

```
public boolean canAuthenticateWithPassword(String password) {
    /** require [valid_password] password != null;  **/
    return digestedString(password).equals(credential());
}
```

There is a usability drawback to the security this adds. If a user forgets their password, it can't be recovered for them. The digest, not the original password, is stored in the database and we have no way of determining the actual password. This eliminates any possibility of having a "show/e-mail me my password" functionality. To accommodate this, you will need to provide a function for the administrator to change the user's password. You can reduce the number of times this will be needed by having the `DigestedPasswordUser` object also record a reminder phrase that can be sent to the user when (not if!) they forget their password.

Encrypting the Password

An alternative to storing a digest of the password is to use a cipher algorithm to create and store an encrypted version of the password. Unlike a digest, the encrypted password can be decrypted if needed. This allows a "show me my password" functionality to be implemented.

To encrypt and decrypt the password, we need to use the same secret key (confusingly also called a password!) for both the encryption and decryption operations. Extra information, in the form of a block of specially processed data, is often mixed in with the secret key to conceal it and also to produce a stronger (less guessable) secret key. More information on such password-based cryptography can be found at `http://www.rsasecurity.com/rsalabs/pkcs/pkcs-5/index.html`.

Encryption has the advantage over obscuring in being able to recover the password. The original password can be recovered by simply decrypting the stored credential. This allows the password to be revealed to a forgetful user. But this comes at the price of being less secure due to the need to store the secret key (not to mention the lack of security if the password is sent by e-mail!). Any reasonably knowledgeable person with access to the source code (or a decompiled version) will be able to determine the secret key and the method of encryption used. With that knowledge it is trivial to decrypt the information. This is simply not possible to do with the cryptographically secure hash functions. Regardless of where we get the secret key from (the user identity, a hard-coded value, a configuration file, etc.), if our code can access it then someone else can, too.

The Java Cryptography Extension (JCE) provides cryptographic support in Java. The JCE is an add-on to JDK 1.3 (it is part of JDK 1.4) so there is no direct support for encryption in JDK 1.3. You will need to install the JCE from `http://java.sun.com/products/jce/` or use a third-party product. Two good places to start looking for third-party products are `http://www.bouncycastle.org/index.html` and `http://www.cryptix.org/`. We will stick with the JCE implementation from Sun because that is what is in JDK 1.4.

Encryption and decryption support from the JCE is accessed via the `javax.crypto.Cipher` class. Encrypting a string is a straightforward process of three steps: get a `Cipher` instance, initialize its mode (`encrypt` or `decrypt`) and password, and then process the string.

Here is a simple example encrypting `inputString`:

```
Cipher pbeCipher = Cipher.getInstance("PBEWithMD5AndDES");
pbeCipher.init(Cipher.ENCRYPT_MODE, secretKey, obfuscator);
byte[] processedBytes = pbeCipher.doFinal(inputString.getBytes());
```

This code is discussed in more detail further on.

CAUTION For some reason we fail to understand, Eclipse puts all of the Jar files in the JRE Extensions directory on the boot classpath when starting the JVM. This has the effect of preventing settings in the `java.security` file from working. When you launch an application that uses the JCE from within Eclipse, you will get an exception similar to `java.lang.ExceptionInInitializerError: java.lang.Security-Exception: Cannot set up certs for trusted CAs: java.security.PrivilegedAction-Exception <<java.net.MalformedURLException: no protocol: US_export_policy.jar at javax.crypto.SunJCE_b.<clinit>(DashoA6275)`. To work around this, you need to edit the JRE definition and remove the Jar files that are in the JRE Extensions directory (see Installed JREs under the Java preferences).

The `EncryptedPasswordUser` in this chapter's example application is a subclass of `AbstractUser` that uses encryption to secure the password. Listing 4-6 shows that setting the encrypted password and authenticating a password is much the same as with the digested password discussed earlier.

Listing 4-6. *Setting and Authenticating the Password for the* `EncryptedPasswordUser`

```
/**
 * Produces authentication credential from password.
 */
public void setPassword(String password) {
    /** require [valid_password] password != null;  **/
    setCredential(transformString(password, Cipher.ENCRYPT_MODE));
    /** ensure [credential_set] credential() != null;
               [credential_is_digest] credential().equals(password); **/
}

/**
 * Return <code>true</code> if this user can be authenticated with password.
 */
public boolean canAuthenticateWithPassword(String password) {
    /** require [valid_password] password != null;  **/
    return transformString(password, Cipher.ENCRYPT_MODE).equals(credential());
}
```

The real work comes in processing the encryption and decryption. As with the digested password, we store the encrypted version encoded in Base64 to ensure the integrity of the binary data (see Listing 4-7).

Listing 4-7. *Handling Password Encryption and Decryption for the* `EncryptedPasswordUser`

```
/**
 * Encrypts or decrypts (determined by mode) inputString. Results of encryption
 * are encoded in Base64. Strings to be decrypted are assumed to have been
 * encoded in Base64 and are decoded before being decrypted.
 */
public String transformString(String inputString, int mode) {
    /** require [valid_input] inputString != null;
                [valid_mode] (mode == Ciper.ENCRYPT_MODE) ||
                             (mode == Cipher.DECRYPT_MODE);  **/

    String transformedString;

    try {
        // Create a Password Based Encryption cipher and initialize with
        // mode, key, and obfuscator
        Cipher pbeCipher = Cipher.getInstance("PBEWithMD5AndDES");
        pbeCipher.init(mode, secretKey, obfuscator);

        if (mode == Cipher.ENCRYPT_MODE) {
            byte[] processedBytes = pbeCipher.doFinal(inputString.getBytes());
            transformedString = new sun.misc.BASE64Encoder().
                encode(processedBytes);
        }
        else {
            byte[] bytesToProcess =
                new sun.misc.BASE64Decoder().decodeBuffer(inputString);
            transformedString = new String(pbeCipher.doFinal(bytesToProcess));
        }
    catch (Exception e) {
        throw new NSForwardException(e);
    }

    return transformedString;
    /** ensure [valid_result] Result != null;  **/
}
```

Listing 4-8 shows how the all-important `secretKey` ("Our(v@rys*c.r.tK!~") and `obfuscator` are created statically.

Listing 4-8. *Creation of the* `secretKey` *and* `obfuscator`

```
protected static PBEParameterSpec obfuscator;
protected static SecretKey secretKey;
    static {
    try {
        // Create parameters for Password Based Encryption. If someone can
        // get this information they can decrypt anything we encrypt!
        obfuscator = new PBEParameterSpec(
            new byte[] { (byte)0xc8, (byte)0xee, (byte)0xc7, (byte)0x73,
                         (byte)0x7e,  (byte)0x99, (byte)0x21, (byte)0x8c},
            100);
        secretKey = SecretKeyFactory.getInstance("PBEWithMD5AndDES").
            generateSecret(new PBEKeySpec("Our(v@rys*c.r.tK!~".toCharArray()));
    }
    catch (Exception e) {
        throw new NSForwardException(e);
    }
}
```

■ **NOTE** When you look at the code in the example application, you will see that it does not use a static initializer block like the example in Listing 4-8. That is because Jass has a parsing bug that prevents it from properly handling static initializer blocks. We had to reorganize the code to accommodate Jass.

Encryption of the password is not suitable for situations with high security requirements due to the ease of decrypting the information. It works best when you want to keep prying eyes (such as those of your staff with access to the database) away but also need to be able to recover a cleartext password. If you are sending the password in a mail-back scenario, you are probably not that worried about security to begin with, as e-mail can be intercepted.

Using Encryption for Secure Data Storage

A better use of encryption is to protect other sensitive information (credit card numbers, for example). Obscured passwords combined with other attributes encrypted using the original password as the secret key can achieve a high level of security for all the information.

To make this work, we keep a copy of the cleartext password that the user enters in the session. When the user logs in, we authenticate with the password they enter. Once we have authenticated the user, we cache the password in the session for later use in encrypting and decrypting other information. This cleartext password goes away when the session terminates. Data items such as credit card numbers can be encrypted and decrypted on demand using the password provided by the user's session.

Special care is needed if the password is changed. All of the encrypted information will need to be decrypted with the old password and re-encrypted with the new password at the same time. If the user forgets their password, the encrypted information will be rendered unreadable and will have to be discarded and re-created. That is the price of security.

Using LDAP for Authentication

In this section we will take a brief look at authentication using LDAP (Lightweight Directory Access Protocol, "el-dap"). What is this thing called LDAP, you ask? And why would you want to use it for user authentication? Those are both good questions, and we will answer them shortly. However, before we begin, we will warn you that LDAP is a large and complex topic. We're only going to scratch the surface of LDAP for what is needed for authentication in WebObjects.

LDAP is a protocol for accessing databases of information. LDAP does not actually refer to the database itself, though it is often used that way in conversation. From our point of view, the terminology is irrelevant; there is information and we can use LDAP to get at it. Often there is no other way to access the information, so calling it an LDAP database is perhaps not so unreasonable.

The sort of databases that have LDAP access have some unique characteristics that set them off from the more common RDBMS (relational database management system—an SQL database, in other words). The major difference is that the entries are organized in a treelike hierarchy with a single root. Like an SQL database, the LDAP database has a unique identifier for each entry (a DN or Distinguished Name in LDAP terms). Unlike the primary key in an SQL database, the DN is composed of several pieces identifying the path from the entry up to the root. If you look carefully at the entries, you will start to notice attributes with more than one value. Unlike an SQL database, the LDAP database has no "one value per column" restriction. This makes the schema much, much more flexible. And unlike those in an SQL database, the LDAP entries can't be related; each stands in isolation. It won't be very obvious from looking, but LDAP databases are also highly optimized for reading rather than writing.

The flexible schema and optimization for reading make LDAP databases great places for storing lists of mostly static information. If you look around where you work, you can probably find many such lists. Employee lists, contact lists, equipment inventories, configuration information, team members—the list of lists goes on. You probably won't be surprised that lists of user names and passwords also fall into this category. While not dedicated to authentication, LDAP is often used to store user information. If you are working for larger (or foresighted) organizations, you will likely find them increasingly using LDAP information sources.

If you are not already familiar with LDAP, we encourage you to at least read Michael Donnelly's "An Introduction to LDAP" (`http://ldapman.org/articles/intro_to_ldap.html`) before going further in this section. It will all seem quite foreign if you don't. LDAP is a very useful technology and becoming more common all the time. If you want to learn more, you will find other good articles and links on Michael Donnelly's site `http://ldapman.org/`. There is enough there to keep you reading for a long time.

The JNDI (Java Naming and Directory Interface, `http://java.sun.com/products/jndi/`) is an extension to the core Java classes that provides access to LDAP from Java. It provides access to a lot of other things, too, but we are only concerned with LDAP for now. Unlike the JCE, this is part of JDK 1.3 so there is nothing more to download.

WebObjects comes with a JNDI `EOAdaptor`, the `JavaJNDIAdaptor`, that provides easy access to data via LDAP. Does this mean that all the work is done? Unfortunately, the answer is "No." The JNDI adaptor is not suitable for our authentication needs. It is great for general LDAP access, but our needs are a bit too specialized.

To authenticate correctly (a.k.a. The Right Way) with LDAP, a *bind* operation needs to be done. In simple terms, this means that you need to use LDAP to log in as the user you are trying to authenticate. If you can log in, the user information is valid; otherwise it is not valid.

The JavaJNDIAdaptor only does a bind (login) with the information in the connection dictionary. This happens the first time it attempts to connect to the LDAP source specified in the connection dictionary. After that it keeps the connection open and does not authenticate again.

To authenticate the wrong way with LDAP, you can simply query for an entry matching the user identity and password that the user entered. In many cases this probably produces the same result as doing a bind, so the JNDI adaptor could be used for authentication. The problem is that it is not always the right way, and a bind operation may enforce other restrictions. Additionally, it is a bit easier to authenticate securely (i.e., not send the password in cleartext) when not using the JNDI adaptor.

We'll need an LDAP server to run this example code against. We've chosen OpenLDAP because it is common on Unix systems, comes preinstalled on OS X, and has a partial implementation that runs on Windows 2000. See Appendix A, "Installation and Configuration of OpenLDAP," for a brief guide on what is needed to run the examples.

We'll create a new AbstractUser subclass, LDAPAuthenticatedUser (see Listing 4-9), to demonstrate correct LDAP authentication. The *Login with SimpleLoginPage* link on the main page will take you to a login form to test this authentication mechanism. As we mentioned earlier, what we are doing is logging in via LDAP to verify the correctness of the information provided by the user. Authentication failures are indicated by exceptions that we need to handle.

Listing 4-9. *Authenticating a User with an LDAP Server*

```
public static final String BASE_DN = ",dc=practicalwebobjects,dc=apress,dc=com";

/**
 * Return <code>true</code> if this user can be authenticated with password.
 * This is implemented by attempting an LDAP login with the credential.
 */
public boolean canAuthenticateWithPassword(String password) {
    boolean canAuthenticateWithPassword = false;

    Hashtable ldapEnvironment = ldapEnvironment();
    ldapEnvironment.put(Context.SECURITY_PRINCIPAL,
                        "userid=" + userID() + BASE_DN);
    ldapEnvironment.put(Context.SECURITY_CREDENTIALS, password);

    try {
        DirContext ctx = new InitialDirContext(ldapEnvironment);
        canAuthenticateWithPassword = true;
        ctx.close ();
    }
    catch (javax.naming.AuthenticationException authException) {
    }
    catch (NamingException e) {
        if (e.getRootCause() instanceof java.net.ConnectException) {
            throw new NSForwardException(e, "Failed to contact LDAP server");
        } else {
            throw new NSForwardException(e);
        }
    }
    return canAuthenticateWithPassword;
}
```

We can't authenticate on the user identity alone, as that is a Relative Distinguished Name (RDN). LDAP bind requires that the security principal (the person being authenticated) be an absolute Distinguished Name (DN), a relative name with additional qualifiers. This can usually be handled by determining in advance what the rest of the DN is. In the code in Listing 4-9 this is handled by the `BASE_DN` constant, which says that all users will be authenticated in `practical-webobjects.apress.com`. If this `BASE_DN` is not the same for all users, you will need to use some other mechanism to determine it. One possible solution is to record it as an attribute on the `LDAPAuthenticatedUser` object. Another alternative is to use the JNDI adaptor to look up the DN based on some other piece of information, such as the person's e-mail address.

The actual authentication process is only three lines:

```
DirContext ctx = new InitialDirContext(ldapEnvironment);
canAuthenticateWithPassword = true;
ctx.close();
```

The first line uses the `ldapEnvironment()` information to attempt to create an initial directory context that, in the process, logs in via LDAP. The second line records success if creating the initial directory context does not raise an exception. The last line closes the context, as we have no further need for it; we only wanted to see if we could create it. The rest of the method just handles exceptions. The only one we expect and are really interested in is `javax.naming.AuthenticationException`. This indicates that either the user identity or password was incorrect. The other exceptions indicate a communications or other unforeseen problem.

The `ldapEnvironment()` method in Listing 4-10 sets up some parameters for the LDAP connection that are not user related.

Listing 4-10. *The* `ldapEnvironment` *Method*

```
public static final String LDAP_URL = "ldap://localhost:389";
protected Hashtable ldapEnvironment() {
    Hashtable ldapEnvironment = new Hashtable();
    ldapEnvironment.put(Context.INITIAL_CONTEXT_FACTORY,
        "com.sun.jndi.ldap.LdapCtxFactory");
    ldapEnvironment.put(Context.PROVIDER_URL, LDAP_URL);

    ldapEnvironment.put(Context.SECURITY_AUTHENTICATION, "simple");

    return ldapEnvironment;

    /** ensure [valid_result] Result != null;
    [has_factory] Result.get(Context.INITIAL_CONTEXT_FACTORY) != null;
    [has_url] Result.get(Context.PROVIDER_URL) != null;
    [has_auth_method] Result.get(Context.SECURITY_AUTHENTICATION) != null;
     **/
}
```

The PROVIDER_URL parameter specifies the LDAP URL for the server to authenticate with. The SECURITY_AUTHENTICATION parameter specifies how the authentication is done. The value in the example code, simple, is dangerous, as it sends the password in cleartext. Unless you are certain that it can't be intercepted, you don't want to use this. Encrypted alternatives are not difficult to code but are somewhat complex to explain. We will stick to WebObjects and instead refer you to the JNDI tutorial on the subject, http://java.sun.com/products/jndi/tutorial/ldap/security/ldap.html.

Password maintenance can usually be delegated to the applications that maintain the LDAP database. Due to security concerns, most places won't want your application changing this anyway! That lets us off the hook for dealing with forgotten passwords and such. Because we do not store the password, the setPassword() method is implemented as an empty method:

```
/**
 * Does nothing. The password is maintained externally by the LDAP server.
 */
public void setPassword(String password) {
}
```

Using Kerberos for Authentication

Kerberos is the Cadillac of user authentication schemes. Authentication is the whole reason for the existence of Kerberos. You are likely to run across it at universities and larger organizations. Using Kerberos for authentication is somewhat similar to using LDAP in that the Kerberos server, not your application, stores the password and handles the authentication process. This makes authentication a bit more involved but frees you from having to manage passwords. Rather than explain what Kerberos is and how it works, we will refer you to Brian Tung's eloquent "The Moron's Guide to Kerberos," http://www.isi.edu/~brian/security/kerberos.html.

The bad news is that there is no free support for Kerberos authentication in JDK 1.3. There is Kerberos support in JDK 1.4 in the form of the JAAS (Java Authentication and Authorization Service) framework and the Kerberos mechanism required by the Java GSS-API (Generic Security Services Application Program Interface) methods.

The only support for Kerberos when using JDK 1.3 comes from WedgeTail Communications (http://www.wedgetail.com/jcsi/kerberos/). While this is not free, it is a very complete and robust implementation that goes way beyond simple authentication. It is also considerably simpler to use than the Kerberos support in JDK 1.4, so even if you are using JDK 1.4, there are substantial advantages to using the WedgeTail classes. We use WedgeTail's classes because we like the cleaner API that is not so determined to inflict all of the gory details on the developer.

The next piece of example code won't run. It won't even compile with the code uncommented unless you have the WedgeTail libraries installed! You can request an evaluation copy of the WedgeTail libraries, but then you will need a Kerberos server to run against. While there are free Kerberos servers available, installation and configuration are decidedly non-trivial. If you are up to the task, look here: http://web.mit.edu/kerberos/www/. Otherwise take this code as an example of the steps needed, not a shining example of great design. This code will actually work and is closely based on code we have in production. However, most of the logic would be best moved to another class, and we've removed some optimizations. We've kept it simple and in one place to make it easier to explain.

Predictably, we'll create a new AbstractUser subclass, KerberosAuthenticatedUser, to demonstrate Kerberos authentication. In general, the authentication process is very similar to LDAP: we try to do something, and if an exception is raised we know that the user ID or password was incorrect.

Unlike LDAP, authentication with Kerberos does not send the password to the server. Instead, it requests a certificate encrypted with the user's password. If the code in our application (in WedgeTail's code, to be precise) can decrypt it with the password that the user entered, that password is valid. If it can't be decrypted, then the password or user ID is wrong. This code is a bit more involved than some of the previous examples, so we will look at it piece by piece.

Special classes represent the user (principal) and password (credential). The first thing we do is convert the string representations entered by the user into instances of those classes:

```
PrincipalName principal = new PrincipalName(userID().toLowerCase());
KerberosPassword kerberosPassword = new KerberosPassword(password.getBytes());
```

We convert the userID() to lowercase before constructing the PrincipalName, as that is what was required by the Kerberos servers we've worked with.

The next task is to get a *context* specifying the realm, user, and server and to use that to get a reference to the actual server that will be processing the authentication:

```
KerberosContext context = new KerberosContext(REALM,
                                              principal,
                                              keyDistributionCenter(KDC_HOST));
Kerberos kerberos = Kerberos.getInstance(context);
```

Kerberos authenticates users in a particular realm. This functions to uniquely identify a user much as the base Distinguished Name did previously for LDAP authentication. The realm must be in uppercase and is usually the domain name. Our example realm is PRACTICALWEBOBJECTS.APRESS.COM. The principal is the special representation of the user ID that we created earlier. Notice how the password is not used when creating the context. The last part of a context is the Key Distribution Center (the Kerberos server). This is just the java.net.InetAddress of the machine.

We are now ready to authenticate. We ask the Kerberos server for a *ticket-granting ticket*, the encrypted certificate that we need to try to decrypt. The Kerberos server will return the encrypted ticket, which requestTicketGrantingTicket() will attempt to decrypt with the Kerberos password (derived from the user-entered password) that we provide. If it succeeds, we have an authentic user ID and password:

```
kerberos.requestTicketGrantingTicket(kerberosPassword, new KDCOptions(),
                                     null, null, null, null);
canAuthenticateWithPassword = true;
```

If requestTicketGrantingTicket() either does not get an encrypted ticket back or can't decrypt what it gets back, then we have a problem. We will need to catch a few exceptions to handle all the cases:

```
catch (com.dstc.security.kerberos.CryptoException e) {
    // Authentication failed: Password incorrect
}
catch (KerberosException e) {
    // Authentication failed: Client not found in Kerberos database
}
catch (java.io.IOException e) {
    // This probably means that the server could not be reached
    throw new NSForwardException(e, "Failed to authenticate");
}
```

The first two exceptions indicate an error in either the user ID or the password. In either case, the user should get the same failure message. There is no point in giving a hacker hints about which part is incorrect. The only other failure is a communications failure, and there is nothing we can do about this so we wrap it in an `NSForwardException` and let some other piece of code deal with it. Listing 4-11 gives the whole method in all of its glory.

Listing 4-11. *Authenticating a User with a Kerberos Server*

```
public static final String REALM = "PRACTICALWEBOBJECTS.APRESS.COM";
public static final String KDC_HOST = "kerberos.practicalwebobject.apress.com";

/**
 * Return <code>true</code> if this user can be authenticated with password.
 * This is implemented by attempting Kerberos authentication with the
 * password.
 */
public boolean canAuthenticateWithPassword(String password) {
    boolean canAuthenticateWithPassword = false;

    PrincipalName principal = new PrincipalName(userID().toLowerCase());
    KerberosPassword credential = new KerberosPassword(password.getBytes());

    KerberosContext context = new KerberosContext(REALM,
                                                  principal,
                                                  keyDistributionCenter(KDC_HOST));
    Kerberos kerberos = Kerberos.getInstance(context);

    try {
        kerberos.requestTicketGrantingTicket(credential, new KDCOptions(),
                                             null, null, null, null);
        canAuthenticateWithPassword = true;
    }
    catch (com.dstc.security.kerberos.CryptoException e) {
            // Authentication failed: Password incorrect
    }
    catch (KerberosException e) {
```

```
        // Authentication failed: Client not found in Kerberos database
    }
    catch (java.io.IOException e) {
        // This probably means that the server could not be reached
        throw new NSForwardException(e, "Failed to authenticate");
    }

    return canAuthenticateWithPassword;
}
```

The WedgeTail Kerberos authentication also requires that their security provider be installed (registered). A provider (`java.lang.Provider`) is basically a factory returning implementations of algorithms, key generation, management facilities, etc. for the Java Security API. In this case, the WedgeTail provider implements cryptographic functions.

The normal way to install a provider is to edit the `JRE/lib/security/java.security` file. It can also be done in code. In general, we prefer the code-based approach because it does not require hand-editing the `java.security` file when installing the application. That is one less step to go wrong. Simpler installations are better installations.

Here is a method that registers the provider and then verifies that this was successful by checking to ensure that the cipher needed for Kerberos is available. This installation needs to be done each time you run the application. Listing 4-12 shows how this can be done in the `Application` constructor.

Listing 4-12. *Registering a Security Provider in Code*

```
/**
 * Installs the com.dstc.security.provider.DSTC Cryptography Package Provider.
 * See the file JRE/lib/security/java.security file for more information and
 * an alternative installation procedure.
 */
protected static void installCryptoProvider() {
   java.security.Provider dtsc = new com.dstc.security.provider.DSTC();

    // Make sure it has not already been installed
    if (java.security.Security.getProvider(dtsc.getName()) == null) {
        java.security.Security.insertProviderAt(dtsc, 2);
    }

    // Verify that we can get the Cipher that we need
    try {
        javax.crypto.Cipher ciph =
            javax.crypto.Cipher.getInstance("DES/CBC/NoPadding");
    }
    catch (Exception e) {
        throw new NSForwardException(e);
    }
}
```

Advanced Login Topics

So far we've looked at secure transmission of information, secure storage of information, how to handle a request to log in, and various methods of authentication. In this section we will look at two pieces of functionality that add some ease of use to the authentication process. The first is producing the login page automatically rather than forcing the user to click a login link. The login page will appear automatically whenever an unauthenticated user makes any request that can only be fulfilled for an authenticated user. The second piece is a "remember me" functionality that reduces the amount of typing needed to log in. We'll also take a quick look at extending this to automatically log in remembered users.

Just in Time Login

You've already seen how to generate a login page when the user clicks on a login link. For some situations, this is just fine. If you can separate your application into two areas, a public one and one requiring authentication, this is a perfectly workable solution. However, imagine an investment advice site where some of the content is public but other content is for registered (fee-paying!) users only. We'd like to be able to show the unregistered users the headlines as an incentive for them to register for our service. We can't do this if the headlines are hidden behind a login panel. It would also be nice if registered users could just click on a headline to see the article and be automatically prompted to log in at the first headline they clicked on. Unregistered users would be asked to register.

Here is how we want it to work. When the user clicks on a headline link, we will check whether they have already logged in or not. If they have logged in, we will show the article; otherwise we will show the login page. When the user has successfully logged in, we will then show the originally requested article.

We need to be able to do three things to accomplish this: we need to know if the user has logged in or not, we need to be able to return either the login page or the originally requested page (the article) from the same link, and we need to be able to return an arbitrary page (the article) after login.

Detecting a Logged-in User

The first requirement, to know whether the user has logged in, is trivial. The code for this was shown earlier in the simple `Session` class in the "Tracking the User After Authentication" section. All that is needed is this test:

```
if ( ! ((Session)session()).isUserAuthenticated()) {
    // Force user to log in
}
```

Returning the Login Page

The second requirement, to be able to return either the login page or the article from the same link, can be met in a couple of ways. The obvious place to do this is in the action method for the article link:

```
public WOComponent showArticle() {
    WOComponent nextPage;
    if ( ! ((Session)session()).isUserAuthenticated()) {
        nextPage = pageWithName("LoginPage");
    } else {
        nextPage = pageWithName("ArticleDisplayPage");
        ((ArticleDisplayPage)nextPage).setArticle(selectedArticle());
    }

    return nextPage;
}
```

The eagle-eyed will notice a problem with this solution. The login page is not going to be displayed securely (over HTTPS) unless the article link has a `secure` binding of `true`. To secure the user's information, the `LoginPage` would then have to generate a HTTPS action URL for the `WOForm` so that the information is submitted securely. HTTPS form action URLs were demonstrated earlier in the section "Using HTTPS with WOForm." We don't want to stay in HTTPS after login, so there is also going to have to be a redirect back to HTTP after the form is submitted and before the article is finally displayed. It is important to think about these transitions between HTTP and HTTPS when designing a login process.

Initiating the login from the action method will work, but it is going to be a bit tedious if we need to do this in many different action methods. Wouldn't it be nice if the article display page could assume responsibility for ensuring that it only displayed itself to registered, authenticated users? After all, what is the point of using objects if we have to run around managing them?

The article display page can take over this responsibility by tapping into the request—response loop. The place in the request—response loop to change what gets returned is the method `appendToResponse()`. We will move the authentication from the action method to the article display page by overriding `appendToResponse()` on `ArticleDisplayPage` like this:

```
public void appendToResponse(WOResponse response, WOContext context) {
    if ( ! ((Session)session()).isUserAuthenticated()) {
        WOComponent loginPage = pageWithName("JITLoginPage");
        response.setContent(loginPage.generateResponse().content());
    } else {
        super.appendToResponse(response, context);
    }
}
```

This solution has the same weakness already noted: the login page will not be shown via HTTPS. Securitywise this is OK as long as the form submits to a secure URL, but your users might feel more comfortable if the login form had the familiar HTTPS URL. We could do this by making the links to the articles secure, but we don't really need the article itself to be displayed via HTTPS. After all, the article does not contain very secret information. That leaves us with only one solution. We must redirect to an HTTPS URL. We will look at two options, URLs for Component Actions and URLs for Direct Actions.

To do this with Component Actions, we just redirect to the article link but with HTTPS instead of HTTP. The URL for the article can be extracted from the request by going through the context like this: `context.request().uri()`. That gets us a secure request but still no user. Once the redirection happens, we need to transition to the login page. That gives us a two-stage process in `appendToResponse()`:

Stage 1: If there is no authenticated user and the request was not made securely, switch to secure mode.

Stage 2: If there is no authenticated user and the request was made securely, transition to the login page.

Of course, if there is an authenticated user the article proceeds normally. Listing 4-13 shows how `appendToResponse()` is put together.

Listing 4-13. *How to Transition to HTTPS and Force Login in* `appendToResponse`

```
public void appendToResponse(WOResponse response, WOContext context) {
    if ( ! ((Session)session()).isUserAuthenticated()) {
        if ( ! WORequestAdditions.isSecure(context.request ())) {
            WORedirect secureRedirect = (WORedirect)pageWithName("WORedirect");
            secureRedirect.setUrl("https://" +
                                  WORequestAdditions.hostName(context.request()) +
                                  context.request().uri());
            secureRedirect.appendToResponse(response, context);
        } else {
            JITLoginPage loginPage = (JITLoginPage)pageWithName("JITLoginPage");
            response.setContent(loginPage.generateResponse().content());
        }
    } else {
        super.appendToResponse(response, context);
    }
}
```

Using a Direct Action we can blend these two steps into one: return a secure Direct Action URL to display the login page. Here is the simplified code:

```
public void appendToResponse(WOResponse response, WOContext context) {
    if ( ! ((Session)session()).isUserAuthenticated()) {
        WORedirect loginPageRedirect = (WORedirect)pageWithName("WORedirect");
        loginPageRedirect.setUrl(DirectAction.secureLoginUrl(context));
        loginPageRedirect.appendToResponse(response, context);
    } else {
        super.appendToResponse(response, context);
    }
}
```

All the magic happens in the convenience method `secureLoginUrl()` that we added to `DirectAction`. At this point (it will get more complicated shortly), it is pretty much a wrapper around:

```
return "https://" + WORequestAdditions.hostName(context.request()) +
       context.directActionURLForActionNamed("login", null);
```

The login Direct Action that this invokes is a single line of code:

```
public WOActionResults loginAction() {
     return pageWithName("JITLoginPage");
}
```

TIP If you need to switch the contents of one page for another, don't just call `appendToResponse()` on the other page like this: `otherPage.appendToResponse(response, context)`. This will result in a page that looks OK, but the action links on the page will not function. Instead, generate the response on the other page and copy the contents like this: `response.setContent(otherPage.generateResponse().content())`. There is an important exception to this: `WORedirect`. With `WORedirect` you must use `secureRedirect.appendToResponse(response, context)` or the redirect won't function.

Returning from the Login Page

The last requirement, to be able to return an arbitrary page (the article) as the page to show after login, requires us to remember where the user was trying to go in the first place. If we can remember the destination, the login page can process the login and redirect (out of HTTPS) to the original destination as demonstrated in Listing 4-14.

Listing 4-14. *Returning the Originally Requested Page After Login*

```
public WOComponent login() {
    WOComponent nextPage = context().page();
    wasLoginInvalid = true;

    if ((userID != null) && (password != null)) {
        try {
            ((Session)session()).authenticateUser(userID, password);

            String insecurePostLoginActionUrl = "http://" +
                WORequestAdditions.hostName(context().request()) +
                destinationUrl();

            nextPage =  pageWithName("WORedirect");
            ((WORedirect)nextPage).setUrl(insecurePostLoginActionUrl);
        } catch (EOObjectNotAvailableException e) {
```

```
            // Login was invalid, nothing else to do
        }
    }
    return nextPage;
}
```

The task of getting the destination URL to the login page depends on which of the two solutions, Component or Direct Action, we are using. In either case, it starts with the URL taken from `context.request().uri()`. For the Component Action approach, this is trivial indeed:

```
JITLoginPage loginPage = (JITLoginPage)pageWithName("JITLoginPage");
loginPage.setDestinationUrl(context.request().uri());
```

Predictably, the example we saved until last is a bit more involved. The way to pass parameters to a Direct Action is through form values. We are not submitting a form, so we need to somehow tack these onto the end of the URL that we redirect to. `WOContext` lets us do this by putting the name and value of each parameter into a dictionary and passing it to `directActionURLForActionNamed()`. The `secureLoginUrl()` method presented earlier needs to be extended to add a parameter for the destination URL, which we have cleverly named `destinationUrl`:

```
public static final String DESTINATION_URL = "destinationUrl";

public static String secureLoginUrl(WOContext aContext) {
    String encodedUrl = java.net.URLEncoder.encode(aContext.request().uri());
    NSDictionary destination = new NSDictionary(encodedUrl,
                                                DirectAction.DESTINATION_URL);
    String loginActionUrl = "https://" +
        WORequestAdditions.hostName(aContext.request()) +
        aContext.directActionURLForActionNamed("login", destination);

    return loginActionUrl;
}
```

Listing 4-15 shows how the action method that this calls is extended to extract the parameter.

Listing 4-15. *Extracting a URL-Encoded Parameter in a Direct Action*

```
public WOActionResults loginAction() {
    String destinationUrl = (String)request().formValueForKey(DESTINATION_URL);
    if (destinationUrl == null) {
        throw new RuntimeException(DESTINATION_URL + " missing from login URL");
    }

    JITLoginPage loginPage = (JITLoginPage)pageWithName("JITLoginPage");
    try {
```

```
            loginPage.setDestinationUrl(java.net.URLDecoder.decode(destinationUrl,
                                                                   "UTF-8"));
        }
        catch (UnsupportedEncodingException e) {
            throw new NSForwardException(e);
        }
        return loginPage;
    }
```

Did you notice that we did not use Design by Contract to check for a missing parameter? That is because this qualifies as user input, and as such errors need to be handled rather than excluded by a contract. Yes, the URL is being generated by code, but it could also be typed by hand. Design by Contract is not appropriate to handle errors of this type.

■ **TIP** One thing to be careful of when creating parameters for Direct Actions is that there are strict rules about which characters can appear in a URL. For details, see `http://www.w3.org/TR/html401/interact/forms.html#h-17.13.4.1`. It is entirely possible that one of your parameters might contain an unacceptable value that will prevent the URL from being processed correctly. It is good practice to always encode the parameters using `java.net.URLEncoder`. Remember to also decode them with `java.net.URLDecoder` before trying to use them. The versions of these methods in JDK 1.3 do not take a string encoding. As of JDK 1.4, they must specify the string encoding. We pass `"UTF-8"` (as recommended by W3C) for the second parameter and handle the potential exception by converting it into a runtime one. For details, see `http://www.w3.org/TR/html40/appendix/notes.html#non-ascii-chars`.

That concludes our look at Just in Time Login. You can find the code in the example application for this chapter in the classes `DirectAction`, `ArticleDisplayPage`, and `ArticleDisplayPage2`. The links in the *Test Just In Time Login* section on the main page can be used to test this. We've looked at two basic options, Component Actions and Direct Actions. Both methods are equally functional and there are a lot of variations possible. One very useful variation is to check not only that the user is authenticated but also that they have permission to view that page. The Direct Action way might be more flexible, as it is easier to reuse the Direct Action. In either case, the code in `appendToResponse()` should be moved to a superclass for easier reuse.

Automating User Login

If you need to log in frequently it can get very annoying to repeatedly type your user name and password. It is so annoying that many modern browsers have started to include an integrated identity manager to take away the drudgery of this. Even with this built-in support, it can still be useful to provide this functionality for those who use an older browser or who don't use the integrated browser support. You can even take it a step further and automatically log the user in when they approach your site. You obviously don't want to do this for a high-security site, but it can be useful when you are more interested in tracking who the user is than in preventing unauthorized access.

Using Cookies for User Tracking

There are only two places we can get information about a user when they request something from our site: the URL and cookies. The URL is less dependable, as it requires a URL that has information about the user embedded it in. Cookies are more reliable, as the browser manages them and sends them when appropriate. While some users block cookies due to various concerns, we haven't found this to be very common. Even if someone does block cookies, it will just prevent this convenience from working for them, not prevent them from using our application.

Cookies come into your application with the user's request and are sent back in the response to the browser for storage. WebObjects provides the `WOCookie` class to represent the cookies that arrive with the request and to create cookies to add to the response. When planning how to handle cookies, it is important to keep straight the difference between the request's cookies (the ones the browser sent for you to read) and the response's cookies (the ones you create in code to send to the browser for storage). It is worth reading up on cookies if you plan on using them. The documentation for the `WOCookie` class has pointers to a couple of good documents that are worth reading. The following discussion is a simplification.

Working with Cookies

We will start with a method to record the authenticated user's userID in a cookie, shown in Listing 4-16.

Listing 4-16. *Method to Store User ID in a Cookie*

```
public static final String USER_COOKIE_NAME = "PracticalWOUser";
/**
 * Adds a cookie to the next response that will allow the userID of the
 * authenticated user to be retrieved later. This cookie will expire two
 * months after the most recent login.
 */
public void rememberUser() {
    /** require [authenticated_user] isUserAuthenticated();  **/
    WOCookie userCookie = new WOCookie(USER_COOKIE_NAME,
                                       authenticatedUser().userID());
    userCookie.setDomain(null);  // Let the browser set the domain
    userCookie.setPath("/");     // Return for all paths in this domain
    userCookie.setExpires(new NSTimestamp().
        timestampByAddingGregorianUnits(0, 2, 0, 0, 0, 0));
    context().response().addCookie(userCookie);
    /** ensure [cookie_added] true;  **/
}
```

First off we'll note that there are `WOCookie` constructors that can make this code simpler. We aren't using them, which makes it is easier to explain what is going on. The constructor we are using just takes a name for the cookie and a value for the cookie. The value can be anything; the name must be unique within the domain and path. If you use the same name for two different cookies in the same domain and path, the browser will not be able to tell them apart and one will overwrite the other. WebObjects does not gracefully handle access to cookies in the same domain that have the same name but different paths. It is a good idea to always try to ensure that the cookie name is unique. It will make your life easier.

■ **TIP** You should consider cookie names and values to be subject to the same allowed character rules as URLs are. Other characters can cause problems. If you think you might need to use such characters, use `java.net.URLEncoder` and `java.net.URLDecoder` to avoid problems.

The domain and the path together tell the browser when to send the cookie back. The domain the cookie is set with (i.e., sent to the browser in the request) must match the domain in the URL of a later request in order for the browser to send the cookie back. Be careful here—the match is done on a name basis, not an IP address basis. Localhost and 127.0.0.1 are considered to be different. If you have set cookies that are not being sent back, then domain differences are likely why. Because of this, it is usually best to just set the domain of the cookie to `null` and let the browser decide. A `null` value tells the browser to record the cookie under the domain that the browser is using.

The path restricts when the cookie is sent within a domain. Paths work like subdirectories in a file system. The browser will send the cookie when the URL requested contains that path exactly, or any path below it. The default path is the application's path, something like `/cgi-bin/WebObjects/Chap4App.woa`. The exact value depends on your configuration and application name. If you only want the cookie sent to this one application, the default is fine. If you want it sent to all WebObjects applications in the domain, you can use `/cgi-bin/WebObjects`. If you are using URL rewriting so that your URLs don't contain `/cgi-bin/WebObjects`, or you want the cookie sent for all requests in that domain, then you can set the path to `/`.

The browser uses the expiry date of a cookie to determine how long to keep the cookie around. If no date is set, then the cookie is deleted when the browser application is terminated. If the cookie has a date in the future, the browser will retain it until that time and then delete it. In the example in Listing 4-16, the cookie will expire and be deleted in two months' time.

There is no direct way to delete a cookie. To have the browser discard a cookie, you need to set it again with a date in the past. The browser should remove it immediately. The method to remove the user cookie looks just like the previous method except that it sets the expired date two months in the past. Don't use dates too far in the past—`NSTimestamp.DistantPast`, for example—as some browsers may not interpret this correctly.

To get the value for a cookie that the browser sent with a request, use the `WORequest` method `cookieValueForKey()`. The parameter for this method is actually the name of the cookie whose value you want. To access the userID previously saved in a cookie, we add this method to our `Session` class:

```
/**
 * Returns the userID from the user cookie, or null if there is no cookie.
 */
public String rememberedUserID() {
    return context().request().cookieValueForKey(USER_COOKIE_NAME);
}
```

Adding User Recall to a Login Page

Our login form will have one additional control (see Figure 4-5): a check box bound to `shouldRememberUser` to indicate whether the user wants to use the "remember me" functionality. If the box is checked and login succeeds, the user will be remembered. If the box is not checked and login succeeds, any remembered user will be forgotten. No change will be made if authentication fails.

User Name:
Password:
Remember Me
Login

Figure 4-5. *A login form with Remember Me*

The user identity and state of the check box are initialized in the page's constructor based on the `rememberedUserID()` provided by the session:

```
public MemoryLoginPage(WOContext context) {
    super(context);
    userID = ((Session)session()).rememberedUserID();
    shouldRememberUser = (userID  != null);
}
```

The only change to the `login()` method is to check and see if we need to add or remove a cookie after login; see Listing 4-17.

Listing 4-17. *Login Method Extended to Handle "Remember Me" Functionality*

```
try {
    ((Session)session()).authenticateUser(userID, password);

    String insecurePostLoginActionUrl = "http://" +
        WORequestAdditions.hostName(context().request()) +
        context().directActionURLForActionNamed("default", null);

    if (shouldRememberUser) {
        ((Session)session()).rememberUser();
    } else {
        ((Session)session()).forgetUser();
    }

    nextPage =  pageWithName("WORedirect");
    ((WORedirect)nextPage).setUrl(insecurePostLoginActionUrl);
} catch (EOObjectNotAvailableException e) {
     // Login was invalid, nothing else to do
}
```

The cookie is set again even if it is already there, so that the expiry date gets advanced to two months in the future at every login. If we don't set it every time, the remembered user will be forgotten every two months.

Implementing Automatic Login

With this support in place, only a small addition to Session is needed to perform automatic login. With this done, the user is automatically logged in when the userID cookie is detected upon waking the Session:

```
/**
 * Overridden to implement auto-login.
 */
public void awake() {
    super.awake();
    if ( ( ! isUserAuthenticated()) && (rememberedUserID() != null)) {
        try {
            authenticatedUser = (AbstractUser)EOUtilities.
                objectMatchingKeyAndValue(defaultEditingContext(),
                    "AbstractUser", AbstractUser.USERID, rememberedUserID());
        } catch (Throwable t) {
            // Authentication failed, nothing to do - the cookie is bad
        }
    }
}
```

As we mentioned, this makes no check other than that the userID in the cookie matches a real user. Therefore it is not suitable where identity fraud is a concern. Even so, you might want to consider using a less explicit cookie name and encrypting the userID so that it is not quite so obvious how to impersonate someone. You can also add additional cookies, such as an obscured password or other identifying data, to make impersonation more difficult.

Advanced Security Topics

In this final section we will take a look at some things you can do to make your application a little less vulnerable to hacking.

Preventing Session Hijacking

The only connection between a request and a particular session in your application is the Session ID. The Session ID is usually passed in the URL:

...Chap4App.woa/wo/**QJUqI2OG9qbj56CAhQnBtg**/0.12
...Chap4App.woa/wa/login?wosid=**QJUqI2OG9qbj56CAhQnBtg**

If someone gets access to this Session ID, they can easily take over (hijack) your session unless you have logged out or it has timed out. Someone could get the Session ID just by looking over your shoulder (though they would need a good memory for this!). A more likely scenario is that someone sits down at the computer after you leave and backtracks or otherwise looks at the URL history. It can also happen if you bookmark such a URL, if the URL is sent in e-mail, or if someone is intercepting the network traffic (sniffing). Also be careful of where you go after using a web application. Your browser will send the previous URL to the new website as the referrer. A malicious site could use this to determine the Session ID and assume control of your abandoned session.

■ **NOTE** Session hijacking is not a WebObjects-specific problem. Any application maintaining state and using HTTP for communication is going to suffer from the same problem. The HTTP protocol is stateless, so the application needs to pass some token, either on the URL or in the headers, to indicate which session an HTTP request is for. There is no way to avoid this weakness, only ways to make your application less vulnerable to it.

Using Cookies to Hide the Session ID

You can make things more difficult for a hacker by keeping the Session ID in a cookie instead of the URL. See the `WOSession` methods `setStoresIDsInURLs()` and `storesIDsInCookies()` for details on how to do this. A hacker could still get access to this and build a fake cookie, but it does require more knowledge and effort. The drawback to this is that it requires users to allow cookies if they want to use your application. You could even get very fancy and detect whether the user is allowing cookies and switch between the Session ID in the URL and in cookies on a session-by-session basis. We'll leave that as another of those infamous "exercise for the reader" solutions.

Verifying an Unchanged IP Address

You can be a bit more certain that the request is authentic if you record the originating IP address when a session is created. For each subsequent request, check that the source IP address matches the original. One place to do this is the `awake()` method on `Session`. If the addresses are different you might have a hacker. Before you run off and implement this, you should know that it is not exactly bulletproof. The most common problem is that some network setups (e.g., the use of gateways or proxies) can result in different users appearing to have the same IP address, or the same user appearing to have different IP addresses. A less common problem is the possibility of IP address spoofing. If you still want to go ahead with this, see the method `originatingIPAddress()` in `WORequestAdditions` in the PracticalUtilities framework.

Managing Session Life Expectancy

Reducing the length of time that a session survives is an important consideration in preventing session hijacking. Terminated sessions don't exist so they can't be hijacked! There are two things that you can do to ensure that sessions terminate as early as possible.

The first thing to do is provide the users with an easily accessible logout function that terminates the session. You will probably also need to educate your users on the importance of logging out, as this is not a normal practice when visiting web sites.

The other thing you should do is keep the session timeout as low as possible. The session timeout is the length of time that can pass since the last request from the user before the session is terminated. The default is one hour. That means that someone can click a link, go for lunch, come back, and continue using the old session. That, we feel, is way, way too long for most applications. A more appropriate length of time is five to fifteen minutes, though this will depend on the usage patterns of your application. This will also reduce your application's memory usage, as there will be fewer abandoned sessions waiting around.

You can set the default timeout for the `Session` object with the `WOApplication` method `setTimeOut()` or the command-line option `WOSessionTimeOut`. The `WOSession` method `setTimeOut()` can be used to fine-tune this on a session-by-session basis. You can increase and decrease a session's timeout at any time. You might want to increase it to keep the session alive longer after a user logs in. You might want to decrease it if the user clicks a link to go to another site and is expected back in a few minutes or not at all.

Preventing Direct Component Access

Start up the example application from this chapter and add `/wo/SecretPage.wo` to the end of the URL in the browser, e.g.:

```
http://localhost/cgi-bin/WebObjects/Chap4App.woa/-1697/wo/SecretPage.wo
```

Press Enter and see what happens. Surprised? If you know the name of a page you can go directly to it without using any navigation links provided by the application. This works a lot like Direct Actions and can even be useful.

This can also be exploited to gain unauthorized access to pages. If you are using on-demand login (an explicit login link), users can bypass your login mechanism and access pages directly. However, if all your pages use the Just in Time Login demonstrated earlier, there is no problem; they will be shown the login page regardless of what URL they use.

Direct component access can also be a problem if your application has a permissions (authorization) system such that not all authenticated users are allowed to access all pages. In that case, you could extend the Just in Time Login code to check for the user's authorization to view a page after checking that they are authenticated. If the user is authenticated but not authorized to view that page, you would return some other page—for example, a page stating that permission was denied.

If you do not want to use this sort of access (Direct Actions are a better way to accomplish the same result), it is best to just disable it. The most comprehensive way is to have the web server detect such URLs and send them elsewhere. For example, this Apache Rewrite Rule will direct all such requests to the main page:

```
RewriteRule ^/(.+)/wo/(.+).wo$ /$1 [last,passthrough]
```

If you can't get the web server to do this, you can do it in code by overriding `pageWithName()` in `Application`:

```
public WOComponent pageWithName(String pageName, WOContext context) {
    if ((context.senderID() == null) &&
```

```
            (componentRequestHandlerKey().equals(
                context.request().requestHandlerKey()))) {
            pageName = "Main";
        }

        return super.pageWithName(pageName, context);
    }
```

`context.request().requestHandlerKey()` is used to detect the `/wo/` in the URL. The request handler key is a series of characters that identify the `WORequestHandler` that is dealing with this request. The two most common request handler keys are `wo` for Component Actions and `wa` for Direct Actions. `context.senderID()` holds the last segment of the URL. This is discussed in more detail in Chapter 6. All we are concerned with at this point is that a `null senderID()` indicates that there is nothing following the final `.wo` in the URL. If these two conditions are met, we have a request we do not want to honor. Instead we return the page named Main. Of course, if you don't have a page named Main you will have to use a different name.

Summary

Securing your application might not be the most exciting task but it is a necessary one. Much like locking the door behind you when you leave the house, not doing so is an invitation to disaster. In this chapter we've taken a look at the fundamentals of securing access to your application. These alone won't produce Fort Knox, but they will make the job of penetration much more difficult.

We started with the fundamentals of using HTTPS/SSL to secure transmissions between the client and server. The support in WebObjects for this is lacking, so we introduced how to use secure hyperlinks and how to get secure `WOForm` submission.

We then looked at a flexible design for user authentication in which user and session cooperate in authentication and identity tracking. This was implemented with simple authentication and used to provide a basic login form and logout functionality.

Storing cleartext passwords in the database is not a best practice. We've seen how to use digests and encryption to add another layer of security to these and other sensitive pieces of data. We've also seen how to extend authentication using the external services of LDAP and Kerberos.

The basic login form is not suitable for all situations and lacks some user-friendly features. We've shown how to extend this to allow authentication to be delayed until necessary with Just in Time Login and how to use cookies to recall users and to allow automatic login.

We finished by tying off a few loose ends in WebObjects that allow security breaches. Session hijacking will always be possible, but we can at least make it a little more difficult. Direct component access is a little-known feature of WO that is best disabled, as it can be used to bypass security checks.

CHAPTER 5

Input and State Validation of Enterprise Objects

A program is a spell cast over a computer, turning input into error messages.

—Anonymous

It is said that to err is human, and nowhere is that more the case than in data entry. Every application must have a way of validating input and state. Validating enterprise objects is more simple than you might expect, especially if you are used to doing manual validation. In this chapter we will discuss validation WebObjects style, some of the limitations and workarounds, and advanced techniques. Finally, we will describe a set of classes in the PracticalUtilities framework that provides a complete solution to most of the issues described.

Validation Basics

We'll start our discussion of validation with a quick overview of the basic WebObjects validation method as specified by the `NSValidation` interface and its subinterface, `EOValidation`.

NSValidation

The `NSValidation` interface specifies a way of validating arbitrary attributes of any object using key-value coding. It defines a method, `validateValueForKey`, which (by default, as implemented by `NSValidation.DefaultImplementation`) validates the value by looking for a method on the class with a name of `validate<Key>`, where `<Key>` is the name of the attribute to validate. For example, assuming `anObject` had a default implementation of `validateValueForKey`, then the following

```
anObject.validateValueForKey(someValue, "aKey");
```

would end up calling `validateAKey(someValue)` on `anObject` (if `validateAKey` exists—if it doesn't exist, then the value is always valid!).

The validation method itself, `validateAKey`, will return the (possibly coerced) valid value or will throw an exception. Listing 5-1 shows an example validation method for an attribute called `"date"` that attempts to coerce the value to an `NSTimestamp` and raises an exception if the value cannot be so coerced or is `null`.

Listing 5-1. *Validation of Attribute "date"*

```
public Object validateDate(Object value)
        throws NSValidation.ValidationException {
    if (value == null) {
        throw new ValidationException("Null value");
    }

    // If the value was already formatted
    if (value instanceof NSTimestamp) {
            return value;
    }

    // Only have to do this if WO didn't use a formatter already
    // Assume value is a String from here on
    // Use the default date formatter...
    NSTimestampFormatter formatter = new NSTimestampFormatter();
    NSTimestamp coercedValue = (NSTimestamp)
        formatter.parseObject((String)value);
    if (coercedValue == null) {
        throw new ValidationException("Invalid date format");
    }
    return coercedValue;
}
```

Note that the method can take either an `NSTimestamp`, in which case it just returns the value it received (if it is not `null`), or a `String`, in which case it attempts to coerce the value to an `NSTimestamp` and raises an exception if it can't. Which type gets passed in depends on how the value is getting set; by default, values coming from a `WOComponent` are of type `String` unless there is a formatter on the field (see the discussion of formatters later in this chapter). You will rarely write coercion code like this, as it's much easier to just use a formatter.

The other method that `NSValidation` specifies is `validateTakeValueForKeyPath`. This method validates a value using `validateValueForKey` on the final destination object of the key path and then assigns it to the attribute (using the default implementation of `takeValueForKey`) if it is valid.

NOTE The fact that the value is only assigned if it is valid will become important later on as we discuss some of the limitations of WebObjects validation.

EOValidation

The EOValidation interface extends the NSValidation interface by adding several new methods that aid in validating enterprise objects. Specifically, it extends the concept of validating an object from the attribute level to the object level by adding the following methods:

- validateForSave
- validateForInsert
- validateForDelete
- validateForUpdate
- validateClientUpdate

For the most part, these methods are self-explanatory. validateForInsert, validateForDelete, and validateForUpdate are each called when an attempt to save an inserted, deleted, or updated object is made. You can use these methods to validate that an enterprise object is ready to be inserted, deleted, or updated. EOCustomObject's implementation of those methods, in turn, calls validateForSave, which should be used when a more specific method is not appropriate.

■ **TIP** When overriding these methods, you should call the superclass's implementation before doing our own validation. The superclass's implementation of validateForInsert, validateForDelete, and validateForUpdate each calls validateForSave, which in turn is responsible for doing the default EOF validation (discussed further on). If the default validations fail, the superclass will throw an exception. You'll need to catch this exception and aggregate it with any custom validation exceptions that you want to raise.

The only remaining method is validateClientUpdate, which is used with Java Client. We won't be discussing that here.

Getting into the Details

So how does this all actually work? In this section, we'll be looking under the hood to get a clearer understanding of what is happening when objects are validated. There are three times when WebObjects validation occurs: during the take values phase of a request, on save from an EOEditingContext, and when an input field has a formatter. It is important to know when each occurs and what exactly is validated.

Validation During Take Values

During the take values phase (also called the Sync stage in recent Apple documentation), WebObjects takes form values and attempts to assign them to the attributes on the page to which they are bound. The page eventually gets a `takeValuesFromRequest`, which calls `takeValuesFromRequest` for each binding to a dynamic input element on the page. Each dynamic element, in turn, calls `validateTakeValueForKeyPath` on the page with the value taken from the form. This method validates the value using `validateValueForKey` on the final destination object. `validateValueForKey` does EOF's default validation and finally calls your custom `validate<Key>` method, if it exists (see Figure 5-1).

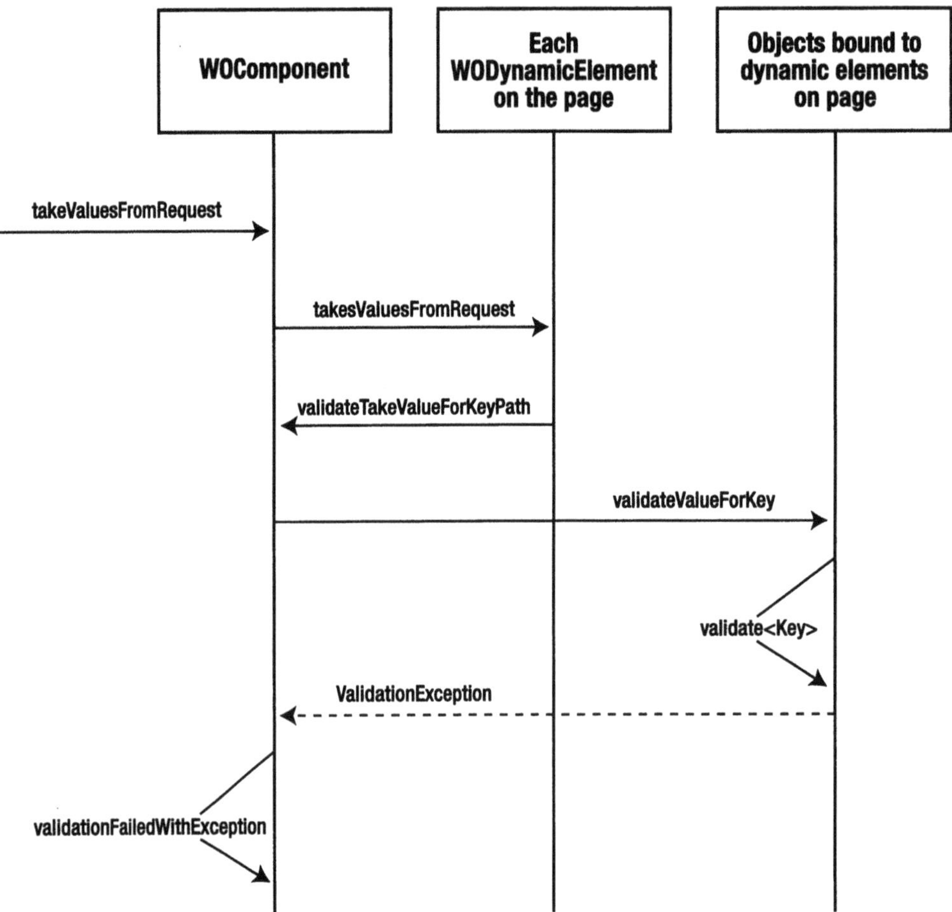

Figure 5-1. *Validation during take values. The default validation, which occurs in* `validateValueForKey`, *has been omitted for clarity.*

As shown in Figure 5-1, values that are invalid will cause an exception to be raised. When it occurs, `WOComponent` will take that exception and call `validationFailedWithException` (this will get called once for each validation failure). This is one of the methods that often gets overridden to handle validation. Usually you will merely store the exception for later use, as in Listing 5-2:

Listing 5-2. *Example Implementation of* validationFailedWithException

```
NSMutableArray errors = new NSMutableArray();
public void validationFailedWithException
        (java.lang.Throwable exception,
        java.lang.Object value,
        java.lang.String keyPath) {
    errors.addError(exception);
}
```

See the ValidatingPage class in the PracticalUtilities framework for a more complete implementation.

During the take values phase, the fact that a form value is bound to an enterprise object is irrelevant, as far as WebObjects is concerned. An attempt is made to validate every value before it is assigned to its binding. It could be an eo, but it might not be: WebObjects attempts to call the validateValueForKey method on any destination object, regardless of its type. For most objects, the default implementation (as specified by NSValidation.DefaultImplementation) is all you need. This forces you to write a method for each attribute that you want to validate. EOF, however, adds some simple validation to every enterprise object.

Automatic EOF Property Validation

Usually you have to write your own validation methods for every kind of error that might occur. EOF, however, does some of that work for you when validating enterprise objects. In a nutshell, when validateValueForKey is called on an eo, the implementation in EOCustomObject first asks the eo's class description to attempt to coerce and validate the value with information from the EOModel. EOF does the following:

- **check not null**: If the model specifies that the property is not null, EOF checks to make sure that the value assigned is not null. Required relationships also fall under this category.
- **coercion of attributes**: EOF attempts to coerce the value into the correct type for the attribute. This coercion is limited to Boolean and number values.
- **check maximum length**: For attributes that have a width property, EOF checks to make sure the value assigned does not exceed that maximum.

TIP As you can see, EOF doesn't provide much automatic validation. It does give us some indication of what we might do when extending the standard EOF validation: override the class description. We will discuss this in a later section, "The Practical Solution."

After doing as much validating as it can from information in the EOModel, EOF then sends a validate<Key> message to your eo, where you can write your validations as usual. The only difference here is that you no longer have to check for things that are already checked for by default: you can be guaranteed, for example, that if you've set an attribute to be not null in your model, when your validate<Key> method gets called, the value won't be null.

This behavior is also the first limitation of WebObjects' validation that we've hit: if the value for an attribute doesn't pass the default validations, then your `validate<Key>` method will never get called (note that only enterprise objects have default validations, but see our later discussion of formatters). This makes a lot of sense; there isn't much other validation you can do on a `null` value, and values that are too long cannot be saved to a database, so custom validation in `validate<Key>` is irrelevant.

Well, not quite. Sometimes, for example, users enter values that are too long and fail some other validation as well. Your app might allow users to enter XML into a form's `textarea`. If the user entered XML that was both malformed and too long, the only validation message they would see would be the one about the value being too long. Only after the user had shortened the XML and resubmitted the page would they get a message about the XML being malformed. We will discuss this and other problems later and will offer some solutions for them.

Validation on saveChanges

Before saving an eo to the database, EOF first makes sure that the object is valid. Since there is no guarantee that the eo's values came from form values on a `WOComponent` (where they would be validated on assignment, as described earlier), the editing context has to validate each attribute. This means that some values might be validated twice, once on assignment from a `WOComponent` and once again when `saveChanges` is called.

In addition to validating each attribute of an eo, EOF also calls `validateForSave` on your eo to allow you to perform any object-level validations—ones that aren't defined on a single attribute. You might, for example, want to make sure that if one attribute is present, another attribute takes on certain values.

EOF also defines three other methods—`validateForInsert`, `validateForDelete`, and `validateForUpdate`—that are called when applying inserts, deletes, or updates to an object. You'll find that you don't use these three methods as often as `validateForSave`, but they are sometimes useful.

One big difference between validation that occurs at other times and validation that occurs during `saveChanges` is that during `saveChanges`, `validationFailedWithException` is not called. Instead, `saveChanges` raises a `ValidationException`, which contains all the validation exceptions that occurred (see Listing 5-3).

Listing 5-3. *Simple Example of Handling Validation Failures During* `saveChanges`

```
public WOComponent saveChanges() {
    try {
        session().defaultEditingContext().saveChanges();
    } catch (NSValidation.ValidationException e) {
        validationFailedWithException(e, null, null);
        // or extract all the exceptions inside e and call
        // validationFailedWithException for each
    }
    return this;
}
```

Formatters

Part of validating a value, at least as far as WebObjects is concerned, is coercing the value to the correct type. Usually the coercion is done automatically, either as part of `validateTakeValueForKey` of a value going to an eo (as already described) or, as we're about to discuss, when you use a formatter.

Formatters are basically little coercion machines. They take string data and translate that somehow into an object of another type. They also do the reverse, though we won't be discussing that here.

There are two standard formatters included with WebObjects—`NSNumberFormatter` and `NSTimestampFormatter`. Their use is fairly obvious: define a format that numbers or dates should be entered and displayed as. As you saw earlier, one way to use a formatter is to instantiate it directly and use it. WebObjects makes using formatters significantly easier by allowing you to bind formatters directly to the input fields on your form (see Figure 5-2).

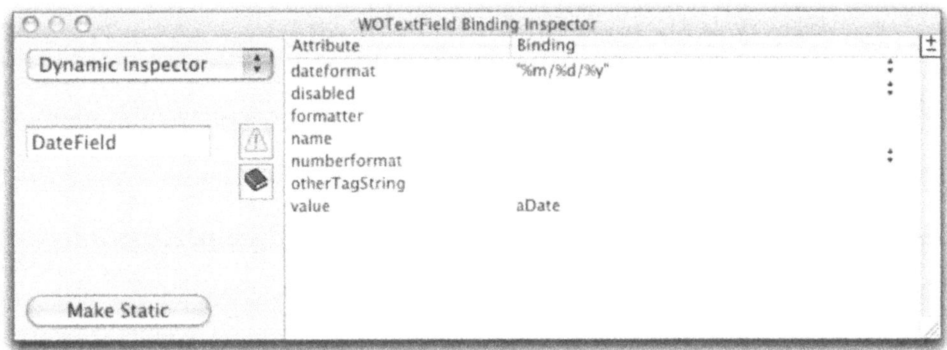

Figure 5-2. *Binding a date formatter to a field*

Values are coerced by the formatter before any other validation happens. If a formatter fails to coerce a value, the assignment does not occur and a validation exception is raised.

You can also define your own custom formatter classes and assign them to fields on a form in a similar way.

Limitations of WebObjects Validation

Despite the power and ease of use of validation in WebObjects, there are several limitations that you need to be aware of. In this section, we'll discuss the limitations and offer solutions or workarounds.

Values Are Not Assigned If Not Valid

When a value is determined to be invalid during a `validateTakeValueForKeyPath`, an exception is raised, and the value is not assigned. This can be annoying to users: consider typing in a phone number and accidentally typing one number too many. When you click Submit on the page and get a validation error, you'd like to be able to just remove the one extra digit you typed and resubmit. But by default in WO, you just get a blank field and have to retype the entire phone number. Worse, if this phone attribute already had a valid phone number and you replaced it with an invalid one, clicking Submit would discard your new, invalid phone number and redisplay the old, valid one. This can get downright confusing, especially to novice users.

There are a couple of things you can do to mitigate this situation. The first is to force the invalid values into the object anyway. The second is to provide a holding area for user-entered values, which only get assigned to their final destination after the values are deemed valid.

Forcing Invalid Values

This is a simple workaround to the problem, and only works when the invalid value can be assigned to the attribute. Override `validationFailedWithException` as in Listing 5-4:

Listing 5-4. *Forcing Invalid Values into an Attribute*

```
public void validationFailedWithException
        (java.lang.Throwable exception,
        java.lang.Object value, java.lang.String keyPath) {
    // Add the exception to the errors array as before
    errors.addObject(exception);

    // Now try to force the value into the attribute
    try {
        takeValueForKeyPath(value, keyPath);
    }
    catch (IllegalArgumentException e) {
        // Just ignore it... we've already added the exception to
        // the array of errors
    }
}
```

The only issue here is when we try to push a value that cannot be held (or coerced) to the attribute, such as trying to assign `Hello` to an integer. Trying to do that causes an `Illegal-ArgumentException` to be raised. As you can see in the listing, you can just ignore this exception. If you need to have such values displayed back to the user, you'll need the next solution: a holding area.

Using a Holding Area

Sometimes you need to display what the user entered, even when it is not the correct type of data. The solution is to use a holding variable (or variables) of type `String` to hold any data that the user might have entered. Since any user-entered value can be represented as a string (well, almost: we'll leave binary data via a file upload as an exercise for the reader), storing these values as a `String` will allow you to let the user know what exactly they entered.

As you might have guessed, this requires a bit more work. For starters, you cannot use a formatter; since it coerces the data, there isn't much point in attempting to store that in a `String`. You must also manually perform the validation, unless you want to duplicate the validation code for these holding variables (something that we strongly recommend against).

There are a couple of implementations possible here: you can provide a separate instance variable for each attribute, or you can store all the values in an `NSMutableDictionary`.

Using an `NSMutableDictionary` frees you from having to create a new instance variable for each binding, and so makes your life a little easier. You can simply bind the dictionary to the form (as in Figure 5-3), adding the attribute to store at the end of the key path, and key-value coding will take care of the rest. Note that you don't have to bind *all* of your attributes to the dictionary, only the ones where you need to have invalid values displayed to the user. You still have to validate manually, as mentioned previously. (See Listing 5-5.)

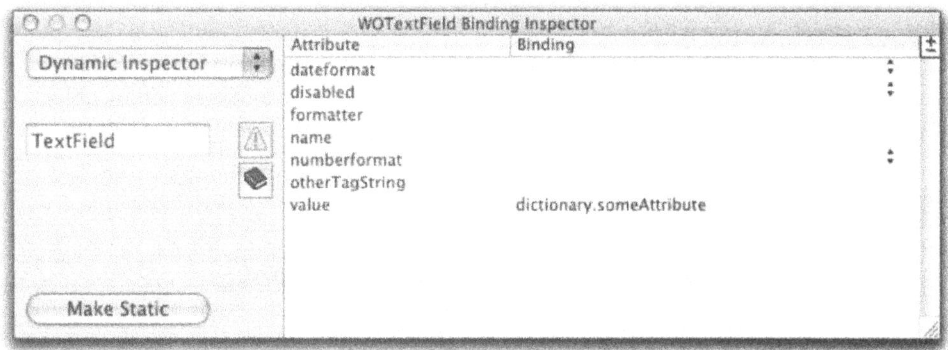

Figure 5-3. *Binding an attribute ("someAttribute") to a dictionary*

Listing 5-5. *Validating with an* `NSMutableDictionary` *As a Holding Area*

```
public WOComponent submitAction() {
    Object aValue = null;
    try {
        aValue = dictionary.objectForKey("someAttribute");
        validateTakeValueForKeyPath(aValue, "myEO.someAttribute");
    }
    catch (ValidationException e) {
        validationFailedWithException(e, aValue, "myEO.someAttribute");
    }
    if (errors.count() == 0) {
        try {
            editingContext.saveChanges();
        }
        catch (ValidationException e) {
            errors.addObject(e.getLocalizedMessage());
        }
    }
    return this;
}
```

Only One Validation Error per Attribute

When submitting a page that saves an eo, validation could be said to occur in several stages: formatter validation, attribute-level validation, and, finally, object-level validation. If ever there is a validation error in one stage, the latter stages are not done. For example, if a formatter cannot coerce the value to the correct type, your custom `validate<Key>` method will not be called. This is certainly the best default behavior: a value that fails formatting won't be much use when validating the attribute, and similarly, if your object has invalid attributes, it's quite likely that validating the object as a whole doesn't make much sense. However, this all means that a user might have to submit a page as many as three separate times in order to see all the validation failures for a given value.

The solutions here are pretty specific to the application involved, but are basically just manually doing validation where appropriate. Most often, you'll be looking at doing object-level validation after an attribute validation has failed.

No Immediate Validation

With a desktop (or Java Client) application, you can immediately inform the user when they have entered an invalid value. For a web application, you are limited to waiting for the user to submit the page before you can perform any validation.

Well, not quite: using JavaScript, you too can immediately verify that the user's values are valid. As usual, this is easier said than done. Most web browsers (probably all, quite frankly) have broken, or at least quirky, JavaScript interpreters. Fortunately, most of what we need with respect to validation is pretty simple, so shouldn't require as much work as trying to implement something more substantial in JavaScript.

Listings 5-6a and 5-6b show a simple extract from a WOComponent that provides some JavaScript validation. Also see the example application for this chapter.

Listing 5-6a. *HTML File for a Page Using JavaScript to Validate*

```
<!DOCTYPE HTML PUBLIC "-//W3C//DTD HTML 3.2//EN">
<html>
    <head>
        <title>PWO Chap 5 - JavaScript Validation</title>
        <script  language="JavaScript">
            <!-- // Protect against non-compliant browsers
            function validateRequired(formField,fieldLabel)
            {
                var result = true;
                if (formField.value == "") {
                    alert('Please enter a value for the "' +
                        fieldLabel +'" field.');
                    formField.focus();
                    result = false;
                }
                return result;
            }
            -->
```

```
        </script>
    </head>
    <body>
        <webobject name=Form>
            <p>Non-negative integer:
                <webobject name=IntegerField></webobject>
                (not negative)</p>
            <p><webobject name=ValidateSubmitButton></webobject></p>
        </webobject>
    </body>
</html>
```

Listing 5-6b. *.wod File for a Page Using JavaScript to Validate*

```
Form: WOForm {
    // This executes the script when the user clicks submit
    onSubmit = "return validateRequired(this.anInteger,"an integer")";
}
IntegerField: WOTextField {
    value = anIntegerToValidate;
    numberformat = "0";
    // Note that we must provide a name here so we can reference
    // this field
    name = "anInteger";
}
ValidateSubmitButton: WOSubmitButton {
    action = anAction;
    value = "Validate Values";
}
```

You may notice that unless you provide a constraint propagation scheme, your validation code is duplicated in your eo and in your JavaScript. For this reason, if you need to provide immediate validation for your application, you should look more closely at using Java Client instead.

Making Changes While Validating an EO

When writing your validation methods for an eo, you need to be careful to not modify any attributes. This is because, during a saveChanges, the object graph is assumed to remain in one state. Updating an attribute, for example, normally adds the eo to the list of updated objects. Since this list is determined at the beginning of saveChanges, changes will make EOF confused. Don't do it.

Lack of Customization of Validation Messages

Often you can get away with just displaying the exception message to the user and leaving it at that. Unfortunately, if you want to customize these messages, you have to do a little work. There are several possible ways to customize messages. The simplest is probably to just override `validationFailedWithException` on a `WOComponent` and map any messages you get from exceptions onto messages you want to display to the user (Listing 5-7).

Listing 5-7. *Mapping Default Validation Messages to Custom Messages*

```
NSMutableArray errors = new NSMutableArray();
public void validationFailedWithException
        (java.lang.Throwable exception,
        java.lang.Object value,
        java.lang.String keyPath) {
    // Map from default messages to custom messages. We can load
    // this from a file, the userInfo dictionary in the eomodel,
    // or use some other method to create it.
    NSBundle bundle = NSBundle.bundleForClass(this.getClass());
    String mappingFileName =
        bundle.resourcePathForLocalizedResourceNamed
            ("validationMessageFile.strings", null);
    byte[] tableBytes = bundle.bytesForResourcePath(mappingFileName);
    String tableString = "{" + new String(tableBytes) + "}";
    mapping = (NSDictionary)NSPropertyListSerialization.
        propertyListFromString(tableString);

    if (mapping.objectForKey(exception.getMessage()) != null)
        errors.addObject(mapping.objectForKey(exception.getMessage()));
    else
        errors.addObject(exception.getMessage());
}
```

This solution, however, deals only with attribute-level validations. Also, you'll have to be careful, since some default validation messages are not constant. If you're using those, you'll need to provide a more robust mapping technique. See the section "The Practical Solution" later in the chapter for a description of a complete solution provided in the PracticalUtilities framework.

Lack of Localization of Validation Messages

A related limitation is the lack of localization of messages. Using the built-in localization methods in `WebObjects`, we can customize these messages fairly simply. In Listing 5-8, we show a simple modification to Listing 5-7 that enables localization:

Listing 5-8. *Getting a Localized Mapping File*

```
WOResourceManager resManager = WOApplication.application().resourceManager();
byte[] tableBytes = resManager.bytesForResourceNamed(
    "validationMessageFile.strings", null, session().languages());
String tableString = "{" + new String(tableBytes) + "}";
mapping = (NSDictionary)NSPropertyListSerialization.
    propertyListFromString(tableString);
```

Missing Database Validations

There are a few validation errors that can occur "below the radar" of WebObjects. These are exceptions that the database adaptor can raise when attempting to save changes to the database. Usually these exceptions are optimistic locking failures, but violation of any database integrity constraint is possible:

- Violation of unique constraint on a column
- Not `null` constraint violation—occurs if your model specifies one of your attributes as nullable, but the database says it is not `null`
- Any other, database-specific violation

It is perhaps a misnomer to call these validation failures, but since they occur in the same general place (that is, on `saveChanges`) as true validation failures, it is convenient to treat them similarly.

Catching these database problems involves writing an exception handler to catch exceptions of type `EOGeneralAdaptorException` around your call to `saveChanges`, as in Listing 5-9.

Listing 5-9. *Catching Database-Level Exceptions*

```
public WOComponent myAction() {
    try {
        editingContext.saveChanges();
    }
    catch (EOGeneralAdaptorException e) {
        interpretEOGeneralAdaptorException(e);
    }
}
```

Now what about that call to `interpretEOGeneralAdaptorException`? You can see a more complete implementation in the PracticalUtilities framework in the `ValidatingEditingContext` class, but the basic idea is to query the `userInfo` dictionary of the `EOGeneralAdaptorException` for the existence of certain keys. For example, if the exception is an optimistic locking exception, the key `EOAdaptorChannel.AdaptorFailureKey` will be present in the `userInfo` dictionary with a value equal to `EOAdaptorChannel.AdaptorOptimisticLockingFailure` (see Listing 5-10). Note that we are referring here to the constants defined in the Java classes.

Listing 5-10. *Interpreting an Optimistic Locking Exception*

```
public boolean isOptimisticLockingFailure
        (EOGeneralAdaptorException exception) {
    boolean isOptimisticLockingFailure = false;
    if (exception.userInfo() != null) {
        String adaptorFailureKey = (String)exception.userInfo().
            objectForKey(EOAdaptorChannel.AdaptorFailureKey);
        if (adaptorFailureKey != null) {
            isOptimisticLockingFailure = adaptorFailureKey.equals
                (EOAdaptorChannel.AdaptorOptimisticLockingFailure);
        }
    }
    return isOptimisticLockingFailure;
}
```

See the `ValidatingEditingContext` class for more information.

The Practical Solution

So now that we've seen how validation works, and what its limitations are, we can provide a complete solution. The PracticalUtilities framework contains various classes that provide that solution. In this section we will discuss how these classes work together to provide a mechanism for customizing standard and arbitrary validation messages.

The Classes

There are several classes involved in the Practical WebObjects solution, each one overriding the standard WebObjects way of doing things to allow you to create customizable messages. Here are the classes and a brief description of each:

- **`EOFValidation`**: The "gateway" class for the Practical solution, and one of only three classes that your application will generally interact with. Contains the method `installValidation`, which is responsible for setting up necessary delegates and notifications for the rest of the classes to work.

- **`EOFValidationException`**: Another class that your application will often interact directly with—your custom `validate<Key>` methods will instantiate and throw `EOFValidationExceptions`. Responsible mainly for holding failed values and "message key paths," which specify which error message to display. Uses `LocalizationEngine` to get the correct message to display and `TemplateSubstitution` to merge variable values with the message.

- **`LocalizationEngine`**: Responsible for determining the correct message to use from the message key path, not for localizing the message into another language!

- **TemplateSubstitution**: Merges the variable parts of a message with the values they represent. For example, given a message of "<<failedValue>> is below the acceptable limit for <<propertyName>> for <<entityName>>.", will use a dictionary to replace <<failedValue>>, <<propertyName>>, and <<entityName>> with the values they represent.

- **EOFValidationEOEntityClassDescription**: A subclass of EOEntityClassDescription, uses EOAttributeValidator and EORelationshipValidator to validate the entity. One important consequence of this is that where EOF used to throw ValidationExceptions, this class uses EOFValidationExceptions.

- **EOAttributeValidator**: Validates attributes.

- **EORelationshipValidator**: Validates relationships.

- **EOModelNotificationProxy**: Catches model-added notifications so that every entity can have an EOFValidationEOEntityClassDescription.

- **ValidatingEditingContext**: Catches adaptor-level exceptions (optimistic locking, unique index violations, etc.) and transforms the exceptions to EOFValidationExceptions. If you don't use a ValidatingPage, you will need to instantiate and use this class directly.

- **ValidatingPage**: The third class that you will generally interact with. Makes use of a private ValidatingEditingContext, and exposes an errors array, used in displaying validation error messages.

Getting Started

In order to use the validation facilities in the PracticalUtilities framework, each entity must have an EOFValidationEOEntityClassDescription. To do this, use

```
EOFValidation.installValidation();
```

Class descriptions are assigned when a model is loaded, so this call must occur before any models are loaded. The best place for this call is in your application subclass's constructor.

Using Message Key Paths

Message key paths are the basic way of customizing your validation messages. You use them in both your validation exceptions and your message files, to specify the messages used by your exceptions. They are constructed similarly to regular key paths, the difference being that they specify a message to display instead of an attribute of an object. A message key path always has two or three parts:

- **Entity specification**: The name of the entity, or the generic name "Entity".

- **Attribute specification**: The name of the attribute. Optional if the message applies to the entire object instead of an attribute.

- **Failure key**: A key that specifies the specific error.

Here are some example message key paths:

- **OrderItem.cost.nullNotAllowed**: Used in a message file, specifies the error message to display when the cost attribute of the OrderItem entity is null. Used in an EOFValidation-Exception, specifies that the cost attribute has violated the not null validation.
- **OrderItem.cost.belowMinimum**: Same as previous, but specifies that the value is too small.
- **Entity.aboveMaximum**: Used in a message file, specifies the global default message to use for any aboveMaximum exceptions (for any entity), unless "overridden" by more specific messages, such as the next example ...
- **OrderItem.aboveMaximum**: Also only usable in a message file, specifies that any attribute of the OrderItem entity that raises an aboveMaximum validation exception should use this message by default unless "overridden" by a more specific message, such as the next example...
- **OrderItem.cost.aboveMaximum**: Can be used in an EOFValidationException, as the first two examples, but in a message file overrides the default aboveMaximum message.
- **OrderItem.optimisticLockingFailure**: An example of a message key path that applies to the whole entity. You cannot specify an attribute with key paths of this type.

Failure Keys

A failure key is the last part of a message key path. Failure keys specify which type of validation has failed, from not null to too long. Here are some of the common failure keys:

- nullNotAllowed
- tooLong
- invalidValue
- belowMinimum
- aboveMaximum

Their meanings should be obvious, except, perhaps, for invalidValue, which specifies a formatter failure. There are several other failure keys that are used less often, mostly dealing with adaptor-level exceptions.

There is also a special failure key, displayName, which specifies a custom display name for an entity (<my entity>.displayName) or an attribute (<my entity>.<my attribute>.displayName). The default is to pretty-print the entity or attribute name by lowercasing it and putting a space wherever a capital was found. For example, by default, entity OrderItem would be displayed as "order item".

Message Key Path Search Order

The defaulting mechanism introduced in the "Using Message Key Paths" section is a powerful technique you can use to avoid having to write the same error messages over and over. Let's take a closer look at how it works.

We start by looking in the main (application) bundle for a file with the most specific message that applies to the message key path that we are interested in:

- First, look for a fully qualified message key path, such as `OrderItem.cost.belowMimimum`, in a `.strings` file with the same name as the entity (e.g., `OrderItem.strings`).
- Next, look in the same file for a default for the specific entity: `OrderItem.belowMinimum`.
- Then, look for a fully qualified message key path in a `.strings` file with the same name as the bundle (e.g., `MyApplication.strings`).
- Next, look in the same file for a default for the specific entity.
- Finally, look for a global default in this second file: `Entity.belowMinimum`.

If we cannot find the message or an appropriate default for the given message key path, we try the next bundle, searching for the same files as before. Bundles are searched in the following order:

- First, look in the main bundle (the application bundle).
- Next, look in the bundle that contains the entity in question.
- Next, traverse up the entity hierarchy, searching each bundle in which the entity is contained.
- Finally, if no other bundle contains an appropriate message, use the global defaults provided in the PracticalUtilities framework (in a file called, not surprisingly, `Practical-Utilities.strings`).

This might seem like a lot of complication just for validation messages, and it is. We've found, however, that it provides a simple solution when you want it (you can do nothing and still get meaningful validation messages), but affords you the power to customize your messages arbitrarily when you need it.

Messages and Variable Substitution

Creating message files is pretty easy; you just create a file using the standard ".strings" format, which is

```
Message.Key.Path = "Some message";
```

For example:

```
OrderItem.cost.belowMinimum="Order items can't have cost lower than 0";
```

A powerful feature of the Practical solution is the ability to substitute variable values in your message. This allows you to create messages like

```
OrderItem.datePurchased.invalidValue =
    "We couldn't interpret <<failedValue>> as a date!";
```

where <<failedValue>> will get replaced by the value that the user entered. Variables that can be substituted are

- **failedValue**: The value that the user entered
- **propertyName**: The name (or displayName) of the property (attribute or relationship) that failed
- **entityName**: The name (or displayName) of the entity
- **attribute**: The EOAttribute of the attribute that failed

You can even use key-value coding on any of these variables. So, for example, the following would produce the expected message:

```
Entity.tooLong = "The value you entered, <<failedValue>>, is↵
    longer than the <<attribute.width>> characters allowed for↵
    <<propertyName>> on <<entityName>>."
```

Validation Methods

Your validate<Key> and validateFor<Operation> methods are written as usual. However, instead of raising a ValidationException, you use EOFValidationException (Listing 5-11).

Listing 5-11. *Validation Method Showing the Use of* EOFValidationExceptions

```
public Number validateChildren(Number value)
        throws NSValidation.ValidationException {
    if (value.intValue() < 0) {
        EOFValidationException exception = new EOFValidationException
            ("PracticalEntity.children.belowMinimum",
            this,
            "children");
        exception.setFailedValue(value);
        throw exception;
    }
    return value;
}
```

Summary

A lot of things happen behind the scenes when using WebObjects validation. It can be a little daunting if you don't know what is going on. However, with the power of key-value coding and the well-defined interfaces for providing validation, it is very easy. With a little work (or a third-party framework, such as PracticalUtilities or Validity—part of Project WONDER), you can easily create quick and completely customizable validation messages for your application.

CHAPTER 6

The Secret Life of Components

Action springs not from thought, but from a readiness for responsibility.

—Dietrich Bonhoffer

Understanding the request—response loop is as essential to success with WebObjects as understanding object graph management is to success with EOF. You can accomplish a fair bit with a rudimentary understanding of the request—response loop but you will soon reach a point where you can no longer understand what is happening in your code. In this chapter we are going to take a quick look at the HTTP protocol that drives this loop. Then we will dive into an in-depth look at all of the stages of the request—response and how they interact with the frameworks to produce a specific response for a specific request.

The Hypertext Transfer Protocol

You don't have to know much about the Hypertext Transfer Protocol (HTTP) to write web applications with WebObjects. That said, a basic understanding helps with the terminology you'll come across and makes it a lot easier to figure out what is happening when things go wrong. And things *will* go wrong! We will take a brief tour of the basics of HTTP protocol, version 1.1, before pushing on.

We will start by figuring out what HTTP is. Simply put, it is a network protocol used to access many of the resources on the World Wide Web. HTTP takes the form of messages *requesting* resources (usually originating from a user's browser) and the corresponding *response* messages returning the resource to the requester. A *client* sends requests and a *server* sends responses. HTTP defines the form and content of these request and response messages.

Both the request and response messages have a similar format that consists of:

- A start line
- Header lines
- A blank line (properly CRLF)
- An optional message body

As a very simple example, let's look at a request message for some WebObjects documentation:

```
GET /documentation/WebObjects/WebObjects.html HTTP/1.1
Host: developer.apple.com
-- a blank line --
```

The start line of a request has three parts, separated by spaces. The first part is the HTTP method name, usually GET or POST when working with web applications. The second part is the path of the requested resource. The last part is the HTTP version being used, almost always HTTP/1.1 nowadays. There are usually a lot more headers, but Host is the only one required. Headers are where extra information, such as cookies or your IP address, are sent between the client and server.

See Listing 6-1 for an example response, the beginning of the response message to the documentation request. Just a like a request, the start line of a response also has three parts separated by spaces. The first part is the HTTP version being used, again almost always HTTP/1.1. The second part is the numeric status code. You are probably familiar with another one as well: 404 (not found). The last part is a description of the status code. The headers, a blank line, and then the resource we requested—an HTML file—follow the start line.

Listing 6-1. *A Partial HTTP Response Message*

```
HTTP/1.1 200 OK
Date: Fri, 19 Dec 2003 00:28:35 GMT
Server: Apache/1.3.27 (Darwin) PHP/4.1.2
Cache-Control: max-age=60
Expires: Fri, 19 Dec 2003 00:29:35 GMT
Connection: close
Content-Type: text/html
-- a blank line --
<!DOCTYPE HTML PUBLIC "-//W3C//DTD HTML 4.01 Transitional//EN"
 "http://www.w3.org/TR/html4/loose.dtd">
<HTML>
<HEAD>
<META NAME=generator CONTENT="Hammerhead 3.0">
<META NAME="ROBOTS" CONTENT="NOINDEX">
<title>WebObjects Documentation</title>
etc.
```

That is enough HTTP for our purposes. If you want to know more, we recommend James Marshall's readable "HTTP Made Really Easy" (http://www.jmarshall.com/easy/http/). If you absolutely must know all of the gruesome details, the RFC is at http://www.w3.org/Protocols/rfc2616/rfc2616.html.

Spying on HTTP

We have often found it useful to get a closer look at this HTTP traffic, both to learn more about what is sent back and forth and to debug problems with such things as misbehaving cookies and special responses (e.g., downloads). One way to do this is to use an HTTP proxy server that logs the requests and responses that go through it. We prefer working at a higher level, but sometimes digging into the details is the only way to troubleshoot a problem. Debugging based on information is much more productive than debugging based on guessing.

WebScarab from the Open Web Application Security Project (`http://www.owasp.org/development/webscarab`) is a good, and free, Java implementation that is quite helpful. It includes some tools that are useful for examining and testing your application. It is a good application to have in your toolbox. It is, however, a little flaky UI-wise, as it is still under development.

Here is a brief guide to using WebScarab. When it starts, it wants a directory to write session information into. You might want to create a specific directory for this, as some useful debugging information, notably the requests and responses, are written here.

Click on the Proxy tab. It will look like Figure 6-1. We can see that it is using ports 8008 and 8009. You can use the Address/Port/Base URL form on the tab to add a different address if you want. You need to set this proxy information into your browser so that all requests are directed though WebScarab. Figure 6-2 shows the proxy settings in Internet Explorer on Windows; other browsers will be similar. Figure 6-3 shows the proxy settings on OS X.

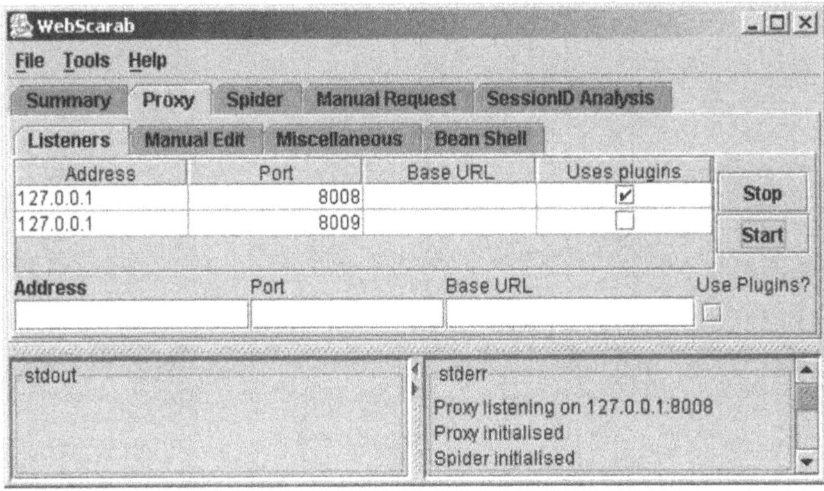

Figure 6-1. *The Proxy tab in WebScarab*

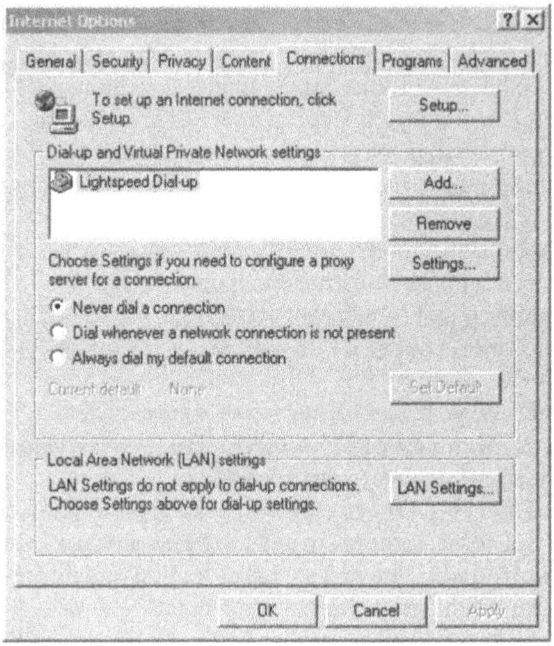

Figure 6-2. *Proxy settings in Windows Internet Explorer*

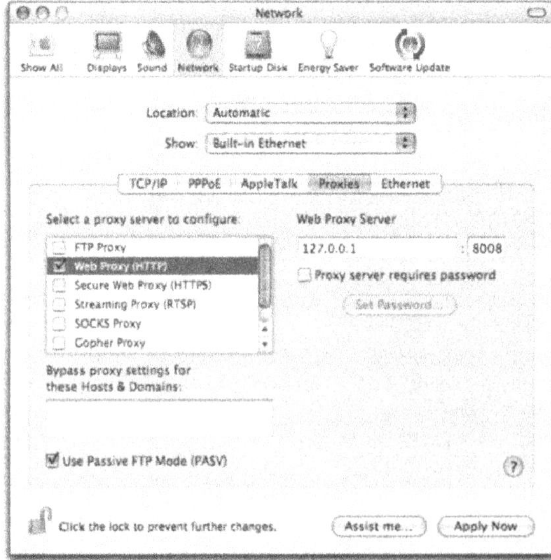

Figure 6-3. *Proxy settings in OS X*

Start up your application, or just surf the Web, and WebScarab will capture all that happens. WebScarab shows an overview of the HTTP conversations on the Summary tab; see Figure 6-4. The top panel shows a summary by host. The middle panel shows a summary of each conversation next to its ID number.

Double-click a conversation to drill down into its details. Figure 6-5 shows the details of an example conversation. The top panel shows the request, including all of the headers and form values (both raw text and URL encoded). The bottom panel shows the response in various forms. Finally, you can create a fine-tuned request manually on the Manual Request page. This can be useful to see how invalid cookies and hack attempts are handled.

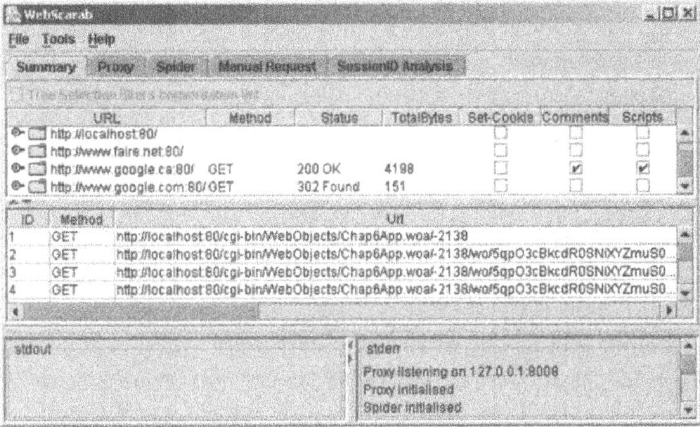

Figure 6-4. *Summary page in WebScarab*

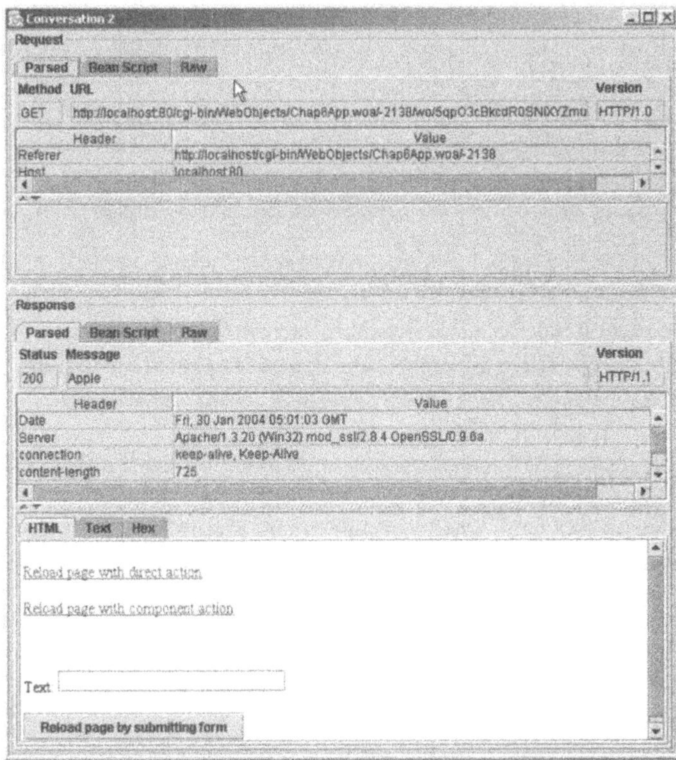

Figure 6-5. *Example HTTP conversation in WebScarab*

An alternative to a proxy like WebScarab is to use utilities such as wget (see `http://xoomer.virgilio.it/hherold/` for a Windows version) or curl (part of OS X) to dump out the headers and content from a response. While this works, using a proxy server will give you a better overall picture of the flow of information.

■ **TIP** It's best to run a WebObjects application through a web server (even during development) instead of using Direct Connect mode, to get a true representation of all of the HTTP communication across the wire. Also, resources are accessed differently when you use Direct Connect, making deployment more difficult.

The Request—Response Loop, Briefly

You can consider a web application to be like a complicated assembly-line factory for text. Raw materials in the form of streams of text (the request) are created externally, usually by a browser, and delivered to the factory (web application). The materials are processed in a variety of ways, and the final result is a new stream of text (the response) that is transported away from the factory and to the consumer (again, usually a browser). While what happens in the factory is the most interesting part, it is also important to know something about the transportation of raw materials and finished goods.

There is an important distinction between a factory and a web application. This distinction lies in how the raw materials arrive. A factory orders the raw materials and knows approximately what will arrive and when it will arrive. A web application is purely event driven. It has no knowledge of, nor control over, which requests arrive and when they arrive. It has to be prepared for anything at any time.

We said that most requests will come from a browser, and that is what we will assume in our discussion. They can also originate from Java Client, applications using web services, and similar sources. None of those change the basic event-driven response to a request pattern.

The Role of the WebObjects Frameworks

The WebObjects frameworks provide a nice object-oriented abstraction of the process and contents of this request—response loop. There are objects and methods to get at the request, the response, headers, cookies, content, etc. There are methods to set cookies and headers, and methods to help you generate the content of the response.

The frameworks control the progress of the request—response loop. Your code only needs to override methods here and there to provide customized behavior for specific situations. The most common thing to do by far is to write small methods in a `WOComponent` subclass to generate custom output, but WebObjects allows you to tweak any stage of the request—response loop: there are many methods that you can optionally override to fine-tune what happens, when it happens, how it happens, and to whom it happens. We will be looking at each of these control points as we pass through the phases of the request—response loop.

Different types of requests (Component Actions, Direct Actions, web service requests) have different paths through the frameworks as they are processed through the request—response loop. The general pattern of progress is the same and you rarely need to be aware of the exact type of request being handled; the frameworks assume that burden. Our discussion in this chapter will be focused on the most common request, the Component Action request.

The Big Picture

The high-level flow through the request—response loop is shown in Figure 6-6. The request flows from the client (usually browser) through the web server to the application by way of the WebObjects adaptor. Within the application, the objects that represent and process the request are created and/or woken up from their sleeping state. The three main phases of the Component Action loop are: getting the submitted form values (if any), performing the requested action, and generating the response. Once this is finished the objects are discarded or put to sleep, and the response flows from the application through the web server, again by way of the WebObjects adaptor, to the client.

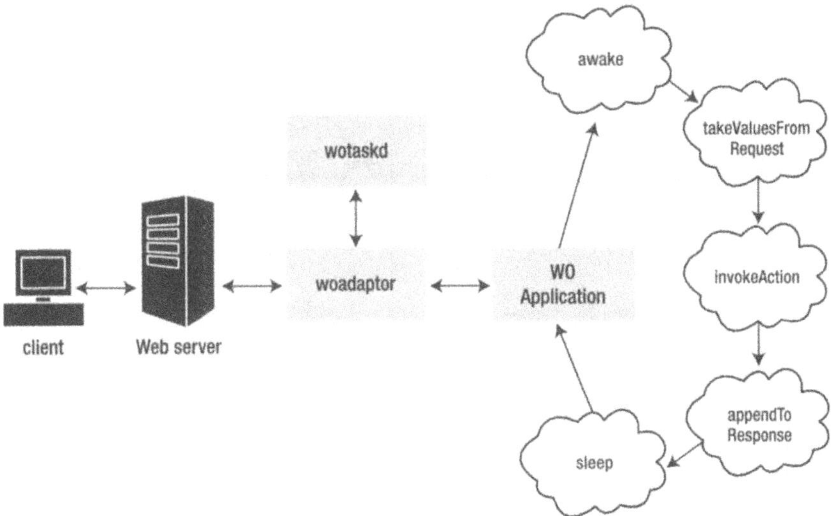

Figure 6-6. *High-level flow through the request—response loop*

Within the application there are four distinct layers that the request—response loop is processed through. These layers are application, session, page, and subcomponents. Each phase, except sleep, starts at the application level and progresses down to the lowest component. The next phase starts again at the application level. The sleep phase progresses in the opposite order as the awake phase. Figure 6-7 shows an overview of how this works. This allows control of the behavior during each phase to be delegated to the most appropriate part of your application.

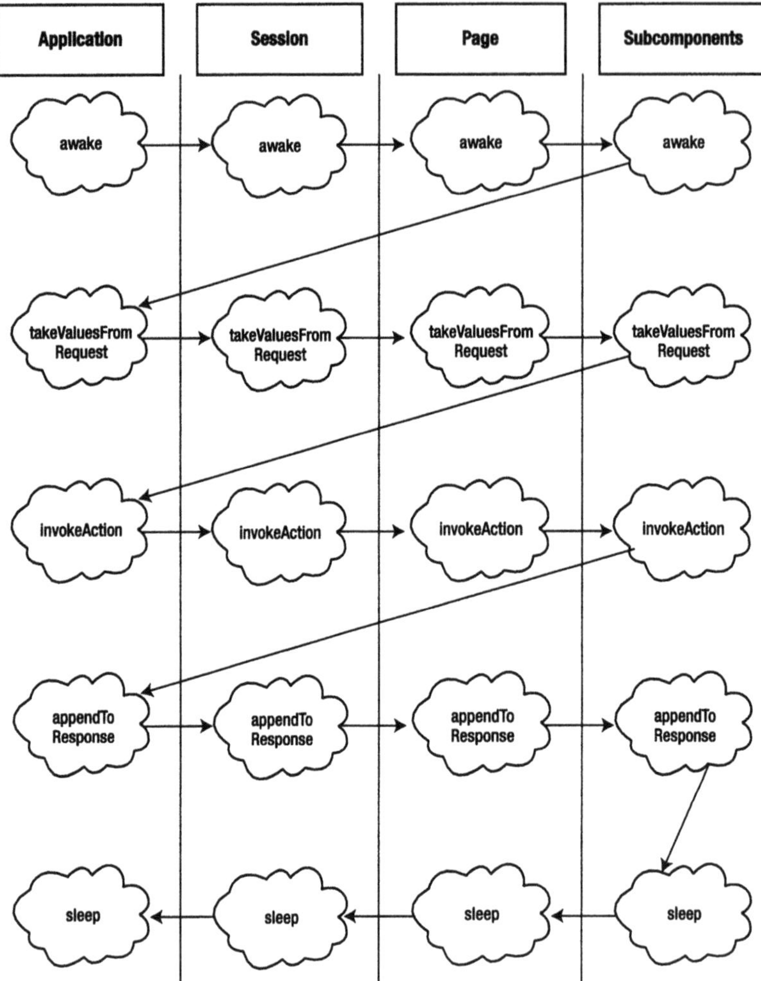

Figure 6-7. *The pattern of awake, take, invoke, append, and sleep calls through application, session, page, and subcomponents*

The Request—Response Loop, Deeply

We are now going to creep through the request—response loop, carefully examining each facet. We have several goals in doing this:

- Learn how the process works so we can handle special situations.
- Learn where to extend and how to configure the process.

- Learn where specific things happen so we can debug effectively.
- Look at various failure points so we can troubleshoot configuration problems.

Figure 6-8 shows a call trace of the most important methods in the request—response loop. Some of the method calls in the text have been omitted in the interests of clarity.

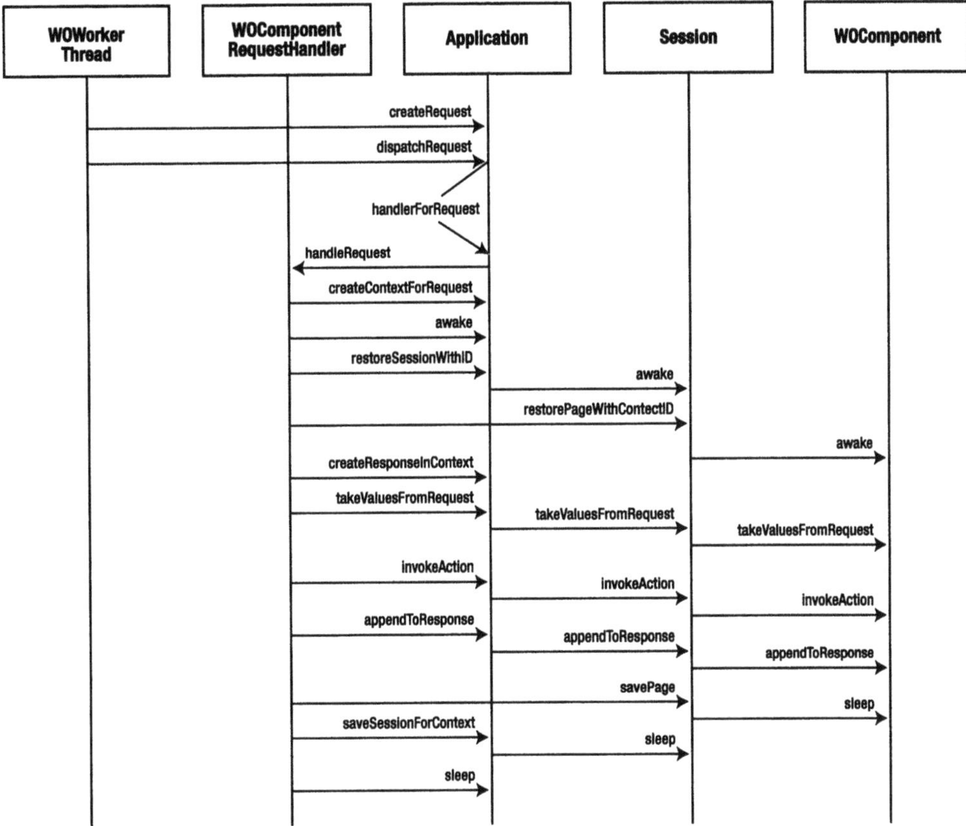

Figure 6-8. *The order of the main methods in the request—response loop*

The Beginning: The Request Is Made

The beginning of this loop, or cycle, starts with a request initiated in a client. This is usually the result of the user clicking on something. The browser takes the URL from the element clicked on, and forms an HTTP request containing the URL, the form values if a form is being posted, and some headers, and forwards this to a web server.

The Web Server Receives the Request

The web server either fulfills the request itself or forwards the request on to a process that can fulfill it. Requests for static resources such as HTML files and images that are stored in the web server's document root are fulfilled directly. The type of requests that we are really interested in (that is, requests for dynamic content) need to be handled by a process outside of the web server. This is where the WebObjects adaptor comes into the picture.

If the web server can't find the adaptor (you have not installed it, or the server is incorrectly configured) the result will be a standard 404 Not Found error message. Any other message indicates that the WebObjects adaptor has at least accepted the request from the web server.

The woadaptor and wotaskd Forward the Request

The discussion that follows assumes that you are using the standard WebObjects deployment with JavaMonitor and WebObjects Task Daemon (wotaskd). The initial request processing is slightly different when deploying in a J2EE application server. The two paths come together (and diverge) at the `dispatchRequest` method in `WOApplication`.

The job of the WebObjects HTTP adaptor (woadaptor, not to be confused with `com.webobjects.appserver.WOAdaptor`) is to act as an intermediary between the web server and the WebObjects application. The adaptor receives the request from the web server, massages it, and hands it off to the application for processing. Once the application is finished, it returns the response to the WebObjects HTTP adaptor, which in turn massages it and passes it back to the web server.

In the default configuration, the woadaptor queries wotaskd via a request to port 1085, and wotaskd responds with the list of available applications, and their instances and the ports they're listening on. (You can also configure the woadaptor to read this information from a configuration file on the file system by changing the `WebObjectsConfig` setting in httpd.conf.) The task of wotaskd is to monitor the WebObjects applications that are running and to start and stop them if scheduled to do so. The JavaMonitor application is just used to configure wotaskd. The woadaptor consults with wotaskd to find the server and port number to forward the request to.

You can see the state of things according to wotaskd by pointing your browser to port 1085—e.g., `http://localhost:1085`. As an example, wotaskd reports this for the application from Chapter 4 running in development mode.

```
<?xml version="1.0" encoding="ASCII"?>
<adaptor>
  <application name="Chap4App">
    <instance id="-1608" port="1608" host="lisbon"/>
  </application>
</adaptor>
```

If wotaskd does not see your application running, no requests will be sent to it (unless you are using Direct Connect and connecting directly to the application). If wotaskd does not see your application running, the result of any requests for the application will be

```
The requested application was not found on this server.
```

If wotaskd can see your application running but no instances are available to service the request (all are shutting down, starting up, refusing sessions, or not responding), your response will be the curt

```
No instance available.
```

To debug problems such as this, start by checking that wotaskd is running and correctly configured by pointing your browser to port 1085. If everything looks OK there, the next step is to enable logging at the WebObjects HTTP adaptor level. For non-Windows platforms this is done with

```
touch /tmp/logWebObjects
```

On Windows you need to create an empty file at

```
C:\Temp\logWebObjects
```

Both of these will result in the creation of a `WebObjects.log` file in the same directory as `logWebObjects`. The `WebObjects.log` file contains a detailed description of what the woadaptor does when dispatching the request. Much of the information will not be useful to you but it can pinpoint where a failure is happening. Simply delete the `logWebObjects` to stop logging.

Assuming that wotaskd returns information about the application instance to connect to, the WebObjects HTTP adaptor opens a socket, sends the request to the application, and waits for a response.

The Application Receives the Request

At last the request has reached our application! Don't expect things to get simple now. When the WebObjects HTTP adaptor opens a socket to talk to our application, it is usually an instance of `com.webobjects.appserver._private.WOWorkerThread` that it is communicating with. These worker threads are created by `com.webobjects.appserver._private.WODefault-Adaptor`, which uses them to handle incoming requests on its behalf. `WODefaultAdaptor` is a subclass of the abstract `com.webobjects.appserver.WOAdaptor`.

The `WOWorkerThread` then calls the `WOApplication` method `createRequest` to create a `WORequest` from the HTTP request. `WORequest` provides an object encapsulation of an HTTP request. Override the `createRequest` method if you want to use a subclass of `WORequest`, if you want to alter the request before the `WORequest` is created, or if you want to pass extra information to `WORequest` in the form of its `infoDictionary`. We do this in the example application for this chapter to use a WORequest subclass, `LoggingRequest`, which logs some of what it is doing.

With the `WORequest` in hand, the `WOWorkerThread` is done for now. It passes the newly created request and control to the application by calling `dispatchRequest`.

The Application Forwards the Request to the Request Handler

Other than transforming the HTTP request into a `WORequest`, the `Application` object first comes into the loop when its `dispatchRequest` method is called. The first thing that this method does is broadcast the `ApplicationWillDispatchRequestNotification`.

WebObjects applications can handle many different types of requests. Each type is handled by a different `WORequestHandler` subclass. A `WORequestHandler` can be considered an adaptor of sorts that adapts a set `WORequest` into various types of handling. By default WebObjects applications have multiple request handlers; see Table 6-1.

The normal way for a request to be associated with a particular handler is by the presence of a key in the URL. For example, the `/wo/` in the URL

```
http://localhost/cgi-bin/WebObjects/App.woa/-1234/wo/EgcbgtQmbDaRCNp856aQjO/0.1
```

indicates that it is intended for the `WOComponentRequestHandler`.

Table 6-1. *Three Common Request Handlers*

Name	Function	Key
`WOComponentRequestHandler`	Handles requests for actions implemented in a WOComponent	`wo`
`WODirectActionRequestHandler`	Handles requests for actions implemented in a WODirectAction	`wa`
`WOResourceRequestHandler`	Handles resource requests	`wr`

You can write your own `WORequestHandler`, though it is unusual to need to do so. A new request handler was added to WebObjects 5.2 to handle web service requests. Another reason to do so might be to handle RSS requests, as described in "Having Fun With WORequestHandler: A RSS Feed" at `http://www.wodeveloper.com/omniLists/webobjects-dev/2002/August/msg00010.html`.

To write a `WORequestHandler` you only need to implement a single method, `handleRequest`. You will also need to tell the application about your request handler by calling `registerRequestHandler` with an instance of your handler and the key (or URL component) identifying your handler. You can generate URLs for this new handler by passing the key to the `WOContext` method `completeURLWithRequestHandlerKey` or `urlWithRequestHandlerKey`.

The application determines the request handler to use by calling `handlerForRequest`. The WOApplication implementation of this method goes to the request and gets its `requestHandlerKey` and then returns the handler registered for that key. You could override this to use a different method of determining the handler to use. If a `null` key is returned, the application will use its `defaultRequestHandler`. This is how requests without a handler key, such as `http://somehost/cgi-bin/WebObjects/AppName.woa`, get to a handler.

Once the handler has been found, the application passes the request to it by calling `handleRequest`. This ends the request dispatch section of the request—response loop until the response is ready to be returned.

The Request Handler Forwards the Request to the Component

Each request handler works differently; this is the whole point of having different request handlers. We are only going to look at one in the context of the request—response loop. We will focus on the `WOComponentRequestHandler`, as it is by far the most interesting. You can use the logging techniques shown in the example application to explore the behavior of the other request handlers.

The first thing the component request handler (which we will refer to simply as *handler* from here on) does is ask the application to create a context by calling `createContextForRequest`. `WOContext` is the glue that holds all of the bits in the request—response loop together: the session, the request, the response, and the page(s) involved. The context also plays a central and crucial role in determining where form values go and which actions are invoked. We will take a closer look at how this works later. Both the session and the components track the context, and it is also passed to several methods as a parameter. Finally, the context provides services for URL generation that are used during the `appendToResponse` phase.

Each context is given an integer identifier called the context ID. This context ID is unique within a session; the context ID starts at zero and increases by one with each new request in that session. The context ID appears in the URL after the session ID and immediately before the element ID (which we will discuss later). In this URL, the context ID is 27 and the element ID is 1:

```
http://localhost/cgi-bin/WebObjects/App.woa/-1234/wo/EgcbgtQmbDaRCNp856aQjO/27.1
```

Replacing `WOContext` with a subclass can be useful, as we saw in Chapter 4 when we did this to fix secure URL generation. You could also change how URLs are generated to support a custom format. `com.webobjects.jspservlet.WOServletContext` is one example of custom URL generation from a `WOContext` subclass.

There are several ways to change the class used as the context. Defining `WOContextClassName` when the application is launched is the most flexible way to use a `WOContext` subclass. This is useful to temporarily switch to using a debugging context. A more permanent way is to call `setContextClassName` in your application constructor or override `contextClassName`. If you need to pass new parameters to the constructor, you will have to override `createContextForRequest`.

The Main Event

Here is where things really get rolling. The awake method is called on the application to give it a chance to do any application-wide preparation needed for handling the request. We've never found any need to use this method. If you do, take care to make it thread-safe so that dispatching requests concurrently does not break your code. The best practice is to treat any shared data at the application level as read only.

We are focusing on Component (`WOComponent`) Actions here, and Component Actions require sessions: the session is where the `WOComponent` instances that will perform the actions are stored between when the response is sent to the user and when a request for an action on that page comes back from the user. Each component is associated with the context ID of the context it was returned in. We will look more closely at how this works a bit later.

As a session is required, the next step for the handler is to either create a new session or restore the previously created session. This service is provided by the application methods `createSessionForRequest` and `restoreSessionWithID`. While you could override `createSessionForRequest` to create a different subclass of `WOSession`, there is little point in doing this. Every WebObjects application by default uses exactly such a subclass: `Session`. It makes far more sense to just modify and use `Session`.

The restoreSessionWithID method just delegates the job of restoring the session to the application's sessionStore by asking it to checkOutSessionWithID. There is little need to replace this method unless you have multiple session stores to check. For example, you could check the in-memory WOServerSessionStore, and if the session is not found there fall back to an external (file system–based) server store.

Creating or restoring a session results in a call to the session's awake method. This is the first place where the context is available with meaningful values; however, note that context().page() will still return null here. The awake method is the place to initialize anything in the session that depends on the current context. The defaultEditingContext is locked from this point on. This is also the place to lock any nonthread safe resources needed by the session while responding to the request. We saw an example of this in Chapter 3 where the MultiECLockManager was locked in this method. This method also signals the start of the most interesting phases of the request–response loop; this makes it a good place for some log messages.

Processing can't proceed further without a component instance to work with. Without the page that generated the URL, there's no way to know what the URL is supposed to do. The page that generated the URL is the only connection between the URL and what action is supposed to be invoked and hence what page is supposed to be returned.

WOSession provides services for saving and restoring pages. The handler calls restorePageForContextID on the session to have the page restored. Restoring the page consists of finding the component instance that generated the HTML from which the request originated.

WOSession has a limited amount of storage for pages. The exact amount is controlled, strangely enough, by the WOApplication method pageCacheSize. Once the cache is full, the oldest page will be discarded. This prevents old pages from consuming all available memory. Hence it is entirely possible that restorePageForContextID will not be able to restore the requested page. In this case it will return null to signify the problem. Returning null stops further processing of the request; without a component, the component request handler can't function. Instead, a call is made to the application method handlePageRestorationErrorInContext to get the result being returned.

You might be tempted at some point to try to replace the default page cache mechanism. Our advice is to proceed with caution. The default page cache has to deal with backtracking and then proceeding upon multiple, parallel paths of execution. The necessary implementation is a great deal more complex than it initially appears.

Restoring the page results in a call to the page component's awake method. This parallels how restoring a session results in a call to the session's awake method. The component's awake method is the place to initialize anything in the component that depends on the current request. You can also use this to do other initialization or to lock resources that the page needs. If the page uses a lot of data that you don't want to keep around between requests, you can set it up here and remove the references in sleep. Values set with bindings are not yet synchronized in awake and should not be accessed here. The next chapter takes a closer look at binding synchronization.

The awake message is also sent to all of the subcomponents on this page. This only applies to WOComponent subclasses and not to WODynamicElement subclasses. It is useful to note that the awake methods are sent from the inside out. That is, the innermost component receives the message first and the containing page receives it last. You can see this in the log messages when clicking on links on the Components In Repetitions page in the demonstration application for this chapter.

TIP Usually the frameworks ensure that the page is awake in the correct context. However, if you are managing pages yourself (for example, storing a page in an instance variable for later use in another request—response cycle) then you are responsible for doing this by calling `ensureAwakeInContext`.

We're almost ready to roll here. We have a request, a session, a context, and a page. All that is lacking is a response. The handler creates a blank response by calling the application method `createResponseInContext`. You can override this method if you need to use a subclass of `WOResponse`. We do this in the example application for this chapter to use a subclass that provides log output.

Now we are at last ready to get on with the business of actually processing the request. This is broken into three independent phases: `takeValuesFromRequest`, `invokeAction`, and `appendToResponse`. We're going to look at each of these in the order that they happen.

Detour: Component Templates

Each page is formed from a tree of static HTML, `WODynamicElement` objects, and `WOComponent` objects. The root of this tree is returned by the `template` method on `WOComponent`. This template is usually automatically constructed from the .html and .wod files of the component. You won't see the root element if you look at the template. The root element is constructed internally by the frameworks, an instance of `com.webobjects.appserver._private.WODynamicGroup`. (We haven't looked at dynamic elements yet. Relax; we will cover them in the next chapter.)

TIP The methods `template` and `templateWithHTMLString` can be used to construct templates on the fly. You could also use them to make templates from string data stored in a database or from across the network.

The Take Values Phase

This phase is not guaranteed to occur. It only happens if the request contains form values. Requests that don't have form values, such as the request that results when a link is clicked, bypass this phase entirely.

If there are form values, the handler initiates this phase by calling `takeValuesFromRequest` on the application. The application simply forwards this to the session by calling `takeValues-FromRequest` on the session. We can't think of anything very useful to do to the request at this stage, but if you need to, either the session or application `takeValuesFromRequest` method can be used.

The session does pretty much as the application does and calls `takeValuesFromRequest` on the page. There is not much point in overriding this method at the page level either. It is usually not a good place to do initialization, as it might not get called. The `awake` method is a far better choice.

The implementation of takeValuesFromRequest in WOComponent is both very similar to and very different from the implementations in WOApplication and WOSession. It is the same in that it does not do very much; page components are not directly tied to form values. It simply passes the buck, and the message, to the WOElement that forms the root of its template. It is different in that the work of moving the form values though bindings and into instance variables now starts.

The WODynamicGroup that is the root of the template in turn forwards the takeValuesFromRequest message to each of its children. The whole process starts over again from here. Some of these children will be WOComponent subclasses; others will be WODynamicElement subclasses. A WODynamicGroup can include any other element or component, including other WODynamicGroups or subclasses such as WOConditional. In all cases, these elements forward the message on to the elements below them.

The Connection Between HTML Inputs and Elements

Before we go deeper into this, we need to investigate how the components and dynamic elements in our code are linked to the HTML shown in the browser. Run the application for this chapter and click on the link *Links and Simple Form*. Now look at the source of the page you see. Listing 6-2 shows a reformatted and annotated version of the source. The first line, URL, is the URL as shown in the browser and not actually part of the page source.

Listing 6-2: *The Source of the First Request for the Links and Simple Form Page*

```
URL: http://localhost/cgi-bin/WebObjects/Chap6App.woa/-4618/wo/
     wSiKlTmD4HYMHj9XcOhpoO/0.1
0:   <!DOCTYPE HTML PUBLIC "-//W3C//DTD HTML 3.2//EN"><html><head><meta
     name="generator" content="WOLips Core"><title>PWO Chap 6 - RR Loop Tests
     </title></head><body bgcolor=#FFFFFF><p>
1:   <a href="/cgi-bin/WebObjects/Chap6App.woa/-4618/wa/RRLoop
     ?wosid=wSiKlTmD4HYMHj9XcOhpoO">Reload page with direct action</a>
2:   </p><p>
3:   <a href="/cgi-bin/WebObjects/Chap6App.woa/-4618/wo
     /wSiKlTmD4HYMHj9XcOhpoO/1.3">Reload page with component action</a>
4:   </p>
5:   <form method="post" action="/cgi-bin/WebObjects/Chap6App.woa/-4618
     /wo/wSiKlTmD4HYMHj9XcOhpoO/1.5">
     5.0: <p></p><p>Text:
     5.1: <input type=text name="5.1">
     5.2: </p><p>
     5.3: <input type=submit value="Reload page by submitting form" name="5.3">
     5.4: </p>
5:   </form>
6:   <p></p>
7: <a href="/cgi-bin/WebObjects/Chap6App.woa/-2134/wo/k4tPTOv1UB52i4zvA3SRrM/
   1.7">Return to main page</a>
8: </body></html>
```

The numbers on the subsequent lines break the HTML into nine parts, one of which, part 5, has five subparts. Numbering starts from zero, which corresponds to the zero-based index of an NSArray. We've numbered these parts to match the scheme used internally by WebObjects. It will be a bit confusing when, for example, we refer to the fourth part, numbered 3.

The first part, 0, is copied directly from the component's HTML template. The next part is a hyperlink generated dynamically by WOHyperlink. The next three parts are more copied HTML, another hyperlink, and yet more copied HTML.

The sixth part, numbered 5, is more interesting. This is a form and it has other parts between its open and close tags. Section 5 spans from the beginning of the form open tag to the end of the form close tag. The subparts of part 5 are copied HTML (5.0), a textual input generated dynamically by WOTextField (5.1), more copied HTML (5.2), a submit input generated dynamically by WOSubmitButton (5.3), and still more copied HTML (5.4).

Following section number 5 is, well, section number 5 again. The closing tag is at the same level/number as the opening tag. Following that is more boring copied HTML (6), a hyperlink generated dynamically (7), and yet more boring copied HTML (8).

The default naming scheme for these parts is based on numbers separated by dots. The numbers represent relative position in the HTML (or an index into an NSArray, if you prefer). Every part, including static HTML copied from the template, gets a number starting with zero. The static HTML is also numbered, as it is represented in the template by an object instance of WOHTMLBareString. The naming scheme also indicates the child elements of a WODynamicGroup. When one group contains another (e.g., forms, conditionals, repetitions), a dot is added and numbering starts again from zero.

There are two kinds of names: action names and element names. Action names have an extra number, the context ID, added onto the beginning. You can see action names in Listing 6-2 in sections 3 and 5. The context ID for these names is **1**. This context ID is used in the WOSession method restorePageForContextID to ensure that the action goes to the correct page instance.

Element names don't have a context ID. Their context ID is implicit in the action name that the page is submitted to. The lines 5.1 and 5.3 show examples of element names. These element names are only used to associate form values with objects in our application.

As befits its central role, the context is deeply involved with managing these names. At the heart of this is the method elementID. This is a somewhat unusual method in that the value it returns is constantly on the move. The elementID tracks the progress of the takeValuesFromRequest, invokeAction, and appendToResponse methods through the tree of objects that make up a page. The value returned by elementID changes as focus and control passes from one object to another. Although at first this may appear as magic, it is not. The components and elements are also involved: they update the context on what is going on.

The WOContext methods central to tracking the elementID are appendZeroElementIDComponent, incrementLastElementIDComponent, and deleteLastElementIDComponent. The method appendElementIDComponent can be used to create nonstandard names. Listing 6-3 shows an outline of how takeValuesFromRequest in WODynamicGroup is probably implemented using these methods.

Listing 6-3. *Outline of Possible Implementation of* WODynamicGroup*'s* takeValuesFromRequest

```
public void takeValuesFromRequest(WORequest aRequest,
                                  WOContext aContext) {
    aContext.appendZeroElementIDComponent();
```

```
    Enumerator childElements = childEnumerator();
    while (childElements.hasMoreElements()) {
        WOElement element = childElements.nextElement();
        element.takeValuesFromRequest(aRequest, aContext);
        aContext.incrementLastElementIDComponent();
    }
    aContext.deleteLastElementIDComponent();
}
```

Groups add another particle to the element ID; the call to `appendZeroElementIDComponent` achieves this by, for example, changing 1.5 to 1.5.0. After each child is given the chance to handle `takeValuesFromRequest`, the `elementID` is updated by a call to `incrementLastElement-IDComponent`, which in our example changes 1.5.0 to 1.5.1. Once all of the children have been processed, `deleteLastElementIDComponent` is called to restore the element ID to its original state, which in our example changes 1.5.7 to 1.5. The `invokeAction` and `appendToResponse` methods would follow a similar pattern to ensure that the element ID was consistent for a particular element across all three phases.

The context function of generating URLs is also tied in with the element ID. The element ID forms a part of every action URL. Calls to `componentActionURL` will return a URL with the current value of `elementID`.

Text Input Example Component

We will put this theory into practice now and create a replacement for `WOTextField`, cleverly called `TextInput`. We will caution you that this is *definitely* not the best way to do this. It is just a demonstration of how things work and proof that you can take values in a component. In the real world `WOGenericElement`, or possibly a subclass of `WODynamicElement`, would be the preferred solution. We'll take those subjects up in the next chapter.

As a reminder, the basic form of an HTML text input is

```
<input type="text" name="SomeName" value="SomeValue">
```

We will use a `WOString` to replace the *SomeName* and *SomeValue* parts. Here is what the `TextInput.html` template looks like:

```
<input type=text name="<webobject name="Name"></webobject>"
       value="<webobject name="Value"></webobject>">
```

We can guess from the earlier example that this will be broken into five parts:

0 <input type=text name="

1 <webobject name="Name"></webobject>

2 " value="

3 <webobject name="Value"></webobject>

4 ">

The bindings are straightforward. The name is just `context.elementID`—WebObjects takes care of ensuring that this is current. We will take the initial value for the input directly from this page's `value` binding:

```
Name: WOString {
    value = context.elementID;
}
Value: WOString {
    value = ^value;
}
```

Run the demonstration application for this chapter and click on *Demonstrate Form Inputs* to see how this works. If you view the source for the page, the top part should look similar to Listing 6-4. There are two nested groups in this example. The outer group is the `WOForm` nested in the ElementNames page. This group is identified as part 1 in the listing. The second group is from our TextInput component nested in the form; this is shown as part 1.1. Within part 1.1 we can see the five parts, 0 through 4, that we identified in the previous example. The name of the input is 1.1.1, which matches the expected element ID (i.e., the second part—confusingly numbered 1—within the 1.1 part).

Listing 6-4. *Annotated HTML Source Generated from the ElementNames Page*

```
0: <!DOCTYPE HTML PUBLIC "-//W3C//DTD HTML 3.2//EN"><HTML><HEAD>
   <META NAME="generator" CONTENT="WOLips Core"><TITLE>Untitled</TITLE>
   </HEAD><BODY BGCOLOR=#FFFFFF>
1: <form method="post" action="/cgi-bin/WebObjects/Chap6App.woa/-3998/wo
   /4RqHAcLrhftt8DSUCks1xw/1.1">
    1.0: Text:
    1.1: WOComponent sub-group
         1.1.0: <input type=text name="
         1.1.1: 1.1.1
         1.1.2: " value="
         1.1.3: no output (empty value)
         1.1.4: ">
    1.2: <P>
    1.3:  <input type=submit value="Submit" name="1.3">
    1.4: </P>
1: </form>
2: Value submitted:
3: null, empty, no value
4: <P>
```

Now let's take a look at the code behind this; see Listing 6-5. We don't want WebObjects to push and pull the bindings for this component, so we implement `synchronizesVariablesWithBindings` to return `false`. The component could be implemented to allow binding synchronization, but doing it manually makes the component easier to understand. The binding will be taken from our parent during the appendToResponse phase by the binding value = ^value. We'll take a closer look at the mechanics of binding synchronization in the next chapter.

Getting the submitted value out of the request and into its destination instance variable is where all of the excitement takes place. We had to cheat a little bit because of the way we constructed this example. When this takeValuesFromRequest method is executing, the TextInput component has the focus and elementID returns 1.1. When the HTML for the input name is being generated, the WOString *Name* has the focus and its element ID is 1.1.1. The first line in this method slaps another 1 on the element ID to make it match that of the WOString *Name*. We could also have cached the element ID of the TextInput component and used that, but this seemed cleaner. In practice, dealing with the element ID is not this messy, as there is no need to cheat for the sake of making an example as we did.

With the adjusted elementID in hand, we just ask the request object for the form value matching that name. It is interesting to notice that the frameworks do not force the form values into the element. Instead, the component is given the opportunity to get its own form value. The element remains in control of the process. It could even peek at or take the value for another element, though there seems little reason to do so. The downside of this is that if you change the contents of the template, input elements *will* take the value intended for another element.

Now that we have the form value, we need to get it into the instance variable in our parent. The value is forced up into the parent by calling setValueForBinding. We need to do this, as we have disabled binding synchronization so WebObjects is not going to do it for us. Finally, we reverse the change we made to the element ID by telling the context to deleteLast-ElementIDComponent.

The eagle-eyed in the crowd are probably waving their hands and asking, "What is that call to _wasFormSubmitted for?" We discovered the need for this when we added the second form to the bottom of the ElementNames page. If one form was submitted, the input in the other form would also go through takeValuesFromRequest. Of course there were no form values, as that form had not been submitted. This resulted in the value in one form being cleared when the other form was submitted.

We tried using isInForm first, but that did not change the result. The standard WOTextField did not show this behavior, so we knew it must be something we were doing or not doing. It was time for another round of class browsing, which turned up the _wasFormSubmitted method. Experimentation showed that _wasFormSubmitted returns true while in any element of the form that was submitted, and false at all other times. That is why we check to ensure that our parent form was submitted before trying to get the form values.

CAUTION Don't use private API unless necessary. Use unit tests to help mitigate the risk of changing semantics between versions.

Listing 6-5: *The Implementation of the TextInput Component*

```
public boolean synchronizesVariablesWithBindings() {
    return false;
}
```

```
public void takeValuesFromRequest(WORequest aRequest, WOContext aContext) {
    if (aContext._wasFormSubmitted()) {
        aContext.appendElementIDComponent("1");
        String formValue = aRequest.stringFormValueForKey(aContext.elementID());
        setValueForBinding(formValue, "value");
        aContext.deleteLastElementIDComponent();
    }
}
```

Performing the Requested Action

The next phase, invokeAction, happens for most, but not all, component requests. It does not happen for the first request in a session where there is no context ID nor element ID. The first request goes directly to the last phase, appendToResponse. invokeAction is the first phase to occur if there are no form values to process. The processing in invokeAction is very similar to that of takeValuesFromRequest. The element ID is reset and control passes down the component tree again.

There is one crucial difference in how invokeAction is processed. A form can have many values and each element in the component tree is given the opportunity to take any of the form values it is interested in. But only a single response can be returned, so invokeAction stops processing as soon as an element indicates that it has performed an action for the request. An element indicates that it was the target of the action by returning a non-null value from invokeAction.

We can guess that invokeAction in WODynamicGroup is implemented something like the code in Listing 6-6. The only material difference between this and the takeValuesFromRequest implementation in Listing 6-5 is the check for a non-null result page to terminate the loop early.

Listing 6-6. *One Possible Implementation of* invokeAction *in* WODynamicGroup

```
public void invokeAction(WORequest aRequest, WOContext aContext) {
    aContext.appendZeroElementIDComponent();
    Enumerator childElements = childEnumerator();
    WOActionResults resultPage = null;
    while (childElements.hasMoreElements() && (resultPage == null)) {
        WOElement element = childElements.nextElement();
        resultPage = element.invokeAction(aRequest, aContext);
        aContext.incrementLastElementIDComponent();
    }
    aContext.deleteLastElementIDComponent();
}
```

Hyperlink Example Component

We are going to look at another example component to show how to use invokeAction. This time we will create a more usable replacement component. This one is for WOHyperlink, cleverly called Hyperlink. While this is perhaps not the best way to implement this, it is closer to the intended use of the frameworks.

As a reminder, the basic form of an HTML hyperlink is

```
<a href="someURL">someText</a>
```

In a departure from the previous example, we are not going to use the .html/.wod pair to generate the HTML. Instead, we are going to do it manually in `appendToResponse` (shown further on in Listing 6-7). As we are not using dynamic elements to generate the HTML, we will not have to deal with changes in the element ID. This makes generating the HTML a little more difficult but makes handling the action straightforward.

It is also worth noticing that we do not call the superclass's implementation in either `invokeAction` or `appendToResponse`. As we fully handle these ourselves, and have no children to worry about, there is no need to call the superclass's implementation. Failing to call `super` will result in no log messages (as they are generated in our `LoggingComponent` parent), so we provide these manually. If we did make use of the superclass implementation, we would override the `template` method to return `null` so that the frameworks know to not waste time looking for a .wo resource for this component.

TIP If you override `template` to return something different than `null` or `super.template()`, it is a good idea to cache your template. This method will get called for each phase of the request—response loop, and time-consuming operations can bog your application down.

Run the demonstration application for this chapter and click on *Demonstrate Element Names* to see an example use of this component. The *Return to Main Page* link at the bottom uses our Hyperlink component.

Now let's take a look at the code behind this; see Listing 6-7. The `appendToResponse` method shows how to generate HTML the hard way. Resorting to manual HTML generation is only needed in `WODynamicElement` subclasses and a few other odd situations. We don't want Web-Objects to push and pull the bindings for this component either, so we implement `synchronizes-VariablesWithBindings` to return `false`. The implementation of `invokeAction` is surprising simple. We check to see if the sender ID (i.e., the element ID from the URL) and our element ID are equal and, if so, return the value for our `action` binding. These two values being equal indicates that the requested action is the one that we provide. If they do not match, we return `null` to indicate that this action was not directed to us.

We could have used `performParentAction` to handle the action for the hyperlink. We didn't, as we don't like this method. It requires the action to be defined as a string, not something that WOBuilder does automatically. While doing without `performParentAction` makes the code a little less obvious, it makes binding the `action` a lot easier, as you can click and drag to bind the action. We won't be reading this code much but we will be setting this binding often (well, we would if this was a real component). Using `(WOActionResults) valueForBinding("action")` to perform the action makes your component much more WOBuilder.

Listing 6-7. *Implementation of the Hyperlink Component*

```
public void appendToResponse(WOResponse aResponse, WOContext aContext) {
    rrLogger.debug(name() + " starting appendToResponse");
    aResponse.appendContentString("<a href=\"");
    aResponse.appendContentString(aContext.componentActionURL());
    aResponse.appendContentString("\">");
    aResponse.appendContentString((String) valueForBinding("linkText"));
    aResponse.appendContentString("</a>");
    rrLogger.debug(name() + " finished appendToResponse");
}

public boolean synchronizesVariablesWithBindings() {
    return false;
}

public WOActionResults invokeAction(WORequest aRequest, WOContext aContext) {
    if (aContext.elementID().equals(aContext.senderID())) {
        return (WOActionResults) valueForBinding("action");
    }
    return null;
}
```

In our ElementNames page, the hyperlink is bound to a method that returns a new instance of the page Main. This is done with `pageWithName`, which creates a new instance and wakes it in the current context. With our response page created we are now ready to start the final phase.

Generating the Response

The next phase, `appendToResponse`, happens for all component requests. It is a simpler matter than the earlier phases because there are no element ID comparisons to worry about. All we need to do is to generate HTML (or DHTML or XML or ...) and put the element ID in the right place.

An important change in the context occurs at the start of this phase. In the first two pages, `context.page` returns the page that generated the request. This is now changed to be the page that `invokeAction` returned, the response page. The `appendToResponse` phase follows the template of the response page, as does the context's element ID.

This phase proceeds in the same pattern as the others: the element ID is initialized and control passes down the component tree again. The elements of this tree are created the first time that the `WOComponent` method `template` is called. If you look at the log messages when this happens, you will notice something interesting. The subclasses of `WODynamicElement` are only created the first time this method is called on a particular component. Subclasses of `WOComponent` are created for each instance of that component. In either case, one instance is created for each reference in the .html file, even if there are multiple references to the same bindings in the .wod file.

This difference between WOComponent and WODynamicElement subclasses has some important implications. First, as fewer instances of WODynamicElement subclasses need to be created, this can reduce memory usage. Second, as the WODynamicElement subclass instances are shared across all instances of a component, even across sessions, they must be thread-safe. We will return to WODynamicElement subclasses in the next chapter.

The WODynamicElement instances are created by the WOApplication method dynamicElementWithName. One reason to override this method is to change the name parameter if you want to replace one of the standard components with your own subclass. This is a lot easier to do than updating all of the .wod files. This can be particularly useful to introduce debugging versions that output log messages. It can also be a useful method to override if you need to add bindings not present in the .wod file.

For example, we can make all of the hyperlinks in an application use HTTPS by forcing the hyperlink to have a secure=true binding:

```
public WOElement dynamicElementWithName(String name,
                                        NSDictionary bindings,
                                        WOElement children,
                                        NSArray languages) {
    if ("com.webobjects.appserver._private.WOHyperlink".equals(name)) {
        bindings = new NSMutableDictionary(bindings);
        ((NSMutableDictionary)bindings).setObjectForKey(WOAssociation
            .associationWithValue(Boolean.TRUE), "secure");
    }
    return super.dynamicElementWithName(name, bindings, children, languages);
}
```

Reprise of the Text Input Example Component

As a final example component, we are going to return to the replacement for WOTextField. This version, following our clever naming scheme, will be called TextInput2. This one will be a much better implementation, but a WODynamicElement subclass is probably still the way to go. As a reminder, the basic form of an HTML text input is

```
<input type="text" name="SomeName" value="SomeValue">
```

We will do the same thing as we did in the previous example and override appendToResponse to generate this HTML manually. takeValuesFromRequest is simpler this time, as we are generating our own HTML and so don't need to fiddle with the element ID. The code for this is shown in Listing 6-8.

Listing 6-8. *Implementation of the* TextInput2 *Component*

```
public boolean synchronizesVariablesWithBindings() {
    return false;
}

public void takeValuesFromRequest(WORequest aRequest, WOContext aContext) {
    if (aContext._wasFormSubmitted()) {
        String formValue = aRequest.stringFormValueForKey(aContext.elementID());
```

```
        setValueForBinding(formValue, "value");
    }
}

public void appendToResponse(WOResponse aResponse, WOContext aContext) {
    aResponse.appendContentString("<input type=\"text\" name=\"");
    aResponse.appendContentString(aContext.elementID());
    aResponse.appendContentString("\" value=\"");

    String aValue = (String)valueForBinding("value");
    if (aValue != null) {
        aResponse.appendContentString(aValue);
    }

    aResponse.appendContentString("\">");
}
```

The End of the World As WO Knows It

At this point we are pretty much done. We have the content for our response. All that remains is a bit of last-minute polishing and then closing everything down and putting it to sleep until that next request rolls in.

As soon as the application has finished with its `appendToResponse`, the handler saves the page returned in the session's page cache. You can intercept this in the `WOSession` method `savePage`. You might want to do this if you know the page will not be needed again—for example, with a page returned by a Direct Action that has no Component Action links on it. In this case you simply don't call `super.savePage`. You can save a fair bit of memory by not caching pages that you no longer have a need for.

All of the components that have been told to `awake` are now told to `sleep`. The handler calls the application method `saveSessionForContext` to check the session back into the session store. As part of this process, the session is also told to `sleep`.

There is a very important point to be aware of here. If the session is not checked into the session store, it will not be available for a subsequent request to use. If you are not dispatching requests concurrently, the next request for that session will deadlock your application. If you are dispatching requests concurrently, the next request for that session will deadlock the session. Either way you will have a lot of annoyed users. Prevent this by making sure that the `sleep` method in `Session` can't throw an exception.

The application is now sent the `sleep` message. At this point the `WOResponse` method `_finalizeInContext` is called. We mention this as it appears that cookies set after this point never make it back to the client. If you need to set a cookie, do it before this point! Do not try to set them in `dispatchRequest` after calling `super.dispatchRequest`. That just does not work.

...And Beyond

`DispatchRequest` has now done its job. The last thing that this method does is to broadcast the `ApplicationDidDispatchRequestNotification`. Following that, it returns the response to the worker thread.

The worker thread returns it to the WebObjects adaptor. The WebObjects adaptor turns it over to the web server; the web server sends it back to the client application. The HTML is rendered, the user clicks, and the whole thing starts over again!

Complications

One of the most vexing questions that plague web developers is what to do when an identical request comes in. Identical requests can result from several different things:

- The browser plug-in asks for a second copy of content that the browser has already downloaded.
- A refresh request is submitted by the browser when the window is resized.
- The user clicks on the refresh/reload button.
- The user double-clicks on a link or a submit button.
- The user backtracks.

There are two fundamental choices that can be made. The first is to handle the request as if it is the first time we have seen it. This works just fine if the request is simply to view some information. It is not nearly as fine when the previous request deleted something that no longer exists or made a payment or took some similar action that either cannot or should not be repeated.

The second choice is to skip some, or all, of the request—response loop processing and return something else. A common thing to return is an error page. Log on to your personal banking site and try backtracking to pay several bills with the same $100. We hope you weren't expecting that to work! Another possibility is to return a home page of some sort with an explanation of why the user is seeing that page.

WebObjects is capable of supporting either choice. By default, it re-generates the response from the component that responded last time. That is about as close as a stateful application can come to properly supporting backtracking. WebObjects can also just pass along the request unmolested and the entire request—response loop is repeated.

This behavior is controlled by the `WOApplication` methods `isPageRefreshOnBacktrackEnabled` and `setPageRefreshOnBacktrackEnabled`. When `isPageRefreshOnBacktrackEnabled` returns `true`, the cache control headers on the response are set so that the browser should not cache the page ("should" because some browsers don't honor these headers). When the user backtracks or refreshes, the handler detects this and skips the first two phases of the request—response loop. It jumps directly to `appendToResponse` and re-generates the response from the component that responded last time. If you use this you need to ensure that there is nothing in `appendToResponse` that can't be done a second or third time.

CAUTION When `isPageRefreshOnBacktrackEnabled` returns `true` and the user backtracks, the page's `awake` method will be called twice instead of once. Watch out for code that expects this to happen only once, or that depends on an equal number of calls to `awake` and `sleep`.

When isPageRefreshOnBacktrackEnabled returns false, the cache control headers on the response are not set and the browser is allowed to cache the page locally. The user can then backtrack locally and make another request (or just refresh). The browser will send this request again and a new trip is made through the request—response loop. You need to be careful doing this when the last action either cannot or should not be repeated.

A third variation on this is possible. The cache control headers can be set by calling disableClientCaching directly on the response. If isPageRefreshOnBacktrackEnabled returns false, we then get a hybrid approach. Any backtracking results in a new request to the server and a full trip through the request—response loop. By itself this is usually not what you want; taking the form values and invoking the action again is rarely the right thing to do. What it does allow is the delegation of the decision about how to handle this action to the individual pages, rather than keeping it at the request-handler level.

It doesn't really matter which way you choose to handle user backtracking. Regardless of your choice, it will be insufficient and troublesome. We wish we could tell you an easy, straightforward, always-working solution, but we can't. You will have to pick one of these ways (WebObjects default is probably the least troublesome) and manually handle the kinks when you run into them.

Summary

In this chapter you learned about the aspects of the HTTP protocol that are relevant to us as developers of web applications. We then looked at how using an HTTP proxy can help us see the goings-on that are normally hidden from view. We took a long look at the request—response loop and how it is represented in WebObjects. This is important material to understand. A lack of understanding limits your ability to effectively debug components and to create more sophisticated components. In the next chapter we are going to use and build on this knowledge to debug some common pitfalls and to learn how to create some interesting components.

CHAPTER 7

Components and Elements

What we need to do is learn to work in the system, by which I mean that everybody, every team, every platform, every division, every component is there not for individual competitive profit or recognition, but for contribution to the system as a whole on a win-win basis.

—W. Edwards Deming

It's easy to cry "bug" when the truth is that you've got a complex system and sometimes it takes a while to get all the components to co-exist peacefully.

—Doug Vargas

In this chapter we are going to build upon our request—response loop knowledge from the previous chapter and peer into some of the less well-lit corners of components. You will see how subtle changes in the component graph during the request—response loop can have obscure or difficult-to-understand side effects and learn how to debug these situations. We will reveal what makes `WODynamicElement` an efficient counterpart to `WOComponent`. We will take a close look at how automatic and manual synchronization of values between parent and child components work, and show that stateless components offer an alternative to dynamic elements that combine efficiency with ease of creation. Finally, we will explore the useful, but little known, `WOEvent` functionality as an aid to optimization and debugging.

The Case of the Missing Element

Run the demonstration application for this chapter and click the *Bad Behavior* link. At the top of the page you will see a little form, shown in Figure 7-1. If you click on one of the *Go!* buttons you will be whisked to the appropriate site. So far, things are looking good. Now hit the back button and select the last site for deletion. Click *Save* and notice that WebObjects is no longer listed. Things are looking fine; we are almost done. Now select any site *except* the last one for deletion. Go ahead and pick any one, it doesn't matter which. Now press the *Save* button.
Uh oh!

Figure 7-1. *UI for The Case of the Missing Element*

We've probably all done this at one time or another. Some of us still do it, but we won't admit to it. Does this sound familiar? You put together a fancy new form, maybe with a couple of custom components on it, and it is ready to meet that rather odd requirement the client had. (Of course, we as developers would never come up with odd requirements, would we?) You bring up the page, enter some data, click Submit, and presto! What the heck is that exception from?

This is usually followed by a lot of debugging messages, head-scratching, and trips for yet another caffeine-laden beverage. Only after a while does it dawn on you that you've not been taking the request—response loop into consideration. You are, in fact, the author of your own misfortune.

Request—Response and Component Debugging

You learned (or at least read) a lot about the request—response loop in the last chapter. It is time to put that theoretical knowledge to a practical use. The code for this is in the `ChangedCollection` class in this chapter's sample application. Let's take a closer look at the stack trace, shown in Listing 7-1, and see if we can find some clues as to why this is happening to us. A quick read from the bottom to the top tells us that the problem is happening during the `takeValuesFromRequest` phase, inside the form, inside the repetition. Now why would it be getting an index out of bounds exception?

Listing 7-1. *Stack Trace from the First Bad Behavior Example*

```
Application:  Chap7App
Error:  java.lang.IllegalArgumentException: Index (3) out of bounds [0, 2]
Reason:  Index (2) out of bounds [0, 1]
Stack trace:
File                        Line#  Method
----------------------------------------------------------------------
NSArray.java                  490  objectAtIndex
WORepetition.java              51  _prepareForIterationWithIndex
WORepetition.java             123  takeValuesFromRequest
WODynamicGroup.java            81  takeChildrenValuesFromRequest
WODynamicGroup.java            89  takeValuesFromRequest
WOForm.java                    70  takeValuesFromRequest
```

```
WOComponent.java                 914  takeValuesFromRequest
WOComponentReference.java         97  takeValuesFromRequest
WODynamicGroup.java               81  takeChildrenValuesFromRequest
WODynamicGroup.java               89  takeValuesFromRequest
WOComponent.java                 914  takeValuesFromRequest
WOSession.java                  1137  takeValuesFromRequest
WOApplication.java              1352  takeValuesFromRequest
WOComponentRequestHandler.java   189  _dispatchWithPreparedPage
WOComponentRequestHandler.java   287  _dispatchWithPreparedSession
WOComponentRequestHandler.java   322  _dispatchWithPreparedApplication
WOComponentRequestHandler.java   358  _handleRequest
WOComponentRequestHandler.java   432  handleRequest
WOApplication.java              1308  dispatchRequest
WOWorkerThread.java              173  runOnce
WOWorkerThread.java              254  run
Thread.java                      536  run
```

There is no point in looking at the method that saves the deletion. That will get called in invokeAction and that phase has not been reached yet. The problem is in takeValuesFromRequest. We can deduce that it must be related to form values, as takeValuesFromRequest is only performed when there are form values.

A quick check shows that there is only one form value, the check box for each web site. This check box has one binding, checked = isSiteDeleted. The accessor and mutator for isSiteDeleted are implemented like this:

```
public boolean isSiteDeleted() {
    return false;
}

public void setIsSiteDeleted(boolean isSiteDeleted) {
    if (isSiteDeleted) {
        websites.removeObjectForKey(websiteName);
        websiteNames.removeObject(websiteName);;
    }
}
```

It seems evident that the accessor isSiteDeleted can't be the source of the problem. The problem must lie in the method setIsSiteDeleted. This method does not do anything unless the isSiteDeleted parameter is true. Taking this all together, we can deduce that the problem occurs sometime after setIsSiteDeleted is called for a web site selected for deletion.

Now let's think through how this works. The takeValuesFromRequest message gets passed down from the application level until it reaches the repetition. The repetition then needs to establish some sort of loop over the list binding. We aren't told what kind of loop this is. For each loop iteration, the repetition needs to pass the takeValuesFromRequest message to each of its children. The WOCheckBox is the only one that is going to do anything with this message. When we get to the selected web site, the setIsSiteDeleted method will remove the selected web site from both the websites and websiteNames collections. The repetition knows nothing of this and will continue marching along through its iterations, which means that it won't realize when it is on the last element. It will ask for the element that was there before and the inevitable exception will result:

```
Error:  java.lang.IllegalArgumentException: Index (3) out of bounds [0, 2]
```

The Golden Rule

This leads us to the golden rule of respecting the request—response loop:

> *Don't modify anything that the component or dynamic elements depend on while in the sequence appendToResponse, takeValuesFromRequest, and invokeAction.*

You should notice that this is not the normal order of events that we have presented in the past. It is safe to make modifications after the `invokeAction` phase ends and before the `appendToResponse` phase starts. This is the point where the cycle for one `WOContext` stops and the cycle for the next `WOContext` starts.

So, how do we use this knowledge to fix our little problem? The `setIsSiteDeleted` method is modifying the collection that the repetition depends on, the collection bound to its `list` binding. That is not allowed. What we need to do is to record the fact that this happened but to delay the actual deletion until after `invokeAction`. We will do this by introducing a new instance variable to hold the web sites that have been selected for deletion.

```
protected NSMutableSet deletedSites = new NSMutableSet();
public void setIsSiteDeleted(boolean isSiteDeleted) {
    if (isSiteDeleted) {
        deletedSites.addObject(websiteName);
    }
}
```

Our only problem now is to decide where to process the actual deletion. The choices are after `invokeAction` and before `appendToResponse`. There are three places where this can be done; all of these will work in different situations:

- in `invokeAction` after calling `super.invoke` action (good for general purpose processing)
- in the action method that was invoked (good for processing that is tied to a specific action)
- in `appendToResponse` before calling `super.appendToResponse` (this works only if returning the same page)

In our case we want to process the delete only after the *Save* button is clicked and not when a web site is visited. The most appropriate place to do this is in the action method that the *Save* button is bound to:

```
public WOComponent saveChanges() {
    while (deletedSites.count() > 0) {
        websiteName = (String) deletedSites.anyObject();
        deletedSites.removeObject(websiteName);
        websites.removeObjectForKey(websiteName);
        websiteNames.removeObject(websiteName);;
    }
    // Save any changes here
    return context().page();
}
```

You can see this working by running the application for this chapter and clicking on the *Good Behavior* link. The full code is in the `GoodChangedCollection` class.

The Mystery of the Missing Submit

We'll look at one more example of the type of thing that can go wrong in the request—response loop before we move on to another topic. Run the demonstration application for this chapter and click the *Bad Behavior* link. At the bottom of the page you will see a little form, shown in Figure 7-2. Click *Button One* and notice the message at the bottom change to indicate which button you clicked. Now click *Button Two* and notice the message change to reflect this. Check *Hide Button One* and then click *Button Two*. The message at the bottom still shows that you clicked *Button Two*. OK, that all looks fine. Now uncheck *Hide Button One* and then click *Button Two*. Again, the message at the bottom still shows that you clicked *Button Two*. Now for the problem. Check off *Hide Button One* and then click *Button One*. "No button clicked"—how can that be?

2. Conditionals

Hide Button One

Button One

Button Two

No button clicked

Figure 7-2. *The Bad Behavior Conditionals UI*

We don't have an exception to guide us this time. We are going to have to think this one through. The check box gets its value in `takeValuesFromRequest` and the button name for the message is set in `invokeAction`. The problem must lie somewhere between those. The code for this component is in the `BadConditional` class. The check box is bound directly to an instance variable, so the problem can't be something we wrote in our code. The behavior is happening somewhere in the WebObjects framework.

We're going to have to get down and dirty and look at the UI template, shown in Figure 7-3. The `takeValuesFromRequest` will go first to the page and then to the form. The form will pass this message on to each of its children. The first child is the check box. When it receives this message it will take its value from the request's `formValues`. The other children of this form and the other elements below it do nothing in response to `takeValuesFromRequest`. So far everything seems OK.

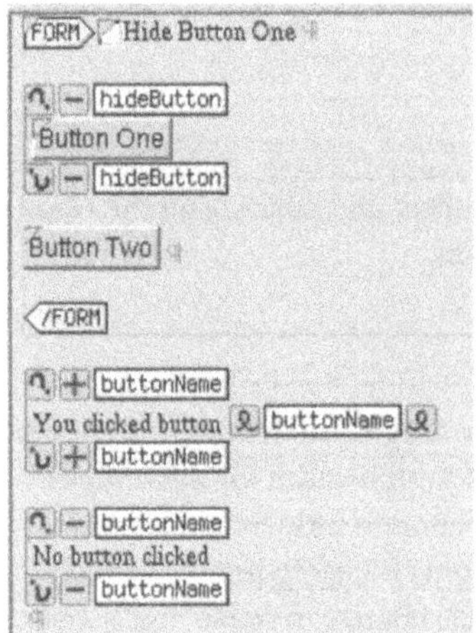

Figure 7-3. *The template for Bad Behavior conditionals*

The next phase is `invokeAction`. The `invokeAction` message will go first to the page and then to the form. The form will pass this message on to each of its children. The first child is the check box; it will do nothing, as check boxes do not have actions. The next child (ignoring the static HTML) is the conditional around Button One. When it receives this message it will pass it on to each of its children. Or will it? If the condition it is bound to evaluates to `false`, a `WOConditional` acts as if it has no children. It does this by not passing messages to its children.

Here, then, is the problem. The value the conditional is bound to, `hideButton`, changed from `true` to `false` during `takeValuesFromRequest`. By the time `invokeAction` is processed, the conditional effectively has no children; the submit button that was clicked has ceased to exist. When no submit button responds to `invokeAction`, the form executes its default action. For this component the form's action is bound to a method that sets `buttonName` to `null`:

```
public WOComponent defaultFormSubmit() {
    buttonName = null;
    return context().page();
}
```

The question now facing us is, "How do we avoid this problem?" Again, the answer is to postpone making the change until a safe time. The `GoodConditional` class shows one example of how this is done. A new `Boolean` value, `hideButtonForConditional`, is introduced and the `condition` binding of the conditional is bound to this method. The new `hideButtonForConditional` value is set from `hideButton` in `appendToResponse` before calling `super`.

```
public void appendToResponse(WOResponse response, WOContext context) {
    hideButtonForConditional = hideButton;
    super.appendToResponse(response, context);
}
```

There are a number of other ways to wreak havoc with your component, but they are all derivatives of this example. With your knowledge of the request—response loop from the previous chapter and the problems and solutions shown in this section, you should be able to figure out any situation you encounter with a minimum of head-scratching. Just remember: there is an answer; you just have to slow down and look for it.

Dynamic Elements

Custom dynamic elements (subclasses of `WODynamicElement`) are useful but seem to be infrequently used by WebObjects developers. We think there are two reasons for this. One reason is that `WODynamicElement` has not been well documented in the past (the documentation is still pretty confusing today). The other reason is that dynamic elements are more difficult to work with than regular components.

The first question we want to answer is, "Why use dynamic elements?" One reason is that a single instance of each is shared among all instances of a `WOComponent` subclass, as we saw in the previous chapter. If 1,000 instances of a page are created, only a single instance of each dynamic element is created. This can save a lot of memory when compared to `WOComponent` subclasses, for which new instances are created for each instance of a parent `WOComponent` subclass. Another reason is access to binding names and values. In previous versions, `WOComponent` did not provide easy access to its bindings—only `WODynamicElement` provided this. We expect that `WODynamicElement` is also faster, as there is less to check, but we have not quantified this.

In summary, `WODynamicElement` is mostly effective when used for small, very frequently used elements where memory usage and speed are a concern. For anything else, a `WOGenericContainer` or `WOGenericElement` will give you the same result for less work (and will make your work easier: WebObjects Builder doesn't seem to like to display the bindings for custom dynamic elements).

Dynamic Elements, Components, and Associations

One complication of having multiple `WOComponent` instances share the same `WODynamicElement` instance is that the `WODynamicElement` subclass must be thread-safe. When requests are being dispatched concurrently, the same page (but not the same instance!) can be used concurrently in multiple sessions and, hence, in multiple threads. As these page instances share the same `WODynamicElement` instance, concurrent access to a `WODynamicElement` instance is a very real possibility. This is why `WODynamicElement` subclasses must be thread-safe. Instance variables are not thread-safe unless object access is synchronized, which would largely defeat the purpose of using `WODynamicElement` instances with concurrent request dispatch.

WebObjects uses the concept of associations (`WOAssociation`) to avoid storing data in instance variables and to allow a single `WODynamicElement` instance to service multiple `WOComponent` instances simultaneously. An association is a pipeline for data transfer between the `WODynamicElement` instance and a specific instance of the `WOComponent` that the element is used in.

Each association knows how to get and/or set one value from a component. The central `WOAssociation` methods for this are `valueInComponent` and `setValue`. These two methods parallel the function of the `WOComponent` methods `valueForBinding` and `setValueForBinding`. These methods are used in conjunction with the `WOContext` method `component`.

```
Object someValue = anAssociation.valueInComponent(aContext.component());
```

This method, unlike `context.page`, changes as progress is made through the tree of elements that compose a page. It always reflects the dynamic element's nearest enclosing `WOComponent`.

If you are thinking that associations sound a lot like bindings in a .wod file, you are right. Each `name = value` pair in the .wod file definition for an element is converted into an association at runtime.

For example, consider this simple binding definition:

```
FullName : WOString {
    value = client.fullName;
}
```

When the .html and .wod files are parsed at runtime, this is converted into an association by calling the static `WOAssociation` method `associationWithKeyPath`. This method creates a `WOAssociation` with the key `client.fullname`. When this association is later asked for its `valueInComponent(aComponent)`, it returns what is effectively

```
aComponent.valueForKeyPath("client.fullname").
```

Other associations can return the value from a binding in the parent component

```
FullName : WOString {
    value = ^fullName;
}
```

or a constant value (created by `associationWithValue`), as in

```
FullName : WOString {
    value = "John Q Public";
}
```

How Dynamic Elements Work

`WODynamicElement`'s constructor is very different from `WOComponent`'s constructor. In place of a `WOContext` it takes a name, a dictionary of associations, and an optional `WOElement` representing its children:

```
WODynamicElement(String name, NSDictionary associations, WOElement children)
```

A context would be meaningless in this situation, as this instance may be used in many contexts at the same time.

We don't know what the name parameter is for, other than logging. Subclasses might use it for something. The dictionary of associations contains all the bindings. This is the important part. The keys into the dictionary are the names of the bindings. In this example, the dictionary would have a single entry. The key would be value, and the object for that key would be the association describing the source of the value. The children element represents the static and dynamic HTML elements and subcomponents contained inside this dynamic element. For example, children would be used for the link text in a WOHyperlink or the components inside a WOConditional. It will be null if there is nothing contained inside this dynamic element (e.g., a form input). If children is not null, it should be forwarded each of the takeValuesFromRequest, invokeAction, and appendToResponse messages.

The dynamic element constructor needs to do three things:

- Validate the associations and children.
- Store the associations for use during a request—response loop.
- Store the children for use during a request—response loop.

The dynamic element also needs to override at least one of takeValuesFromRequest, invokeAction, or appendToResponse. Elements that only display themselves will only need to implement appendToResponse. Form input elements will need to implement both takeValuesFromRequest and appendToResponse. Action elements (submit buttons, hyperlinks) will need to implement invokeAction and appendToResponse. Elements with children may need to implement all three so that each message gets passed on to the children.

An Example Dynamic Element

Since we presented two hyperlink implementations in the last chapter and said that they would be better implemented as a WODynamicElement, we feel that it is only proper to actually do so. Yes, it's true! We are not leaving this one as an infamous "exercise for the reader." We are going to extend the previous example to handle the pageName binding from WOHyperlink and also to mimic the behavior of rendering any unknown bindings as HTML attributes on the opening tag. The *rest* of the WOHyperlink bindings we are, of course, leaving as an exercise for the reader!

Constructing and Validating a Dynamic Element

The instance variables and constructor for our hyperlink are shown in Listing 7-2. In order to be thread-safe, we only store the values passed in the constructor in instance variables. These are all immutable objects, WOAssociation or WOElement.

Validation of the bindings and children is done when the dynamic element is constructed. Either action or pageName is required, and both can't be present. These bindings are obtained from the associations dictionary by name. If these bindings are not valid, we throw a WODynamicElementCreationException to match what the standard WebObjects dynamic elements throw. The children are also required; otherwise there would be nothing to click on to activate the link. The last thing we do is remove the bindings that we know about from associations and keep the rest to render in appendToResponse as optional attributes on the opening tag.

Listing 7-2. *Instance Variables and Constructor for Hyperlink*

```
public static final String ACTION_BINDING_KEY = "action";
public static final String PAGE_NAME_BINDING_KEY = "pageName";

protected WOAssociation action;
protected WOAssociation pageName;
protected NSDictionary extraBindings = null;
protected WOElement children;


/**
 * Constructor.
 *
 * @param name not used
 * @param associations bindings from WOD file
 * @param children HTML inside link
 */
public Hyperlink(String name, NSDictionary associations, WOElement children) {
    super(name, associations, children);

    /** require [associations_valid] associations != null;  **/

    action = (WOAssociation)associations.objectForKey(ACTION_BINDING_KEY);
    pageName = (WOAssociation)associations.objectForKey(PAGE_NAME_BINDING_KEY);

    // Binding validation, one is required.
    if (action() == null && pageName() == null) {
        throw new WODynamicElementCreationException("<" +
            getClass().getName() + "> Missing required attribute: 'action' or " +
                "'pageName'");
    }

    // Binding validation, both are not allowed.
    if (action() != null && pageName() != null){
        throw new WODynamicElementCreationException("<" +
            getClass().getName() + "> Must specify only one of: 'action' or " +
                "'pageName'");
    }

    // Usage validation, <a href="..."></a> is not allowed
    if (children == null) {
        throw new WODynamicElementCreationException("<" +
        getClass().getName() + "> Missing contents.  Hyperlink must be " +
            "wrapped around something");
    }
```

```
    // Handle extra bindings such as style, class, etc.
    if (associations.count() > 1) {
        NSMutableDictionary tempBindings = associations.mutableClone();
        tempBindings.removeObjectForKey(ACTION_BINDING_KEY);
        tempBindings.removeObjectForKey(PAGE_NAME_BINDING_KEY);
        extraBindings = tempBindings.immutableClone();
    }
    this.children = children;
}
```

Generating HTML from a Dynamic Element

Other than the extra bindings, the appendToResponse method (shown in Listing 7-3) is similar to what we used in the example in Chapter 6. We've added HTML comments around the link so that you can identify it when looking at the source for a page. The URL is produced exactly the same way. It has nothing to do with our bindings; those come into play in invokeAction. The values for the extra bindings are obtained from the associations using valueInComponent with the context passed into appendToResponse. Finally, we ask our children to render themselves into HTML before we add our closing tag.

■ **NOTE** Have you ever wondered why the WOComponent request—response loop methods such as appendToResponse take a WOContext as a parameter when WOComponent has a context method that returns the same object? This was done to keep the method signature the same for all levels of the request—response loop. In dynamic elements it stops being redundant and becomes vital.

Listing 7-3. *The* appendToResponse *Method of Hyperlink*

```
/**
 * Add hyperlink to response's content as:
 * <a href="actionUrl>[optional bindings]>children</a>
 */
public void appendToResponse(WOResponse aResponse, WOContext aContext) {
    // Output <a href="url"
    aResponse.appendContentString("<!-- Our Hyperlink -->");
    aResponse.appendContentString("<a href=\"");
    aResponse.appendContentString(aContext.componentActionURL());
    aResponse.appendContentString("\"");

    // Output optional bindings
    if (extraBindings() != null) {
        Enumeration bindings = extraBindings().keyEnumerator();
        String bindingName;
        WOAssociation binding;
        while (bindings.hasMoreElements()) {
            bindingName = (String) bindings.nextElement();
            binding = (WOAssociation) extraBindings.objectForKey(bindingName);
```

```
                aResponse.appendContentString(" ");
                aResponse.appendContentString(bindingName);
                aResponse.appendContentString("=\"");
                aResponse.appendContentString((String)binding.valueInComponent(
                    aContext.component()));
                aResponse.appendContentString("\"");
            }
        }

        // Close opening tag
        aResponse.appendContentString(">");

        // Output text, image, etc. that will be clicked on
        children().appendToResponse(aResponse, aContext);

        // Output closing tag
        aResponse.appendContentString("</a>");
        aResponse.appendContentString("<!-- Our Hyperlink End -->");
    }
```

Handling Actions in a Dynamic Element

The `action` and `pageName` associations are used in `invokeAction`, shown in Listing 7-4. Again, this is not very different from the example in Chapter 6. Although we have already verified that there is an `action` or `pageName` association, we can't verify that it is associated with a non-`null` value until this method. Here we have access to a component and can check the result of the association. If `pageName` is `null` we don't know which page to return, so we throw an exception. The `action` association can return `null` and that is an acceptable value for `invokeAction` to return. However, we want the processing to stop here, so we translate that into the equivalent `context.page` to signal that we have performed the action.

Listing 7-4. *The* `invokeAction` *Method of Hyperlink*

```
/**
 * If this action is directed at us, either invoke the bound action or create
 * a new instance of the named page and return the result.
 */
public WOActionResults invokeAction(WORequest aRequest, WOContext aContext)
{
    WOActionResults result = null;

    if (aContext.senderID().equals(aContext.elementID())) {
        if (action() != null) {
            // Invoke the bound action.  Binding to a method that returns
            // null is acceptable.
            result = (WOActionResults)action().
                valueInComponent(aContext.component());
```

```
            // Substitute aContext().page() for null so that processing stops
            if (result == null) {
                result = aContext.page();
            }
        } else {
            // Get and validate the page name.  Binding to a null page name
            // is not acceptable.
            String nameInComponent = (String)pageName().
                valueInComponent(aContext.component());
            if (nameInComponent == null) {
                throw new IllegalStateException("<" + getClass().getName() +
                    "> : Missing page name.");
            }

            result = WOApplication.application().pageWithName(nameInComponent,
                                                              aContext);
        }
    }

    return result;
    /** ensure [result_if_action_invoked] Result != null ||
               ! aContext.senderID().equals(aContext.elementID());      **/
}
```

The entire class can be found in the demonstration application for this chapter. Run the application and click on the *Dynamic Elements* link to see this in action.

Replacing the WebObjects Dynamic Elements

One of the drawbacks of subclassing `WODynamicElement` is that WOBuilder does not show your replacements with the same UI elements as it used for the originals. This does not stop you from using them, but there is no validation, the design-time UI is not as clear, and there are no binding names created for you.

One way around this is to override `dynamicElementWithName` in `Application` to change standard names into custom names before the element is created. We initially mentioned this in Chapter 6. In the current chapter, we have implemented this in the demonstration application so that you can experiment with replacing the standard dynamic elements. Doing this allows you to configure the originals in WOBuilder and use your custom version at runtime.

CAUTION Sometimes you can get away with just subclassing `WODynamicElement`. For other dynamic elements you will need to subclass the more specific class so that it is type compatible.

The mapping between the name requested and what dynamicElementWithName returns is maintained in the file ElementMap.properties. In order for this resource file to be included in the built application, it needs to be added to the resources tag of the woapplication (or woframework) task in the build.xml file (for Eclipse only—Xcode does this for you):

```
<woapplication name="${project.name}" stdFrameworks="false"
               destDir="${dest.dir}">
    <resources dir=".">
        <include name="ElementMap.properties"/>
etc.
```

The ElementMap.properties file is in the standard Java properties format with the original name on the left-hand side and the replacement name on the right-hand side. The fully qualified class names must be used:

```
com.webobjects.appserver._private.WOHyperlink =↵
    com.apress.practicalwo.chap7app.Hyperlink
```

This mapping is loaded in the Application constructor:

```
elementMap = new Properties();
try {
    InputStream mappedElements = resourceManager().inputStreamForResourceNamed(
        "ElementMap.properties", null, null);
    elementMap.load(mappedElements);
}
catch (IOException e) {
    NSLog.err.appendln("ElementMap load failed: " + e.getMessage());
    System.exit(1);
}
```

and is used in dynamicElementWithName:

```
String alternateElement = elementMap.getProperty(name);
if (alternateElement != null) {
    name = alternateElement;
}
```

You can do the same thing in pageWithName. This can be a very useful technique to customize an application for specific clients, and is an easy way to provide UI or functionality tweaks for specific installations without affecting any others.

You should know enough now to start writing your own WODynamicElement subclasses. WODynamicElement does not provide a lot of support for subclasses, so you will find it useful to create a subclass to add some workhorse methods for dealing with associations. Here is an example that may give you some inspiration: http://www.wodev.com/cgi-bin/WebObjects/WODev.woa/wa/Main?wikiPage=CreatingADynamicElement.

Mysteries of Binding Synchronization

One thing that makes creating components in WebObjects so easy is the ability to pass values by describing what to pass and where to pass them, accomplished by setting bindings in WOBuilder. Magically, the frameworks get all the right values to the right places at the right time. One of the mysterious parts about creating components is how this happens. How are the values actually moved around? When are they are moved around? We are going to attempt to demystify this a bit.

Timing

In the section on dynamic elements we learned how `WOAssociation` is involved in accessing the bound values. The first thing that you need to know is that this is a two-way street. The values are not just pulled from the higher-level component down into the lower-level one. They are also pushed up from the lower-level component into the higher-level component. Clearly this exchange of values must be carefully coordinated to avoid overwriting the new values and to ensure that the right value is in the right place at the right time.

The automatic (as contrasted to manual) synchronization of bindings through the `WOAssociation` class will pull and push values at the start and end of each of the three phases of the component action request—response loop: `takeValuesFromRequest`, `invokeAction`, and `appendToResponse`. WebObjects uses key-value coding to synchronize the values. It does not use the `valueForBinding` and `setValueForBinding` methods for this; these methods are only for manual synchronization.

If a child component pulls a value from the parent component, the value will also be pushed back from the child into the parent. This is an all-or-nothing deal; the only way to keep the value from being pulled from or pushed back into the parent is to turn binding synchronization off and move the values manually. We will look at the reasons you might want to do that a bit later.

■ **NOTE** In binding synchronization we see another example of the pattern of decentralizing control. Subcomponents take the values that they want from their parents; parents do not force values into their subcomponents. Subcomponents push the values that they want to update into their parents; parents do not take the values from their subcomponents. This closely parallels how form elements take their own values independently from the form or page. You will see many examples of this pattern throughout the WO and EOF frameworks.

A Binding Synchronization Example

The example application for this chapter includes a page with three levels of component nesting to demonstrate how binding synchronization works. Most of the log messages are generated from the common superclass `LogBindingSynchronizationComponent`. For the implementation details, refer to its subclasses `TopLevelPage`, `SubComponent`, and `SubSubComponent`. These are indicated by color and name in the UI to make things clearer.

Run the application and click the *Binding Synchronization* link. You will see a page, of which the top part looks like Figure 7-4. The log messages generated by a form submission are detailed in Listings 7-5 through 7-7. Taking a close look at these reveals some interesting and useful information.

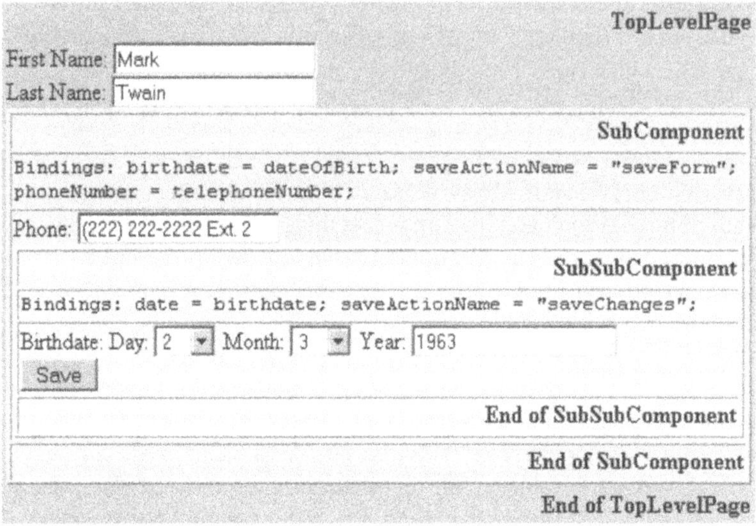

Figure 7-4. *Main UI elements from Binding Synchronization page*

The first thing we see in Listing 7-5 is that binding synchronization occurs after `awake` is called on the component. Thus you should not refer to bound values in the `awake` method. The `awake` method of `SubComponent` is overridden to demonstrate this. The first place where bound values can be accessed is in the `pullValuesFromParent` method. You can also get them before calling `super.takeValuesFromRequest`, etc.

Each component logs out its `bindingKeys`: the named values that it will synchronize with its parent in the `pullValuesFromParent` and `pushValuesToParent` methods. `SubComponent` shows this:

```
SubComponent pulling values for ("birthdate", "saveActionName", "phoneNumber")
```

which matches the bindings declared for this component in TopLevelPage.wod:

```
SubComponent: com.apress.practicalwo.chap7app.SubComponent {
    birthdate = dateOfBirth;
    saveActionName = "saveForm";
    phoneNumber = telephoneNumber;
}
```

The rest of the messages show the progression of `pullValuesFromParent` followed by `takeValuesFromRequest`, and then progression to the next lower level in the hierarchy of components. When the innermost component has invoked `takeValuesFromRequest`, it calls `pushValuesToParent` before returning control to `takeValuesFromRequest` in its parent component. This sequence of calls continues back up to the TopLevelPage. This is the pattern repeated in all phases to ensure that the binding values are moved to the correct place at the correct time.

Listing 7-5. *Flow of Binding Synchronization Methods to End of* takeValuesFromRequest

```
TopLevelPage _awakeInContext
  SubComponent _awakeInContext
    SubSubComponent _awakeInContext
    SubSubComponent awake
  SubComponent awake
TopLevelPage awake
TopLevelPage takeValuesFromRequest starting
  SubComponent pulling values for ("birthdate", "saveActionName", "phoneNumber")
     from parent TopLevelPage
  SubComponent takeValuesFromRequest starting
    SubSubComponent pulling values for ("submitActionName", "date") from parent
       SubComponent
    SubSubComponent takeValuesFromRequest starting
    SubSubComponent takeValuesFromRequest finished
    SubSubComponent pushing values for ("submitActionName", "date") to parent
       SubComponent
  SubComponent takeValuesFromRequest finished
  SubComponent pushing values for ("birthdate", "saveActionName", "phoneNumber")
     to parent TopLevelPage
TopLevelPage takeValuesFromRequest finished
```

The progress of the invokeAction phase is detailed in Listing 7-6. This proceeds exactly as the takeValuesFromRequest phase until the WOSubmitButton invokes the action in SubSubComponent. The save method uses performParentAction to get the response page. This temporarily transfers control back up to the parent component. However, the invokeAction phase has not yet finished, so any changes to the binding values made in SubSubComponent will not yet be reflected in the parent component. To accommodate this, performParentAction calls pushValuesToParent before performing the action and then calls pullValuesFromParent afterward in case the parent has changed any binding values. The log messages show that saveChanges in SubComponent does the same thing, as it also uses performParentAction.

■TIP In the previous chapter we used valueForBinding as an alternative to performParentAction. This differs from using performParentAction in that binding values are not pushed up and pulled down when this method is used. That is not usually a problem, as we rarely change bound values in invokeAction. If you do, then simply call pushValuesToParent before calling valueForBinding and call pullValuesFromParent afterward.

Listing 7-6. *Flow of Binding Synchronization in* `invokeAction` *with* `performParentAction`

```
TopLevelPage invokeAction starting
  SubComponent pulling values for ("birthdate", "saveActionName", "phoneNumber")
     from parent TopLevelPage
  SubComponent invokeAction starting
    SubSubComponent pulling values for ("submitActionName", "date") from parent
       SubComponent
    SubSubComponent invokeAction starting
    SubSubComponent performing parent action named saveChanges on SubComponent
    SubSubComponent pushing values for ("submitActionName", "date") to parent
       SubComponent
  SubComponent performing parent action named saveForm on TopLevelPage
  SubComponent pushing values for ("birthdate", "saveActionName", "phoneNumber")
     to parent TopLevelPage
TopLevelPage invoked saveForm action
  SubComponent pulling values for ("birthdate", "saveActionName", "phoneNumber")
       from parent TopLevelPage
    SubSubComponent pulling values for ("submitActionName", "date") from parent
       SubComponent
    SubSubComponent invokeAction finished
    SubSubComponent pushing values for ("submitActionName", "date") to parent
       SubComponent
  SubComponent invokeAction finished
  SubComponent pushing values for ("birthdate", "saveActionName", "phoneNumber")
     to parent TopLevelPage
TopLevelPage invokeAction finished
```

Listing 7-7 shows the binding synchronization in `appendToResponse`. After the previous two phases there is not much of interest; it follows the same pattern with no divergence.

Listing 7-7. *Flow of Binding Synchronization in* `appendToResponse`

```
TopLevelPage starting appendToResponse
  SubComponent pulling values for ("birthdate", "saveActionName", "phoneNumber")
     from parent TopLevelPage
  SubComponent starting appendToResponse
    SubSubComponent pulling values for ("submitActionName", "date") from parent
       SubComponent
    SubSubComponent starting appendToResponse
    SubSubComponent finished appendToResponse
    SubSubComponent pushing values for ("submitActionName", "date") to parent
       SubComponent
  SubComponent finished appendToResponse
  SubComponent pushing values for ("birthdate", "saveActionName", "phoneNumber")
     to parent TopLevelPage
TopLevelPage finished appendToResponse
TopLevelPage sleep
  SubComponent sleep
    SubSubComponent sleep
```

Binding Instance Variables and Methods

Here are three rules to keep in mind when working with bindings:

- The nearly code-free way to get bindings values to automatically synchronize is to provide a `public` instance variable. Assuming that your code is in packages, the instance variable must be declared `public`, as access is done with key-value coding that requires public access. Yes, you could also use `NSKeyValueCoding.ValueAccessor` and package access variables to allow key-value coding access. This feels like too much of a hack to us. Although `public` instance variables are generally not good OO design, they seem acceptable in this situation if you are not using component inheritance.
- As an alternative to `public` instance variables, you can use `private` instance variables and `public` accessor and mutator methods. This is recommended when component inheritance is used, as it provides better abstraction and the methods can function as hooks for custom behavior in subclasses. As you saw in Listings 7-6 and 7-7, the values are synchronized several times in a request—response loop. Because of this, accessor and mutator methods should have no unwanted side effects and should be implemented as efficiently as possible.
- It is perfectly acceptable to use methods not backed by an instance variable. The `date` value in `SubSubComponent` is a good example of this. If you do this, you must provide both accessor and mutator methods, even if they are empty. This does not apply to methods bound to a dynamic element's `action` binding; these are never set.

■ TIP The API Inspector's "Will Set" check box for a binding simply indicates that your component may need to change the value. The WebObjects Builder uses this to create a validation rule for the binding that raises a warning if it is bound to a constant value. This does not denote any kind of synchronization rule; it only indicates that a value might need to be pushed into the attribute bound to this.

Debugging Binding Synchronization

If you are having problems with binding synchronization (usually not getting the value you expect), you can ask WebObjects to log out every value transfer that it makes. To do this, add a binding `WODebug true` as shown in Figure 7-5. This needs to be done on each component that you want to get this information for; there is no global setting.

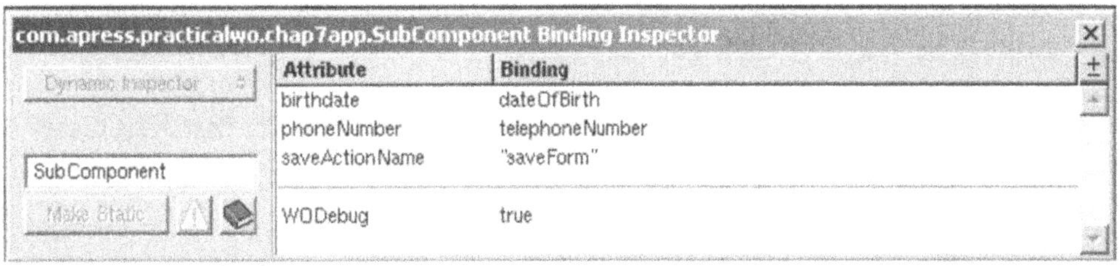

com.apress.practicalwo.chap7app.SubComponent Binding Inspector

Attribute	Binding
birthdate	dateOfBirth
phoneNumber	telephoneNumber
saveActionName	"saveForm"
WODebug	true

Dynamic Inspector | SubComponent | Make Static

Figure 7-5. *Use of the* `WODebug` *binding*

The log message produced does need some explanation. The messages when a value is pulled from the parent or pushed back into the parent are very similar. Here is an example that indicates `SubComponent` is taking the value for its `saveActionName` from the constant value `"saveForm"`:

```
[2004-02-13 21:07:45 PST] <WorkerThread1>
    [SubComponent:com.apress.practicalwo.chap7app.SubComponent]
        saveActionName <==
            (class java.lang.String: "saveForm")
```

The `<==` symbol indicates that the direction of synchronization is pulling from the parent into the component. The opposite symbol, `==>`, indicates that the direction of synchronization is pushing from the component into the parent. This example shows `SubComponent` pushing `2004-02-13 08:00:00 Etc/GMT` into whatever its parent has bound `birthdate` to:

```
[2004-02-13 21:07:45 PST] <WorkerThread1>
    [SubComponent:com.apress.practicalwo.chap7app.SubComponent]
        (birthdate: 2004-02-13 08:00:00 Etc/GMT) ==>
            com.webobjects.appserver._private.WOKeyValueAssociation
```

Manual Synchronization

The alternative to automatic binding value synchronization is manual synchronization. The first question that presents itself is "Why?" Automatic binding synchronization does a lot for you with very little effort required. In what situations would it be more advantageous to do this manually?

- Component synchronization can sometimes lead to values being set when you don't want them to be set. You have no control over when, or how often, the binding value is synchronized.
- Needless binding synchronization wastes CPU cycles. While it may not be a lot, if you don't need the benefit why incur the cost?
- It allows you to make `action` bindings like those on the dynamic element. Trying to synchronize these bindings requires set methods that have no meaning and results in the action being invoked over and over again regardless of what the user clicked on. The latter will waste memory and processor cycles and can lead to even worse results as spurious pages are created and discarded.
- There is no need to declare unused instance variables and accessor or mutator methods to support binding value synchronization.

Now that we know why we might want to do this, let's look at how. The first thing that is needed is to add this method to the component:

```
public boolean synchronizesVariablesWithBindings() {
    return false;
}
```

The next thing we need to learn is how to move the values back and forth. When components are not synchronized, they behave more like dynamic elements in that values need to be pushed or pulled manually in your code. Use valueForBinding and setValueForBinding methods to get and set the binding values as needed. All bindings will be returned as Object. You will need to manually convert them if you need to use an int, Boolean, or other simple type. You can make your component more robust by using the hasBinding method to ensure that required bindings are present and to allow for optional bindings. The canSetValueForBinding can be used to ensure that the value you need to return has not been bound to a constant, such as a quoted string.

The Carat Notation

There is one situation in which using nonsynchronizing components can be a bit of a nuisance. If one of your subcomponents—a WOString, for example—needs a value that comes from your bindings—title, for example—then you must create a method to get and return this value so that it can be bound to the WOString.

```
public String title() {
    return (String) valueForBinding("title");
}
```

This can lead to several little methods cluttering your component. Clearly, this will be a common situation and not code that is an ideal use of our time to write. WebObjects provides a special notation for use in the .wod file to avoid the need to write methods to move binding values. This is the carat (^) notation. A carat placed before a binding value means, "Use the value that my parent bound to this."

For example, to avoid having to write the title method just mentioned, we can change the .wod file from

```
TitleString : WOString {
    value = title;
}
```

to

```
TitleString : WOString {
    value = ^title;
}
```

Stateless Components

In the previous chapter we saw a difference in how WOComponent and WODynamicElement instances are created. Subclasses of WODynamicElement are only created once per use in a component class and then shared after that. Subclasses of WOComponent are created for each instance they are referenced in. This will result in the creation of fewer instances of WODynamicElement subclasses, which makes them a lot easier on memory. Stateless components bring this memory efficiency to WOComponent subclasses without sacrificing the ease of creating components. WODynamicElement subclasses may be efficient, but they are also more work to create, as you need to handle associations and there is no template to ease generation of output.

Stateless components can't have stateful children (i.e., regular `WOComponents`). Only dynamic elements and stateless components can be used as the children of stateless components. If you violate this you will get a `java.lang.IllegalStateException`.

There is an interesting difference between dynamic elements and stateless components in relation to thread safety. Dynamic elements must be thread-safe. To achieve this, no state is held in a dynamic element. All state information is instead accessed using associations. Stateless components aren't thread-safe. The result of this is that, unlike a dynamic element, stateless components can't be shared among threads. Additional instances of stateless components are created when they are simultaneously used in multiple threads. Because a single instance of a stateless component can be reused by many parent components, it is not as tightly tied to its bindings as dynamic elements are. So while using the same dynamic element on a page ten times will result in the creation of ten instances, doing the same thing with a stateless component will only create a single instance. It is difficult to determine which will be more memory efficient, but either is much better than a standard `WOComponent` in this regard.

To make a component stateless, all you need to do is override the `isStateless` method:

```
public boolean isStateless() {
    return true;
}
```

Overriding this method to return `true` will make the component stateless. Statelessness is ideally suited to small, frequently used components. This is where you will get the biggest benefit in terms of reduced memory usage. Such components are also where automatic binding synchronization represents a significant amount of overhead. Therefore, by default, stateless components don't automatically synchronize their bindings. While we recommend sticking with this default behavior, you can override `synchronizesVariablesWithBindings` to return `true` if you want automatic binding synchronization.

The reality of stateless components does not exactly match their name. Stateless components can maintain state, but only for the duration of the current phase of the current request–response loop. At the end of each phase the `reset` method is called. The `reset` method is invoked only if the component is stateless. You should override this to clear any state that you may have been holding. The usual state to hold is the value for a binding. This avoids repeated requests for the same bound value. Listing 7-8 shows the basic pattern for this using a `formatter` binding as an example. If the binding will frequently be `null` and will frequently be accessed in one phase, this pattern can still result in too many requests for the binding value. In that case, you will need to use some sort of flag system to indicate that a binding has been accessed rather than just checking for a `null` value.

Listing 7-8. *Use of Binding Value Caching and the* `reset` *Method in a Stateless Component*

```
protected java.text.Format formatter;

public java.text.Format formatter() {
   if (formatter == null) {
```

```
        formatter = (java.text.Format) valueForBinding(FORMATTER_BINDING);
    }
    return formatter;
}

public void reset() {
    formatter = null;
    super.reset();
}
```

■ **NOTE** If you ever use a stateless component as a child of itself, you will notice that additional instances are created. This is why: the state of the parent must be maintained for the duration of that phase, separate from the child's state.

The Mapped List Popup Stateless Component

It is time again for another example component. This one is actually usable, and we find it useful to boot. Have you ever run into the situation where you wanted the user to pick one object from a list but the object had no attribute appropriate for display to the user? We certainly have, time and again.

The Mapped List Popup (`PWOMappedPopup`) handles this by allowing a list of displayable names to be associated with a list or dictionary of objects. When two lists are used, the items at the same index are expected to relate to each other. Where a list and a dictionary are used, the display names must be the keys into the dictionary. We chose to disallow a single dictionary binding, as we wanted to be able to control the display order of the names and there is no ordering associated with the keys in a dictionary. The other bindings are documented in `WOPopUp` and shown in Figure 7-6.

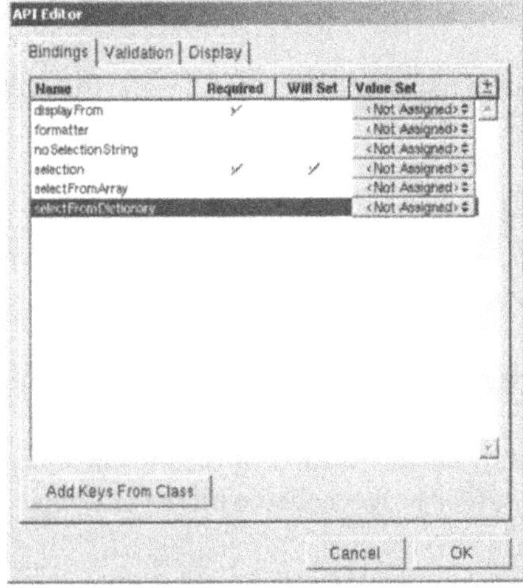

Figure 7-6. *API for* `PWOMappedPopup`

We chose to make this a stateless component as it fit the criteria: it's a small piece of a page that might be used frequently and it has no need to store state. We left it set to the default of nonsynchronizing because we didn't see any great burden in getting and setting binding values manually. You can see this component in action by running the example application and clicking on the *Stateless Components and Manual Binding Synchronization* link. The page using this component is `StatelessManualBindingSynching`.

We are not going to reproduce the code for `PWOMappedPopup` here, as there is nothing particularly interesting in the implementation that you have not seen before. There is another version of this in the PracticalUtilities framework that is not cluttered with demonstration code.

We would like to draw your attention to a few points of interest:

- The component's `hashCode` is logged in a few places so that you can see that it is the same instance taking on a new parent, bindings, and template when it is reused.
- The validation of bindings can't be done just once because the component will be reused with different bindings. To reduce the number of times this is done, we defer validation until a binding is accessed. This does result in a lot of checking, so you might want to consider only performing these checks if a certain `NSLog` debugging level or group has been set.
- We were interested in how and when the parent, bindings, and template were switched when a stateless component was reused. We found the undocumented method `_setParent(WOComponent parent, NSMutableDictionary bindings, WOElement template)` that appears to be doing this job. This method has been overridden to log some messages so that you can see what is happening. You can access the binding values from here, but as it is undocumented and there are alternatives, this seems ill advised.
- The `pullValuesFromParent` method gets called for a stateless component (as does `pushValuesToParent`), even though the values are not automatically synchronized (pulled or pushed). This gives you the chance to implement them manually if you wish, though we don't usually do this. This is the first documented method where binding validation can be done and the binding's values accessed. If you know that you're going to need all the values, you can pull them all there. If you don't need them all, pulling them as needed is more efficient.
- Comment out the `reset` method to see the effect of not resetting internal state: this will result in both popups being identical.

The log messages resulting from the first click on the *Stateless Components and Manual Binding Synchronization* link are shown in Listing 7-9. These messages have been edited a bit to make them easier to read. Because of this, the log messages you will see in the console do not exactly match those in Listing 7-9.

After the page has been awoken, you can see a single `PWOMappedPopup` get created. This is only created a single time, even though there are two on this page. If you go back to the main page and come back to this page again, this creation step will be skipped, as the previously created instance is reused. Once created, we can see `_setParent` get called with the bindings for the first use of `PWOMappedPopup`.

With the current parent, bindings, and template set, awake is called, and the appendToResponse phase runs its regular course with calls to pullValuesFromParent and pushValuesToParent before and after. When this completes, reset is called and the cycle starts over for the next use of PWOMappedPopup.

In the first use we can see three calls to get the formatter binding, one for each value in the popup. This is a defect of using null to indicate that a binding value has not been read yet. The formatter binding is not bound and returns null, which results in our code not realizing that it has already read the value. One way to avoid this is to use a different value than null to indicate the unread state. Creating a singleton NullValue object will fulfill this need. We don't use NSKeyValueCoding.Null for this purpose, as it is treated specially by NSKeyValueCoding and hence may produce undesired side effects.

Listing 7-9. *Log Messages (Edited) from* PWOMappedPopup

```
bindings - StatelessManualBindingSynching _awakeInContext
bindings - StatelessManualBindingSynching awake, context
bindings - StatelessManualBindingSynching starting appendToResponse
nonSynch - Created PWOMappedPopup 6330655
nonSynch - PWOMappedPopup 6330655 _setParent:
nonSynch - PWOMappedPopup
           parent:com.apress.practicalwo.chap7app.StatelessManualBindingSynching
nonSynch - PWOMappedPopup    bindings: {
           noSelectionString = ... value=When will you complete the mission?;
           selectFromArray = ... keyPath=completionDates;
           displayFrom = ... keyPath=completionDescriptions;
           selection = ... keyPath=selectedCompletion; }
nonSynch - PWOMappedPopup    template: null
bindings - PWOMappedPopup _awakeInContext
bindings - PWOMappedPopup awake, context
bindings - PWOMappedPopup pulling values for (
           "noSelectionString","selectFromArray","displayFrom","selection")
           from parent StatelessManualBindingSynching
bindings - PWOMappedPopup starting appendToResponse
bindings - PWOMappedPopup getting Value ("Yesterday", "Today", "Tomorrow")
           for binding displayFrom
bindings - PWOMappedPopup getting Value When will you complete the mission?
           for binding noSelectionString
bindings - PWOMappedPopup getting Value null for binding selection
bindings - PWOMappedPopup getting Value null for binding formatter
bindings - PWOMappedPopup getting Value null for binding formatter
bindings - PWOMappedPopup getting Value null for binding formatter
bindings - PWOMappedPopup finished appendToResponse
bindings - PWOMappedPopup pushing values for
             ("noSelectionString", selectFromArray","displayFrom","selection")
             to parent StatelessManualBindingSynching
nonSynch - PWOMappedPopup resetting
nonSynch - PWOMappedPopup 6330655 _setParent:
```

```
nonSynch - PWOMappedPopup    parent:
           com.apress.practicalwo.chap7app.StatelessManualBindingSynching
nonSynch - PWOMappedPopup    bindings: {
           selectFromDictionary = ... keyPath=booleanChoices;
           noSelectionString = ... value=Do you accept this mission?;
           displayFrom = ... keyPath=booleanChoices.allKeys;
           selection = keyPath=selectedBoolean; }
nonSynch - PWOMappedPopup    template: null
bindings - PWOMappedPopup _awakeInContext
bindings - PWOMappedPopup awake, context
bindings - PWOMappedPopup pulling values for (
           "selectFromDictionary","noSelectionString","displayFrom","selection")
           from parent StatelessManualBindingSynching
bindings - PWOMappedPopup starting appendToResponse
bindings - PWOMappedPopup getting Value ("No", "Yes") for binding displayFrom
bindings - PWOMappedPopup getting Value Do you accept this mission? for
           binding noSelectionString
bindings - PWOMappedPopup getting Value null for binding selection
bindings - PWOMappedPopup getting Value null for binding formatter
bindings - PWOMappedPopup getting Value null for binding formatter
bindings - PWOMappedPopup finished appendToResponse
bindings - PWOMappedPopup pushing values for (
           "selectFromDictionary","noSelectionString","displayFrom","selection")
           to parent StatelessManualBindingSynching
nonSynch -   PWOMappedPopup resetting
bindings - StatelessManualBindingSynching finished appendToResponse
bindings - StatelessManualBindingSynching sleep, context
```

Debugging and Optimization with WOEvent

There are two difficult-to-debug problems with components. One is where a binding causes an exception to be thrown but it is not at all clear which of the 27 `WOHyperlink` components is responsible for the error. We wish we had an easy solution to this one, but we don't. The other problem is a page made slow by binding synchronization. These can be very difficult to debug/optimize because with automatic binding synchronization it is not clear what is getting called nor how many times it is called. *This* we have a solution for!

At the heart of the solution are the classes `EOEvent` and `EOEventCenter`. `EOEvent` provides a structure for storing information (description, duration) about a logged event. The `EOEventCenter` accumulates the `EOEvent` instances so they can be summarized and reported on. This allows you to identify which events occur frequently and/or which consume a lot of time. The `WOEvent` subclass extends `EOEvent` to record events about the application, components, and associations. The JavaWOExtensions framework provides two pages, `WOEventSetup` and `WOEventDisplay`, to configure event logging and display event information.

TIP There are also `EOEvent` subclasses that track activity (primarily fetching and saving objects) in the EO frameworks. This can be used to analyze and optimize those areas of your application.

Preparing for WOEvent Logging

We will jump right in with a quick guide to getting `WOEvent` logging up and running:

1. Set a password for `WOEventSetup` and `WOEventDisplay`. If you don't set a password, you won't be able to access these pages. The password can be set in the launch arguments, `-DEOEventLoggingPassword=secret`. It can also be set in code, usually in the `Application` constructor, `EOEventCenter.setPassword("secret")`.

2. Configure the events that you want to track. Go to the direct action `WOEventSetup` (i.e., `http://localhost/cgi-bin/WebObjects/Chap7App.woa/-1234/wa/WOEventSetup`). You will be asked for a password the first time in each session. Leave the *User* field blank; the *Password* is what you set in Step 1. Figure 7-7 shows the configuration page. The `WOAssociation` and `WOComponent` events are the ones of most interest to us.

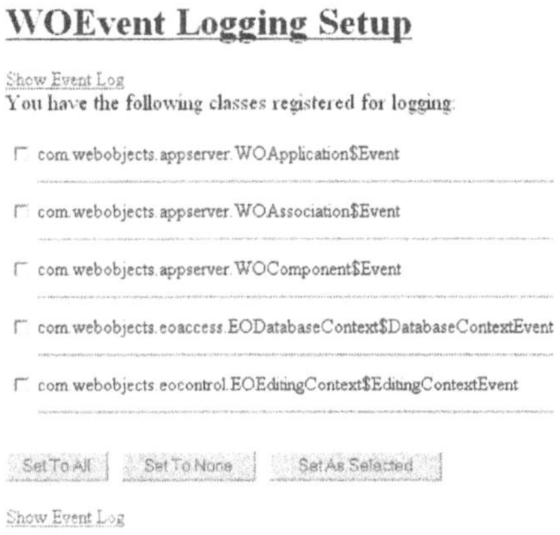

WOEvent Logging Setup

Show Event Log
You have the following classes registered for logging:

- com.webobjects.appserver.WOApplication$Event
- com.webobjects.appserver.WOAssociation$Event
- com.webobjects.appserver.WOComponent$Event
- com.webobjects.eoaccess.EODatabaseContext$DatabaseContextEvent
- com.webobjects.eocontrol.EOEditingContext$EditingContextEvent

Set To All | Set To None | Set As Selected

Show Event Log

Figure 7-7. *The* `WOEventSetup` *page*

3. Exercise your application to generate statistics. You will get the most accurate results by repeating everything several times.

NOTE Some of the documentation claims that you need to enable tracking of `WOEvents` by adding `-DWOEventLoggingEnabled=true` to the launch arguments. We have not needed to do this. The documentation also mentions that you should click around in the application to "warm it up" before configuring event capture because the event classes are registered dynamically. We've never seen that this was needed, but if something appears to be missing this is the place to start fiddling.

CAUTION As of WO 5.2.2, the WebObjects frameworks will throw an exception if you use `valueForBinding` in `awake` while logging `WOAssociation` events. This happens in the `awake` method of `SubComponent`. You will need to comment out the logging statement in that method if you want to use this page when event logging is enabled.

Displaying the Logged Events

Once you have exercised the application enough, you can view the collected statistics by going to the direct action `WOEventDisplay` (i.e., `http://localhost/cgi-bin/WebObjects/Chap7App.woa/-1234/wa/WOEventDisplay`). You may be asked for a password again; reply the same as you did in the `WOEvent` logging setup.

Figure 7-8 shows one mode of the event display. There are several modes, each useful for a purpose. Sometimes you need to experiment to find what works best for a particular need. You can find some documentation on some of these modes and how to read them at `http://developer.apple.com/documentation/WebObjects/Reference/API/com/webobjects/eocontrol/concepts/EOEventCenterConcepts.html`. For our purposes the last mode, Show Events Grouped By Page, Associations Only, seems to work the best.

- ○ Show all root events
- ○ Show aggregated hierarchical events
- ○ Show events grouped by page, then by component
- ○ Show events grouped by page
- ◉ Show events grouped by page, associations only

[Redisplay] [Reset Event Log]

Current Event Log:

based on 90 events -- spent 0 ms in 0 events in EOF, 24055 ms in 90 events in WOF

Title	Comment	Time	Calls	Relative
▼ com.apress.practicalwo.chap7app.SlowBindingPage		48070 ms	65x	
▼ com.webobjects.appserver.WOComponent$Event	com.apress.practicalwo.chap7app.SlowBindingPage	24035 ms	29x	
slowList : com.apress.practicalwo.chap7app.SlowBindingPage	slowList : pull	24035 ms	8x	
anItem : com.apress.practicalwo.chap7app.SlowBindingPage	anItem : pull	0 ms	24x	
com.webobjects.appserver.WOComponent$Event	com.apress.practicalwo.chap7app.Main	0 ms	2x	
refreshPage : com.apress.practicalwo.chap7app.SlowBindingPage	refreshPage : pull	0 ms	2x	
slowList : com.apress.practicalwo.chap7app.SlowBindingPage	slowList : pull	24035 ms	8x	
refreshPage : com.apress.practicalwo.chap7app.SlowBindingPage	refreshPage : pull	0 ms	2x	
anItem : com.apress.practicalwo.chap7app.SlowBindingPage	anItem : pull	0 ms	24x	
com.webobjects.appserver.WOComponent$Event	com.apress.practicalwo.chap7app.Main	0 ms	2x	
▶ com.apress.practicalwo.chap7app.Main		20 ms	25x	

Figure 7-8. *The* `WOEventDisplay` *page*

Some Practice Reading the Event Log

We've added a purposely slow page to this chapter's application so you can see how trouble spots are pinpointed. Start the application and click on the *WOEventSetup* link on the main page. The password is *secret*—no, really, that's the password. Turn on logging for the `WOAssociation` and `WOComponent` events and go back to the main page. The *Slow Bindings* link will take you to a page that is slow to render. Click some of the five links there, visit some other pages if you want to, and then head back to the main page.

Click on the `WOEventDisplay` link and provide the password when asked. Select the last mode, Show Events Grouped By Page, Associations Only, and then click Redisplay. Titles that appear as hyperlinks are aggregates of lower events. You can click on them to drill down into more detail. Expand the SlowBindingPage title and then the WOComponent$Event title. The result should look something like Figure 7-8. It is pretty clear from this that the problem lies in the `slowList` value. Looking at that method on the `SlowBindingPage`, we can see that we are correct:

```
public NSArray slowList() {
    try {
        Thread.sleep(2000);
    }
    catch (InterruptedException e) {
        throw new NSForwardException(e);
    }
    return slowList;
}
```

In practice you won't find the problem quite that glaringly obvious. A more common cause is a method that is a little slow being called from a binding method that is synchronized over and over again. The key to fixing this is to use manual synchronization and/or cache the value that is returned by the slow method. Bindings that result in large fetches can also cause this problem. Indexes on the database might help this, but usually the only way is to fetch objects in a batch and find some way to fetch fewer at a time. Do you really need all those objects right now?

Creating Custom Events

You are by no means limited to the events that we have identified in the previous section. It is quite easy to create your own events to precisely track where time is spent in your code. As an example, imagine that you have added PDF generation to your application and are wondering how much of a drag it is placing on the system. Creating a `WOEvent` to measure this is quick, easy, and effective.

To create a custom event you need to declare a subclass of `EOEvent` (or another `EOEvent` subclass such as `WOEvent`), create a description file with the event's type and subtypes, and register the event with the `EOEventCenter`. We will now go over these steps in detail, creating a class that tracks the amount of time spent in each phase of the request—response loop.

Creating a Subclass of EOEvent

Our goal is to track the amount of time spent in each phase of the request—response loop. A subclass of `WOEvent`, rather than `EOEvent`, seems like the obvious choice here. At the moment there is nothing else we need to add to this new subclass. We are just creating a new type so that it can be tracked.

```
public class RRLoopPhaseEvent extends WOEvent {
}
```

Describing the New Event

Each event needs a description file. This is just a dictionary in plist format that is named as *<class name>*`Event.description`. This file goes in the project's Resources directory. You'll also need to update the build.xml file if you're using Eclipse so that these description files are copied into the built product. To do this, add this line

```
<include name="*.description"/>
```

to the `resources` tag in the `build.woapp` target.

The event's description file defines the main event type (group) and optional subtypes that are used on the WOEventDisplay page. As an example, here are the contents of WOComponentEvent.description:

```
{
    EOEventGroupName = "WOComponent Event";
    takeValuesFromRequest = "takeValuesFromRequest";
    invokeActionForRequest = "invokeAction";
    appendToResponse = "appendToResponse";
    awake = "awake";
    sleep = "sleep";
    init = "init";
}
```

The `EOEventGroupName` key is required; it describes the group of events logged by the class and is used for grouping events for display. All the other keys are specific to the event class itself. These keys, the event subtypes, and the values are user-presentable descriptions. These keys are used for subgroups within this event.

The `EOEvent` class reads this file to configure each event. If it can't find a description file, it creates a default one consisting of a single pair. The key is the mandatory `EOEventGroupName` and the value is the fully qualified name of the event class.

It may appear at first that our example is reimplementing something that is already in `WOComponent.Event`. However, the `EOEvent` implementation to read the description file is broken in WebObjects 5.2.2, which results in the default description being used. We could not find any way to fix this. Instead we changed our event implementation to accommodate this problem. Let's hope this bug will get fixed soon.

Here is our method to create a new event. We use the `EOEventCenter` method `newEvent-OfClass` to create a new event instance. The page and component name need to be set manually. Finally, we mark the start of the event and reuse the `type` as the information parameter so that it gets used as the comment when the event is displayed (see the `WOComponent.Event` class for details):

```
public static RRLoopPhaseEvent newEvent(String type, WOContext aContext) {
    RRLoopPhaseEvent event = (RRLoopPhaseEvent)
        EOEventCenter.newEventOfClass(RRLoopPhaseEvent.class, type);
    event.setComponentName(aContext.component().name());
    event.setPageName(aContext.page().name());
    EOEventCenter.markStartOfEvent(event, type);
    return event;
}
```

Registering the Event Class

The new class needs to be registered with the `EOEventCenter` before it can be used. One way to do this is to create a static initializer block:

```
static {
    EOEventCenter.registerEventClass(RRLoopPhaseEvent.class,
                                     new RRLoopPhaseEventLoggingEnabler());
}
```

This requires the class to be referenced so that the class gets loaded and the initializer run. This is why the documentation advises you to "warm up" the application before enabling logging: if a class has not yet been loaded, you won't see the events in it.

The other way to register a new event class is to do it manually in the `Application` constructor. That avoids the need for warm-up, provided that you are aware of all the event types when you write the constructor. That is not always an option when using third-party frameworks. Manual registration is straightforward:

```
EOEventCenter.registerEventClass(RRLoopPhaseEvent.class,
                                 new RRLoopPhaseEventLoggingEnabler());
```

Our new event also needs to provide an implementation of the `EOEventCenter.EventRecordingHandler` interface. This is implemented in a static inner class that sets a static flag in the event class. Listing 7-10 shows the code that needs to be added to our class to implement this interface.

Listing 7-10. *How to Register a New* `EOEvent` *Subclass*

```
protected static volatile boolean _IsEventLoggingEnabled = false;

public static boolean isLoggingEnabled() {
    return _IsEventLoggingEnabled;
}

public static class RRLoopPhaseEventLoggingEnabler extends Object
    implements EOEventCenter.EventRecordingHandler {

    public void setLoggingEnabled(boolean isLogging, Class aClass) {
        if (aClass.equals(RRLoopPhaseEvent.class)) {
            RRLoopPhaseEvent._IsEventLoggingEnabled = isLogging;
        }
    }
}
```

Implementing the Rest of the Event

So far we have seen how to create our event, how to register our event, and how to enable and disable event logging. The rest of the class is shown in Listing 7-11. The `title` method is the only one we really need, and that is only to accommodate the bug loading the event descriptions. The constants and two static methods are just a convenience for classes that are instrumented with this event.

Listing 7-11. `RRLoopPhaseEvent` *Implementation*

```
public static final String TAKE_VALUES = "takeValuesFromRequest";
public static final String INVOKE = "invokeAction";
public static final String APPEND = "appendToResponse";


public static RRLoopPhaseEvent startEvent(String type, WOContext aContext) {
    RRLoopPhaseEvent newEvent = null;
    if (RRLoopPhaseEvent.isLoggingEnabled()) {
        newEvent = RRLoopPhaseEvent.newEvent(type, aContext);
    }
    return newEvent;
}

public String title() {
    return _componentName;
}
```

Instrumenting Code with Events

To instrument an event you need to check whether logging is enabled for that event, create and start the event if it is, and stop the event at the end of the relevant code. The pattern looks like this:

```
// Start event
EOEvent event = null;
if (RRLoopPhaseEvent .isEventLoggingEnabled()) {
    event = EOEventCenter.newEventOfClass(RRLoopPhaseEvent.class, type);
    EOEventCenter.markStartOfEvent(e, type);
}
// Code to be measured here
// Stop Event
EOEventCenter.markEndOfEvent(event);
```

The second argument to `newEventOfClass` is a key that corresponds to a type entry in the .description file. Or, rather, it would be if this worked. We also pass this to `markStartOfEvent` so that it appears as comments in the display. This makes it easier to understand. The `markEndOfEvent` method handles a `null` parameter, so there is no need to check whether event is `null` or not.

■ **TIP** If you need a customized display for your event, you can override the `displayComponentName` name method and return the name of your custom `WOComponent`. It should follow the formatting of the default display component `/Developer/Examples/JavaWebObjects/Source/JavaWOExtensions/WOEvent.subproj/WOEventRow.wo`.

We created a convenience method (`startEvent` in Listing 7-11), as the event setup is always the same and we need to do some special handling to accommodate the bug loading the .description file. Using the convenience method, the pattern for event instrumentation becomes this:

```
RRLoopPhaseEvent event =
    RRLoopPhaseEvent.startEvent(RRLoopPhaseEvent.TAKE_VALUES, aContext);
// Code to be measured here
EOEventCenter.markEndOfEvent(event);
```

The result of our custom event logging can be seen in Figure 7-9.

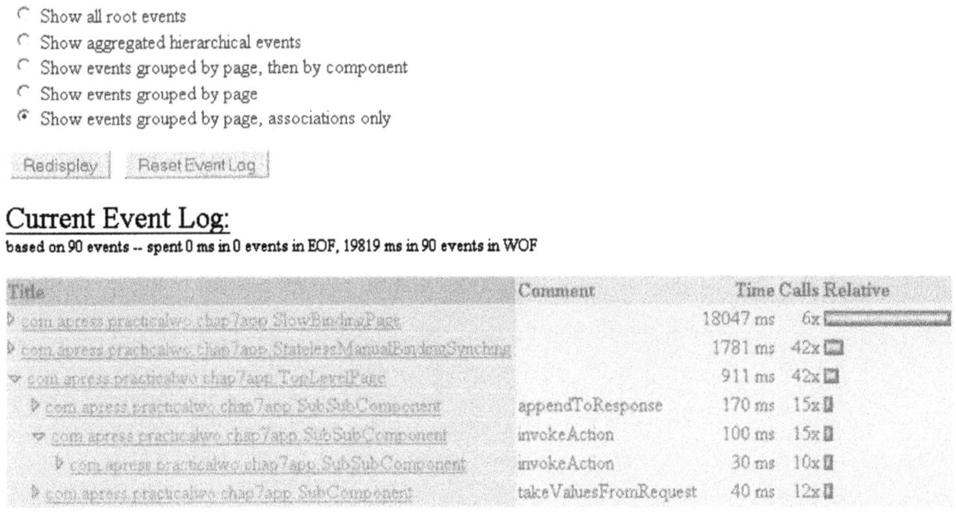

- Show all root events
- Show aggregated hierarchical events
- Show events grouped by page, then by component
- Show events grouped by page
- Show events grouped by page, associations only

Redisplay | Reset Event Log

Current Event Log:

based on 90 events -- spent 0 ms in 0 events in EOF, 19819 ms in 90 events in WOF

Title	Comment	Time	Calls	Relative
▷ com.apress.practicalwo.chap7app.SlowBindingPage		18047 ms	6x	
▷ com.apress.practicalwo.chap7app.StatelessManualBindingSynching		1781 ms	42x	
▽ com.apress.practicalwo.chap7app.TopLevelPage		911 ms	42x	
▷ com.apress.practicalwo.chap7app.SubSubComponent	appendToResponse	170 ms	15x	
▽ com.apress.practicalwo.chap7app.SubSubComponent	invokeAction	100 ms	15x	
▷ com.apress.practicalwo.chap7app.SubSubComponent	invokeAction	30 ms	10x	
▷ com.apress.practicalwo.chap7app.SubComponent	takeValuesFromRequest	40 ms	12x	

Figure 7-9. `EOEventDisplay` *from the custom* `RRLoopPhaseEvent`

Summary

We've covered a lot of ground in this chapter and hope to have given you enough information to tackle tough debugging tasks, such as the result of subtle changes in the component graph during the request—response loop and application slowness caused by slow binding synchronization. You now have the knowledge to add custom dynamic elements, manually synchronized bindings, and stateless components to your application. And in `EOEvent` you have a sharp new tool to measure the amount of time your application spends performing specific tasks.

CHAPTER 8

Localization

If it had been possible to build the Tower of Babel without climbing it, it would have been permitted.

—Franz Kafka

In this chapter we are going to add to our component knowledge by discussing how to build a localized application. We will examine the need for localization and various techniques for localizing a WebObjects application.

Parlez-vous Anglais?

The fraction of the online world population that speaks English is declining. As of 2004 64.2 percent of the online population were non-English speakers; in 2002, that proportion was 59.8 percent. The "English only" Web has lost about 5.5 percent market share in the space of two years. Even in the U.S., a large segment of the population cannot read English well enough to understand what they read, and prefer to access the Web in another language.

Languages are very location-specific. Many regions of the globe share the "same" language, but use it differently. The most obvious example is between the English in the U.S. and the English in England, but the same is true of other languages. There are significant differences between French in France and French in Québec, or Spanish in Spain and Spanish in Mexico.

Date usages vary also from region to region. 1/4/2004 will mean January 4th, 2004 in the U.S. and April 1st, 2004 in France: quite a difference if you are quoting a delivery date. There are even places that don't share our Gregorian calendar.

Then there are different currencies, and here again there are wide variations. Some regions have two commonly used currencies, and some currencies are shared between countries. Having a common currency does not mean having a single notation. Take the euro, for example: it is shared between 12 countries speaking at least 12 different languages, and they don't write their prices the same way! A thousand euros will be written 1.000,00 € in France and € 1,000.00 in Ireland (note the inversion of the punctuation symbols).

Text Encoding

Writing is a way of transcribing language in a systematic way so that it can be recorded and transmitted. As there is such an abundance of languages and cultures around the planet, it is not surprising that there are many ways of writing: a little research on the Internet yields at least 400 writing systems. Quite a few of them are archaic, but more than a few are in common use in some country or another.

Each writing system needs to be represented (encoded) in a way that computers can understand. Unfortunately, when computers were developed, memory was scarce and a very small encoding was chosen, just enough to be able to write English (i.e., seven-bit ASCII). This encoding can only represent 127 characters, which is not enough for many languages.

In the late 1970s and early 1980s a number of encodings were developed to take care of this particular problem, including the Western (ISO Latin 1) and Japanese (Shift JIS) encodings. These encodings represent a slightly larger range of characters, but require the user to maintain the association between the encoding and the language. The same binary value has a different meaning depending on the language! This user-dependent system was not very reliable.

This is why Unicode (ISO-10646) was created. ISO-10646 defines a 31-bit character set that enables the representation of all known characters of all languages. This is known as UCS-4 (Universal Multiple-Octet Coded Character Set), but this format is very awkward to use as it includes numerous `null` bytes and therefore plays havoc in C string manipulation. This is why the UTF-8 and UTF-16 (UCS Transformation Format 8 and 16) encodings were invented.

UTF-16 uses two bytes per Unicode character (except rare character signs that use four bytes). It is much easier to handle for software writers and is more space-efficient for most languages. Generally, "world language–aware" software will use UTF-16 internally. UTF-8 uses a variable number of bytes, in such a way that American English can be represented in one byte, British English occasionally requires two bytes, Western European languages require two bytes in most languages, and the rest of the world needs three or four bytes most of the time. It codes for the same set of characters as UTF-16. UTF-8 contains all of the characters needed for the language structure of HTML in eight-bit characters, which are the same as those in ASCII.

For Web use, our main concern, UTF-8 is usually the best choice. This enables the representation of all characters without relying on the browser detection of the page encoding for character conversion.

ISO-10646 defines the Unicode standard, but there are many other standards that you must be aware of in order to localize effectively. Here are the next in importance:

- Language names and codes are defined by ISO-639.
- Country names and codes are identified by ISO-3166.
- Currencies are identified by ISO-4217.

You probably use these standards without thinking: "FR" for France, "CA" for Canada, "en" for English, "USD" for U.S. currency, etc. Note that country and currency codes always utilize uppercase and language codes always utilize lowercase. These standards are built into Java, and most applications use them. Therefore, if you use these codes in the same way, you will simplify your life and that of your user. It will also be easier to interoperate with others.

Localize Early

Whenever we start a project for a client, we always ask the question of localization; invariably, the answer is, "All of our customers speak English."

As mentioned earlier, the market share of native English speakers is currently declining by some 2.5 percent a year. So inevitably someone is going to discover that "English only" is not good enough, and will come back asking for other languages. And this is where the problems start. Adding localization at the start of development, if it has been well thought out, is very easy. However, it is very difficult to do if the strategy for localization is not in place from the beginning. Don't fool yourself: if you are developing for the Web, chances are that you will have to localize your application.

CAUTION Our experience is that developing for localization adds a small cost to the overall development but that retrofitting an application to add localization is a major undertaking.

If the budget is so tight that you cannot afford to plan a strategy for localization, be very sure that you have raised the issue with your management and/or your customer, as this will likely come back and haunt you.

Detecting User Language Preferences

An important aspect of localization is the ability to respond correctly to the language request of the browser. All modern browsers support language preferences. With the request, the browser sends the HTTP header `Accept-Language`. This header lists all of the language and region codes that the user wishes to receive, in the order of preference.

Here is an example of an `Accept-Language` header:

```
Accept-Language: da, en-gb;q=0.8, en;q=0.7
```

This means that the user prefers Danish, but will accept British English and other types of English. The "q" notes "quality"; it is used to rank the choices, though, since the languages are in order to begin with, we can ignore it.

WebObjects will decode this field for you and create a language list in the session, ordered in the user's preferred order. However, this is a *language* list only; in creating this list, WebObjects strips out any regional (or country) information. In the example, the language list that WebObjects creates would be `Danish, English` and your localized resources would appear in directories Danish.lproj and English.lproj.

NOTE The language list items that WebObjects creates by default are always in English. It would be simple to modify the code in Listing 8-1 to return a non-English language list. Of course, your localized resources have to be in directories that match.

This works in most cases but does not allow fine-grained localization. If you need to distinguish between British English and American English, for example, you are out of luck; you will need to provide your own decoding. Doing this is quite easy, but you need to remember that most browsers will send a lowercase string so you must transform the country code to uppercase before you can match it against the ISO-3166 list.

To decode this information correctly you need to incorporate some code, such as that in Listing 8-1, in your session, and invoke it on session creation.

Listing 8-1. *Retreiving the Browser Language with Regional Information Included*

```
// Assume these mappings exist
NSDictionary countryCodeToCountryName;
NSDictionary languageCodeToLanguageName;

protected String removeTail(String aString) {
    String aCleanedString = aString;
    int index = aString.indexOf(";");
    if (index > 0) {
        aCleanedString = aString.substring(0, index);
    }
    return aCleanedString.trim();
}

/** Return the browser prefs in an array. */
protected NSArray browserLanguagePreferences(String aBrowserString) {
    NSMutableArray aList = new NSMutableArray();
    if (aBrowserString != null) {
        int index = 0;
        String aBrowserCode = "";
        String remainderString = aBrowserString;
        while (remainderString.length() > 0) {
            index = remainderString.indexOf(",", index);
            if (index > 0) {
                aBrowserCode = remainderString.substring(0, index);
                aList.addObject(removeTail(aBrowserCode));
                remainderString = remainderString.substring(index + 1);
            } else {
                aBrowserCode = remainderString;
                aList.addObject(removeTail(aBrowserCode));
                remainderString = "";
            }
        }
    } else { // Use the default...
        aList.addObject("en-US");
    }
    return aList;
}
```

```
public static String countryCode(String aName) {
    // the string is in the form xx-YY
    String aCode = "";
    if (aName.indexOf("-") > 0) {
        aCode = aName.substring(aName.indexOf("-") + 1).toUpperCase();
    }  else {
        aCode = "ZZ"; // Unable to determine country code
    }
    // The standard say that there can be another part after the country
    // so just trim it
    if (aCode.indexOf("-") > 0) {
        aCode = aCode.substring(0, aCode.indexOf("-")).toUpperCase();
    }
    return aCode;
}

public static String languageCode(String aName) {
    // the string is in the form xx-YY
    String aCode = "";
    if (aName.length() > 2) {
        aCode = aName.substring(0,2).toLowerCase();
    } else if (aName.length() == 2) {
        aCode = aName.toLowerCase();
    } else {
        aCode = "zz"; // Unable to determine language code
    }
    return aCode;
}

protected NSArray browserLanguages() {
    NSMutableArray _browserLanguages = new NSMutableArray();
    if (context().request() != null) {
        // So many different ways to specify the accepted languages!
        // Each adaptor has their own...
        String aHeader = context().request().headerForKey("accept-language");
        if ((aHeader == null) || aHeader.equals(""))
               aHeader = context().request().headerForKey("Accept-Language");
        if ( (aHeader == null) || aHeader.equals("") )
               aHeader = context().request().headerForKey("HTTP_ACCEPT_LANGUAGE");

        String aBrowserCode = "";
        java.util.Enumeration anEnumeration =
           browserLanguagePreferences (aHeader).objectEnumerator();
        while (anEnumeration.hasMoreElements()) {
            aBrowserCode = (String)anEnumeration.nextElement();
            String countryName = (String)countryCodeToCountryName.
```

```
                objectForKey(countryCode(aBrowserCode));
            String languageName = (String)languageCodeToLanguageName.
                objectForKey(languageCode(aBrowserCode));
            _browserLanguages.addObject(languageName + " (" + countryName + ")");
        }
    }
    return _browserLanguages;
}
```

This method returns a list of languages that can be given to the session using its setLanguages() method (this is probably best set in the session's constructor):

```
setLanguages(browserLanguages());
```

Although by default WebObjects only supports the use of languages (and not country codes), the session method can be used for the language/country combination without any problem. You can have in your language list entries like "French (Canada)" or "German (Austria)." You will then need to get your application to recognize these localizations. We will see that later.

Encoding in Responses

Character encoding in the browser is a shifting target. In theory, we should decode the Accept-Charset header and respond appropriately. In practice, all modern browsers support UTF-8 encoding (with the notable exception of Internet Explorer 4.0.3 and 4.0.4, but these should have been retired long ago). Instead of managing character encoding, it is much easier to just return a UTF-8 encoded page. This works with all languages and ensures consistent rendering of the pages. You still have to do some work with this strategy: you need to tell the browser that the page you are returning is UTF-8 encoded, and you must also encode it properly.

To give the heads-up to the browser, the best and recommended way is to add a header in your response:

```
Content-Type: text/html; charset=UTF-8
```

Unfortunately, WebObjects does not do this automatically for you. You will have to include a statement in your Application's appendToResponse() method to set the right header in your pages:

```
public void appendToResponse(WOResponse response, WOContext wocontext) {
    super.appendToResponse(response, wocontext);
    // This must be done after the page generation to override the default
    // header created by WO during the page generation.
    if ( _NSUtilities.UTF8StringEncoding.equals(response.contentEncoding()))
        response.setHeader("text/html; charset=UTF-8", "Content-Type");
}
```

As an alternative, you can also include a meta header in the page content. This works fine although it is not the method recommended by W3C.

```
<META http-equiv="Content-Type" content="text/html; charset=UTF-8" />
```

As this doesn't cost much, we do both just to be sure of the browser reaction.

Of course, after doing this, you must make sure that your components are UTF-8 encoded. To achieve this, you should look into WebObjects Builder preferences and change them to UTF-8 (see Figure 8-1).

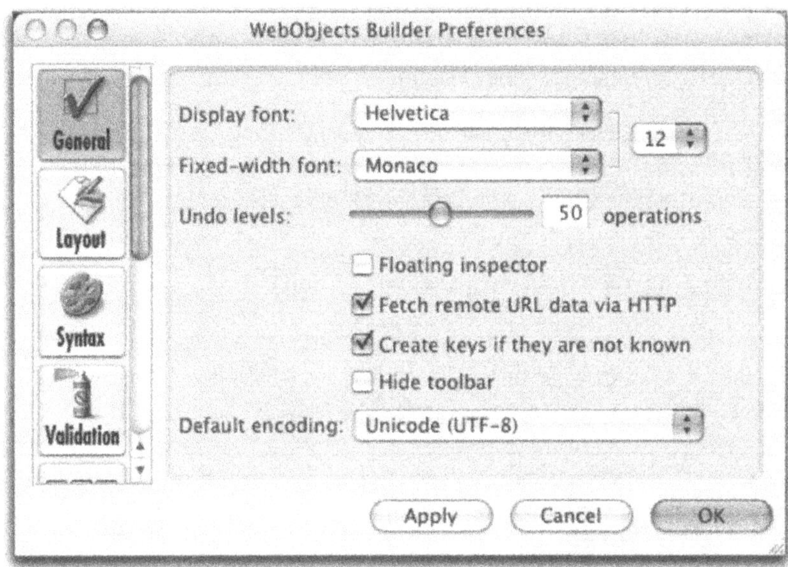

Figure 8-1. *WebObjects Builder Preferences*

Be aware that this will not change existing components. You need to change the encoding for those explicitly by doing a Save As and checking the encoding.

To check that your components are correctly encoded, open the .woo file in the `.wo` package and check the first line. It should read

```
{"WebObjects Release" = "WebObjects 5.0"; encoding = NSUTF8StringEncoding;}
```

If you follow our recommendation and go the UTF-8 route for all of your projects, you can change the component template once and not have to worry about it any more. It is located at

```
/Library/Application Support/Apple/Developer Tools/ ↵
    File Templates/WebObjects/Component.pbfiletemplate
```

Be aware that the wocomponent.wo package in this directory is empty: all of the files that are supposed to be inside this package's directory are, in fact, outside, in the directory that contains the package. The easiest way to replace this component template is to open WebObjects Builder, create a new component, and save it in place of the wocomponent.wo package. Then open the package and move the files inside to the directory containing the package. When you have finished this, all of your new components will be UTF-8 encoded.

The last thing is to set the WOResponse content encoding to UTF-8 so that WebObjects does not re-encode your carefully encoded content. This is done by overwriting WOApplication.createResponseInContext(). The code used should be similar to that in Listing 8-2.

Listing 8-2. *Ensuring That WebObjects Uses Your Encoding*

```
public WOResponse createResponseInContext(WOContext wocontext) {
        WOResponse woresponse = super.createResponseInContext(wocontext);
        woresponse.setContentEncoding( _NSUtilities.UTF8StringEncoding );
        return woresponse;
    }
```

■ **CAUTION** Beware of the two spellings. When setting the encoding in a WOMessage, the name is "UTF8" (or use the private constant _NSUtilities.UTF8StringEncoding). Everywhere else, it is "UTF-8".

Encoding in Requests

Now that we know how to send data to the browser, we need to examine the way we receive it from the browser. There are two ways of receiving data: as part of a form submission (POST) or as part of a request for a page (GET).

The POST requests are the easiest to handle: they are the result of submitting a form on a page that our application has previously generated. The browser submits the form in the same encoding as the original page. As we encode all our pages in UTF-8, this means that data that we will receive is UTF-8 encoded. All we have to do is force WebObjects to recognize the request as UTF-8 encoded. You can easily do this by overriding the takeValueFromRequest method of the session (Listing 8-3).

Listing 8-3. *Ensuring That the Request Is Properly Encoded*

```
public void takeValuesFromRequest(WORequest aRequest, WOContext aContext) {
    aRequest.setDefaultFormValueEncoding( _NSUtilities.UTF8StringEncoding );
    super.takeValuesFromRequest(aRequest, aContext);
}
```

GET requests are a little bit trickier. When doing a GET request, most applications encode some information in the URL query string, the part of the URL after the ?. The common scheme supported by WebObjects is to structure the query string as key=value separated by &. The problem occurs because URLs are supposed to be encoded with seven-bit ASCII. This means that all noncore ASCII characters must be encoded.

The current recommended way of doing this is to translate character sequences into UTF-8 and then use the %HH encoding for all unsafe bytes. Unfortunately, this recommendation (#2718) from W3C only came out in November 1999. Before this, most query strings were encoded first in ISO-Latin. The real problem is that these encoding schemes are incompatible. The good news is that WebObjects supports both schemes. The bad news is that the default encoding is the deprecated ISO-Latin one.

WebObjects makes an attempt at guessing the URL encoding, but this is very unreliable. In version 5.2.*x*, WebObjects introduced a new way of determining the URL encoding: by adding a key in the query string. It is now possible to fix the encoding of the query string by adding a parameter WOURLEncoding=UTF-8.

This can easily be done either by adding the key and value in your query dictionary before encoding or by adding a query binding to your WOHyperLink.

```
myHyperLInk: WOHyperLink {
    ....
    ?WOURLEncoding = "UTF-8";
}
```

With those precautions, all of your URL encoding should now work correctly.

Database Localization Issues

Most WebObjects applications use some kind of database to store information, and need to present on a Web page text retrieved from that database. Here again, UTF-8 encoding is your friend. Having the database store information in UTF-8 format is the best way of guaranteeing that there will be no error in the translation.

When dealing in localization, all databases are not born equal. The more recently developed ones (e.g., FrontBase and OpenBase) use UTF-8 by default, and therefore do not require any action from the developer. Other databases aren't quite so friendly.

For Oracle, you will need to set the default encoding to UTF-8, or if the database already exists you will need to convert it. We will leave this as an exercise for the reader. When this is completed, you need to add three entries to your connection dictionary to tell the driver that it should not convert the values:

```
NLS_DATE_FORMAT = "YYYY-MM-DD HH24:MI:SS";
NLS_LANG = AMERICAN_AMERICA.UTF8;
databaseEncoding = "UTF-8";
```

■ **CAUTION** Beware of column width; most databases (and SQL92) measure the database column in bytes, not characters. If your database is UTF-8 encoded, this is meaningless. If you enter a Chinese name with four characters, you need a column defined as VARCHAR(16) to be able to cover all cases. You will have to manually edit the SQL that EOModeler generates in order to provide this (another case where thinking ahead really helps). Since Java `Strings` handle UTF-8 encoding, failing to provide extra room in your table could result in a string value passing EOF's validation but failing to be inserted into the database due to being too long.

Sorting It All Out

You will commonly be sorting your data for display to the user. Again, English has it easy: you need to make a choice as to whether your sorting will be case-sensitive or case-insensitive, but otherwise there are no surprises.

Unfortunately, other languages aren't quite so simple. For example, in French, "e" and "f" are considered primary differences, while "e" and "é" are secondary differences, "e" and "E" are tertiary differences (tertiary differences are also present in English, obviously), and "e" and "e" are identical. This has a direct impact on the sorting order.

Your database will provide a sorting algorithm, also called a "collation." It is outside the scope of this chapter to cover database collations, but you should check your database behavior if you have unexpected sorting results. If you are sorting strings in memory, use the `java.text.Collator` class to provide for localized sorting. This will provide a result that is compatible with most any database-sorting algorithm.

The Biggest Problem of Our Time (Zone)

One of our most hated development tasks is dealing with dates and times. Never mind that Java has at least two different and complex date/time implementations, but the developers of WebObjects couldn't leave well enough alone and added a further (and buggy!) implementation on top of the original Java ones. Additionally, the assumptions we often make about dates or times (such as "dates or times are contiguous") often turn out to be false.

There are usually three time zones in a WebObjects application: the client browser time zone, the application time zone, and the database time zone. Usually you can just assume that the application and the database reside in the same time zone, but it is quite likely that at least some of the clients of your application do not. Normally, however, you don't really care what time zone your clients are in, since one time zone can easily be converted into another.

But now we get to the heart of the matter: WebObjects and the JDBC specification do not properly handle time zones in date/times. Basically, the time zone is dropped altogether from date/times! For example, if you assign the date/time "October 26, 2004, 11:00 AM PST" to an `NSTimestamp`, it will be represented internally as "October 26, 2004, 7:00 PM GMT" since `NSTimestamp` always uses GMT internally (if you don't specify a time zone with your date/time, `NSTimestamp` will use the server's time zone when converting to GMT).

NOTE The way that NSTimestamp represents dates and times is as a result of the way that JDBC works. We can't lay all of the blame at Apple's feet.

You may already see the problem: when converting back out of an NSTimestamp, WebObjects has no way to recover what time zone the date was created with. It only knows two things: the internal representation of the date/time in the GMT time zone and the server's own time zone. So, not surprisingly, when extracting that date information (such as when displaying it to the user), WebObjects uses the server's time zone.

Sometimes this little oversight in the JDBC specification (and consequently in NSTimestamp) is irrelevant. What do you care if an order comes in at 9 p.m. PST or at 1 p.m. GMT? Both times represent the same instant, so who cares if we lose some time zone information, right? Wrong: it gets more serious if you live in an area (as we do) that observes Daylight Saving Time. Date/times that occur when the time zone moves ahead an hour cannot be represented, while those that occur when the time zone moves back an hour can be represented in two different ways.

NOTE Actually, the problem is not Daylight Saving Time: it is any change in the server's time zone. Obviously, however, your server will not normally spontaneously change time zones ... until it is time to "fall back" again.

Unfortunately, there is no easy fix for this. If you need to know the exact time in a date/time, you are stuck with a workaround: store the time zone separately and convert it manually every time you need it.

Standard WebObjects Localization

The standard localization procedure in WebObjects is to create language directories, one per language to be supported, in the application bundle that contains the localized resources. A typical nonlocalized WebObjects application will have both a Resources and a WebServer-Resources directory. The Resources directory contains all of the components while the WebServerResources directory contains all of the graphics and the like.

A localized application will have a slightly different structure. The Resources and WebServerResources directories will contain a series of subdirectories, one per language. The result is a structure similar to this one:

```
MyApp.woa/
  Resources/
  English.lproj/
    MyApplicationWide.strings
    Main.wo/
      Main.html
      Main.wod
```

```
      Main.woo
  French.lproj/
    MyApplicationWide.strings
    Main.wo/
      Main.html
      Main.wod
      Main.woo
WebServerResources/
  English.lproj/
    Flag.gif
  French.lproj/
    Flag.gif
```

WebObjects provides a class (WOResourceManager) meant to provide access to all of these localized resources, so you don't have to handle traversing this directory structure yourself. Provided you place the file in the correct location, WebObjects will handle the language selection for you.

CAUTION As noted earlier, WebObjects expects languages and countries to have their English name. The French localization is "French" and not "Français"; the German from Germany is "German (Germany)," not "Deutsch (Deutschland)."

Java localization uses resource bundles that are postfixed with language and country code. As it does not bring anything more than traditional WebObjects localization, we do not usually worry about it.

An Alternate Localization Strategy

As mentioned in the previous section, WebObjects' traditional way of handling localization is through duplication of resources. When you create a component, for example, you need to duplicate it (modified for each language) into the different language directories. This offers a great deal of flexibility and enables the application designer to fine-tune all of the elements of the UI for each of the supported languages. It also allows each of the design elements of each page to be adjusted independently. The major drawback of that solution is maintenance. Each time you add new functions to a page, you will need to duplicate the UI work for each language.

There is another strategy for doing this: work directly with strings and localize them instead. In this approach, all localizable elements are abstracted as dynamic elements and loaded dynamically at runtime. Components are not duplicated, but a WebObjects tag replaces all strings and dates. The strings are stored in "tables," which are just resource files in the languages directories. Those strings of formatted text are then loaded at runtime using the resource manager, and the page is generated.

A typical method might look like this:

```
public String localizedString() {
    return WOApplication.application().resourceManager().stringForKey("myKey",
        "myTable", "myDefault", null, this.session().languages());
}
```

String files are property files with an extension “strings”. They use the classic structure

```
{
  AccessRightString = "アクセス権: ";

  AddButton = "追加";

  OwnerString = "所有権者: ";

  Read = "読み取り";

  Modify = "修正";

  Delete = "削除";

  GroupsInPopUp = "グループ";

  UsersInPopUp = "ユーザー";

  AccessControlDisabledString = "アクセスコントロールは使用できません";
}
```

CAUTION Tables must be encoded in UTF-8. And you should be sure to check this, as having the right appearance on the screen does not guarantee UTF-8 encoding.

Using the resource manager to load strings works well but requires a lot of code. Imagine having to write a method for each string on your page! Fortunately WebObjects allows us to build reusable components that make our task a lot easier.

The way to do it is to build a library of components that handles the string localization. We will look here at a localized class, `LocaleString`, which duplicates the functionality of `WOString` but uses a localized string (see Listing 8-4).

Listing 8-4. *A Localized* `WOString` *Example Class*

```
import com.webobjects.appserver.*;

public class LocaleString extends WOComponent {
    public String key = "";
    public Object value = "";
    public String default = "";
    public boolean escapeHTML = false;
    // Defaults to the application
    public String framework = "";

    public LocaleString(WOContext aContext) {
        super(aContext);
    }
```

```
    public String localizedString() {
        String aLocalizedString = "";
        if ( ! key.equals("") ) {
            aLocalizedString = WOApplication.application().resourceManager().
                stringForKey(key, table, default, framework,
                context().request().browserLanguages());
        } else {
            aLocalizedString = default;
        }
        return aLocalizedString;
    }

    public void appendToResponse(WOResponse aResponse, WOContext aContext) {
        super.appendToResponse(aResponse, aContext);
        if (escapeHTML) {
            aResponse.appendContentString(localizedString());
        } else {
            aResponse.appendContentHTMLString(localizedString());
        }
    }
}
```

The .html and .wod files are empty: they are not used because we append the localized string in code. Here is a typical example of the .html file:

```
<webobject name="displayedCategoryLevelNameString"></webobject>
```

and the .wod file:

```
displayedCategoryLevelNameString: LocaleString {
        default = "CategoryLevel Name: ";
        key = "CategoryLevelNameString";
        table = "CategoryLevel";
}
```

This strategy frees your custom pages from localization code. The only drawback is that none of the strings are visible in WOBuilder, making page building slightly cryptic.

You can easily extend the LocaleString component to also handle localized date or number formatting. If you need to show a date, for example, with a specific format, Java provides a very convenient format-parsing class, `java.text.DateFormat`. Using this class, you can construct a formatter that uses localized date format strings such as these:

```
LastPublishDateFormatter = "EEEE, MMMM d, yyyy '@' HH:mm:ss z";
LastPublishDateFormatter = "EEEE, d MMMM yyyy 'à' HH:mm:ss z";
LastPublishDateFormatter = "yyyy'年'M'月'd'日'(EEEE) '@' HH:mm:ss z";
```

These will translate into localized long dates. Here are the example formats, each formatting the same date:

Wednesday, March 31, 2004 @ 13:05:53 PST

mercredi, 31 mars 2004 à 13:05:53 PST

2004年3月31日 (水曜日) @ 13:05:53 PST

To use those formats, you could add code similar to Listing 8-5 to LocaleString.

Listing 8-5. Using Localized Date Formatting

```
// Assume these exist
String value;
String aPattern;
java.util.Locale locale;

java.text.SimpleDateFormat aFormat =
    new java.text.SimpleDateFormat( aPattern,  locale);
aLocalizedString = aFormat.format(value);
```

Strings, All Shapes and Sizes

The next element of a successfully localized application is the internal strings. The solution is obvious: never hard-code any strings in your application. Instead, use a constant and ask the resource manager to localize your constant with a string table.

The last element is to develop a strategy for storing localized values in the database. Suppose you are developing an e-commerce solution and you need to store the description of order items. You will need to store that description for each language you support. There are two ways of providing that support: storing the description as a serialized dictionary in a LOB or providing a lookup table. The serialized dictionary solution is by far the simplest, but does not scale well if the description is too long or the languages numerous (see Chapter 2 for a description of how to do this, as well as the benefits and drawbacks of the technique). As for most projects, the number of languages is likely to grow when managers discover that adding new languages is easy. We do not recommend the first solution.

The way we store localized text in the database is by using a lookup table, indexed by the locale code (i.e., the language and country code). See Figure 8-2.

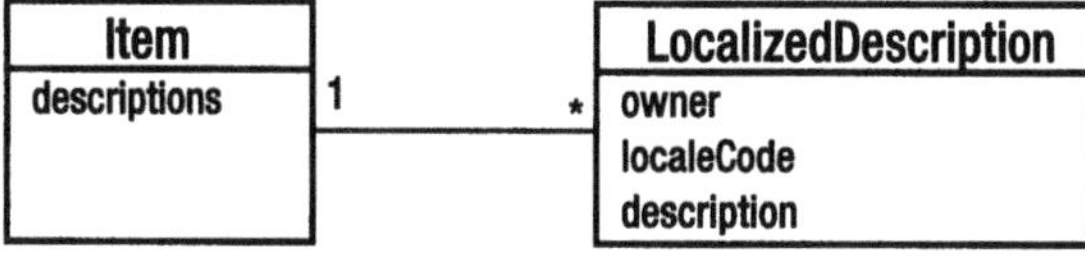

Figure 8-2. *Localized database texts*

You then need to add to your code the management of these lookup tables and some method of retrieving the value given a locale code. We will leave that as an exercise for the reader.

Debugging Issues

Here is a very strong note of caution. WebObjects provides a Rapid Turnaround mode. It is a very nice feature during demonstration. It enables you to quickly change some element of the UI and see your modification on the screen. This feature includes UI localization and it works great if you don't have too many locales. This feature will, however, bring your application to a crawl if you have many locales. So if you are building an application for the European market in 19 official languages, you will need to disable that feature. To do this, add to the launch parameters the following:

```
-WOAllowRapidTurnaround false
```

■ **CAUTION** Remember that Rapid Turnaround and Direct Connect behave slightly differently in the real deployment environment, so use them wisely or not at all. We pretty much shun Rapid Turnaround mode as evil.

One of the problems that need debugging is "forgotten keys." When you develop your application using localized strings with an intelligent default, you are bound to forget updating string table entries—i.e., the result is correct in English (or whatever your primary development language is) because the defaults are written in English, but the keys are missing in the table, and when you give the files for translation, they are forgotten. To enable you to debug this problem, you can create a subclass of the resource manager that logs the problems when they occur.

Summary

Localization may look daunting, but it is not really difficult. It is more a question of methodology and planning than anything else. And finally, don't forget that retrofitting an existing application for localization is much more difficult than planning ahead.

Bonne chance!

CHAPTER 9

Copying Enterprise Objects

Success is dangerous. One begins to copy oneself, and to copy oneself is more dangerous than to copy others.

—Pablo Picasso

Sooner or later you are likely to run into the need to make a copy of one or more enterprise objects. At first this seems trivial: just call `clone` on the objects. You will quickly discover that `EOEnterpriseObject` does not include the `Cloneable` interface. The closer you look at the problem, the more you might feel as if you have fallen down a rabbit hole into a strange world. Unlike most Java objects, enterprise objects seldom exist in isolation. Much of their meaning depends on the context of their relationships to other enterprise objects. Copying objects in such a situation is far from trivial. In this chapter we are going to look at three ways of copying enterprise objects, from the trivial to the fully featured. Along the way we will take a look at how to access object metadata through EOF. We will wrap up with a look at how entire object stores can be copied.

Understanding the Problem

Before we start designing a solution, we ought to make a survey of the problems we are trying to avoid. Copying attributes can be problematic, but the real difficulties arise when copying related objects.

Which attributes should not be copied? The first one that comes to mind is the primary key. The copy is a unique object itself and needs its own primary key. If the primary key is copied, EOF will not recognize that this needs to be replaced. If you provide a value for the primary key of a newly created object, EOF will be happy to use it. The database will not allow this, hence the copy cannot be saved.

Other attributes that should not be copied are those that uniquely identify the object. For example, it can be useful to base a new `Order` object on an existing, similar one, but copying the order number is not the right thing to do. Nor would you want to copy the user ID when creating a new user as a copy of an existing one. Attributes such as the date created do not uniquely identify the object, but they are unique to the object and often should not be copied.

Relationships present much more of a problem. When you copy a relationship, do you just copy the fact that object A is related to object B, or do you also copy object B? The answer to this depends on the context of the relationship and sometimes the context of the copy operation. Consider a task-tracking system. When using an existing task as a template for a new task, you want to copy the fact that the task is for a particular project. You certainly don't want to create an entire new project! However, when copying an Order you probably want to copy the OrderItems as new objects.

Some relationships should not be followed when copying an object. This is somewhat similar to attributes that should not be copied. Consider copying an article in a content management system (CMS) with the intention of basing a new article on it. It would not be appropriate to record the author of the original article as the author of the new article.

Then there is the question of when to stop copying. With many object models it is possible to navigate from one object to many, if not all, of the other objects in the object graph. If you don't take care of this, you can find copying one object turning into copying your entire database! Oops, that's not what you wanted.

Related to this is the problem of cyclic relationships. Consider the simple case shown in Figure 9-1. Copying object A copies object B which copies object C which copies object D which copies object A which copies object B which copies object C and on and on until we have no more memory. That is most certainly not what we want to have happen. We need to keep track of the objects we have copied to avoid copying the same object more than once.

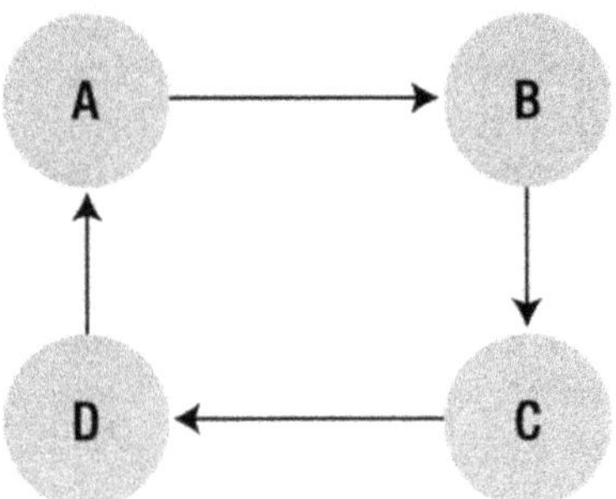

Figure 9-1. *A cyclic graph of objects*

Types of Copies

We will name and define three types of copies: reference, shallow, and deep. These are summarized in Table 9-1. A reference copy is a copy of only the reference to an object; it does not create a new object. Reference copying is appropriate for objects that should not be copied—lookup list values, for example. A shallow copy is a new object with the original's attributes and a reference copy of each of its related objects. This type of copy is suitable for things such as an OrderItem where the duplication of the order's product is not wanted. A deep copy is a new object with the original's attributes and a copy of each of its related objects. A deep copy can result in the creation of many new objects. A deep copy is suitable when the object being copied owns the objects it is related to. In practice, most objects will be copied by a combination of these methods.

Table 9-1. *The Three Types of Copies*

Type	Description	Creates New Object
Reference	A copy of only the reference to an object	No
Shallow	A new object with the original's attributes and a reference copy of each of its related objects	Yes
Deep	A new object with the original's attributes and a copy of each of its related objects	Multiple

Naive Copy

EOF is perfectly capable of copying enterprise objects; it does it all the time when faulting enterprise objects into an editing context. Perhaps we can use this to help us make shallow copies.

First we need the values from the object to be copied. We have a couple of choices here. `EOEditingContext` provides the method `committedSnapshotForObject` that returns a dictionary containing the object's committed values, the values last read from or saved to the database. The `EOEnterpriseObject` interface includes the method `snapshot`. This method returns a dictionary containing the object's current values, which may differ from the committed ones if changes have been made locally in the editing context. We think that using the committed values makes more sense. If changes are needed, they are better made in the copy than the original, but this is, of course, an implementation choice.

Now we need some way to get this dictionary of values into the copy object. Once again the frameworks provide for our needs. `EOEnterpriseObject` includes the `EOKeyValueCodingAdditions` method `takeValuesFromDictionary`. All we need to do to make our copy is

```
copy.takeValuesFromDictionary(ec.committedSnapshotForObject(original));
```

`EOUtilities` even provides an easy way to generically create a new instance with the method `createAndInsertInstance`. This method requires an editing context and the name of the entity to create. The eo object can provide its own entity name via the method `entityName`. Seek and ye shall find!

Combining these two gives us a three-line generic eo copying method:

```
public EOEnterpriseObject copy(EOEnterpriseObject original) {
    EOEnterpriseObject copy =
        EOUtilities.createAndInsertInstance(ec, original.entityName());
    copy.takeValuesFromDictionary(ec.committedSnapshotForObject(original));
    return copy;
}
```

Isn't that nice and simple? Too bad it won't work. Here's why:

- The primary key will also get copied, so the object can't be saved.
- There is no way to handle deep copies of relationships.
- Default values in the copy set in `awakeFromInsertion` won't get overwritten if the original object has a `null` value in the attribute.

EOEnterpriseObject Metadata

The information in an EOModel is used at runtime for creating, relating, fetching, and deleting objects. Not surprisingly, it is easy to access this information for our own purposes. The main objects involved in this are described briefly in this section and shown in Figure 9-2. More details can be found in the EOF documentation and in the Javadocs for the `EOControl` and `EOAccess` packages.

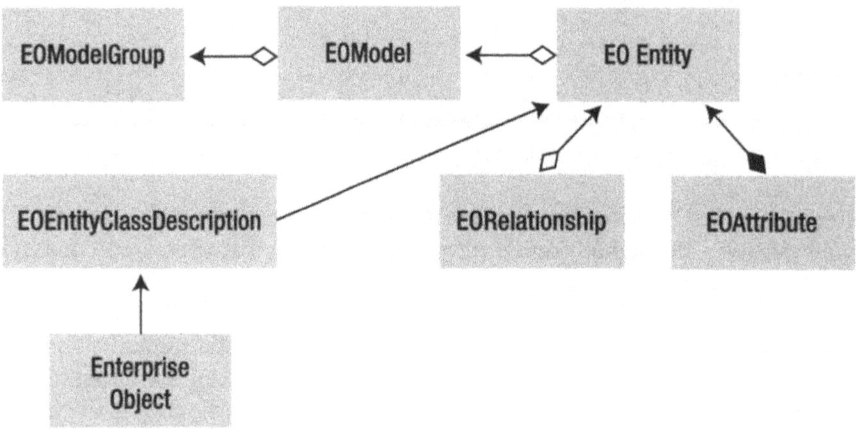

Figure 9-2. *The classes involved with runtime use of EOModel*

EOAttribute

An `EOAttribute` is the runtime representation of an attribute of an entity in an EOModel. It provides a name, a description of how to obtain a value from an external source, and some basic validation. It also indicates whether the attribute is part of the primary key, is used for locking, or is a class property. The last point is the most interesting for us. We only need to copy visible (class property) attributes. EOF will take care of the values used internally.

EORelationship

An `EORelationship` describes a directional association between two entities, based on attributes of those two entities. The two entities that make up a relationship can be in the same model or two different models, but they must be in the same model group.

EOEntity

Each entity in an EOModel is represented at runtime by an instance of `EOEntity`. An `EOEntity` instance knows which attributes and relationships it is composed of, which are collectively called *properties* in EOF terminology.

EOModel

An EOModel object represents the overall EOModel at runtime. Its most important runtime jobs are finding its entities, knowing its EOModelGroup, and storing the information needed to connect to the external object store. It can also determine the EOEntity for a particular enterprise object with the entityForObject method.

EOModelGroup

An EOModelGroup manages a set of related models in which no two models or any two entities have the same name. When a model in the group needs to find a related entity based on a name, it looks for that entity in the model group. Relationships can be formed between entities in different models in one model group. Relationships cannot be formed between entities in models in different model groups.

Every application has a default model group that contains all of the models in an application and any EOModels in frameworks loaded by the application. In most cases, this automatically created default model group is sufficient. However, you should be careful in assuming that the default is the only group in your code. If you create multiple EOF stacks you will also get multiple model groups. The EOAccess class EOUtilities provides the modelGroup method to determine the correct model group for an editing context:

```
static EOModelGroup modelGroup(EOEditingContext ec)
```

EOModelGroup can return the model group associated with an EOObjectStoreCoordinator:

```
static EOModelGroup
    modelGroupForObjectStoreCoordinator(EOObjectStoreCoordinator)
```

The EOObjectStoreCoordinator manages the object stores (usually EODatabaseContext) and editing contexts that perform data operations for the EOModelGroup.

EOClassDescription

EOClassDescription extends the behavior of Java classes by providing a mechanism for accessing metadata not available in the runtime system. This is the crucial difference between an ordinary Java object and an enterprise object. The most common class description used is the EOEntityClassDescription, which derives its metadata from an EOEntity in an EOModel. The information provided by this class is often useful in copying and it is an important player in the world of models and entities—a good class to be familiar with.

EOModel-Based Copy

How can we use this runtime metadata to support copying of enterprise objects? There are several paths from the eo to the metadata. A generic copying method will have no trouble accessing it. The metadata will tell us the name of the attributes and relationships to be copied. It will tell us which relationships are to-one and which are to-many. It will allow us to determine which are class properties and hence need to be copied, and which are private and should be ignored.

The metadata will also allow us to determine when to reference-copy and when to deep-copy relationships. The determination of whether to make a reference or deep copy of the related objects hinges on whether the related object is owned or not (Figure 9-3). This ownership implies that the owned object needs to be copied deeply when the owner is copied.

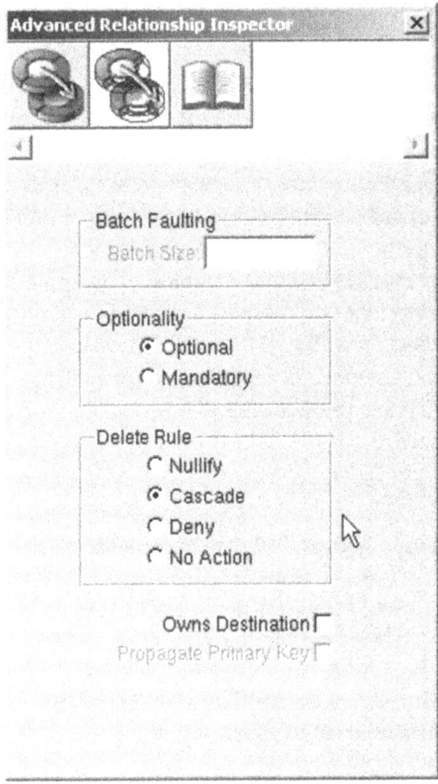

Figure 9-3. *The Owns Destination property of relationships*

The copy will be performed by a single method. The code for this copy method can be found in the `EOEntityCopier` class in the PracticalUtilities framework. Here is the interface:

```
public static synchronized EOEnterpriseObject
    deepCopy(EOEditingContext editingContext, EOEnterpriseObject original)
```

We pass in an editing context to allow the copy to be created in an editing context other than the one that the original object is in. This is useful to keep the changes isolated in their own editing context, or when the object is being copied from one EOF stack to another.

To get set up for copying we need to create a new instance of the same type. This will be the destination of the copy. We also need to get a reference to the metadata for the object being copied. We accomplish this with the help of two `EOUtility` methods:

```
// Get the entity like this to handle editingContext and original being
// in different EOF stacks.
EOEntity entity = EOUtilities.entityForObject(editingContext, original);

// This is the preferred method for creating a new class as it ensures
// that the object is matched to its correct class description and that it
// is inserted into an editing context before being worked with.
EOEnterpriseObject copy = EOUtilities.createAndInsertInstance(editingContext,
                                                          entity.name());
```

As we mentioned, we need to determine which attributes are class properties, as we only want to copy class properties. EOEntity can provide a list of all attributes or all relationships. These lists contain non-class properties as well as class properties. EOEntity can also provide a list of class properties, with both relationships and attributes in the same list. We use NSSet to determine which attributes are class properties by intersecting the attributes and class properties lists.

```
// Non-class properties will be handled by EOF, we should not copy them.
NSSet classProperties = new NSSet(entity.classProperties());
// Find the copyable attributes on the EO, ignoring non-class properties
NSSet allAttributes = new NSSet(entity.attributes());
NSSet publicAttributes = allAttributes.setByIntersectingSet(classProperties);
```

With a list of attributes in hand and key-value coding at our disposal, copying the attributes is a trivial loop:

```
Enumeration attributeEnumerator = publicAttributes.objectEnumerator();
EOAttribute anAttribute;
while (attributeEnumerator.hasMoreElements()) {
    anAttribute = (EOAttribute)attributeEnumerator.nextElement();
    copy.takeValueForKey(original.valueForKey(anAttribute.name()),
                                              anAttribute.name());
}
```

The relationships need to be treated similarly to the attributes in that only class properties should be copied. Flattened relationships are copied as the flattened relationship, not the underlying to-many and to-one relationships. EOF will take care of the underlying relationships for us.

```
// Copy relationships ignoring non-class properties. Owned objects are
// deep-copied, all others are copied by reference.
NSSet allRelationships = new NSSet(entity.relationships());
NSSet publicRelationships = allRelationships.
    setByIntersectingSet(classProperties);
```

Copying relationships is more complex than copying attributes. The copying logic depends on whether a to-many or to-one relationship is being copied. Copying to-one relationships is simpler but we need to handle null values. This aspect is easier with to-many relationships, as "null" values are just empty arrays.

```
Enumeration relationshipEnumerator = publicRelationships.objectEnumerator();
EORelationship aRelationship;
while (relationshipEnumerator.hasMoreElements()) {
    aRelationship = (EORelationship)relationshipEnumerator.nextElement();
    if (aRelationship.isToOne()) {
        EOEnterpriseObject relatedObject = (EOEnterpriseObject)original.
            valueForKey(aRelationship.name());
        // To-one relationships are easier to copy but we need to handle
        // null relationships
        if (original != null) {
```

Here, then, is where we make the distinction between owned objects that get deep-copied and the rest that are copied by reference. As the copy may be produced in an editing context different than the original, we must ensure that reference-copied related objects are faulted into the destination editing context. Recursion enters the picture here as we call deepCopy to make deep copies of the owned related objects. Notice that we use addObjectToBothSides-OfRelationshipWithKey rather than takeValueForKey to allow EOF to set any back-pointing relationships correctly.

```
            EOEnterpriseObject copiedRelationship;
            if (aRelationship.ownsDestination()) {
                copiedRelationship = deepCopy(editingContext, relatedObject);
            }
            else {
                copiedRelationship = EOUtilities.localInstanceOfObject(
                    editingContext, relatedObject);
            }
            copy.addObjectToBothSidesOfRelationshipWithKey(
                copiedRelationship, aRelationship.name());
        }
    }
```

Copying the to-many relationships is a little bit more work but follows the same basic pattern. What we need to do is to iterate over the related objects and process each related object as if it was a to-one relationship. The details of copying to-many relationships can be found in Listing 9-1.

Listing 9-1. *EOModel-Based Copy of To-Many Relationship*

```
        else {
            // Copy each element of the to-many array
            NSArray relatedObjects = (NSArray)original.valueForKey(
                aRelationship.name());
            for (int i = 0, count = relatedObjects.count(); i < count ; i++) {
                EOEnterpriseObject relatedObject =
                    (EOEnterpriseObject)relatedObjects.objectAtIndex(i);
                EOEnterpriseObject copiedRelationship;
                if (aRelationship.ownsDestination()) {
                    copiedRelationship = deepCopy(editingContext, relatedObject);
                }
                else {
                    copiedRelationship = EOUtilities.
                        localInstanceOfObject(editingContext, relatedObject);
                }
                copy.addObjectToBothSidesOfRelationshipWithKey(
                    copiedRelationship, aRelationship.name());
            }
        }
return copy;
}
```

In many cases this algorithm for copying is completely sufficient. If it suits your needs, this is what to use. It is efficient, compact, generic, and model driven—the best of all worlds. However, as with many generic solutions, it covers many but not all situations.

Here are some situations where this algorithm will not be sufficient:

- Owns Destination does not indicate all of the related objects that need to be copied deeply.
- The object graph contains cycles of deep copies: this algorithm will loop endlessly in this situation.
- An object graph can be copied in different contexts in which the decision to reference- or deep-copy depends on the context (e.g., copying an order item in the context of creating a new order item based on the original, and copying an order item in the context of copying an entire order in the context of creating a new order).
- Some attributes (e.g., `dateCreated`) should be taken from `awakeFromInsertion` and not copied.
- Related objects are set in `awakeFromInsertion` and need to be removed before copying proceeds.

The EOCopyable Interface

Our goal is to create a fully flexible copying mechanism. This mechanism should allow for the ease of copying of the EOModel-driven copy while allowing the object being copied to determine exactly how it should be copied. It also needs to transparently handle cycles within the graph of objects being copied. In short, we want it all.

We made two design decisions to support our requirements. The first was that we would maintain, and pass around, a list of the objects we had already processed regardless of how they were copied. This allows us to avoid the problem of endless loops caused by cycles in the object graph. The second was that we would give the object the responsibility to decide for itself how it would be copied rather than allowing the object related to it to determine the copy method. This removed dependencies on how the EOModel was constructed and allowed the type of copy made to vary based on the circumstances.

The foundation of this is the `EOCopyable` interface. This interface, seen in Listing 9-2, contains a constant and a scant two methods that define the process of the copy. The Listing 9-2 code and the remaining code in the chapter can be found in the PracticalUtilities framework. The `copy` method is the root of the copy process. This method is called on the object where the copy is to start to kick off the process. The `copy` method defines the overall logic of the copy process and is responsible for preventing an object from being duplicated twice. The `duplicate` method is the workhorse of the copy process. It performs the actual copy and returns the resulting object.

■ **TIP** If you want the copy to be made in an editing context other than the one the object being copied is in, just use the `localInstanceOfObject` method from `EOUtilities`: `((EOCopyable)EOUtilities .localInstanceOfObject(newEc, source)).copy(new NSMutableDictionary())`. EOF will take care of the rest.

The `copiedObjects` parameter is the key to avoiding infinite recursion due to cycles in the object graph. The keys in this dictionary are the `EOGlobalIDs` of the original objects that have already been copied. The object corresponding to each key is the resulting copy. A quick check in this dictionary determines whether an object has already been copied.

The `copiedObjects` dictionary is not limited to holding the copied objects. It can also be used to pass other information related to the copy. For example, the identity of the user who initiated the copy can also be passed in this dictionary. Additionally, this dictionary is used to communicate the context in which the copy is being made. The constant `COPY_CONTEXT` is for use in those situations where the type of copy depends on the context. It is intended for use as a standard key into `copiedObjects`. We'll look at a use of `COPY_CONTEXT` later.

■ **NOTE** The contracts in the interface are commented out, as Jass does not support contract definition in an interface. We add them like this as a reminder to the implementer of the interface to include these contracts.

Listing 9-2. *The* EOCopyable *Interface*

```
public interface EOCopyable
{
    public static final String COPY_CONTEXT = "copyContext";
    /**
     * Returns a copy of this object, copying related objects as well. The
     * actual copy mechanism (by reference, shallow, deep, or custom) for each
     * object is up to the object being copied. If a copy already exists in
     * <code>copiedObjects</code>, then that is returned instead of making a new
     * copy. This allows complex graphs of objects, including those with cycles,
     * to be copied without producing duplicate objects. The graph of copied
     * objects will be the same regardless of where copy is started with two
     * exceptions: if it is started on a reference-copied object or if a reference-
     * copied object is the only path between two disconnected parts of the graph.
     * In these cases the reference-copied object prevents the copy from following
     * the graph further.
     *
     * @param copiedObjects - the copied objects keyed on the EOGlobalID of the
     * object the copy was made from.
     * @return a copy of this object
     */
    public EOEnterpriseObject copy(NSMutableDictionary copiedObjects);
    //** require [copiedObjects_not_null] copiedObjects != null;  **/
    //** ensure [copy_made] Result != null;
    //          [copy_recorded] copiedObjects.objectForKey(editingContext().
    //                          globalIDForObject(this)) != null;  **/

    /**
     * Returns a copy of this object. Each EOEnterpriseObject should implement
     * this to produce the actual copy by an appropriate mechanism (reference,
     * shallow, deep, or custom).
     *
     * @param copiedObjects - the copied objects keyed on the EOGlobalID of the
     * object the copy was made from.
     * @return a copy of this object
     */
    public EOEnterpriseObject duplicate(NSMutableDictionary copiedObjects);
    //** require [copiedObjects_not_null] copiedObjects != null;  **/
    //** ensure [copy_made] Result != null;   **/
}
```

The EOCopyable Default Implementation

The `DefaultImplementation` inner class (see Listing 9-3) of the `EOCopyable` interface provides a fully functional implementation of the `EOCopyable` interface. This parallels the `DefaultImplementation` of `NSKeyValueCoding`, which allows this class to align well with the other framework classes.

The `copy` method controls the function of the copy process. The default implementation of the `copy` method first gets the `globalId` of the object to be copied. It then looks this up in the `copiedObjects` dictionary. If it finds a match, that means that a copy has already been made and nothing more needs to be done; the object from the dictionary is returned. If a match is not found, the object to be copied is passed to the `DefaultImplementation`'s `duplicate` method. The copy returned from `duplicate` is added to the dictionary under the key of the original object's `globalId`.

The `duplicate` method performs the actual copy of an object once it has been determined that a copy does not already exist and needs to be made. The `DefaultImplementation`'s `duplicate` method passes this task off to the `Utility` inner class's `deepCopy` method. Obviously a deep copy is not right in all situations. We'll get to how to alter this a little later. We'll also be examining the `Utility` class, so don't worry about the details of that for now.

Listing 9-3. *The* `EOCopyable DefaultImplementation` *Inner Class*

```
/**
 * This class provides a default implementation of EOCopyable that handles
 * the most common situations encountered copying Enterprise objects.
 * Debugging information can be turned on with the log4j logger
 * com.apress.practicalwo.practicalutilities.EOCopyable.
 * If you implement your own deep copy of relationships you should register
 * the new object before copying its relationships to so that circular
 * relationships will be copied correctly. For example:
 * EOGlobalID globalID = editingContext().globalIDForObject(this);
 * copiedObjects.setObjectForKey(copy, globalID);
*/
 public static class DefaultImplementation {
/**
       * Returns a copy of this object. The actual copy mechanism (by
       * reference, shallow, deep, or custom) is up to the object being
       * copied. If a copy already exists in <code>copiedObjects</code>,
       * then that is returned instead of making a new copy. This allows
       * complex graphs of objects, including those with cycles, to be
       * copied without producing duplicate objects.
       *
       * @param copiedObjects - the copied objects keyed on the EOGlobalID
       * of the object the copy was made from.
       * @param source - the EOEnterpriseObject to copy
       * @return a copy of this object
       */
```

```
    public static EOEnterpriseObject copy(NSMutableDictionary copiedObjects,
                                          EOEnterpriseObject source) {
        /** require [copiedObjects_not_null] copiedObjects != null;
                    [valid_source] source != null;
                    [source_EOCopyable] source instanceof EOCopyable;  **/

        EOGlobalID globalID = source.editingContext().
            globalIDForObject(source);

        copyLogger("Copying object " + globalID);

        EOEnterpriseObject copy = (EOEnterpriseObject)copiedObjects.
            objectForKey(globalID);

        if (copy == null) {
            copyLogger.debug("Creating duplicate of object " + globalID);

            copy = ((EOCopyable)source).duplicate(copiedObjects);
            copiedObjects.setObjectForKey(copy, globalID);
        }

        return copy;

        /** ensure [copy_made] copy != null;
                   [copy_cached] copiedObjects.objectForKey(
                                     source.editingContext().
                                     globalIDForObject(source)) != null; **/
    }

    /**
     * Returns a deep copy of this object.
     *
     * @param copiedObjects - the copied objects keyed on the EOGlobalID of
     * the object the copy was made from.
     * @return a deep copy of this object
     */
    public static EOEnterpriseObject duplicate(
        NSMutableDictionary copiedObjects, EOEnterpriseObject source) {
        /** require [copiedObjects_not_null] copiedObjects != null;
                    [valid_source] source != null;                  **/
       EOEnterpriseObject duplicate = Utility.deepCopy(copiedObjects,
                                                       source);
       return duplicate;
       /** ensure [duplicate_made] duplicate != null;      **/
    }
}
```

Making Use of the Default Implementation

The easiest way to make use of the default implementation is to use it in a superclass common to all of your enterprise objects. This common superclass should be a subclass of either EOCustomObject or EOGenericRecord, whichever one you are using now. Listing 9-4 shows an example implementation. It also includes a no-parameters version of copy that can be used to start a copy process.

Listing 9-4. *Using the* EOCopyable DefaultImplementation

```
public class CopyableGenericRecord extends EOGenericRecord {

    public EOEnterpriseObject copy(NSMutableDictionary copiedObjects) {
        return EOCopyable.DefaultImplementation.copy(copiedObjects, this);
    }

    public EOEnterpriseObject copy() {
        return copy(new NSMutableDictionary());
    }

    // Subclasses can override this to copy via a different mechanism.
    // This can be anything from EOCopyable.Utility.referenceCopy(this)
    // to a fully customized copy.
    public EOEnterpriseObject duplicate(NSMutableDictionary copiedObjects) {
        return EOCopyable.Utility.deepCopy(copiedObjects, this);
    }
}
```

Creating a common superclass for your enterprise objects is a useful technique even if you are not using EOCopyable. It allows you to add common methods to all of your eo classes without needing to use inheritance in the EOModel. This is yet another good reason to use EOGenerator. You can define the superclass name with

```
-define-EOSuperclass CopyableGenericRecord
```

This defined name is used in the template as

```
public class _<$classNameWithoutPackage$> extends
<$if hasParentEntity$><$parentClassName$><$else$><$EOSuperClass$><$endif$>
```

The EOCopyable Utility Methods

This class provides utility methods for use implementing EOCopyable. They handle the most common situations encountered copying enterprise objects. The DefaultImplementation uses them internally. The implementations of referenceCopy, shallowCopy, and deepCopy should be suitable for most enterprise objects to use for their duplicate method. However, there are some situations that can't be handled with this generic code:

- An attribute or relationship must not be copied (e.g., order numbers).
- An attribute or relationship needs special handling (e.g., dateModified should reflect when the copy was made, not when the original object was created).
- An enterprise object should not be copied the same way in all situations (e.g., should be copied deeply in one situation but be copied by reference in another situation).
- The relationships must be copied in a certain order (e.g., due to side effects in the methods setting the relationships).

In these situations you will need to write a custom implementation of the duplicate method. This can be as simple as invoking the default implementation and then cleaning up the result, or as complex as doing it all by hand.

The Utility class also provides lower-level methods that you can use when creating a custom duplicate method. These are newInstance, copyAttributes, exposedKeyAttributeNames, shallowCopyRelatedObjects, deepCopyRelatedObjects, cleanRelationships, and deepCopy-Relationship.

Debugging information can be turned on with the DEBUG level of the log4j Logger in com.apress.practicalwo.practicalutilities.EOCopyable.

The referenceCopy method is shown in Listing 9-5. There is very little to this method. It exists just to allow for more-consistent and easier-to-understand copying code.

Listing 9-5. *The* referenceCopy *Method of the* Utilities *Inner Class*

```
/**
 * Returns a copy of this object by reference. This is equivalent to
 * <code>return this;</code> on an EOEnterpriseObject. This method of
 * copying is suitable for lookup list items and other objects which
 * should never be duplicated.
 *
 * @param source the EOEnterpriseObject to copy
 * @return a copy of this object
 */
public static EOEnterpriseObject referenceCopy(EOEnterpriseObject source) {
    /** require [valid_source] source != null;
                [source_EOCopyable] source instanceof EOCopyable;  **/

    copyLogger.debug("Reference copying " + globalIDForObject(source));
    return source;

    /** ensure [copy_made] source != null;  **/
}
```

The shallowCopy method, shown in Listing 9-6, is a little more interesting. It copies the attributes by value and the relationships by reference. This kind of copy is useful when using an object as a template to create a new object. All of the real work is done with the lower-level methods newInstance, copyAttributes, and shallowCopyRelatedObjects. We'll get to those methods shortly.

Listing 9-6. *The* shallowCopy *Method of the* Utilities *Inner Class*

```
/**
  * Returns a shallow copy of this object; the attribute values are
  * copied and the relationships are copied by reference. This method
  * of copying is suitable for things like an order item where
  * duplication of the product is not wanted and where the order will
  * not be changed (the copied order item will be added to the orginal
  * order, not a copy of it).
  *
  * @param source the EOEnterpriseObject to copy
  * @return a copy of this object
  */
public static EOEnterpriseObject shallowCopy(EOEnterpriseObject source) {
    /** require [valid_source] source != null;
                [source_EOCopyable] source instanceof EOCopyable;   **/

    copyLogger.debug("Making shallow copy of " + globalIDForObject(source));

    EOEnterpriseObject copy = newInstance(source);
    copyAttributes(source, copy);
    shallowCopyRelatedObjects(source, copy);

    return copy;

    /** ensure [copy_made] copy != null;   **/
}
```

The deepCopy method, shown in Listing 9-7, is the most complex of the standard copy methods provided by the Utilities class. It uses the same newInstance and copyAttributes methods as shallowCopy but uses deepCopyRelatedObjects for the relationships.

There is one important thing to note about making a deep copy. As soon as the copy is created with newInstance it needs to be registered in the copiedObjects dictionary with

```
copiedObjects.setObjectForKey(copy, globalIDForObject(source));
```

You should follow the same pattern if you create your own copy methods that deep-copy one or more relationships. The reason is that the relationships are copied recursively, and if one of the deep-copied relationships can be followed back to this object (a back-pointing relationship in the simplest case), and it has not yet been registered as having been copied, it will be copied again and infinite recursion will result. Registering the copy before copying relationships will prevent this from happening.

Listing 9-7. *The* deepCopy *Method of the* Utilities *Inner Class*

```
/**
  * Returns a deep copy of this object; the attribute values are copied
  * and the relationships are copied by calling copy(NSMutableDictionary)
  * on them. Thus each related object will be copied by its own reference,
  * shallow, deep, or custom duplicate(NSMutableDictionary) method.
  * The copy is registered with copiedObjects as soon as it is created
  * so that circular relationships can be accommodated. This method of
  * copying is suitable for duplicating complex graphs of objects.
  *
  * @param copiedObjects the copied objects keyed on the EOGlobalID of
  * the object the copy was made from.
  * @param source the EOEnterpriseObject to copy
  * @return a copy of this object
  */
public static EOEnterpriseObject deepCopy(
    NSMutableDictionary copiedObjects, EOEnterpriseObject source) {
    /** require
        [copiedObjects_not_null] copiedObjects != null;
        [valid_source] source != null;
        [source_EOCopyable] source instanceof EOCopyable;
        [not_already_copied] copiedObjects.objectForKey(
            globalIDForObject(source)) == null;    **/

    copyLogger.debug("Making deep copy of " + globalIDForObject(source));

    EOEnterpriseObject copy = newInstance(source);

    // Register this object right away to handle circular relationships
    copiedObjects.setObjectForKey(copy, globalIDForObject(source));

    copyAttributes(source, copy);
    deepCopyRelatedObjects(copiedObjects, source, copy);

    return copy;

    /** ensure [copy_made] copy != null;
               [copy_recorded] copiedObjects.objectForKey(
                   globalIDForObject(source)) != null;       **/
}
```

Listing 9-8 shows newInstance, the method the copying process uses to create new object instances when not making a reference copy. The new instance is created with the EOUtilities method createAndInsertInstance to handle cases where the same Java class implements more than one entity. We encourage using this method as the standard way of creating any new enterprise object, as it is guaranteed to do the right thing.

We run into an interesting problem here. Some attributes and relationships can have a non-null value immediately after object creation. These values come from the effects of awakeFromInsertion and from destination objects created by EOF as the result of to-one relationships that are marked as *owns destination*. The attributes are not a problem; we can just copy over them.

The relationships are a problem. If we just copy over them the related objects will still exist and will get saved when the copy is saved. This will often produce validation or database exceptions. We could try to use them for subsequent copies, but what if the copy has already been made or should be a reference copy? To handle this as simply as possible, the method cleanRelationships is called to make these objects go away cleanly.

Listing 9-8. *The* newInstance *Method of the* Utilities *Inner Class*

```
/**
  * This creates and returns a new instance of the same Entity as source.
  * When an EO object is created it can already have some relationships
  * and attributes set. These can come from to-one relationships that
  * are marked as 'owns destination' and also from the effects of
  * awakeFromInsertion(). Preset attributes should be overwritten when
  * all attributes are copied, but the relationships need some special
  * handling. See the method cleanRelationships(NSMutableDictionary,
  * EOEnterpriseObject, EOEnterpriseObject) for details on what is done.
  * This method can be used when creating custom implementations of the
  * duplicate() method in EOCopyable.
  *
  * @param source the EOEnterpriseObject to copy
  * @return a new instance of the same Entity as source
  */
public static EOEnterpriseObject newInstance(EOEnterpriseObject source) {
    /** require [valid_source] source != null;  **/

     copyLogger.debug("Making new instance of " + globalIDForObject(source));

    EOEnterpriseObject newInstance = EOUtilities.
        createAndInsertInstance(source.editingContext(),
                                source.entityName());
    cleanRelationships(source, newInstance);

    return newInstance;

    /** ensure [newInstance_made] newInstance != null;
               [same_entity] source.entityName().equals(
                                 Result.entityName());     **/
}
```

The detail of the cleanRelationships method is shown in Listing 9-9. While the code is long, the pattern is simple. First a non-null relationship is located. Then removeObjectFromBothSidesOfRelationshipWithKey is called to disconnect the related object. Finally, the related object is deleted if it is not already in the database—i.e., if it was just created for this new instance. Newly created objects are detected with this test:

```
globalIDForObject(relatedObject).isTemporary()
```

Both to-one and to-many relationships are checked, though the to-many relationships will only have objects if they were set in awakeFromInsertion.

We'd like to draw your attention to the use of toManyRelationshipKeys, and to compare this to the code used in the EOModel-based copying method shown earlier:

```
NSSet allRelationships = new NSSet(entity.relationships());
NSSet publicRelationships = allRelationships.
    setByIntersectingSet(classProperties);
```

The EOEnterpriseObject method toManyRelationshipKeys is equivalent to classDescription().toManyRelationshipKeys(). As we mentioned earlier, EOClassDescription (and EOEntityClassDescription) provides an alternative way of accessing the information stored in an EOModel. By using toManyRelationshipKeys, we end up with keys (String objects, the name of the relationship) not EORelationship objects; however, we don't have to filter out the non-class properties, as that has been done for us.

Either way will work, but one is often more convenient than the other for a specific situation. For example, all we need of the relationship here is the name, so we chose the toManyRelationshipKeys way of accessing the information. Be aware that in EOAccess (and in EOControl to some extent) there are several different ways of accessing slightly different views of the same information. This can be very confusing at first.

Listing 9-9. *The* cleanRelationships *Method of the* Utilities *Inner Class*

```
/**
 * When an EO object is created it can already have some relationships
 * set. This can come from to-one relationships that are marked as 'owns
 * destination' and also from the effects of awakeFromInsertion() and
 * need some special handling prior to making a copy.
 * <ol>
 * <li>All objects are disconnected from the relationship.</li>
 * <li>If a disconnected object has a temporary EOGlobalID it is deleted.</li>
 * </ol>
 *
 * @param source the EOEnterpriseObject that copy was created from
 * @param copy the newly instantiated copy of source that needs to have
 * its relationships cleaned
 */
public static void cleanRelationships(EOEnterpriseObject source,
                                      EOEnterpriseObject copy) {
```

```
/** require [valid_copy] copy != null;
            [valid_source] source != null;    **/

copyLogger.debug("Cleaning related objects in copy of " +
    globalIDForObject(source));

EOEditingContext ec = source.editingContext();
EOEntity entity = EOUtilities.entityForObject(ec, source);

// To-Many relationships
Enumeration relationshipEnumerator = copy.toManyRelationshipKeys().
    objectEnumerator();
while (relationshipEnumerator.hasMoreElements()) {
    String relationshipName = (String)relationshipEnumerator.nextElement();
    NSArray relatedObjects = (NSArray) copy.valueForKey(relationshipName);

    if (relatedObjects.count() > 0) {
        EORelationship relationship = entity.
            relationshipNamed(relationshipName);

        copyLogger.debug("Removing objects in to-many relationship "
            + relationshipName);

        Enumeration relatedObjectEnumerator = new NSArray(relatedObjects).
            objectEnumerator();
        while (relatedObjectEnumerator.hasMoreElements()){
            EOEnterpriseObject relatedObject = (EOEnterpriseObject)
                relatedObjectEnumerator.nextElement();

            copy.removeObjectFromBothSidesOfRelationshipWithKey(
                relatedObject, relationshipName);
            if (globalIDForObject(relatedObject).isTemporary()) {
                ec.deleteObject(relatedObject);
            }
        }
    }
}

// To-one relationships
relationshipEnumerator =  copy.toOneRelationshipKeys().objectEnumerator();
while (relationshipEnumerator.hasMoreElements()) {
    String relationshipName = (String)relationshipEnumerator.nextElement();
    EOEnterpriseObject relatedObject = (EOEnterpriseObject) copy.
        valueForKey(relationshipName);
    if (relatedObject != null) {
        copyLogger.debug("Removing object in to-one relationship " +
            relationshipName);
```

```
                copy.removeObjectFromBothSidesOfRelationshipWithKey(
                    relatedObject, relationshipName);
                if (globalIDForObject(relatedObject).isTemporary()) {
                    source.editingContext().deleteObject(relatedObject);
                }
            }
        }
    }
```

At this point in the copy we have a newly created instance cleaned of any automatically populated relationships. It's time to look at copying the attributes. Listing 9-10 shows the `copyAttributes` method.

It would be nice if we could just bulk-copy the attributes with a nifty use of a key-value coding extension:

```
NSArray classAttributes = source.attributeKeys();
destination.takeValuesFromDictionary(source.valuesForKeys(classAttributes));
```

However, our life is just not that easy. Although making primary and foreign keys class properties is considered a poor design choice, it still is done for various reasons. We don't want to copy these exposed keys any more than we want to keep automatically created related objects. If we were to copy an exposed primary key, EOF would not replace it with a new one and the save would fail at the database level due to duplicated primary keys. The exposed foreign keys should be `null` after `cleanRelationships` but we will also `null` them in case these utility methods are used in other circumstances. We don't want our code to be too dependent on what gets called and when it gets called.

Listing 9-10. *The* `copyAttributes` *Method of the* `Utilities` *Inner Class*

```
/**
  * This copies the attributes from the source EOEnterpriseObject to the
  * destination. Only attributes which are class properties are copied.
  * However if an attribute is a class property and also used in a
  * relationship it is assumed to be an exposed primary or foreign key and
  * not copied. Such attributes are set to null. See
  * exposedKeyAttributeNames for details on how this is determined. It
  * can be used when creating custom implementations of the duplicate()
  * method in EOCopyable.
  *
  * @param source the EOEnterpriseObject to copy attribute values from
  * @param destination the EOEnterpriseObject to copy attribute values to
  */
public static void copyAttributes(EOEnterpriseObject source,
                                  EOEnterpriseObject destination) {
    /** require [valid_source] source != null;
                [valid_destination] destination != null;     **/

    copyLogger.debug("Copying attributes for  " + globalIDForObject(source));
```

```
    NSArray exposedKeyAttributeNames = exposedKeyAttributeNames(source);
    Enumeration attributeNameEnumerator = source.attributeKeys().
        objectEnumerator();
    while (attributeNameEnumerator.hasMoreElements()) {
        String attributeName = (String)attributeNameEnumerator.nextElement();

        if (exposedKeyAttributeNames.containsObject(attributeName)) {
            copyLogger.debug("Nulling exposed key " + attributeName);
            destination.takeStoredValueForKey(null, attributeName);
        }
        else {
            copyLogger.debug("Copying attribute " + attributeName + ", value "
                + source.valueForKey(attributeName));
            destination.takeStoredValueForKey(
                source.storedValueForKey(attributeName), attributeName);
        }
    }
}
```

The `copyAttributes` method relies on the `exposedKeyAttributeNames` method, seen in Listing 9-11, to tell it which attributes should be copied and which should be set to `null`. This is a rather intensive process so, as an optimization, the results are cached on an entity-name basis. The cache is created using the lazy initialization pattern

```
    if (exposedKeyAttributeDictionary == null) {
        exposedKeyAttributeDictionary = new NSMutableDictionary();
    }
```

and checked for results cached under the source object's entity's name:

```
    EOEntity entity = EOUtilities.entityForObject(source.editingContext(),
                                                  source);
    NSMutableArray exposedKeyAttributeNames = (NSMutableArray)
        exposedKeyAttributeDictionary.objectForKey(entity.name());
```

To determine the exposed key attributes we must first determine the key attributes. This is done by creating a set containing the primary key attribute names and then looking at each relationship and adding its key attribute names as well.

Finally, we determine the exposed key attribute names as the intersection of the key attribute names with the public attribute names and tuck this away in the cache for later use.

Listing 9-11. *The* `exposedKeyAttributeNames` *Method of the* `Utilities` *Inner Class*

```
protected static NSMutableDictionary exposedKeyAttributeDictionary = null;
/**
  * Returns an array of attribute names from the EOEntity of source that
  * are used in the primary key, or in forming relationships. These can
```

```
 * be presumed to be exposed primary or foreign keys and handled
 * accordingly when copying an object.
 *
 * @param source the EOEnterpriseObject to copy attribute values from
 * @return an array of attribute names from the EOEntity of source that
 * are used in forming relationships.
 **/
public static NSArray exposedKeyAttributeNames(EOEnterpriseObject source) {
    /** require [valid_source] source != null;      **/

    // These are cached on EOEntity name as an optimization.
    if (exposedKeyAttributeDictionary == null) {
        exposedKeyAttributeDictionary = new NSMutableDictionary();
    }

    EOEntity entity = EOUtilities.entityForObject(source.editingContext(),
                                                  source);
    NSMutableArray exposedKeyAttributeNames = (NSMutableArray)
        exposedKeyAttributeDictionary.objectForKey(entity.name());

    if (exposedKeyAttributeNames == null) {
        copyLogger.debug("Checking " + entity.name() + " for exposed keys");
        NSMutableSet keyNames = new NSMutableSet();
        keyNames.addObjectsFromArray(entity.primaryKeyAttributeNames());

        Enumeration relationshipEnumerator = entity.relationships().
            objectEnumerator();
        while (relationshipEnumerator.hasMoreElements()) {
            EORelationship relationship = (EORelationship)
                relationshipEnumerator.nextElement();
            keyNames.addObjectsFromArray((NSArray)relationship.
                sourceAttributes().valueForKey("name"));
        }

        NSSet publicAttributeNames = new NSSet(source.attributeKeys());
        exposedKeyAttributeNames = publicAttributeNames.
            setByIntersectingSet(keyNames).allObjects();
        copyLogger.debug("--> Attributes " + exposedKeyAttributeNames +
                                  " are exposed, including...");
        exposedKeyAttributeDictionary.setObjectForKey(exposedKeyAttributeNames,
                                                      entity.name());
    }

    return exposedKeyAttributeNames;
    /** ensure [valid_result] Result != null;  **/
}
```

Now we are ready to look at relationship copying. The simple case, shallowCopyRelatedObjects, is shown in Listing 9-12. To-one and to-many relationships are processed separately but with the same process: the related object is identified, a referenceCopy is made, and the copy is attached to the object being copied with addObjectToBothSidesOfRelationshipWithKey. The call to referenceCopy is just to make the code more explicit and to provide a hook for extra processing that might be needed in the future.

Listing 9-12. *The* shallowCopyRelatedObjects *Method of the* Utilities *Inner Class*

```
/**
 * This copies related objects from the source EOEnterpriseObject to the
 * destination by reference. Only relationships which are class properties
 * are copied. It can be used when creating custom implementations of the
 * duplicate() method in EOCopyable.
 *
 * @param source the EOEnterpriseObject to copy attribute values from
 * @param destination the EOEnterpriseObject to copy attribute values to
 */
public static void shallowCopyRelatedObjects(EOEnterpriseObject source,
                                             EOEnterpriseObject destination)  {
    /** require [valid_source] source != null;
                [source_EOCopyable] source instanceof EOCopyable;
                [valid_destination] destination != null;
                [destination_EOCopyable] destination instanceof EOCopyable;
     **/

    copyLogger.debug("Shallow copying relationships for  " +
        globalIDForObject(source));

    Enumeration relationshipEnumerator =  source.toManyRelationshipKeys().
        objectEnumerator();
    while (relationshipEnumerator.hasMoreElements()) {
        String relationshipName = (String)relationshipEnumerator.nextElement();
        NSArray originalObjects = (NSArray)source.valueForKey(relationshipName);

        copyLogger.debug("Copying " + originalObjects.count() +
            " for relationship " + relationshipName);

        for (int i = 0, count = originalObjects.count(); i < count; i++) {
            EOEnterpriseObject originalRelated =  (EOEnterpriseObject)
                originalObjects.objectAtIndex(i);
            destination.addObjectToBothSidesOfRelationshipWithKey(
                referenceCopy(originalRelated), relationshipName);
        }
    }
```

```
    relationshipEnumerator = source.toOneRelationshipKeys().objectEnumerator();
    while (relationshipEnumerator.hasMoreElements()) {
        String relationshipName = (String)relationshipEnumerator.nextElement();
        EOEnterpriseObject originalRelated = (EOEnterpriseObject)source.
            valueForKey(relationshipName);
        if (originalRelated != null) {
            copyLogger.debug("Copying object for relationship " +
                relationshipName);
            destination.addObjectToBothSidesOfRelationshipWithKey(
                referenceCopy(originalRelated), relationshipName);
        }
    }
}
```

The counterpart to shallowCopyRelatedObjects is deepCopyRelatedObjects, shown in Listing 9-13. This method uses deepCopyRelationship to handle copying to-one and to-many relationships in a uniform manner. In this situation we want the actual EORelationship objects, not just the names, and we want both to-one and to-many relationships. EOClassDescription does not provide this directly so we take it from the object's EOEntity.

Listing 9-13. *The* deepCopyRelatedObjects *Method of the* Utilities *Inner Class*

```
/**
 * This copies related objects from the source EOEnterpriseObject to the
 * destination by calling deepCopyRelationship on them. It can be used
 * when creating custom implementations of the duplicate() method in
 * EOCopyable. Only relationships which are class properties are copied.
 *
 * @param copiedObjects the copied objects keyed on the EOGlobalID of the
 * object the copy was made from
 * @param source the EOEnterpriseObject to copy attribute values from
 * @param destination the EOEnterpriseObject to copy attribute values to
 */
public static void deepCopyRelatedObjects(NSMutableDictionary copiedObjects,
                                          EOEnterpriseObject source,
                                          EOEnterpriseObject destination) {
    /** require [valid_source] source != null;
                [source_EOCopyable] source instanceof EOCopyable;
                [valid_destination] destination != null;
                [destination_EOCopyable] destination instanceof EOCopyable;
                [valid_copiedObjects] copiedObjects != null;    **/

    copyLogger.debug("Shallow copying relationships for  " +
                     globalIDForObject(source));
    EOEntity entity = EOUtilities.entityForObject(source.editingContext(),
                                                  source);
```

```
        Enumeration relationshipEnumerator = entity.relationships().
            objectEnumerator();
        while (relationshipEnumerator.hasMoreElements()) {
            EORelationship relationship = (EORelationship)
                relationshipEnumerator.nextElement();
            if (entity.classProperties().containsObject(relationship)) {
                deepCopyRelationship(copiedObjects, source, destination,
                                     relationship);
            }
        }
    }
```

The most interesting part of the copy process is in the deepCopyRelationship method shown in Listing 9-14. This is where the recursion comes into play. The method is structured much like shallowCopyRelatedObjects shown in Listing 9-12. The crucial difference is that it calls copy, not referenceCopy, to get a copy of the related objects. Because the recursion goes back up to the root copy method of the EOCopyable interface, each related object will get copied by the mechanism that it implements in its duplicate method: reference, shallow, deep, or custom. The deepCopyRelationship method is most useful when implementing a custom duplicate method in which different relationships are copied by different methods.

There is an added complexity that must be handled for to-many relationships. This can be a little tricky to understand. The call to copy will continue the copy process as far as it can reach in the object graph before returning. Due to cycles in the object graph (as simple as a back-pointing relationship) and the way addObjectToBothSidesOfRelationshipWithKey sets both relationships, it is possible that the relationship we are trying to create has already been formed when copy returns. Therefore we must make an explicit test for this to avoid creating duplicates in the to-many relationships:

```
EOEnterpriseObject copy = ((EOCopyable)original).copy(copiedObjects);
if ( ! destinationObjects.containsObject(originalCopy)) {
    destination.addObjectToBothSidesOfRelationshipWithKey(copy,relationshipName);
}
```

Listing 9-14. *The* deepCopyRelationship *Method of the* Utilities *Inner Class*

```
/**
 * This copies the object(s) for the named relationship from the source
 * EOEnterpriseObject to the destination by calling
 * copy(NSMutableDictionary) on them. Thus each related object will be
 * copied by its own reference, shallow, deep, or custom
 * duplicate(NSMutableDictionary) method. It can be used when creating
 * custom implementations of the duplicate() method in EOCopyable.
 *
 * @param copiedObjects the copied objects keyed on the EOGlobalID of the
 * object the copy was made from
 * @param source the EOEnterpriseObject to copy attribute values from
 * @param destination the EOEnterpriseObject to copy attribute values to
 * @param relationship the EORelationship to copy
 */
```

```
public static void deepCopyRelationship(NSMutableDictionary copiedObjects,
                                        EOEnterpriseObject source,
                                        EOEnterpriseObject destination,
                                        EORelationship relationship) {
    /** require
        [valid_copiedObjects] copiedObjects != null;
        [valid_source] source != null;
        [source_EOCopyable] source instanceof EOCopyable;
        [valid_destination] destination != null;
        [destination_EOCopyable] destination instanceof EOCopyable;
        [valid_relationship] relationship != null;  **/

    String relationshipName = relationship.name();
    if (relationship.isToMany()) {
         copyLogger.debug("Copying 2-M relationship " + relationshipName);
         copyLogger.debug("        from " + globalIDForObject(source));

        NSArray originalObjects = (NSArray)source.valueForKey(relationshipName);
        NSArray destinationObjects = (NSArray)destination.valueForKey(
            relationshipName);

        copyLogger.debug("Copying " + originalObjects.count() +
            " for relationship " + relationshipName);

        for (int i = 0, count = originalObjects.count(); i < count; i++) {
            EOEnterpriseObject original =
                (EOEnterpriseObject)originalObjects.objectAtIndex(i);

            EOEnterpriseObject originalCopy = ((EOCopyable)original).
                copy(copiedObjects);

            // This is a tricky part. Making the copy in the previous
            // copiedObjects line can set the relationship that we are
            // about to set. We need to check for this so that we do not
            // create duplicated relationships.
            if ( ! destinationObjects.containsObject(originalCopy)) {
                destination.addObjectToBothSidesOfRelationshipWithKey(
                    originalCopy, relationshipName);
            }
        }
    }
    else {
        EOEnterpriseObject original = (EOEnterpriseObject)source.
            valueForKey(relationshipName);
        copyLogger.debug("Copying 2-1 relationship " + relationshipName);
        copyLogger.debug("        from " + globalIDForObject(source));

        if (original != null) {
```

```
                copyLogger.debug("Copying object for relationship " +
                    relationshipName);
                destination.addObjectToBothSidesOfRelationshipWithKey(
                    ((EOCopyable)original).copy(copiedObjects),
                     relationshipName);
            }
        }
}
```

Tweaking the Copy Process

The most useful aspect of the EOCopyable interface is that it allows you to fine-tune the copy process in each object. In this section we are going to look at some examples of what might be done.

Listing 9-15 shows one such customized duplicate method. Two things are being customized here. The first is that two attributes, dateCreated and dateModified, should show the date of the copy, not the dates from the original. This could have been handled by copying the attributes one by one, but it was easier to copy all of the attributes at once using copyAttributes and then to replace the two values with the current time.

The second thing is that not all of the relationships should get copied. This particular copy method is creating a new object using the existing one as a template. Some of the relationships apply only to the original and have no meaning on the copy. To accommodate this, each relationship is copied manually using EOCopying.Utility.deepCopyRelationship. Using this method to copy relationships individually is also useful when implementation dependencies require that relationships be copied in a specific order.

Listing 9-15. *Custom Attribute and Relationship Copying in Duplicate*

```
public EOEnterpriseObject duplicate(NSMutableDictionary copiedObjects) {
    /** require [copiedObjects_not_null] copiedObjects != null;  **/

    // Handle circular relationships by registering this object right away.
    EOEnterpriseObject copy = EOCopying.Utility.newInstance(this);
    EOGlobalID globalID = editingContext().globalIDForObject(this);
    copiedObjects.setObjectForKey(copy, globalID);

    EOCopying.Utility.copyAttributes(this, copy);
    // These need to reflect the date of copying, not the original site.
    copy.takeValueForKey(new NSTimestamp(), "dateCreated");
    copy.takeValueForKey(new NSTimestamp(), "dateLastModified");

    EOEntity entity = ((EOEntityClassDescription)classDescription()).entity();
    EOCopying.Utility.deepCopyRelationship(copiedObjects, this, copy,
        entity.relationshipNamed("childGroups"));
    EOCopying.Utility.deepCopyRelationship(copiedObjects, this, copy,
        entity.relationshipNamed("configureGroup"));
    EOCopying.Utility.deepCopyRelationship(copiedObjects, this, copy,
        entity.relationshipNamed("files"));
```

```
    EOCopying.Utility.deepCopyRelationship(copiedObjects, this, copy,
        entity.relationshipNamed("folders"));
    EOCopying.Utility.deepCopyRelationship(copiedObjects, this, copy,
        entity.relationshipNamed("footer"));
    EOCopying.Utility.deepCopyRelationship(copiedObjects, this, copy,
        entity.relationshipNamed("sections"));
    EOCopying.Utility.deepCopyRelationship(copiedObjects, this, copy,
        entity.relationshipNamed("owner"));

    return copy;
    /** ensure [copy_made] Result != null;    **/
}
```

Here is an example in which a different type of copy is made depending on what the object represents. It would cause serious problems if one of the unique system groups were duplicated, so they are reference-copied. Ordinary groups are copied normally.

```
public EOEnterpriseObject duplicate(NSMutableDictionary copiedObjects) {
    /** require [copiedObjects_not_null] copiedObjects != null;  **/

    Group copy = this;  // Reference-copy system groups
    if ( ! isSystemGroup()) {
        copy = (Group) super.duplicate(copiedObjects);
    }

    return copy;
    /** ensure [copy_made] Result != null;   **/
}
```

For objects that should never be duplicated, implement the duplicate method like this:

```
public EOEnterpriseObject duplicate(NSMutableDictionary copiedObjects) {
    /** require [copiedObjects_not_null] copiedObjects != null;  **/
    return EOCopyable.Utility.referenceCopy(this);
    /** ensure [copy_made] Result != null;   **/
}
```

Earlier we mentioned using a "copy context" to control the behavior of a copy. Listing 9-16 shows an example in which either a reference copy or a deep copy is made. If the copy context indicates that the object is being copied as part of a template, then a deep copy is made. For all other cases the object is copied by reference only.

Listing 9-16. *Using the Copy Context to Control Copy Behavior*

```
public EOEnterpriseObject duplicate(NSMutableDictionary copiedObjects) {
    /** require [copiedObjects_not_null] copiedObjects != null;  **/
    String context = (String)copiedObjects.objectForKey(
        EOCopyable.COPY_CONTEXT);
```

```
    if (context.equals("template") {
        return EOCopyable.Utility.deepCopy(this);
    } else {
        return EOCopyable.Utility.referenceCopy(this);
    }
    /** ensure [copy_made] Result != null;   **/
}
```

Object Migration

Migrating objects between one database and another is a topic closely related to copying enterprise objects. The most common reason to do this is to move from one vendor's database to another, but it can also be useful when migrating data from one version of an application to the next if the changes are not too drastic. Moving data from one vendor's database to another can be quite easy with EOF if you have planned ahead and used prototype attributes. In this section we are going to look at three ways of doing this.

Using javaeoutil

Hidden in each developer installation of WebObjects is a little data migration command-line tool masquerading as a web application. This is javaeoutil (a.k.a. eoutil), found at /Library/WebObjects/JavaApplications/javaeoutil.woa. While this comes with WebObjects, it is not an official part of WebObjects. In short, this means that it is even more poorly documented than the rest of WebObjects. The real purpose of this application is to support the demos that come with WebObjects. However, with a bit of patience and coaxing, it can do much more for us.

First, a word of warning: javaeoutil is not intended to be production-quality code; it is just there to support the demo applications. This application has bugs, not all of the features work or work as documented. If it is not working for you, well, it might not be something you are doing wrong. That said, there is usually another way to do the same thing with a bit more effort.

Although javaeoutil looks like a web application when it starts, it is really just a command-line tool. All of the official documentation that exists is output when javaeoutil is started with a command-line parameter of `help`. A reformatted version of this is shown in Listing 9-17.

Listing 9-17. *The Documentation Output from* `javaeoutil help`

```
Command line utility to perform database and EOF oriented tasks.
Syntax: javaeoutil dump/connect/convert
  javaeoutil dump <model> [-source <source> [sourcefile]]
                          -dest <dest> [destfile]
                          [-schemaCreate <options>]
                          [-schemaDrop <options>]
                          [-postInstall]
                          [-force]
                          [-connDict <connection dictionary>]
                          [-entities <entities>]
                          [-modelGroup <modelGroup>]
```

```
This command reads data from <source> and dumps it to <dest>. The dump may
include bits of DML that create bits of database schema. The -source flags is
optional if only schema is to be created (i.e. no data is being dumped.) The
following is a list of possible values for each of the arguments in the
command:
  model       -- must be the name of an eomodel or eomodeld file
  source      -- plist or database(uses model to connect)
  sourcefile  -- name of file to read plist from
  dest        -- plist or script(both are written to stdout unless destfile is
                 specified) or database(uses model to connect)
  destfile    -- name of file to write plist
  entities    -- a subset of the entities in the model (all used by default)
  options     -- tables, primaryKeySupport, primaryKeyConstraints, or
                 foreignKeyConstraints
  postInstall -- looks in the userInfo dictionary for an array of SQL strings
                 to process after any schema creation and data dumping is done
  force       -- Do not quit processing after database error
  connDict    -- A substitute connection dictionary
  modelGroup  -- A list of models to create a model group. Allows you to use
                 models not in a framework. Model names must be absolute paths.

Example: javaeoutil dump Movies.eomodeld \
          -source plist \
          -dest database \
          -schemaCreate tables primaryKeySupport foreignKeyConstraints \
          < MovieData.plist
Creates the tables in the database, reads data in plist format from stdin,
stores the data in the database listed in the connection dictionary of model,
creates primary key support in the database, and creates foreign key
constraints corresponding to the relationship definitions.


javaeoutil convert <model> <adaptorName> <connectionDictionary> <outFileName>
This command converts the type mapping in a model for the data source specified
by the connection dictionary URL. The connection dictionary in the new model is
set to connectionDictionary.

  model                -- must be the name of an eomodel or eomodeld file
  adaptorName          -- JDBC or JNDI
  connectionDictionary -- string in property list format specifying the URL for
                          the data source (required) and username and password
                          (if required by that data source)
  outFileName          -- the name of a directory to write the converted model


Example: javaeoutil convert Movies.eomodeld JDBC \
          '{ URL = jdbc:openbase://127.0.0.1/Movies; }' \
          M.eomodeld
```

```
Converts types in Movies.eomodeld file to OpenBase types and writes the
converted model to ./M.eomodel


javaeoutil connect <adaptorName> <connectionDictionary>
This command attempts to connect to a data source using the adaptor named
adaptorName with connectionDictionary. It returns an exit status of 0 if
successful and 1 otherwise. This is primarily useful for scripts.

  model                -- must be the name of an eomodel or eomodeld file
  adaptorName          -- JDBC or JNDI
  connectionDictionary -- string in property list format specifying the URL for
                          the data source (required) and username and password
                          (if required by that data source)

Example: javaeoutil connect JDBC
           '{ URL = "jdbc:oracle:thin:@sqasun2:1521:sqa"; username = movies; \
            password = movies; }'
 Attempts to connect to an Oracle database via JDBC at the given URL.


javaeoutil help
      Prints this text.
```

We have had the most success with the dump command. We have had problems with the connDict parameter in the past. We have found it easiest to just have copies of the model that contain the correct connection information. The modelGroup parameter has also given us trouble. We wanted to use this to include prototypes and models in other frameworks. In the end we copied these into the model that we used with javaeoutil. That said, we have not used javaeoutil recently and some of these may function correctly now.

Another problem with javaeoutil has more to do with how EOF works. The problem is that it is very memory intensive. It is quite willing to pull the entire database into memory. If you have more data than free memory, this will not be a success. For larger databases, we found it necessary to give javaeoutil a lot of memory and to process only one entity at a time. To make this work, you need to drop all of the foreign key constraints on the destination database, import the data, and then re-create the foreign key constraints. This is because you are loading one table at a time and foreign keys may reference data in a table that has not yet been loaded.

Listing 9-18 shows part of a script that exports and imports the data for one entity. Notice that two different models, which have two different connection dictionaries, are used. The maximum heap size will need to be increased if you have a lot of data.

Listing 9-18. *Example Script to Export and Import Data for the User Entity*

```
# Export User Data
./javaeoutil \
  -Xms128m -Xmx256m \
  dump ~/Conversion/SourceModel.eomodeld \
  -source database \
  -dest plist ~/Conversion/User_Data.plist \
  -entities User

# Import User Data
./javaeoutil \
  -Xms128m -Xmx256m \
  dump ~/Conversion/DestinationModel.eomodeld \
  -source plist ~/Conversion/User_Data.plist \
  -dest database
```

Using BulkMover

Jesse Barnum of 360works created an application that uses raw rows and EOF to extract all of the data from one database (based on its EOModel) and transfer it to another database (using a different EOModel). This has an advantage over javaeoutil in that it comes with full source code so that you can tweak or extend it to meet your needs. You can get BulkMover at `http://www.360works.com/developertools.html`.

EOF is not an ideal tool for moving large amounts of data, as it is not tuned for bulk inserts and can be memory intensive. BulkMover might also need some work to be able to handle large data sets.

Using Dedicated Migration Tool

The final solution, for when all else fails, is to plunk down your cash for a real data migration tool. We have never used it, but we have heard good things about SRTransport; see `http://www.schemaresearch.com/products/srtransport/`.

If you are looking for an open source alternative, have a look at the Database Migration Tool (dbmt). This is a tool written in Java to migrate data from one schema to another via JDBC. It is reported to be at a "stable/production" state. An XML file defines the source and target schemas and configures the migration and any needed transformations of the data. See `http://sourceforge.net/projects/dbmt/`.

Summary

We have shown three methods of copying enterprise objects in this chapter. No matter what your copying needs, one or more of them will meet your requirements. In the process we have introduced the classes that are used for runtime access to the metadata stored in EOModels. This is useful for a lot more than copying. You will find uses for this again and again. Finally, we have looked at some ways to migrate objects between databases. We have shown how this can be done with a tool that comes with WebObjects, and identified some free and some commercial alternatives.

CHAPTER 10

WebObjects in a J2EE World

WebObjects can be considered the granddaddy of the application server world. It is certainly the most mature product of the bunch, having been demonstrated by NeXT in 1995 and officially released in March 1996. Microsoft Active Server Page technology debuted at the end of 1996. Java also had its introduction in May 1995.

Since then, the software universe has undergone huge changes and large paradigm shifts. Java has been in a continual state of evolution. The core API has grown to several hundred classes and interfaces.

WebObjects, on the other hand, has evolved at a much slower and deliberate pace, in part because Apple hasn't committed the resources needed to bring WebObjects to the masses and because they haven't had to! WebObjects/EOF has enjoyed a very strong architectural advantage for the past ten years that other technologies are just starting to emulate. As we delve deeper into this chapter, you will gain a greater appreciation for the sheer genius of the WebObjects developers.

In this chapter we will compare and contrast WebObjects technology with the J2EE (Java 2 Enterprise Edition) world and show the similarities and the differences between them. We will step behind the scenes and learn how a J2EE application works and how our WebObjects applications can peacefully coexist with other J2EE applications in the corporate data center. Finally, we will explore the practical side of building and deploying a simple J2EE application using WebObjects and JavaServer Pages.

What Is J2EE and Why Is It Important?

When people talk about Java 2 Enterprise Edition (J2EE), they often only think of Enterprise JavaBeans (EJB). In fact, J2EE has turned into a catchall brand for a wide range of seemingly unrelated technologies. Some of the current J2EE technologies are

Common Object Request Broker Architecture (CORBA)

Enterprise JavaBeans (EJB)

Extensible Markup Language (XML)

Java Authentication and Authorization Service (JAAS)

Java Cryptography Extension (JCE)

Java Database Connectivity (JDBC)

Java Mail

Java Message Service (JMS)

Java Naming and Directory Interface (JNDI)

Java Secure Socket Extension (JSSE)

Java Servlet Technology

JavaServer Faces

JavaServer Pages (JSP)

Web Services

The list continues to grow with no end in sight. All of the major software vendors (except for one who shall remain nameless) have developed products that provide compliant implementations of most of the J2EE technologies.

The promise of J2EE is to provide a vendor-neutral, platform-independent foundation for developing complex business applications that can interoperate with each other in a seamless fashion. To a large extent, Sun has succeeded—it is possible to move EJBs and Java servlets from one vendor's server container to another without much difficulty.

In order to continue to move WebObjects forward into the corporate development shops, Apple has chosen to embrace those technologies that provide complementary services and has added support for deploying WebObjects applications in J2EE-compliant app servers.

This strategy provides support for developers who need to answer the eternal question "Why do you want to use software from Apple?" and the related "Is WebObjects J2EE compliant?" Choose a technology from the list and say yes!

Before we get into the internals of J2EE deployment, we will go over a few of the more relevant J2EE technologies and discuss how they relate to WebObjects.

Servlets

The Java Servlet specification has been around for a few years now. The original intention of the Servlet specification was to replace CGI programming with Java code. The Servlet API provides the hooks to communicate between the servlet container and the programmer's code.

The Servlet API has familiar constructs such as session, request, response, and cookie. These constructs have direct parallels to the WebObjects world, as we will see later.

To a certain extent, you can almost equate a WebObjects Direct Action or `WOComponent` to a servlet. They both accept requests and generate responses that get served out to the requestor.

Servlets can be used to perform just about any server-side task you can think of, including form processing, business logic implementation, interface to legacy systems, etc.

Typically, servlets are divided into two camps: flow controllers and business logic engines. Flow control servlets are used to control access to the rest of the Java application. A flow control servlet can be used as the entry point for all servlet requests. When a request comes in to the flow control servlet, the request is examined and routed to the appropriate business logic engine for servicing. Flow control servlets act as traffic cops for your application. You can use flow control servlets to perform load balancing, security, or filtering prior to redirecting to your business logic servlets.

Servlets can be chained from one to another, making it possible to develop very complex business logic engines from a handful of modular servlets that pass the requests around to each other.

Servlets can be deployed into servlet containers such as Tomcat, Jetty, or any of the numerous servlet containers that are available. Servlet containers provide the life-cycle services: security, class loading, Java Virtual Machine (JVM) environment, and resource pools to the servlets loaded within them. Deployment descriptors define the runtime characteristics of the servlet in the servlet container. These deployment descriptors allow the behaviors of the servlets and the environment they live in to be modified without having to recompile the servlet.

Imagine the hassle involved if you needed to recompile your code every time you wanted to change the number of concurrent threads your servlet could use or to modify the security roles required to use the servlet. The deployment descriptors eliminate that headache.

The Servlet specification only mandates a single deployment descriptor for web applications that use servlets. The web.xml file is located in the WEB-INF directory of the web application and contains all of the initialization parameters needed to initialize your servlet when the servlet container has the need. Vendors are free to create their own deployment descriptors for their containers. The Servlet specification does not specify the format or location of these vendor-specific deployment descriptors.

A WebObjects application does not have a direct equivalent to the deployment descriptor concept. Instead, much of the runtime configuration of a WebObjects application relies on property files, command-line arguments, or environment variables.

JavaServer Pages

Even though learning Java is not difficult, web designers and other nontechnical personnel would find it difficult to create anything more complex than a Hello World application if they were required to develop servlets each time they needed to interact with a web page.

JavaServer Pages (JSP) was developed as a direct competitor to Microsoft's Active Server Page (ASP) technology. The structure and syntax were designed to make it very easy for ASP developers to migrate to JSP development.

While there are many similarities between JSP and ASP, especially at the API level, there is a fundamental difference between the two technologies: JSPs are compiled into Java servlets by the servlet container they are hosted in before they are actually run, providing much better performance than an interpreted model such as the ASP one. As a side note, ASP.Net has moved to a compiled code model similar to JSP for the same reasons.

Web designers can use tools such as Macromedia Dreamweaver to create their JSP pages instead of hard-coding the designs into a servlet. Servlet containers are usually smart enough to detect when a JSP page has changed and recompile it on the fly.

If we consider Direct Actions to be the WebObjects equivalent of a servlet, then the HTML portion of a `WOComponent` could be loosely considered the equivalent of a JSP page. Like a `WOComponent`, a JSP page is loaded on demand and information is passed to it via the `Request` objects. When the request—response loop is completed, both the JSP and the `WOComponent` return their response in a `Response` object.

JSP Tag Libraries

JSP custom tag libraries are the mechanism used to encapsulate functionality into re-usable pieces that can be deployed separately from your servlets or JSP pages. A JSP tag library essentially allows you to create your own reusable components and expose them to your web designer in a manner that integrates well with the tools that they currently use. As long as you don't break your tag library API, you can change the behavior of your tags without affecting the JSP pages that use them.

JSP tag libraries are the functional equivalent of creating custom `WOComponents` with bindings that can be linked from a JSP page. The act of placing a JSP tag on a page provides the same type of interaction as a .wod file does to the HTML component. Changing the values of the binding can change the behavior of the page without your having to recompile and redeploy the web application.

Sun has encouraged the development of the Java Standard Tag Library (JSTL) through the Java Community Process. JSTL has evolved into a very useful collection of JSP tags that provide a wide range of functionality including XML processing, SQL access, and conditional processing. The JSTL can be downloaded from Sun at `http://java.sun.com/products/jsp/jstl/`. The JSTL library can be used concurrently with the WebObjects tag library or your own custom-designed tag library. Tag libraries are registered in the WEB-INF/web.xml. The Tag Library Descriptor (TLD) provides the documentation on how the tags are to be used and the parameters required for each tag (similar to the .api file of a component).

Enterprise JavaBeans

Enterprise JavaBeans (EJB) is the primary thing most people think about when they hear J2EE. EJBs are server-side components that encapsulate business logic. The idea behind EJB is that business logic can be written once and deployed in any vendor-supplied container. There are two main classifications of EJBs: entity beans and session beans.

Entity beans are the closest things to EnterpriseObjects that J2EE has. Entity beans are roughly equivalent to eo entities. They provide the object-relational mapping between the database and the Java world. The EJB container is responsible for doing the work of actually getting a connection and executing the required changes. The EJB container performs similar actions to the EOAccess framework. It interacts with the EJBs through the `EJBHome` interface. The entity bean maintains the state of the data associated with the bean in a manner analogous to the EOF `EOEditingContext`.

An entity bean can use container-managed persistence (CMP) or bean-managed persistence (BMP). CMP is similar to creating an EOModel and letting the EOF framework take care of the data interaction. Initially the vendors' CMP implementations were very lightweight in comparison to EOF. They have closed the gap, but EOF has the benefit of ten years of development on its side. BMP requires the entity bean to take care of the database interactions. As the CMP implementations improve, many developers will move away from BMP.

When an EJB is deployed into an EJB container, a deployment descriptor must be provided to tell the EJB container how to interact with the bean. The deployment descriptors can include security information, life cycle information, or transaction information. These deployment descriptors can be very complex and tedious to build. Many of the modern IDEs provide some type of GUI tool to build these deployment descriptors for your EJBs.

EJBs have a complex mechanism of interaction based on the CORBA design pattern; all of the client interactions are through proxy interfaces. Remote procedure calls (some containers are smart enough to recognize that calls to the local server do not need to be "remote" calls) are made to the EJB from the client code. While this gives a great deal of flexibility in deploying EJBs on your network, it has the potential for serious performance bottlenecks if not managed properly.

Understanding WebObjects Servlet Deployment

Starting with WebObjects 5.*x* it has been possible to deploy regular WebObjects applications using servlet containers such as BEA WebLogic or Apache Tomcat. The Apple documentation has some basic information on deploying WebObjects applications as servlets, but they failed to mention that you can just as easily create your own servlets that use the power of WebObjects/EOF and deploy them in the same fashion.

When deploying in the traditional fashion, a WebObjects application typically talks to the outside world through a web server adaptor that provides the interface between the web server and the WebObjects application. The web server adaptor receives the request from the web server and routes the request to the appropriate WebObjects instance.

In a J2EE world our WebObjects application doesn't talk to a web server, it talks to a servlet container. The process flow is slightly more complicated with a J2EE deployment. Figure 10-1 shows the interaction between the servlet container and the WebObjects runtime environment.

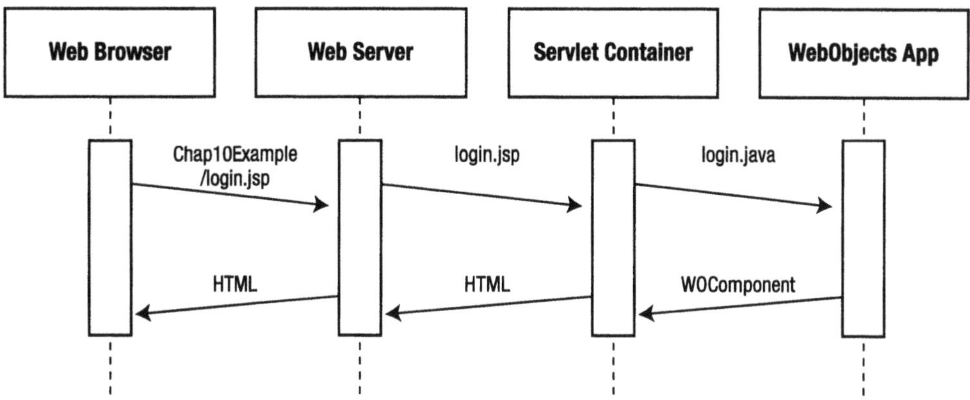

Figure 10-1. *J2EE/WebObjects process flow*

The web server passes the request to the servlet container through a native adaptor similar to the WebObjects adaptor. With a J2EE deployment there is another layer—the native adaptor talks to the servlet container, then the servlet container passes the request to the appropriate web application.

Single Servlet Deployment vs. Standard Deployment

With a typical WebObjects application deployment using the WebObjects Monitor application, you typically create multiple instances of your application using Monitor and let the WebObjects adaptor do the load balancing between instances. Each of those instances of your application spawns a new instance of the JVM. While this is more resource intensive from a runtime perspective, it does have the side benefit of making your application more fault tolerant. Monitor also provides some nice features to schedule cycling of your application and e-mail notification of instance failures.

With a servlet-based deployment, only a single instance of your application is typically deployed. It is very important that your WebObjects application is thread-safe and can handle concurrent requests efficiently. The servlet container is responsible for managing the requests coming in and distributing them to the various web applications. Servlet container vendors have come up with their own fault-tolerant and load-balancing schemes that are independent of the web application. The strategies and implementations are vendor specific and vary widely in capabilities.

There are two different mechanisms available for deploying WebObjects applications as servlets. The first method involves installing the WebObjects deployment license on the server; the second method does not require WebObjects to be installed on the server. If you have multiple WebObjects-based applications that you are developing, it is much easier to install WebObjects Deployment on the server. Doing so makes your final deployment much smaller, as you only need to deploy your custom code.

The second method does not require any previous WebObjects installation on the server. This makes your application easier to distribute and is also useful when your code has to coexist with other applications, or if you want to be able to deploy your WebObjects application on platforms that don't have native support for a regular WebObjects deployment. Linux is a good example; although it is possible to deploy the Unix version of WebObjects on a Linux box, it is much easier to use method 2 for single servlet deployment. The downside of the second method is that you have multiple copies of the WebObjects runtime installed on your server in multiple places.

■ **NOTE** The licensing for WebObjects is server based. You can have any number of WebObjects applications on a single server, but each physical server must be licensed separately, regardless of which method you choose to deploy your application with. If you choose the second method, each application will have its own license, but they can all use the same license key. The license key for WebObjects deployment is stored in the JavaWebObjects.framework/Resources/License.key file.

Class Loading

One of the questions that comes up frequently when deploying WebObjects applications in a servlet container is, "How do my classes get loaded?" The answer is, "It depends on your servlet container." The Servlet spec (`http://jcp.org/aboutJava/communityprocess/first/jsr053/index.html`) specifies a default class-loading behavior that each application server must support; however, most servlet container vendors have implemented their own class loaders in addition to the Servlet specification. JBoss is a good example of this.

JBoss utilizes its own class loader as the default behavior as opposed to the standard servlet class-loading scheme. The JBoss class loader is optimized for runtime memory performance and can share classes between web applications. This can cause strange unexpected behaviors. If your application behaves differently under JBoss than Apache Tomcat in stand-alone mode, suspect issues with the JBoss class-loading scheme.

The default class-loading scheme specified by the Servlet specification is

WEB-INF/classes

WEB-INF/lib

JAVA_HOME/jre/lib/ext

Most servlet containers ignore the CLASSPATH environment variable. Most servlet containers also load classes/Jars from shared directories. In a Java 2 (that is, JDK 1.2 or later) environment, class loaders are arranged in a parent-child tree. Normally, when a class loader is asked to load a particular class or resource, it delegates the request to a parent class loader first, and then looks in its own repositories only if the parent class loader(s) cannot find the requested class or resource. In Tomcat stand-alone mode, classes are loaded from the following directories as well:

CATALINA_HOME/common/classes

CATALINA_HOME/common/endorsed

CATALINA_HOME/common/lib

CATALINA_HOME/server/classes

CATALINA_HOME/server/lib

CATALINA_HOME/shared/classes

CATALINA_HOME/shared/lib

If Tomcat is running as an embedded server as it does under JBoss (Tomcat 4.1.*x*), the class-loading behavior is controlled by the primary server, and it may not behave the same as in the stand-alone mode.

Typically, once a class is loaded it stays in memory until the web application is restarted or undeployed. Some servers (e.g., JBoss) provide dynamic loading/unloading of classes, but the behavior is not specified by the Servlet specification and is vendor specific.

Resource Location

One of the first questions that WebObjects developers ask is, "How do resources like EOModels and images embedded in frameworks get loaded?"

For the most part, WebObjects servlet resources such as EOModels will get loaded from the same place that a regular WebObjects application loads them from. The launch scripts provided by the Eclipse/WOLips build process set the necessary environment variables properly.

WebObjects provides a default Java-style Properties file located in WEB-INF/<Project-Name>.woa/Contents/Resources/Properties. This file is read when the application starts and the properties are merged into the System properties. These properties are then available using standard Java calls.

If your properties file looks like

```
application.name=myproject
```

then

```
String prop = System.getProperty("application.name");
```

will yield

```
prop = myproject
```

You can also create your own Java-style properties files and locate them anywhere on the runtime classpath (WEB-INF/classes is designed for this mechanism) of your web application and reference them at runtime using code like

```
...
Properties logProperties.load(this.getClass().getClassLoader().
    getResourceAsStream("myapp.properties"));
...
```

Differences Between WebObjects Applications and WebObjects Servlets

Thankfully, Apple has made it very easy to migrate applications from a stand-alone deployment to a servlet-based one. This makes it much easier to debug and test your WebObjects applications using Eclipse and then deploy your application as a servlet. The differences between environments from a developer's perspective are minor. Here is a brief list of some of those differences:

1. Applications are deployed to servlet containers instead of through Monitor.
2. wotaskd is not used for servlet deployments.
3. Servlet applications are multithreaded single JVMs; Monitor-based deployments usually create multiple instances of the application and are less dependent on multithreading design patterns.
4. The runtime classpath is controlled by the servlet container, not the `CLASSPATH` environment variable. The WOLips/Xcode build process creates a web.xml with some environment variables that are initialized at runtime that point to the frameworks associated with your project. These runtime parameters are passed to the `WOServlet-Adaptor` as web application context parameters in the WEB-INF/web.xml file.
5. `System.out` and `System.err` are typically swallowed by the servlet container's logging mechanism unless specifically overridden. It is useful to use an external logging mechanism such as log4j where you can configure the output file for your debugging output.
6. The `main()` method in your application class will not be called while running as a servlet. Your `Application()` default constructor will be called, however.

7. Instead of getting `WOContext` classes, your WebObjects application will use `WOServlet-Context` classes. They are functionally the same and should not cause any issue unless you are doing something very specific with the `WOContext`.

8. The `WOSession` and JSP `Sessions` are tied together. If you set the session timeout in the WEB-INF/web.xml file for the JSP `Session`, it is supposed to get passed along to the `WOSession`.

Multithreaded Servlet Containers

A significant difference between standard WebObjects applications deployed through Monitor or other means and those deployed as a servlet is that servlet containers are inherently multi-threaded. Standard WebObjects applications can be thread-safe—but many developers simply deploy multiple instances of their application and hope for the best. By default the WebObjects attribute WOAllowsConcurrentRequestHandling is turned off, so even if you have a deployment license installed, the WebObjects request handling will be single threaded. This can have a negative effect on your application's overall performance.

So what makes a WebObjects application thread-safe? Here are a few guidelines to follow:

1. Limit use of public instance variables in your classes. Control access to your variables using `get`/`set` methods, which can be synchronized if necessary.

2. Lock/unlock your `EOEditingContexts` before and after using them. Here is an excerpt from the `EOEditingContext` API documentation on this matter.

   Locks access to this EOEditingContext to prevent other threads from accessing it. If it has a shared editing context, this EOEditingContext takes a reader lock on it as well. You should lock an editing context when you are accessing or modifying objects managed by the editing context. The thread safety provided by Enterprise Objects Framework allows you to have one thread to be active in each EOEditingContext and one thread to be active in each EODatabaseContext (EOAccess). In other words, multiple threads can access and modify objects concurrently in different editing contexts, but only one thread can access the database at a time (to save, fetch, or fault).

3. Be careful of using static variables, especially if your application changes the state of the variable for any reason. Static variables are the Java equivalent of global variables. Debugging problems caused by value changes in a multithreaded environment can be very tricky and frustrating.

4. Follow normal Java optimizations for multithreaded access such as synchronizing access to locally managed hashtables, etc.

EAR, WAR, WOA

In the J2EE world, deploying applications to servlet containers can be an adventure! While simple in theory, there are quite a few mudholes to step in along the way. Over the past few years, Sun and the Java community have done a lot to standardize the deployment methodology across vendors.

At runtime, a servlet application may have a URL like `http://localhost:8080/myapp/myservlet?param1=abc¶m2=def`, where

myapp is the web application context.

myservlet is the name of the servlet being called.

param1, *param2* are parameters being passed to the current request going to myservlet.

A WebObjects application deployed as a servlet will have a URL like `http://localhost:8080/myapp/WebObjects/myapplication.woa`, where

myapp is the servlet context that will receive the request from the web server.

WebObjects is the name of the servlet handling the incoming request. This servlet is the `WOServletAdaptor` that replaces the functionality of the `WOAdaptor` used in a regular WebObjects deployment.

Most servlet containers let you specify a different name for the servlet context than the directory name. The servlet context you choose will be reflected in the URL needed to access your application.

■NOTE All relative references to other JSP files or images are made from the directory represented by the servlet context. In addition, most servlet containers have a ROOT context that is roughly equivalent to a web server's DOCROOT directory. Items stored in the servlet can be accessed as they were in the DOCROOT directory of a web server only if the servlet container is also set up to act like a web server. If you use an external web server such as Apache, you will need to create aliases for your resource directories instead.

There are three basic deployment mechanisms available to the J2EE developer (we can honestly call ourselves that nowadays!). Each mechanism has advantages in different stages of a web application's lifecycle.

Directory Deployment

Directory deployment of a J2EE web application (including our WebObjects applications) is a useful mechanism when you are in development mode and need to test JSP pages and make changes in real time. It is similar to WebObjects' quick turnaround mode in ProjectBuilder/Xcode. Most servlet containers can be set to automatically recompile JSP pages if they change. Tomcat sometimes has problems detecting pages that have been changed if they are nested inside JSP `INCLUDE` directives. In those cases you may have to force a page to recompile by touching the top-level page so the modify date is changed.

Just as the name implies, directory-based deployment simply involves copying your JSPs and servlets into your web application deployment directory. JSPs go into the root directory of your web applications; servlets go into the WEB-INF directory. All of the files are expanded out and ready to run. You must register your servlets in the WEB-INF/web.xml file prior to using them. Most servlet containers will detect when the web.xml has changed and automatically reload your web application.

■ **CAUTION** Be aware that even if your web application is reloaded, your `Servlet` classes may or may not get reloaded in the JVM they are running in. Some servlet containers tend to keep the classes loaded until the servlet container is restarted manually. If you make a change to your web application and your application doesn't behave as expected, stop your servlet container, delete any precompiled classes that are being cached by it, and then restart it.

WAR File Deployment

WAR is an acronym for web application archive. A WAR file is similar to a Jar file and contains all of the resources needed for a web application. The WAR file is basically a tar-style archive of your application deployed expanded into the proper directory structure as described previously. WAR files can contain JSPs, servlets, frameworks, images, or any other files needed for a web application.

Creating a WAR file is very easy. Use the Java `jar` command

```
jar cvf myapp.war <application directory to recursively archive>
```

There are Ant tasks available to create WAR files as well.

When a WAR file is created and copied to your servlet container's deployment directory, the WAR file is automatically extracted into the servlet engine's runtime directory. If a new WAR file is placed into the deployment directory, the older expanded version of the app is deleted and replaced with the newer version. The only requirement is that your WAR files have a .war extension on them.

■ **TIP** Some servlet engines (e.g., JBoss) only understand WAR and EAR files (more on EARs later) and not directory-based deployments. JBoss can be tricked into thinking that your directory-deployed application is a WAR simply by changing the name of the directory to end with .war.

WAR files simplify the process of deploying a web application by allowing a single file to be deployed instead of directories full of files that need to be in the proper place with the proper permissions. WAR files do have a drawback: changing any of the files in the WAR file will require that a new WAR be generated and placed into the deployment directory. This can be a hassle during development, when everything is in a big state of continual change.

EAR File Deployment

EAR (Enterprise Archive) files are another method of deploying servlet-based applications. EAR files are typically used to deploy EJB-based applications, but they can be used to deploy servlet-only applications as well.

An EAR file is similar to a WAR file with a couple of differences:

1. An EAR is composed of one or more modules and their associated deployment descriptors (*.xml). Module types include EJB modules, Web modules (WAR files), Application client modules, and Resource Adaptor modules.
2. An EAR file can contain multiple WAR files. Typically there is an application.xml file located in META-INF that details which WAR file gets deployed to which location and provides a context name. Listing 10-1 shows a sample META-INF/application.xml. This makes it very easy to deploy multiple web applications from a single file.
3. If your web application uses EJBs, the EJBs can be deployed in the same package as your web applications.

Figure 10-2 shows the structure of an EAR file.

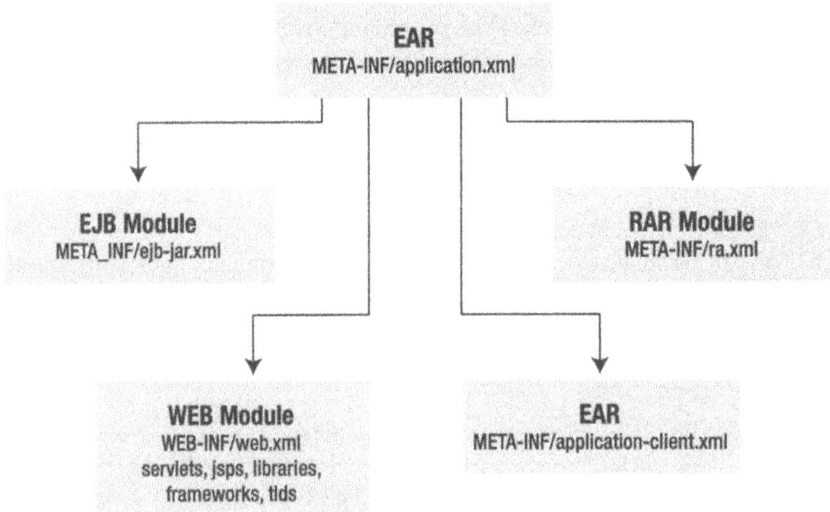

Figure 10-2. *EAR file layout*

Listing 10-1. *Sample META-INF/application.xml*

```
<?xml version="1.0"?>
<!DOCTYPE application PUBLIC "-//Sun Microsystems, Inc.//DTD↩
    J2EE Application 1.3//EN" "http://java.sun.com/dtd/application_1_3.dtd">
<application>
  <display-name>My Application</display-name>
  <module>
    <web>
```

```
      <web-uri>myapp.war</web-uri>
      <context-root>/myapp</context-root>
    </web>
  </module>
</application>
```

EAR files can be easily created using the Ant EAR task, or the `jar` command as shown under "WAR File Deployment" except using a .ear extension:

```
jar cvf myapp.ear <directory containing all of my web apps to deploy>
```

The end result is a single file containing all parts of your web application.

WOA Files

In the good old days, a WebObjects application was contained inside its .woa folder. First you installed a deployment license of WebObjects onto your Windows, Solaris, or OS X server. Then you copied your WebObjects application to the `NEXT_ROOT`/Local/Library/WebObjects/ Applications directory. At runtime your system frameworks were found based on the value of the `NEXT_ROOT` environment variable.

In the servlet world, your application is still packaged inside its .woa directory, but your .woa directory is packaged inside of the WEB-INF directory of the web application. All of the runtime classes for your application should be available within the runtime classpath of your servlet container, WEB-INF/classes, or the WEB-INF/lib directories. System or other WebObjects frameworks are located in the WEB-INF/Library directory.

Tips and Tricks

The ability to play in the J2EE world as a full-fledged member in good standing has given us WebObjects developers a vast playground. In order to take advantage of our newfound freedom, here are some tips and tricks that will help us play safer with the big bullies.

Packages

Apple's ProjectBuilder and Xcode IDEs have always been designed as a multilanguage development tool. These tools use Makefiles or derivatives to build the projects and create the final outputs required for each environment. As a consequence, most WebObjects developers have neglected to use Java packages to contain their EOModel and component classes. There are two good reasons for this: first, it wasn't necessary because the WebObjects frameworks were designed with anonymous classes in mind; second, Apple never told us we could use packages. When deploying our WebObjects applications in a servlet environment, it is a good idea to package all of your classes inside Java packages. Here are some things you can do to use Java packages in your WebObjects applications:

- Use Eclipse with WOLips to refactor your source code. Eclipse does a good job of helping you move code around. Eclipse/WOLips provides tools that work great when your classes are in packages. Code completion and Javadoc lookup make coding much more fun.

- In your EOModel, fully qualify your classes in EOModeler. If you use the native Java code generator, it will read the class name from the EOModel and build your code with the correct package statement. If you use tools such as RubiCode's EOGenerator (`http://www.rubicode.com/Software/EOGenerator/`), you may have to adjust your generation scripts to put the code in the proper location.

- For `WOComponent` actions, binding instance variables or methods that are usually private need to be made public; otherwise the WebObjects runtime has problems finding your bindings. You will see errors that look something like

```
com.webobjects.foundation.NSKeyValueCoding$UnknownKeyException:⏎
    [ valueForKey()]: lookup of unknown key: 'username'. This⏎
    WOComponent does not have an instance variable of the name⏎
    username or _username, nor a method of the name username,⏎
    _username, getUsername, or _getUsername
```

Using WebObjects with JavaServer Pages

Now that you have some basic background on how servlet containers work, we'll jump into building some WebObjects-based components that can be used in JavaServer Pages. Our example will show how to use WebObjects components within a JSP page. We will set some bindings in the JSP side for our `WOComponent`, execute WebObjects Java code, and then pass back some values to the JSP side.

For the example projects you will need WebObjects 5.2.*x* installed, Eclipse/WOLips, and Tomcat 5.*x* (available for free from `http://jakarta.apache.org/tomcat`). The example project should build on both Windows and OS X.

WOComponent Integration with JSP Example

This first example is pretty simple but illustrates the basics of communicating back and forth between the JSP world and the WebObjects world. This project is a simple login `WOComponent` that is called out from a JSP page with some bindings that fill a drop-down list in the component. When the user clicks the submit button, WebObjects takes over and processes the request. We then show two different methods to pass back information to the JSP side so that it can be processed and shown to the user.

WO Login Component

We will start with the login component that we are going to build in WebObjects Builder. When we are done, it will look like Figure 10-3.

Since all of our classes (including `Application`, `Session`, `Main`, and `DirectAction`) are in packages, we need to make our bindings public or provide public `get`/`set` methods so that the WebObjects runtime can find them. Listing 10-2 shows the source code for our `Login.java` class.

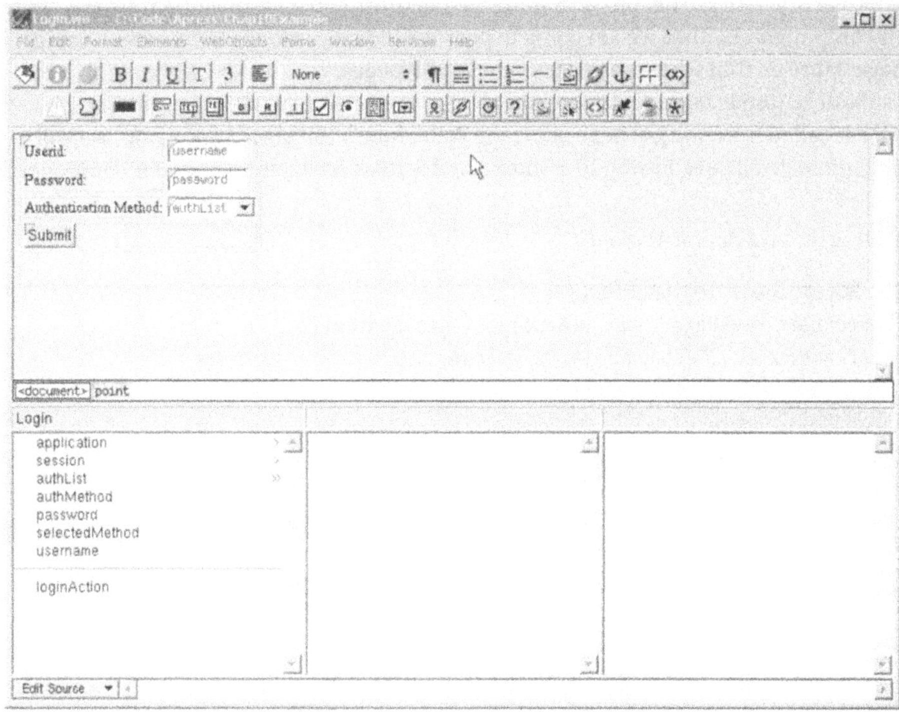

Figure 10-3. *Login.wo component layout*

Listing 10-2. `Login.java` *Header Source Code*

```
package com.apress.practicalwo.chap10;
import javax.servlet.http.HttpSession;

import com.webobjects.appserver.*;
import com.webobjects.foundation.*;
import com.webobjects.jspservlet.WOServletContext;

public class Login extends WOComponent {
    /*
     Here are our form bindings, notice they are PUBLIC since the
     WO runtime can't find them otherwise since the class is in a package
     */
    public String username;
    public String password;
    public String authMethod;

    /** @TypeInfo java.lang.String */
    public NSArray authList;
    public String selectedMethod;
...
```

For this example, we are not going to initialize the drop-down list of authentication types inside our component. Instead we are going to pass the NSArray into the WOComponent using the JSP page. More on that when we go through the JSP pages.

The submit button is bound into the loginAction method of our WOComponent. The WOComponent is called from the JSP page using the WebObjects JSP tag library. Again, we will cover that in more detail later. Listing 10-3 shows the loginAction method from our component.

Listing 10-3. Login.java *Action Method*

```
public WOComponent loginAction() {
    WORedirect nextPage = new WORedirect(this.context());
    nextPage.setUrl("/Chap10Example/welcome.jsp?user="+username+
        "&authmeth="+selectedMethod);

    NSMutableDictionary userinfo = new NSMutableDictionary();
    userinfo.setObjectForKey("John Doe","name");
    userinfo.setObjectForKey("123 Sesame Street", "address");
    userinfo.setObjectForKey("Anywhere", "city");

    HttpSession httpSession = ((WOServletContext)context()).httpSession ();
    if (httpSession !=null ){
        httpSession.setAttribute("userinfo", userinfo);
    }

    return nextPage;
}
```

This method demonstrates two different ways to send information back to a JSP after processing. Chances are you will only use one at a time in your code. In either case you will need to use a WORedirect class to get back to the required JSP page after processing is completed. You can call out other WOComponents using pageWithName() calls if you like, but this example focuses strictly on talking back and forth between WebObjects and JSP.

The setURL() method needs a URL that includes the JSP context of our web application in order to get directed to the proper application from the web server.

```
WORedirect nextPage = new WORedirect(this.context());
nextPage.setUrl("/Chap10Example/welcome.jsp?user=" + username +
    "&authmeth="+selectedMethod);
```

By adding URL parameters user and authmeth to the target page, the supplied values will be available in the JSP page as part of the request. This is a simple method of passing String data back and forth between the WebObjects side and the JSP side.

In a lot of cases, however, it is not sufficient to only pass strings back and forth. You may need to pass other Java objects such as Hashtables or NSArrays. In that case, putting them in the URL is not an option. The second method, shown in Listing 10-4, allows us to pass any arbitrary object back and forth.

Listing 10-4. `Login.java` *Passing Objects Back to JSP* `Session`

```
...
NSMutableDictionary userinfo = new NSMutableDictionary();
userinfo.setObjectForKey("John Doe","name");
userinfo.setObjectForKey("123 Sesame Street", "address");
userinfo.setObjectForKey("Anywhere", "city");

HttpSession httpSession = ((WOServletContext)context()).httpSession ();
if (httpSession !=null ){
    httpSession.setAttribute("userinfo", userinfo);
}
...
```

First we create an `NSMutableDictionary` and set some values in it. Next we need to get a reference to the JSP `Session` from our `WOComponent`. When we include the JavaWOJSPServlet.framework and run our application as a servlet deployed in a JSP container, WebObjects behaves slightly differently. The `context()` of a `WOComponent` normally returns a `WOContext` object. In a JSP environment, `context()` returns a `WOServletContext` object instead. `WOServletContext` extends `WOContext` and provides us the necessary hooks into the JSP side. Through the `WOServletContext` we can access some important JSP-side objects including

- **ServletConfig**: This `Servlet` object gives us access to any servlet configuration parameters defined in the WEB-INF/web.xml.
- **ServletContext**: The `ServletContext` object provides methods to read/write initialization parameters and context parameters. Context parameters are similar to `Application`-scoped parameters that can be shared across instances within a servlet.
- **JspWriter**: The `JspWriter` object is responsible for outputting information onto the JSP after it has been processed.
- **HttpSession**: The `HttpSession` object provides an interface to the JSP `Session`. We can store information at the session level and use it from the JSP side.

In our example application we are going to use the `HttpSession` object to store the `NSMutableDictionary` object that we created and then retrieve it and display it from the JSP page.

Login.jsp

Our example application starts off with Login.jsp. This page uses the WebObjects custom tag library to integrate `WOComponents` with our JSP environment. Listing 10-5 shows the code for Login.jsp.

Listing 10-5. *Login.jsp Code Listing*

```
<%@ taglib uri="/WOtaglib" prefix="wo" %>
<%-- Import statements --%>
<%@ page import="com.webobjects.foundation.*" %>
<%-- Create authentication list --%>
<% NSMutableArray authtypes = new NSMutableArray();
    authtypes.addObject(new String("password"));
    authtypes.addObject(new String("LDAP"));
    authtypes.addObject(new String("Active Directory"));
    authtypes.addObject(new String("Kerberos"));
    authtypes.addObject(new String("PAM"));
    authtypes.addObject(new String("pinkie shake"));
%>
<HTML>
<HEAD>
<TITLE>Chapter 10 JSP Login Example</TITLE>
</HEAD>
<BODY>
    <wo:component className="Login">
        <wo:binding key="authList" value='<%= authtypes %>' />
    </wo:component>
</BODY>
</HTML>
```

The first line in our JSP page, `<%@ taglib uri="/WOtaglib" prefix="wo" %>`, defines the JSP custom tag library. The prefix attribute "wo" specifies the namespace to be used for the WebObjects-related custom tags. Each tag library referenced on a page must have a unique namespace prefix. A JSP page can use many different tag libraries on the same page. The uri attribute references the tag library definition in the WEB-INF/web.xml file.

```
...
<taglib>
    <taglib-uri>/WOtaglib</taglib-uri>
    <taglib-location>/WEB-INF/tlds/WOtaglib_1_0.tld</taglib-location>
  </taglib>
...
```

The next line in our JSP page, `<%@ page import="com.webobjects.foundation.*" %>`, imports the WebObjects Foundation framework. In order to use any class within a JSP page, it must be found on the runtime classpath of the web application. Prior to being used, each JSP page is compiled into a Java servlet. If a class can't be found at runtime, a `NoClassDefFoundException` will be thrown. The WEB-INF/lib directory will always be on the runtime classpath of all application servers. During the Ant build process, all of the Jar files needed for the application should be copied to the WEB-INF/lib directory. For installations where WebObjects is installed on the server, make sure the runtime classpath can find the WebObjects System frameworks.

After we create an NSMutableDictionary, we add some string objects to it that will be used to populate our drop-down list on our Login form. This will be bound into the drop-down list of our login component using the WebObjects tag library as shown here:

```
...
<wo:component className="Login">
    <wo:binding key="authList" value='<%= authtypes %>' />
</wo:component>
...
```

The className attribute of the wo:component tag specifies the WOComponent that we are going to load into our JSP page at runtime. This is the same name used in the pageWithName() in the WebObjects environment.

The binding key attribute of the wo:binding tag is the name of the binding in the Login.wod that we are attaching our NSMutableDictionary onto.

We are using two of the custom WebObjects tags: the wo:component tag and the wo:binding tag. The wo:binding tag must be nested inside of a wo:component tag in order to function properly. If you make a mistake while building your page, the JSP compiler will throw an error indicating that the tags are not properly nested. Some containers have mechanisms to precompile the JSP pages into servlets; these compile-time issues will prevent your page from loading and must be corrected prior to use.

A JSP tag is self-documenting using the Tag Library Descriptor (TLD). The TLD is normally located in the WEB-INF. Its exact position is specified by the web.xml. The properties for the wo:component tag are documented in Listing 10-6.

Listing 10-6. wo:component *Tag Library Descriptor*

```
...
<!-- WOComponentTag enables the use of a WOComponent within a JSP.
       See comments for individual attributes as well. -->
  <tag>
    <name>component</name>
    <tagclass>com.webobjects.jspservlet.WOComponentTag</tagclass>
    <bodycontent>jsp</bodycontent>
    <info>Tag handler for WOComponent</info>

    <!-- The WOComponent class name. Required. -->
    <attribute>
      <name>className</name>
      <required>true</required>
      <rtexprvalue>true</rtexprvalue>
    </attribute>

    <!-- Indicates if only the WOResponse body content is required.
         The HTML headers will be stripped off if this is true.
         Default is true. Optional. -->
    <attribute>
      <name>bodyContentOnly</name>
    </attribute>
```

```
    <!-- Indicates if only the WOResponse headers should be merged
         with the ServletResponse's headers.
         Default is false. Optional. -->
    <attribute>
      <name>mergeResponseHeaders</name>
    </attribute>
  </tag>
...
```

The TLD defines the Java class that is run when the tag is processed. This class must be on the runtime classpath of the web application. The `<bodycontent>` element of the `wo:component` tag tells whether or not the tag can contain other JSP code that can be processed in the scope of the tag. Valid values are either `jsp`, meaning that it will process the JSP code, or `empty`, indicating that any JSP code will be ignored.

Each tag can have zero or more attributes associated with it. These attributes are passed to the JSP tag at runtime and are used to specify parameters for the underlying Java class. Each attribute specifies

- **name**: This is the name of the attribute that will be used in the JSP code. The names are case sensitive since they are converted to Java code at compile time.
- **required**: This attribute determines whether or not the JSP compiler will check at compile time to see if the attribute is available.
- **rtxprvalue**: This optional element indicates whether the value of the attribute can be supplied at runtime from the JSP code. If it is `false`, the value must be coded into the tag directly, using data that is available at compile time.
- **type**: This optional element indicates the data type of the value that the attribute is expecting. The data type can be any of the `java.lang` datatypes or it can be one of your own design if the class is available at JSP compile time.

A tool such as Dreamweaver MX can read your TLDs and integrate them into its IDE and allow you to use its capabilities for tasks such as auto-completion, type checking, etc. Consult your IDE manual for more information on integrating JSP custom tags with the IDE.

Welcome.jsp

The welcome.jsp is the final part of our mini-application. This is the page that our login component redirects to after the WebObjects application processes our requests and is ready to send us back our data. Listing 10-7 shows the JSP code for the welcome page.

Listing 10-7. *Welcome.jsp Source Code*

```
<%@ taglib uri="/WOtaglib" prefix="wo" %>
<%@ page import="com.webobjects.foundation.*" %>
<HTML>
<HEAD>
<TITLE>Chapter 10 JSP Example</TITLE>
</HEAD>
```

```
<BODY>
    Welcome <b><%= request.getParameter("user") %></b>, you used
        <b><%= request.getParameter("authmeth") %></b> to authenticate your
        access!!
    <%
        NSMutableDictionary userinfo = new NSMutableDictionary();
        userinfo = (NSMutableDictionary)session.getAttribute("userinfo");
    %>
    <%= userinfo %>
</BODY>
</HTML>
```

This page is pretty simple; it retrieves the data passed to it from both methods and displays it on the page. Our first piece of data was passed via the URL from the Login.java component when we built up our URL for the `WORedirect.setURL()` call. Here is what we passed in the Login.java:

```
nextPage.setUrl("/Chap10Example/welcome.jsp?user="+username+"&↵
    authmeth="+selectedMethod);
```

Our JSP page looks in the request for the `user` and `authmeth` parameters and formats the resulting information into a string to be displayed using the following code:

```
Welcome <b><%= request.getParameter("user") %></b>, you used
<b><%= request.getParameter("authmeth") %></b> to authenticate your access!!
```

The `NSMutableDictionary` of user information that we created in the `Login.java` class can be retrieved from the JSP `Session` using the following code:

```
...
userinfo = (NSMutableDictionary)session.getAttribute("userinfo");
...
```

As long as the proper imports are added to the JSP page and the class can be found on the runtime classpath, any WebObjects framework Java class can be accessed and used within a JSP page. EOF-based classes should *not* be used on the JSP side, since the editing context the EO belongs to may get garbage collected. There is a very loose tie between JSP `Sessions` and `WOSessions`, making the use of `session.defaultEditingContext()` dangerous.

Deploying the Sample Application

Once we develop our servlet-based WebObjects applications, we need to get them deployed so we can test them and eventually move them out to production. The number of steps in deploying a WebObjects-based servlet application depends on whether you're doing a production deployment. First, the application needs to be built in a manner that can be deployed to a servlet engine; second, it needs to be deployed to the servlet engine; third, for a production environment, the servlet engine must be configured to talk to our external web server.

We will package our application as a single servlet deployment that can be deployed to any servlet container on any platform. We will *not* require WebObjects to be installed in order to run our application. Our deployment package will consist of a single WAR that can be hot-deployed to our servlet container. For this exercise we will use Apache Tomcat 5.*x*. You can download the latest version from the Apache Foundation web site at `http://jakarta.apache.org/tomcat`. Follow the instructions to install Tomcat for your system. In most cases, if you download a binary build, you can simply unzip it and start the server from the `CATALINA_HOME/bin` directory using the ./startup.sh or startup.bat scripts. Once Tomcat is installed and running, you should be able to view the Tomcat homepage at `http://localhost:8080`.

Apache's Ant build system provides the basis for building our project. If you have never used Ant before, you can find the most current documentation and software at `http://ant.apache.org`. Using Eclipse and WOLips simplifies the process of creating the Ant-based build scripts we need. Our build script is contained in the build.xml file located in the root directory of our example project. There are several build targets inside the build.xml file; the one we will focus on is the single servlet deployment directory (SSDD) target.

Build.xml

The build.xml is automatically created for us when we use Eclipse/WOLips to create a new project. By default the SSDD and WAR targets are included but disabled, so they are not run when the project is built. Make sure to remove the `if =${never}` attribute from the target for new projects.

In order to create the proper deployment directory structure, our application must first be built. The `build.woapp` target is used to create the .woa structure that we normally deploy to Monitor for a standard WebObjects application. The `build.woapp` target uses WOProject Ant build tasks to create the deployment package. These are documented at `http://www.objectstyle.org/woproject/` in some detail. WOProject can be used in other non-Eclipse projects, but they are nicely integrated into Eclipse.

After the .woa project is built, we use the `ssdd` target to assemble the servlet deployment files into a single place. In our project we put all of the build products in the dist directory under the root of our project. The `ssdd` target is designed to run in sequence from the default target for the project. The default target looks like

```
<target name="build" depends="setProps,init.build,build.woapp,ssdd,war"/>
```

The order of the default `build` target was changed to build the WAR file after the `ssdd` target was run, in order to create a complete WAR file that could be deployed anywhere.

The default `ssdd` target that Eclipse/WOLips builds assumes that your target deployment machine has WebObjects already installed on it. That is a good assumption for Windows and OS X deployment machines, but not useful on Linux. While it is possible to install WebObjects on a Linux machine, it is a hassle and, thankfully, not necessary.

Our final directory structure for our example application must look like the following before we create the WAR file to deploy it:

```
dist/
    Chap10Example/
        login.jsp
        welcome.jsp
```

```
WEB-INF/
    classes/
    lib/
    Library/
    Chap10Example.woa/
    tlds/
    web.xml
```

The lib directory will contain all of our Jar files that are needed at runtime for our application, including the WebObjects framework Jar files. The Library directory contains all of the frameworks used in our project including custom-developed frameworks and WebObjects System frameworks. All of your `WOComponents` get loaded out of this directory. The Chap10Example.woa is our binary build of our application created by the `build.woapp` target. The web.xml file is our deployment descriptor that allows our servlet container to launch our application.

The first part of our build.xml `ssdd` target simply copies over our tag library descriptor, a plain text LICENSE file, and our binary build of our web application into the WEB-INF directory. All web applications must have a WEB-INF (case sensitive—all caps) directory. This is where the classes are run from. Listings 10-8, 10-9, and 10-10 show portions of the single servlet deployment target from our build.xml.

Listing 10-8. `ssdd` *Target in build.xml*

```
...
<!-- ssdd target-->
    <!-- To use this target remove the if="${never}" statement and create the
        LICENSE in your project
        and create the web.xml file with the woapplication task.-->
    <target name="ssdd">
        <mkdir dir="${dest.dir}/${project.name}/WEB-INF/tlds"/>
        <copy todir="${dest.dir}/${project.name}/">
            <fileset dir="web/." />
        </copy>
        <copy todir="${dest.dir}/${project.name}/WEB-INF/">
            <fileset dir="..">
                <include name="LICENSE"/>
            </fileset>
        </copy>
        <copy todir="${dest.dir}/${project.name}/WEB-INF/">
            <fileset dir="${dest.dir}">
                <include name="${project.name}.woa/**"/>
            </fileset>
        </copy>
        <copy todir="${dest.dir}/${project.name}/WEB-INF/tlds">
            <fileset dir="${wo.wosystemroot}/Library/Frameworks/↵
                JavaWOJSPServlet.framework/Resources/">
                <include name="WOtaglib_1_0.tld"/>
            </fileset>
        </copy>
```

The next section of the ssdd target copies the referenced frameworks into the WEB-INF/Library directory. All frameworks used in your project that need to be deployed must be copied into the WEB-INF/Library directory so the WOComponents and resources can be loaded at runtime. There are some files maintained in the Eclipse project directory structure by WOLips that can be used to build these entries in a more generic fashion. These files are named ant.classpaths.xxx.xxx and ant.frameworks.xxx.xxx; they contain directory names and Jar file names for items added to your project. The frameworks used in Listing 10-9 are the bare minimum needed to deploy your WebObjects application as a servlet.

Listing 10-9. *SSDD Framework Copy in build.xml*

```
<copy todir="${dest.dir}/${project.name}/WEB-INF/⏎
            Library/Frameworks/JavaEOAccess.framework">
            <fileset dir="${wo.wosystemroot}/Library/Frameworks/⏎
                JavaEOAccess.framework"/>
        </copy>
        <copy todir="${dest.dir}/${project.name}/WEB-INF/⏎
            Library/Frameworks/JavaEOControl.framework">
            <fileset dir="${wo.wosystemroot}/Library/Frameworks/⏎
                JavaEOControl.framework"/>
        </copy>
        <copy todir="${dest.dir}/${project.name}/WEB-INF/⏎
            Library/Frameworks/JavaFoundation.framework">
            <fileset dir="${wo.wosystemroot}/Library/Frameworks/⏎
                JavaFoundation.framework"/>
        </copy>
        <copy todir="${dest.dir}/${project.name}/WEB-INF/⏎
            Library/Frameworks/JavaJDBCAdaptor.framework">
            <fileset dir="${wo.wosystemroot}/Library/Frameworks/⏎
                JavaJDBCAdaptor.framework"/>
        </copy>
        <copy todir="${dest.dir}/${project.name}/WEB-INF/⏎
            Library/Frameworks/JavaWebObjects.framework">
            <fileset dir="${wo.wosystemroot}/Library/Frameworks/⏎
                JavaWebObjects.framework"/>
        </copy>
        <copy todir="${dest.dir}/${project.name}/WEB-INF/⏎
            Library/Frameworks/JavaWOExtensions.framework">
            <fileset dir="${wo.wosystemroot}/Library/Frameworks/⏎
                JavaWOExtensions.framework"/>
        </copy>
        <copy todir="${dest.dir}/${project.name}/WEB-INF/⏎
            Library/Frameworks/JavaWOJSPServlet.framework">
            <fileset dir="${wo.wosystemroot}/Library/Frameworks/⏎
                JavaWOJSPServlet.framework"/>
        </copy>
        <copy todir="${dest.dir}/${project.name}/WEB-INF/⏎
```

```
        Library/Frameworks/JavaEOProject.framework">
        <fileset dir="${wo.wosystemroot}/Library/Frameworks/↵
            JavaEOProject.framework"/>
    </copy>
```

The next part of the ssdd target copies all of the Jar files to the WEB-INF/lib directory. The lib directory is part of the runtime classpath of the web application. In order for the JSP files to properly compile and run, the classes they use must be found in the runtime classpath. The WebObjects System framework Jar files must be loaded here in order to use them in your JSP pages. For installations where WebObjects is already installed on the machine, these steps aren't necessary; the WebObjects launch scripts can usually find the installed classes.

Listing 10-10. *SSDD Jar Copy in build.xml*

```
<copy todir="${dest.dir}/${project.name}/WEB-INF/lib">
        <fileset dir="${dest.dir}/${project.name}.woa/↵
            Contents/Resources/Java/">
            <include name="*.jar"/>
        </fileset>
    </copy>
    <copy todir="${dest.dir}/${project.name}/WEB-INF/lib"
        file="${dest.dir}/${project.name}/WEB-INF/Library/Frameworks/↵
        JavaEOAccess.framework/Resources/Java/javaeoaccess.jar"/>
    <copy todir="${dest.dir}/${project.name}/WEB-INF/lib"
        file="${dest.dir}/${project.name}/WEB-INF/Library/Frameworks/↵
        JavaEOControl.framework/Resources/Java/javaeocontrol.jar"/>
    <copy todir="${dest.dir}/${project.name}/WEB-INF/lib"
        file="${dest.dir}/${project.name}/WEB-INF/Library/Frameworks/↵
        JavaEOProject.framework/Resources/Java/javaeoproject.jar"/>
    <copy todir="${dest.dir}/${project.name}/WEB-INF/lib"
        file="${dest.dir}/${project.name}/WEB-INF/Library/Frameworks/↵
        JavaFoundation.framework/Resources/Java/javafoundation.jar"/>
    <copy todir="${dest.dir}/${project.name}/WEB-INF/lib"
        file="${dest.dir}/${project.name}/WEB-INF/Library/Frameworks/↵
        JavaJDBCAdaptor.framework/Resources/Java/javajdbcadaptor.jar"/>
    <copy todir="${dest.dir}/${project.name}/WEB-INF/lib"
        file="${dest.dir}/${project.name}/WEB-INF/Library/Frameworks/↵
        JavaWOExtensions.framework/Resources/Java/JavaWOExtensions.jar"/>
    <copy todir="${dest.dir}/${project.name}/WEB-INF/lib"
        file="${dest.dir}/${project.name}/WEB-INF/Library/Frameworks/↵
        JavaJDBCAdaptor.framework/Resources/Java/javajdbcadaptor.jar"/>
    <copy todir="${dest.dir}/${project.name}/WEB-INF/lib"
        file="${dest.dir}/${project.name}/WEB-INF/Library/Frameworks/↵
        JavaWOJSPServlet.framework/Resources/Java/javawojspservlet.jar"/>
    <copy todir="${dest.dir}/${project.name}/WEB-INF/lib"
        file="${dest.dir}/${project.name}/WEB-INF/Library/Frameworks/↵
        JavaWOJSPServlet.framework/WebServerResources/Java/↵
```

```
        JavaWOJSPServlet_client.jar"/>
    <copy todir="${dest.dir}/${project.name}/WEB-INF/lib"
        file="${dest.dir}/${project.name}/WEB-INF/Library/Frameworks/↵
        JavaWebObjects.framework/Resources/Java/javawebobjects.jar"/>
</target>
...
```

Once the ssdd target is run, our directory structure should be ready to go. We could directly deploy our dist/Chap10Example directory (not the dist/Chap10Example.woa directory) to our servlet container. The default target on our build.xml will create a WAR file that can be hot-deployed to our servlet container. The WAR file is created using the war target. Once the war target is run, our Chap10Example.war file will be located in our dist directory.

Start your Tomcat server and copy the Chap10Example.war file into CATALINA_HOME/webapps directory. Tomcat should recognize the WAR file and auto-deploy it to your servlet container and unpack the contents automatically.

After Tomcat deploys your application, it should be available at http://localhost:8080/Chap10Example/login.jsp. To view the login component in the native WebObjects application, go to http://localhost:8080/Chap10Example/WebObjects/Chap10Example.woa; this will load the component using the WebObjects servlet instead of the WebObjects adaptor. In both cases Chap10Example is the name of the servlet context. All URLs are always relative to the servlet context in the JSP world.

Figure 10-4 shows our sample application loaded through a JSP page. One of the things you will notice is that the URL does not contain any reference to WebObjects. Some managers still have issues with Apple in the enterprise, even though tools such as WebObjects allow much quicker development at a much higher level.

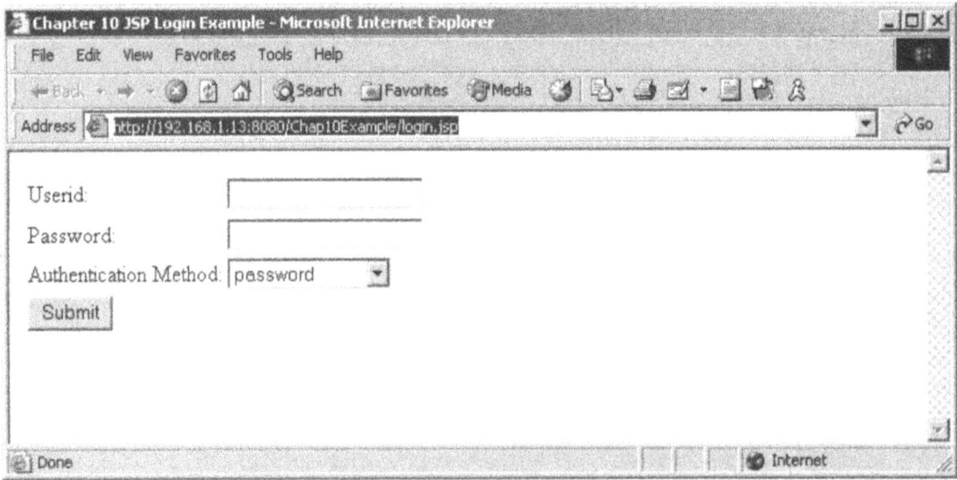

Figure 10-4. *Sample application running in Tomcat from JSP*

JSP/WO Best Practices

Here are some tips and tricks that can be useful in working with a mixed environment such as JSP/WebObjects.

Troubleshooting Application Startup

One of the most common frustrations in this mixed environment is the difficulty getting your first WO-based servlet application to launch properly. Many of the problems often stem from missing classes at runtime and problems in the WEB-INF/web.xml file.

If your application depends on third-party Jar files, you need to make sure the Jar files are deployed to the WEB-INF/lib directory of your web application. Check your application server's `System.out` and `System.err` log file output. A normal WebObjects servlet application startup will look something like Listing 10-11.

Listing 10-11. `System.out` *from a Nominal Servlet Startup*

```
INFO: Installing web application at context path /Chap10Example from URL ↵
    file:/Users/dov/jakarta-tomcat-5.0.12/webapps/Chap10Example
Found MainBundle at: /Users/dov/jakarta-tomcat-5.0.12/webapps/Chap10Example↵
    /WEB-INF/Chap10Example.woa
Classpath for WebObjects classloader is /Users/dov/jakarta-tomcat-5.0.12/↵
    webapps/Chap10Example/WEB-INF/Chap10Example.woa/Contents/Resources/↵
    Java/chap10example.jar:/Users/dov/jakarta-tomcat-5.0.12/webapps/↵
    Chap10Example/WEB-INF/Library/Frameworks/JavaEOAccess.framework/Resources/↵
    Java/javaeoaccess.jar:/Users/dov/jakarta-tomcat-5.0.12/webapps/Chap10Example/↵
    WEB-INF/Library/Frameworks/JavaEOControl.framework/Resources/Java/↵
    javaeocontrol.jar:/Users/dov/jakarta-tomcat-5.0.12/webapps/Chap10Example/↵
    WEB-INF/Library/Frameworks/JavaFoundation.framework/Resources/Java/↵
    javafoundation.jar:/Users/dov/jakarta-tomcat-5.0.12/webapps/Chap10Example/↵
    WEB-INF/Library/Frameworks/JavaWebObjects.framework/Resources/Java/↵
    javawebobjects.jar:/Users/dov/jakarta-tomcat-5.0.12/webapps/Chap10Example/↵
    WEB-INF/Library/Frameworks/JavaWOExtensions.framework/Resources/Java/↵
    JavaWOExtensions.jar:/Users/dov/jakarta-tomcat-5.0.12/webapps/Chap10Example/↵
    WEB-INF/Library/Frameworks/JavaWOJSPServlet.framework/Resources/Java/↵
    javawojspservlet.jar:/Users/dov/jakarta-tomcat-5.0.12/webapps/Chap10Example/↵
    WEB-INF/Library/Frameworks/JavaXML.framework/Resources/Java/javaxml.jar:↵
    /Library/WebObjects/Extensions/avalon-framework-4.1.2.jar:/Library/↵
    WebObjects/Extensions/axis-ant.jar:/Library/WebObjects/Extensions/axis.jar:↵
    /Library/WebObjects/Extensions/commons-discovery.jar:/Library/WebObjects↵
    /Extensions/commons-logging.jar:/Library/WebObjects/Extensions/jaxrpc.jar:↵
    /Library/WebObjects/Extensions/log4j-1.2.4.jar:/Library/WebObjects/↵
    Extensions/logkit-1.0.1.jar:/Library/WebObjects/Extensions/saaj.jar:↵
    /Library/WebObjects/Extensions/servlet.jar:/Library/WebObjects/Extensions/↵
    wsdl4j.jar:/Library/WebObjects/Extensions/
<Chap10Example>[2004-04-24 22:26:10 EDT] <main> WODefaultUndoStackLimit=10
<Chap10Example>[2004-04-24 22:26:10 EDT] <main> NSProjectSearchPath=("..")
<Chap10Example>[2004-04-24 22:26:10 EDT] <main> WOGenerateWSDL=true
```

```
<Chap10Example>[2004-04-24 22:26:10 EDT] <main> WOMaxHeaders=200
<Chap10Example>[2004-04-24 22:26:10 EDT] <main> WOCachingEnabled=false
<Chap10Example>[2004-04-24 22:26:10 EDT] <main> WOFrameworksBaseURL=↵
    /WebObjects/Frameworks
<Chap10Example>[2004-04-24 22:26:10 EDT] <main> WOAllowRapidTurnaround=true
<Chap10Example>[2004-04-24 22:26:10 EDT] <main> ↵
    WOAllowsConcurrentRequestHandling=false
<Chap10Example>[2004-04-24 22:26:10 EDT] <main> WOAllowsCacheControlHeader=true
<Chap10Example>[2004-04-24 22:26:10 EDT] <main> WOSMTPHost=smtp
<Chap10Example>[2004-04-24 22:26:10 EDT] <main> WOAcceptMalformedCookies=false
<Chap10Example>[2004-04-24 22:26:10 EDT] <main> ↵
    WOContextClassName=com.webobjects.jspservlet.WOServletContext
<Chap10Example>[2004-04-24 22:26:10 EDT] <main> ↵
    WOMissingResourceSearchEnabled=true
<Chap10Example>[2004-04-24 22:26:10 EDT] <main> ↵
    WOSessionStoreClassName=com.webobjects.jspservlet.WOServletSessionStore
<Chap10Example>[2004-04-24 22:26:10 EDT] <main> WODebuggingEnabled=true
<Chap10Example>[2004-04-24 22:26:10 EDT] <main> WODisplayExceptionPages=true
<Chap10Example>[2004-04-24 22:26:10 EDT] <main> WOAutoOpenClientApplication=false
<Chap10Example>[2004-04-24 22:26:10 EDT] <main> ↵
    WOAdaptorURL=http://localhost//Chap10Example/WebObjects
<Chap10Example>[2004-04-24 22:26:10 EDT] <main> WOApplicationBaseURL=/WebObjects
<Chap10Example>[2004-04-24 22:26:10 EDT] <main> WOAutoOpenInBrowser=false
<Chap10Example>[2004-04-24 22:26:10 EDT] <main> WOIncludeCommentsInResponse=false
<Chap10Example>[2004-04-24 22:26:10 EDT] <main> -----------------------
<Chap10Example>[2004-04-24 22:26:10 EDT] <main> NSBundle is unable to find ↵
    "ExtensionsForResources.plist" in the main bundle.  Ignoring optional ↵
    configuration file.
<Chap10Example>[2004-04-24 22:26:11 EDT] <main> Cannot use rapid turnaround. ↵
    Please start Xcode and open the project for this application.
Welcome to Chap10Example !
<Chap10Example>[2004-04-24 22:26:10 EDT] ↵
    <main> <WOApplication>.primeApplication: The Application name is Chap10Example
<Chap10Example>[2004-04-24 22:26:11 EDT] <main> The URL for webserver connect ↵
    through Servlet Container is:
http://dov.local//Chap10Example/WebObjects/Chap10Example.woa
<Chap10Example>[2004-04-24 22:26:10 EDT] <main> Waiting for requests...
```

You should first see a line indicating that the main bundle was found. This is an indication that the `WOServletAdaptor` was able to find your Application.class file. If this fails, usually the `WOServletAdaptor` did not initialize properly. A likely cause is that the `WOApplicationClass` parameter in the WEB-INF/web.xml is not properly defined.

Next you should see the `WOClasspath` displayed; this is read from the WEB-INF/web.xml as well. The web.xml file contains some shortcut variables that will be replaced at runtime with the absolute path to the location of the Jar files. If there is a problem running your application, carefully inspect the classpaths displayed and make sure they are correct. If the paths are incorrect, you may have to hard-code the paths in the WEB-INF/web.xml file.

After the classpaths are displayed, you should see the runtime WebObjects properties displayed as the application starts up. Once your application is running you should see the final message indicating that the application is waiting for requests.

Ant Builds

Eclipse keeps the Java class files updated. The Ant build script is designed to build the deployment products. The WOProject Ant tasks can automatically build the web.xml file. Once a project has matured and the basic architecture is laid out, automatically recreating the web.xml file might not be a good idea. If you develop custom servlets, integrate third-party tag libraries, or use custom parameters stored in the web.xml, WOProject cannot generate your custom changes. Once you have modified the web.xml, it is a good idea (and not very difficult) to maintain it yourself. The build.xml for the example project uses a web.xml file that is stored in a separate folder within the project (web folder). An alternative to maintaining the web.xml file manually is to use Xdoclet (`http://xdoclet.sourceforge.net`) to maintain your web.xml file. Xdoclet is very powerful and can be used to generate Java classes, or deployment descriptors from your code.

Another useful trick is to store your JSP pages within the Eclipse project. Our sample files are stored in the web folder. When the Ant script is run, the JSP files are copied into the proper place in our deployment directory.

■ **NOTE** When deploying your project to a new server without WebObjects installed, you will need to update the WebObjects license key with the deployment license key. This key is located in the WEB-INF/Library/Frameworks/JavaWebObjects.framework/Resources/License.key file. Your Ant script can read your deployment key from the build.properties file and make the necessary changes before the WAR gets created.

Debugging

It can be difficult debugging a web application built using any technology. Debugging our WebObjects application using Eclipse is no exception. However, since our WebObjects application can also be run as a Java application, we can make use of the built-in Eclipse Java debugging tools. We can set breakpoints, inspect variables, and do all of the wonderful things a modern IDE is supposed to allow you to do. Of course, `System.out.println()` is always available.

Eclipse can also be used to attach to a running Java application that has been started in debug mode. To run our example application in debug mode using Tomcat, start Tomcat using the Java Platform Debugger Architecture (JPDA):

```
$CATALINA_HOME/bin/catalina.sh [.bat for Windows] jpda start
```

This will start Tomcat and any applications deployed in Tomcat in debug mode. You can connect to the application on port 8000 using the Remote Java Application debug mode in Eclipse. Breakpoints can be set in the WebObjects Java code and the value of variables can be viewed. As you browse around the example application from the JSP side, any WebObjects Java code with breakpoints should be able to be debugged.

Connecting with External Web Servers

Using your servlet container's built-in web server may be suitable for your development needs, but chances are it won't be suitable for your production deployment. You can't run your application on port 8080 in production out in the real world either, since most firewalls are configured to block access to nonstandard ports (i.e., not 80 or 443). In addition, you may want to do fancy things such as URL rewriting.

Deploying your WebObjects application in a servlet container requires the use of native libraries provided by your container vendor to interact with external web servers such as Apache or Microsoft Internet Information Server. These external servers do not natively know anything about JSP or WebObjects. In a pure WebObjects world, the WebObjects adaptor was our link between the web server and the WebObjects application. In the servlet world, we need to rely on the vendor-provided mechanisms to route requests from the web server to our applications. One side benefit to using the vendor-supplied interface is that the connectors tend to be well tested and high performing.

The biggest issue with the vendor-supplied web server connectors is the ease of integration with your web server. The commercial products such as Macromedia JRun and BEA WebLogic provide web server connectors that are easy to integrate with the most popular web servers and are documented very well. The open source containers such as JBoss, Jetty, and Tomcat provide web server connectors that can be challenging to install and configure. The documentation on the open source connectors can be difficult to follow and is frequently out of date as the connector architecture evolves.

A large percentage of the posts to the Tomcat forums involve web server connector configuration issues with the JK or JK2 connectors. Thankfully, there have been a lot of solutions posted to the forums and on individual web sites to cover most of the problems that will be encountered. A resourceful administrator can probably get most problems fixed by doing some web searches.

While open source containers such as Tomcat are cost effective, managers of high-volume, mission-critical projects would do well to consider purchasing commercial products to gain access to better documentation and support.

Summary

WebObjects has made a huge leap into the mainstream Java world with the ability to be deployed into any J2EE servlet container. A recent SYS-CON (`http://www.sys-con.com/`) survey awarded WebObjects *Best Java Framework* and second place in *Best Java Component*. These accolades indicate a new role for WebObjects in the future: partner, not competitor!

CHAPTER 11

XML and WebObjects

Syntax, my lad. It has been restored to the highest place in the republic.

—John Steinbeck

Sometimes when we read the hype and hyperbole about XML (Extensible Markup Language) we really have to wonder about the state of the industry. Despite its name, XML is not a language. XML is not a protocol. XML is a not a silver bullet. XML won't guarantee platform independence. It doesn't provide automatic internationalization. It will not future-proof your application. Unlike HTML, XML does not do anything.

In this chapter we will discuss how to use WebObjects to manipulate XML, including serializing objects, parsing XML, and transforming XML via XSLT (a language for transforming XML documents).

What About XML?

What XML is: all those angle brackets, Unicode, a constraint language (the Document Type Definition, DTD), data models, trees, and an ever-expanding family of specifications. It is a subset of SGML (Standard Generalized Markup Language), which has been around for a long time. In a nutshell, XML is a strictly defined syntax, plain and simple. It is just pure information wrapped in XML tags. And that is precisely the source of its usefulness—it is a simple yet extremely powerful syntax for representing structured data. XML is a cross-platform software- and hardware-independent tool for representing information.

NOTE XHTML (Extensible HyperText Markup Language) is HTML 4.01 with the strictness of XML syntax. The idea is that markup code that is required to be correct will lead to more consistent rendering. It should also lead to faster, smaller browsers. Take a look at `http://www.csszengarden.com/` to see some of the neat things that can be done with XHTML and Cascading Style Sheets.

What XML does for you is remove a major roadblock, format incompatibility, when exchanging information with other systems. We now have a common syntax, but not a common vocabulary, for exchanging information. We don't have to write formatting code for output nor parsers to handle input. These are standard components we can pick up and use.

With a standard syntax comes the possibility of standard, generic transformations. There are a multitude of tools out there that are configured with XML or can manipulate XML to produce everything from more XML to graphics.

There is at least one XML file in every WebObjects application and framework. Under the Resources directory is the misleadingly named Info.plist, shown in Listing 11-1. This file describes the contents of the bundle but is of little interest to us other than as an example of an XML document. In previous versions of WebObjects this was actually in plist format, hence the name. For more details on XML and the related topics in the following sections, see the clear, concise, and free tutorials at `http://www.w3schools.com/default.asp`. This site also has clear (though Microsoft-based) examples illustrating each of these technologies.

Listing 11-1. *Example XML Contents of Info.plist*

```
<?xml version="1.0" encoding="UTF-8"?>
<!DOCTYPE plist PUBLIC "-//Apple Computer//DTD PLIST 1.0//EN"
    "http://www.apple.com/DTDs/PropertyList-1.0.dtd">
<plist version="1.0">
<dict>
    <key>CFBundleDevelopmentRegion</key>
    <string>English</string>
    <key>CFBundleExecutable</key>
    <string>PracticalUtilities</string>
    <key>CFBundleInfoDictionaryVersion</key>
    <string>6.0</string>
    <key>CFBundlePackageType</key>
    <string>FMWK</string>
    <key>CFBundleSignature</key>
    <string>webo</string>
    <key>CFBundleVersion</key>
    <string>0.0.1d1</string>
    <key>Has_WOComponents</key>
    <true/>
    <key>Java</key>
    <dict>
        <key>JVMVersion</key>
        <string>1.4+</string>
    </dict>
    <key>NSExecutable</key>
    <string>PracticalUtilities</string>
    <key>NSJavaClientRoot</key>
    <string>WebServerResources/Java</string>
    <key>NSJavaPathClient</key>
    <string>practicalutilities.ja</string>
</dict>
</plist>
```

Document Type Definitions

A Document Type Definition (DTD) defines the legal elements of an XML document. See Figure 11-2 for an example. A DTD can be declared inline in the XML document, or as an external reference. A DTD is the difference between well-formed and valid XML. XML with correct syntax is well formed; XML validated against a DTD is valid. All valid XML is well formed but well-formed XML is not necessarily valid.

A DTD is needed for validation because XML, unlike HTML, is not marked up with predefined tags. The structure of HTML documents and the tags (`<br />`, `<table>`, etc.) used for markup are predefined and unalterable. In XML you define your own tags and document structure. Interestingly, the syntax used in a DTD is not XML syntax.

A DTD is optional in an XML document. Why would you want to use a DTD?

- The data you receive from external sources can be validated against a standard DTD.
- You can verify your own data with a DTD.
- With an inline DTD, your XML files can provide a description of its own format.
- A common or standard DTD allows independent groups to reliably exchange data.

The XML file in Listing 11-1 references an external DTD on the Apple web site. The DTD referenced is shown in Listing 11-2.

Listing 11-2. *The External DTD Referenced in Listing 11-1*

```
<!ENTITY % plistObject "(array | data | date | dict | real | integer | string |
    true | false )" >
<!ELEMENT plist %plistObject;>
<!ATTLIST plist version CDATA "1.0" >

<!-- Collections -->
<!ELEMENT array (%plistObject;)*>
<!ELEMENT dict (key, %plistObject;)*>
<!ELEMENT key (#PCDATA)>

<!--- Primitive types -->
<!ELEMENT string (#PCDATA)>
<!ELEMENT data (#PCDATA)> <!-- Contents interpreted as Base-64 encoded -->
<!ELEMENT date (#PCDATA)> <!-- Contents should conform to a subset of ISO 8601
    (in particular, YYYY '-' MM '-' DD 'T' HH ':' MM ':' SS 'Z'.  Smaller units
    may be omitted with a loss of precision) -->

<!-- Numerical primitives -->
<!ELEMENT true EMPTY>  <!-- Boolean constant true -->
<!ELEMENT false EMPTY> <!-- Boolean constant false -->
<!ELEMENT real (#PCDATA)> <!-- Contents should represent a floating point number
    matching ("+" | "-")? d+ ("."d*)? ("E" ("+" | "-") d+)? where d is a digit 0-9.
-->
<!ELEMENT integer (#PCDATA)> <!-- Contents should represent a (possibly signed)
    integer number in base 10 -->
```

XML Schema

XML Schema is the successor to DTD. Like a DTD, an XML Schema describes the structure of an XML document. The most noticeable difference is that it is in XML syntax. What the originators of DTDs were thinking we'll never understand. You might also see the XML Schema language referred to as XML Schema Definition (XSD).

Although DTDs are still in use, we expect that XML Schemas will eventually replace them. XML Schemas provide several important advantages:

- XML Schemas support namespaces. This is important, as packages are in Java.
- XML Schemas are extensible: a schema can be reused in other schemas; custom data types can be derived from existing types; multiple schemas can be referenced in the same document.
- XML Schemas describe the syntax in a more complete manner.
- XML Schemas are written in XML: you don't have to learn another language; a standard XML editor can edit Schema files; a standard XML parser will parse Schema files; Schema can be manipulated and transformed with standard tools.

XSL and Related Technologies

XML describes data, but not how to display that data. Having data that you can't display is often not that useful. You can use CSS (Cascading Style Sheets) to add display information to an XML document. The class names in the stylesheet must match the entity and attribute names in the XML document. An XML document indicates the CSS definition to use by including a line like

```
<?xml-stylesheet type="text/css"
    href="http://www.apple.com/DTDs/PropertyList-1.0.css"?>
```

Don't bother looking for this file; it does not exist. We just used that as an example. Despite the fact that this works, we don't think that it is the way to go. The better solution involves (are you surprised?) yet more XML.

XSL (the Extensible Stylesheet Language) is a far more sophisticated technology than CSS. Today XSL consists of three parts: XSLT (XSL Transformations) for transforming XML documents; XPath for defining and accessing the parts of an XML document; and XSL-FO for formatting XML documents into some presentation format.

XSL Transformations

XSLT focuses on transforming XML documents into other documents, often into other XML documents. Why would you want to do this? One reason would be to convert the XML structure to one that an existing application could more easily work with. For simple output purposes you can also convert it directly into XHTML. XSLT means you are not restricted to one representation of the data.

XSLT can do more than just a straight "A to B" transformation. It can add new elements and remove elements. It can test the data described in XML and, based on the test, make decisions about which elements to display. It allows the data described in XML to be arranged and sorted.

XPath

XPath defines the syntax for expressions describing the parts of an XML document. It uses paths that are similar in structure and concept to file system paths to identify nodes in an XML document. XPath is central to XSLT; XSLT uses XPath to define the matching patterns for transformations. XPath includes a library of standard functions, similar to what you find in Java, for working with strings, numbers, and Boolean expressions.

XSL-FO

XSL-FO (Extensible Stylesheet Language Formatting Objects) is a language for formatting XML data. It should come as no surprise that it is an XML-based markup language. XSL-FO describes how to format XML data for output to screen, paper, or other media. Confusingly, the World Wide Web Consortium (W3C) has formally named XSL-FO as XSL. You will probably see the names used interchangeably in general documentation.

XSL-FO documents are just XML files describing how to format output. They describe the contents and layout of the final product. They don't, however, do anything. For that, you need a program, an XSL-FO processor. A popular example of such a program is the Apache FOP (Formatting Objects Processor), found at `http://xml.apache.org/fop/`.

An interesting tutorial on XSL-FO can be found at `http://www.renderx.com/Tests/doc/html/tutorial.html`.

But WebObjects Already Has a Data-to-Display Transformer

Yes, it does. And it is a fine one. Although it does not produce really great, modern HTML, we are not suggesting using XSLT to replace it. There are a lot of useful tools out there based on this technology and you may well find a home for one or more in your project.

XML Parsers

If you have an XML file, how do you use it? You need some way of converting the data into something your Java code can use. This is the job of an XML parser. There are two common types of XML parsers. One is called SAX (Simple API for XML) and the other DOM (Domain Object Model). SAX and DOM both give you access to the information stored in XML documents. However, they take very different approaches to giving you access to your information.

DOM Parsers

The Document Object Model (DOM) builds an in-memory tree structure that contains the data from an entire XML document. The `org.w3c.dom` package defines the DOM interfaces for accessing the XML information in a tree rooted in a `Document` object. This tree is conceptually similar to how JavaScript treats an HTML document. This tree maintains information about elements, attributes, character data sections, etc.

The advantage of a DOM tree is that it mirrors the original document's structure and content. This form is useful for XML processing tools such as XPath and XSLT processors. This form is also well suited when your XML documents contain data from traditional document sources such as Word and Excel files.

One result of holding the entire tree model in memory is that random navigation is possible. As SAX processes the XML document sequentially, backward navigation is not possible. If you need to search and navigate, you will be at a serious disadvantage when using SAX. You would need to write a considerable amount of extra code to work around this.

The key problem with DOM has to do with scalability. As the entire tree is held in memory, memory is the limiting factor in the size of document that can be processed. It is also not the optimal form for dealing with structured data. Consider the case of reading a database schema from XML and creating a database from it. DOM is probably not the right choice for this scenario; this is when SAX might be a better fit.

SAX Parsers

The Simple API for XML (SAX) is a low-level API used to access the contents of an XML document. The simple part is talking about what it does, not what you as the user of the parser have to do. SAX is simple because it offloads the work onto you.

SAX provides the contents of an XML document as a sequence of events. You need to write the code to catch, interpret, and process these events. You'll be notified at the start and finish of parsing the document; when each start or end tag is parsed; and when character data is read. While this is efficient from the parser's point of view (information is not held in memory and little processing is needed), the information in a single SAX event is not of much use. Without knowing the context of the event you won't know what to do with the information. Thus, to make use of SAX you end up having to record the relevant state information as parsing proceeds.

We are not trying to say that SAX is useless. It is efficient and it has its place. A specific application will know what data it needs and know when each piece of data is no longer needed. SAX allows the optimization to be done at the place of greatest knowledge. SAX lets you build efficient XML-handling code, but like any low-level API it is cumbersome to use. It is particularly well suited when the information in the XML document is machine-readable, such as a database schema or serialized objects. You will need to create Java classes to hold, manage, and manipulate this kind of data. Tying this into SAX is not a great deal of effort.

Other Parsers

While SAX and DOM are the main/core parsing Java APIs for XML, they are by no means the only ones. A quick search of Google will turn up more variants and derivatives than you can shake the proverbial stick at. Google tends to do that. We'll point out one interesting one.

Digester is part of the Jakarta Commons Project found at `http://jakarta.apache.org/commons/`. It uses a syntax similar to XPath to map the elements in the XML file to a data structure in your code. This allows you to easily select the needed elements out of an XML document without resorting to parsing it node-by-node using SAX or walking through the treelike data structure created by the DOM.

XML and Object Serialization

According to JavaSoft's Object Serialization documentation:

> *Object Serialization supports the encoding of objects, and the objects reachable from them, into a stream of bytes; and it supports the complementary reconstruction of the object graph from the stream. Serialization is used for lightweight persistence and for communication via sockets or Remote Method Invocation (RMI).*

Serialization is often used to save the state of an application as a binary representation of all of the objects with their current values. Unfortunately, serialized components are fragile, being sensitive to changes in the classes used to produce them. Therefore XML APIs that handle Java serialization provide a useful alternative: a human-readable (and editable) persistent-state format. This enables you to keep data in a form you can examine if software fails (as opposed to keeping data in objects that can only be accessed via methods).

XMLEncoder is designed to archive graphs of objects. This means that if an object has properties that reference other objects, those objects will also be archived. Note, though, that XMLEncoder will only traverse properties that are exposed via the JavaBean naming conventions (e.g., `set<X>`, `get<X>`) or a `BeanInfo` class.

WebObjects Application Support

Starting with version 5.2, WebObjects has fully embraced XML all through the core frameworks. There are several new classes that support XML serialization, XSLT transformation, and XML parsing. WebObjects XML support is based on the Apache Foundation Xerces XML parser and Xalan XSL processor.

There are several new classes that are used to implement XML serialization in WebObjects.

- **`NSXMLOutputStream`**: An `NSXMLOutputStream` writes primitive data types and graphs of Java objects to an `OutputStream` as XML data.
- **`NSXMLOutputFormat`**: This class is used to specify an output format used to display the formatted XML stream, mostly for human-readable consumption.
- **`NSXMLInputStream`**: An `NSXMLInputStream` deserializes primitive data and objects previously written as XML data using an `NSXMLOutputStream`.
- **`NSXMLObjectOutput`**: This interface provides for converting data from any of the Java primitive types to a series of XML elements. There are also facilities for converting a Java object in an XML element, which then includes sub-XML elements.

Sample Application

The best way to showcase the XML support built into WebObjects is with a sample application. This simple example is designed to show how XML serialization and XSL transformation can be performed using WebObjects. The sample application is a mini shopping cart that displays a list of products retrieved from a database. The user has the option of adding products to the "cart." Once products are in the cart, the data can be serialized, transformed into HTML, or converted dynamically to a PDF document.

All of these technologies can come in handy in many applications. XML serialization can be used as an import/export format for your data. XSL transformation is useful when it is necessary to transform data from one data structure to another.

Our sample application has a single entity called Product. Figure 11-1 shows the layout of our Product entity.

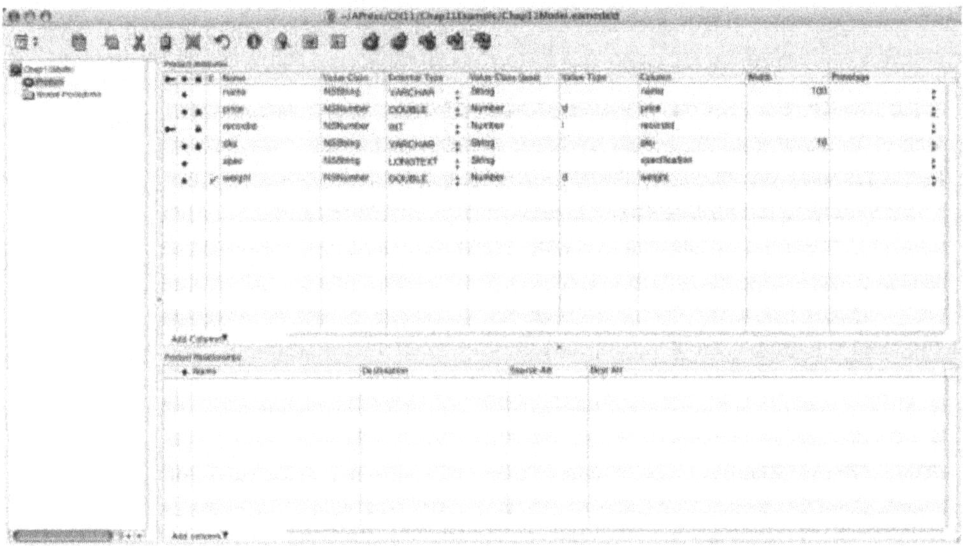

Figure 11-1. *Product entity EOModel*

Serializing EO Data into XML

In general, the basic procedure for serializing EOs into an XML data stream is as follows:

- Add `writeObject()` to EOModel classes.
- Create an `NSXMLOutputstream`.
- Assign an `NSXMLOutputFormat` to the output stream.
- Call `writeObject()` on the EO objects that are to be serialized.

Step 1: Adding Serialization Support to EOModel Classes

The first step in preparing our EO entities to be serialized is to implement the `writeObject()` method in all of the model classes. The `writeObject` method is responsible for writing the state of the object for its particular class so that the corresponding `readObject` method can restore it. This method is defined in the Java interface `java.io.Serializable`. When traversing an object graph, an object may be encountered that does not support the `Serializable` interface. In this case the `NotSerializableException` will be thrown and will identify the class of the non-serializable object. If a class requires special handling to be serialized, it will need to override the default `writeObject` behavior.

EOModeler generates a template for the `readObject()` (used to deserialize an object) and `writeObject()` (used to serialize an object). These methods are commented out by default. If you require any special handling for an `EOEntity` or attribute during the serialization or deserialization, you can override the default `readObject()` and `writeObject()` methods.

In order to have access to the attribute-level data in our shopping cart, we are going to serialize the attributes with key value names. Otherwise the `NSXMLOutputStream` only serializes the EO data as faults and we won't have access to the information we need later on in our sample application. Listing 11-3 shows the serialization method for the Product entity.

Listing 11-3. *Product* `writeObject()`

```
/**
  * If you add instance variables to store property values you
  * should add empty implementions of the Serialization methods
  * to avoid unnecessary overhead (the properties will be
  * serialized for you in the superclass).
  */
private void writeObject(ObjectOutputStream stream) throws IOException {
    NSXMLOutputStream xml_stream = (NSXMLOutputStream)stream;
    xml_stream.writeObject(name(), "name");
    xml_stream.writeObject(spec(), "spec");
    xml_stream.writeObject(price(), "price");
    xml_stream.writeObject(weight(), "weight");
    xml_stream.writeObject(sku(), "sku");
}
```

When the `NSXMLOutputStream` calls `writeObject()` on the object being serialized, all references to the object are also serialized. If you do not provide the methods to serialize your attributes, the eo will be serialized but it won't contain any of your data, only the eo fault required to refetch the data when the object is deserialized. By providing a string key for each of the attributes defined in the `writeObject()` method, `NSXMLOutputStream` will output our data as part of the XML fault information. Listing 11-4 shows a portion of the sample application after the shopping cart was serialized. The keys are highlighted in bold.

Listing 11-4. *Portion of a Serialized Product Entity*

```
...
<object id="47">
            <class idRef="6" name="com.apress.practicalwo.chap11.Product"/>
            <long field="version">5000</long>
            <object field="editingContext" idRef="24"/>
            <object field="globalID" id="48">
                <class idRef="25"
                  name="com.webobjects.eocontrol._EOIntegralKeyGlobalID"/>
                <string field="entityName" idRef="33"/>
                <object field="guessedName"/>
                <string field="subEntityName" idRef="33" ignoreEDB="1"/>
                <object field="keyValue" id="49" ignoreEDB="1">
                    <class idRef="34" name="java.lang.Integer"/>
                    <int field="value">3</int>
                </object>
            </object>
            <object field="properties" ignoreEDB="1"/>
            <object field="classDescription" idRef="40" ignoreEDB="1"/>
            <string id="50" key="name" xml:space="preserve">Power Mac
              G5</string>
            <string id="51" key="spec" xml:space="preserve">↵
              Dual 2GHz PowerPC G5 1GHz frontside bus/processor ↵
              512K L2 cache/processor 512MB DDR400 128-bit SDRAM ↵
              Expandable to 8GB SDRAM 160GB Serial ATA SuperDrive ↵
              Three PCI-X Slots ATI Radeon 9600 Pro 64MB DDR video↵
              memory 56K internal modem </string>
            <object id="52" key="price">
                <class idRef="43" name="java.lang.Double"/>
                <double field="value">2999.0</double>
            </object>
            <object key="weight"/>
            <string id="53" ignoreEDB="1" key="sku"
              xml:space="preserve">dual-g5</string>
        </object>
...
```

The serialized version of an NSArray of Products contains information about the state of the editing context and a serialized representation of the NSArray. Serializing even a simple data structure such as a list of selected Products can generate large files. For our sample application, selecting two of the products generated a 8595-byte file that was 120 lines long!

If you implement all of the attributes and relationships in your eo object's `writeObject()`, you may traverse those relationships when you serialize your objects. Depending on the nature of the data model and the amount of data in your database, the serialization process could take a great deal of time and disk space, generate a lot of disk and database activity, and require large amounts of memory. Be sure of the underlying environment before embarking on large-scale serialization schemes.

Step 2: Serializing the Cart

Once we have plumbed out our EOModel Java classes with serialization support, we are all set to go. The next step is to actually cause the serialization to happen. Serialization is a Java-defined process, not a WebObjects one. There is no mechanism that specifies the format of your serialized data. You just need to be able to reconstitute the object using the `readObject()` method. We could serialize our shopping cart into a binary format if we wanted to, but we are going to use an XML format instead (so we can show how to use WebObjects' nifty `NSXMLOutputStream` class).

Our WebObjects page is pretty simple; we are using standard WebObjects conventions to talk to our EOModel and displaying a list of products retrieved from the database. Our `WODisplayGroup` simply retrieves all of the Products from the database and displays them in a repetition. Next to each product is an "Add to Cart" button that will store a reference to the selected Product into an `NSArray`. Figure 11-2 shows the layout of our shopping cart page.

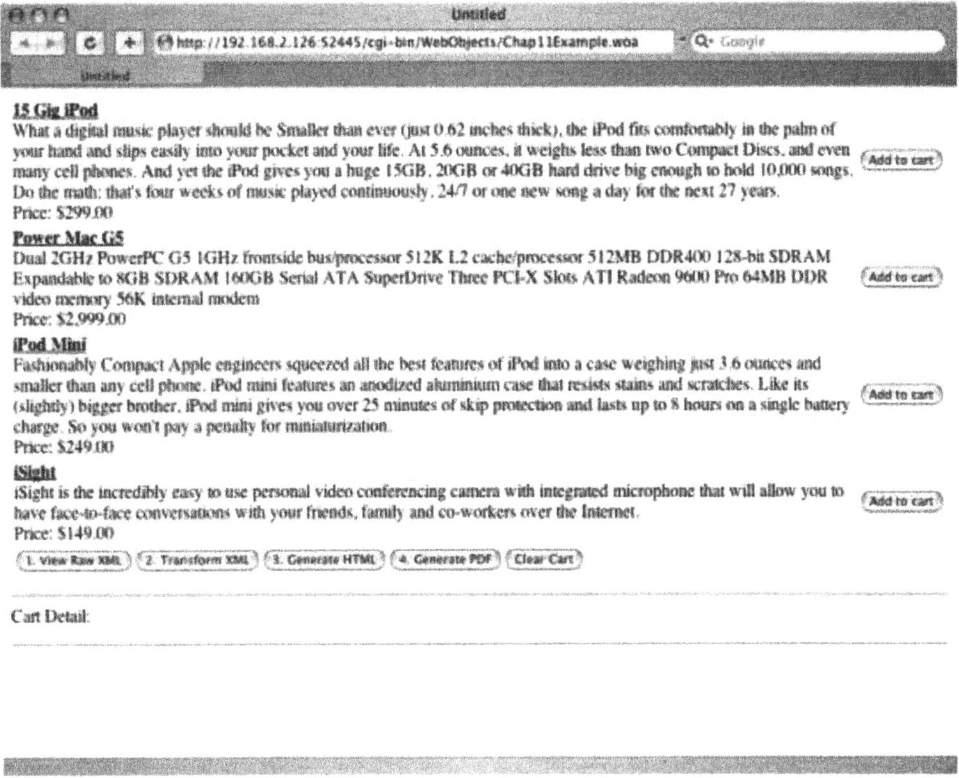

Figure 11-2. *XML shopping cart application*

Listing 11-5 shows the `WOComponent` method used to add a selected Product into the `NSMutableArray` (our shopping cart).

TIP Notice in Listing 11-5 that we did not simply return `null` for the method. Instead we created a new page with the same name and assigned the data into the new page. The primary reason for doing this is that it helps prevent problems when the user clicks the back button in their browser. Creating a new page adds a new page into the WebObjects page cache with current data. If the `Application`'s `pageRefreshOnBackTrackEnabled` is `false`, the pages are delivered to the browser pre-expired and the browser will retrieve a fresh copy. The new page should have the most current data if you set all of the instance variables needed each time.

Listing 11-5. `ProductList.addToCart()` *Method*

```
public WOComponent addToCart() {
    WOComponent nextPage = pageWithName("ProductList");
    if (selectedProducts == null) {
        selectedProducts = new NSMutableArray();
    }
    selectedProducts.addObject(product);
    ((ProductList) nextPage).selectedProducts = selectedProducts;
    return nextPage;
}
```

After we have our shopping cart filled with products, we can serialize the shopping cart using the WebObjects serialization classes. Listing 11-6 shows the `WOComponent` code that kicks off the serialization process.

Listing 11-6. `ProductList.viewXML()` *Method*

```
public WOComponent viewXML() {
    WOComponent nextPage = pageWithName("ProductList");
    cartXML = XMLSerializer.serializeArray(selectedProducts);
    ((ProductList) nextPage).selectedProducts = selectedProducts;
    ((ProductList) nextPage).cartXML = cartXML;
    ((ProductList) nextPage).hidexml = false;
    return nextPage;
}
```

The `XMLSerializer` class does all of the heavy lifting. The `serializeArray()` takes the array of selected products (our shopping cart) and serializes the `NSArray` object. As the object graph contained in the `NSArray` is processed, the `writeObject()` method we added to our Product entity is automatically called. Listing 11-7 shows the code that generates the XML formatted string that gets returned to the ProductList component.

Listing 11-7. `XMLSerializer.serializeArray()` *Method*

```
public static String serializeArray(NSArray list) {
    ByteArrayOutputStream out = new ByteArrayOutputStream();
    try {
        // Create a stream to the output file.
        BufferedOutputStream byte_output_stream = new BufferedOutputStream(out);
        NSXMLOutputStream stream = new NSXMLOutputStream(byte_output_stream);

        // Set the format of the output document (XML).
        NSXMLOutputFormat format = new NSXMLOutputFormat(true);

        // Serialize data to object output stream.
        stream.writeObject(list);

        format.setEncoding("UTF-8");
        //turn indentation on
        stream.setOutputFormat(format);

        stream.flush();
        stream.close();
        byte_output_stream.close();

    } catch (IOException e) {
        // TODO Auto-generated catch block
        e.printStackTrace();
    }
    return out.toString();
}
```

The `NSXMLOutputStream` is constructed with a `BufferedOutputStream` because it is much more efficient than using a plain `ByteArrayOutputStream`. This output stream is going to contain our serialized data when the process is completed. The `ByteArrayOutputStream` could be replaced with a `FileOutputStream` to save the resulting serialized objects to a file on the local file system.

The real magic happens when the `stream.writeObject(list)` method is called. The `NSXMLOutputStream` class walks down the object graph calling the `writeObject()` for each object it comes across, passing itself as a reference. The `NSXMLOutputFormat` class is used to apply a human-readable format to the resulting output stream. You can set various encoding schemes using the `setEncoding()` method, but the XML parsers and XSLT engines currently only support UTF-8, which is the default if not otherwise specified. The resulting string is bound to a WOString component on the ProductList page to be displayed in the bottom half of the screen.

The resulting serialized data dump is large and complex. If you added a bunch of products into the cart, your dump will be even bigger. The data dump is a snapshot of the state of the `NSArray` at the time of serialization. Because the objects we serialized were part of an `EOEditingContext`, that information is also serialized, adding to the complexity of the data.

If we had serialized that data to a file we could rebuild the shopping cart to the same state as it was by deserializing the file back into Java objects.

The format of the output generated by the NSXMLOutputStream is specified by the WebObjects default XML serialization schema. This schema is maintained on Apple's servers and can be accessed to validate the data structure by tools and parsers. The schema for WebObjects 5.2 is located at http://www.apple.com/webobjects/5.2/schemas/woxml.xsd. NSXMLOutputStream specifies the validation schema in the header of the XML dump. Listing 11-8 shows the header information generated by our writeObject() method.

Listing 11-8. *XML Schema Declaration in XML Data Dump*

```
<?xml version="1.0" encoding="UTF-8"?>
<content xmlns="http://www.apple.com/webobjects/XMLSerialization"
    xmlns:xsi="http://www.w3.org/2001/XMLSchema-instance"
    xsi:schemaLocation="http://www.apple.com/webobjects/XMLSerialization
    http://www.apple.com/webobjects/5.2/schemas/woxml.xsd">
...
```

The definition and understanding of XML Schemas are beyond the scope of this book, but there are a lot of great resources on the Web to help you. The official specification is located at http://www.w3.org/XML/Schema along with some materials to help you learn about using XML Schemas. The basic purpose of an XML Schema is to define the structure of an XML document so that the structure can be validated. XML parsers such Apache's Xerces can validate an XML document prior to parsing to ensure that it is complete. These types of XML parsers are called validating parsers. Most XML parsers support this functionality. It is not necessary to embed the schema definition information at the top of the file for the XML file to be considered valid. If there is no schema associated with an XML document, it is assumed to be a valid document if it is well formed (matching tags).

Step 3: XML Transformation

Now that we have the shopping cart serialized, we could do all sorts of things with the resulting XML structure. The biggest problem is that the raw XML from the serialization is very complex and difficult to understand. The XML structure was designed to capture all of the information needed to reconstitute the objects, not for the convenience of mere mortals. In order to do something useful with our serialized shopping cart, we need to transform the complex XML structure into something more manageable.

The general procedure for executing an XSL transformation uses an XSLT transformation engine. WebObjects uses the Apache Foundation's Xalan classes (http://xml.apache.org/xalan-j/index.html). The Transformer takes an input source of the XML to be transformed and the XSL stylesheet to use for the transformation. The output stream of the Transformer can be directed to a file or a bytestream as required.

We are going to use an XSLT (XML Stylesheet Language Transformations) script to convert the data from one format to another. This initial transformation requires a rather complex XSL script to process the raw serialized data. Fortunately Apple provides a sample transformation script in their *XML Serialization* documentation. This script is called, strangely enough, SimpleTransformation.xsl (Listing 11-9).

Listing 11-9. *SimpleTransformation.xsl*

```
<?xml version="1.0" encoding="UTF-8"?>
<xsl:stylesheet xmlns:xsl="http://www.w3.org/1999/XSL/Transform"
      xmlns:woxml="http://www.apple.com/webobjects/XMLSerialization"
      exclude-result-prefixes="woxml" version="1.0">
    <xsl:output method="xml" encoding="UTF-8"
        omit-xml-declaration="no" indent="yes"/>
    <!-- ** Constants ** -->
    <!-- Indicates how dictionaries are encoded: key-value or two-array. -->
    <xsl:variable name="dictionary_encoding">
        <xsl:value-of select="'key-value'"/>
    </xsl:variable>
    <!-- ** Utilities ** -->
    <!-- Gets the base class name from a fully-qualified class name. -->
    <xsl:template name="basename">
        <xsl:param name="path"/>
        <xsl:choose>
            <xsl:when test="contains($path, '.')">
                <xsl:call-template name="basename">
                    <xsl:with-param name="path"
                        select="substring-after($path, '.')"/>
                </xsl:call-template>
            </xsl:when>
            <xsl:otherwise>
                <xsl:value-of select="$path"/>
            </xsl:otherwise>
        </xsl:choose>
    </xsl:template>
    <!-- ** Element Processing ** -->
    <!-- Processes the tree root. -->
    <xsl:template match="/">
        <xsl:element name="content">
            <xsl:apply-templates select="woxml:content"/>
        </xsl:element>
    </xsl:template>
    <!-- Processes the root element (woxml:content). -->
    <xsl:template match="woxml:content">
        <xsl:apply-templates select="*"/>
    </xsl:template>
    <!-- Processes woxml:object elements. -->
    <xsl:template name="process_object" match="woxml:object">
        <!-- extract class name -->
        <xsl:variable name="className">
            <xsl:value-of select="woxml:class/@name"/>
        </xsl:variable>
        <!-- get base class name -->
        <xsl:variable name="class">
```

```
            <xsl:call-template name="basename">
                <xsl:with-param name="path" select="$className"/>
            </xsl:call-template>
        </xsl:variable>
        <!-- determine the element name -->
        <xsl:variable name="tag">
            <xsl:choose>
                <xsl:when test="$class='NSDictionary' or
                      $class='NSMutableDictionary'">
                    <xsl:value-of select="'dictionary'"/>
                </xsl:when>
                <xsl:when test="$class='NSArray' or $class='NSMutableArray'">
                    <xsl:value-of select="'array'"/>
                </xsl:when>
                <xsl:otherwise>
                    <xsl:value-of select="$class"/>
                </xsl:otherwise>
            </xsl:choose>
        </xsl:variable>
        <!-- create the element -->
        <xsl:element name="{$tag}">
            <xsl:choose>
                <xsl:when test="$class='NSDictionary' or
                      $class='NSMutableDictionary'">
                    <xsl:call-template name="process_dictionary"/>
                </xsl:when>
                <xsl:otherwise>
                    <xsl:call-template name="process_object_content"/>
                </xsl:otherwise>
            </xsl:choose>
        </xsl:element>
    </xsl:template>
    <!-- Processes the content of a woxml:object element. -->
    <xsl:template name="process_object_content">
        <xsl:apply-templates select="*"/>
    </xsl:template>
    <!-- Processes woxml:class elements. -->
    <xsl:template match="woxml:class"/>
    <!-- Processes woxml:array elements. -->
    <xsl:template match="woxml:array">
        <xsl:for-each select="woxml:object">
            <xsl:call-template name="process_object"/>
        </xsl:for-each>
    </xsl:template>
    <!-- Processes primitive-type and woxml:string elements. -->
    <xsl:template match="woxml:boolean|woxml:byte|woxml:ch|woxml:short|↵
      woxml:int|woxml:long|woxml:float|woxml:double|woxml:string">
```

```
    <!-- determine the element name -->
    <xsl:variable name="element_name">
        <xsl:choose>
            <xsl:when test="@key">
                <xsl:value-of select="@key"/>
            </xsl:when>
            <xsl:when test="@field">
                <xsl:value-of select="@field"/>
            </xsl:when>
            <xsl:otherwise>
                <xsl:value-of select="name()"/>
            </xsl:otherwise>
        </xsl:choose>
    </xsl:variable>
    <!-- store possible reference to another element -->
    <xsl:variable name="ref">
        <xsl:value-of select="@idRef"/>
    </xsl:variable>
    <!-- create the element -->
    <xsl:element name="{$element_name}">
        <xsl:choose>
            <xsl:when test="string(number($ref))='NaN'">
                <!-- $ref is not a number, therefore there's no reference -->
                <xsl:value-of select="."/>
            </xsl:when>
            <xsl:otherwise>
                <!-- $ref is a number and, by extension, a reference -->
                <xsl:value-of select="//*[@id=$ref]"/>
            </xsl:otherwise>
        </xsl:choose>
    </xsl:element>
</xsl:template>
<!-- Processes woxml:object elements that contain a NSDictionary or
    NSMutableDictionary.  -->
<xsl:template name="process_dictionary">
    <xsl:choose>
        <xsl:when test="$dictionary_encoding='key-value'">
            <!-- output the two arrays as key-value pairs within item
              elements -->
            <xsl:for-each select="woxml:array[1]">
                <xsl:for-each select="*">
                    <xsl:variable name="current_position">
                        <xsl:value-of select="position()"/>
                    </xsl:variable>
                    <xsl:element name="item">
                        <xsl:element name="key">
                            <xsl:apply-templates select="."/>
```

```
                            </xsl:element>
                            <xsl:element name="value">
                                <xsl:apply-templates
                                 select="ancestor::*[position()=2]/⏎
                                 child::woxml:array[2]/child::*[position()=⏎
                                 $current_position]"/>
                            </xsl:element>
                        </xsl:element>
                    </xsl:for-each>
                </xsl:for-each>
            </xsl:when>
            <xsl:otherwise>
                <!-- output the two arrays on separate nodes -->
                <xsl:for-each select="woxml:array">
                    <xsl:element name="array">
                        <xsl:apply-templates select="*"/>
                    </xsl:element>
                </xsl:for-each>
            </xsl:otherwise>
        </xsl:choose>
    </xsl:template>
</xsl:stylesheet>
```

Instead of diving into this complex script, we are just going to use it to transform our raw data into a much simpler data structure. The `XMLSerializer` class has a `transformXML()` that takes the XML string that will be transformed and the file name of the XSL stylesheet that will be used to do the actual transformation. Listing 11-10 shows the source for the `transformXML()` method.

Listing 11-10. `XMLSerializer.transformXML()`

```
public static String transformXML(String xml, String xslfile) {
    String result = null;
    try {
        Result output = new StreamResult(new ByteArrayOutputStream());
        // get the XSL stylesheet
        WOApplication application = WOApplication.application();
        WOResourceManager resource_manager = application.resourceManager();
        String xsl = new String(resource_manager.bytesForResourceNamed(
            xslfile, null, null));

        // create the XSL Transformer
        TransformerFactory tFactory = TransformerFactory.newInstance();
        Transformer transformer = tFactory.newTransformer(new StreamSource(
            new StringReader(xsl)));
```

```
        // Perform the XSL transformation
        transformer.transform(new StreamSource(new StringReader(xml)), output);

        result = ((StreamResult) output).getOutputStream().toString();
    } catch (TransformerConfigurationException e1) {
        // TODO Auto-generated catch block
        e1.printStackTrace();
    } catch (TransformerFactoryConfigurationError e1) {
        // TODO Auto-generated catch block
        e1.printStackTrace();
    } catch (TransformerException e) {
        // TODO Auto-generated catch block
        e.printStackTrace();
    }

    return result;
}
```

The first thing we need to do is read the XSL script and get the data from it into a `String` that we can use with our `Transformer`. For this sample we stored the XSL file in the root of our Eclipse project. We modified the Ant build script to copy the XSL files to the Chap11Example.woa/Contents/Resources directory after the build is completed. Once the XSL files are in the Resources directory of our application, we can use the `WOResourceManager` to locate the files by name without having to hard-code a full path or URL.

Next, we need to get a Transformer to perform the actual XSL transformation. We could use the native Xalan API to get a reference to the Xalan transformation engine, but that ties us to a specific XSL parser. When our application has hard-coded references to a specific version of an XML or XSL parser, it can cause severe compatibility issues when trying to deploy in environments that have their own XML parsers. A good example is a Servlet container such as Apache Tomcat or Oracle Application Server. Apache uses Xerces/Xalan whereas Oracle uses an in-house-developed XML/XSL parser. Oracle requires some proprietary services that their parsers provide.

Sun resolved these issues by introducing the Java API for XML Processing (JAXP). It is a set of interfaces and classes that abstract the services needed for XML and XSL parsing. The full specification for JAXP can be found at `http://java.sun.com/xml/jaxp/index.jsp`.

As long as our code only uses the published org.w3c.xxx APIs and Java interfaces, JAXP ensures that we can swap out any JAXP-compliant XML/XSL parser at runtime and expect to get the same results. This allows us to move our code between Tomcat and Oracle Application Server without worrying about the services provided by each parser.

Our code uses the `TransformerFactory` class to create an instance of the XSL parser we will use. At runtime the `TransformerFactory` finds us the first available `Transformer` from all of the available class loaders (if you are using Java 1.4.*x*, there is a built-in XML and XSL parser that will be used unless there is another `Transformer` subclass on the classpath).

When the `transform()` method is called, the XML document is parsed and, as each XML element is read, the associated stylesheet is applied. If there is an instruction for the XML element, its XSL template is applied to that element. If there are no instructions, the node is skipped.

After the transform is complete, our simplified XML document looks like Listing 11-11.

Listing 11-11. *Simplified XML Shopping Cart*

```
<?xml version="1.0" encoding="utf-8"?>
<content>
  <array>
    <Product>
      <version>5000</version>
      <EOEditingContext>
        <version>5000</version>
      </EOEditingContext>
      <_EOIntegralKeyGlobalID>
        <entityName>Product</entityName>
        <subEntityName>Product</subEntityName>
        <Integer>
          <value>1</value>
        </Integer>
      </_EOIntegralKeyGlobalID>
      <EOEntityClassDescription>
        <entityName>Product</entityName>
      </EOEntityClassDescription>
      <name>15 Gig iPod</name>
      <spec>What a digital music player should be Smaller than ever (just 0.62↵
        inches thick), the iPod fits comfortably in the palm of your hand and↵
        slips easily into your pocket \u0014 and your life. At 5.6 ounces, it↵
        weighs less than two Compact Discs, and even many cell phones. And↵
        yet the iPod gives you a huge 15GB, 20GB or 40GB hard drive \u0014↵
        big enough to hold 10,000 songs. Do the math: that\u0019s four weeks↵
        of music \u0014 played continuously, 24/7 \u0014 or one new song a↵
        day for the next 27 years.</spec>
      <Double>
        <value>299.0</value>
      </Double>
      <Double>
        <value>5.6</value>
      </Double>
      <sku>15g-ipod</sku>
    </Product>
    <Product>
      <version>5000</version>
      <_EOIntegralKeyGlobalID>
        <entityName>Product</entityName>
        <subEntityName>Product</subEntityName>
        <Integer>
          <value>3</value>
        </Integer>
```

```
        </_EOIntegralKeyGlobalID>
        <name>Power Mac G5</name>
        <spec>Dual 2GHz PowerPC G5 1GHz frontside bus/processor 512K L2↩
           cache/processor 512MB DDR400 128-bit SDRAM Expandable to 8GB↩
           SDRAM 160GB Serial ATA SuperDrive Three PCI-X Slots ATI Radeon 9600↩
           Pro 64MB DDR video memory 56K internal modem </spec>
        <Double>
           <value>2999.0</value>
        </Double>
        <sku>dual-g5</sku>
     </Product>
  </array>
</content>
```

Even this simplified XML still contains some extraneous information that we are not going to use. But you can now see the general structure of the XML document and you can pick out the items in our shopping cart more easily. This initial transformation showed us the mechanics of how to perform an XSL transformation. Our next step will be to take this simplified XML structure and perform a much simpler XSL transformation into an HTML document that can be displayed in the browser.

Step 4: HTML Transformation

This step will show how to create an XSL stylesheet and will explain how the XSL engine processes our XML document using the instructions contained in the XSL stylesheet. We will not go into all of the capabilities of XSL transformation. That subject alone has already filled many large books.

This transformation will take the output from the previous step and apply a different stylesheet to generate HTML instead of XML. This is a prime example of the cool things you can do with XSL. You can easily chain the output from one process into the input of another process.

We are going to take the output shown in Listing 11-11 and use our `XMLSerializer` class with a different stylesheet. Listing 11-12 shows our new (and much simpler) XSL stylesheet that we are going to apply to Listing 11-11.

Listing 11-12. *CartHTML.xsl*

```
<?xml version="1.0" encoding="UTF-8" ?>
<xsl:stylesheet xmlns:xsl="http://www.w3.org/1999/XSL/Transform" version="1.0">
    <xsl:output method="html" encoding="UTF-8" omit-xml-declaration="no"
        indent="yes"/>
    <!-- Processes the tree root. -->
    <xsl:template match="/">
        <html>
            <head/>
            <body>
                <xsl:apply-templates select="*"/>
```

```
            </body>
        </html>
    </xsl:template>
    <xsl:template match="array">
        <table border="1">
            <tr>
                <td>Name</td>
                <td>Description</td>
                <td>Price</td>
            </tr>
            <xsl:apply-templates select="Product"/>
            <xsl:call-template name="total"/>
        </table>
    </xsl:template>
    <xsl:template match="Product">
        <tr>
            <td>
                <xsl:value-of select="name"/>
            </td>
            <td>
                <xsl:value-of select="spec"/>
            </td>
            <td align="right">
                <xsl:value-of select="format-number(⏎
                    Double[1]/value,'$#,###.00')"/>
            </td>
        </tr>
    </xsl:template>
    <xsl:template name="total">
        <tr>
            <td colspan="2" align="right">Total:</td>
            <td align="right">
                <xsl:value-of select="format-number(⏎
                    sum(Product/Double[1]/value),'$#,###.00')"/>
            </td>
        </tr>
    </xsl:template>
</xsl:stylesheet>
```

The XSL engine loads the XML document and starts parsing it from the top. As it comes to each element, it checks the XSL stylesheet that it loaded for matching xsl:templates for instructions on what to do. If there is no matching instruction, it proceeds along its happy trail. The first element processed is the root node of the XML document.

In Listing 11-11, the root node is called <content>. The XSL engine checks the stylesheet and finds a template match:

```
<!-- Processes the tree root. -->
    <xsl:template match="/">
...
```

The XSL engine then starts processing the instructions inside the template match. The first XSL directive that the engine comes to is `<xsl:apply-templates select="*"/>`; the current node is <array> since it is the first child under the root node. The apply-templates directive will cause the XSL engine to search for the matching template. Each xsl:template directive specifies an XPath pattern that can be applied to an XML document to return a collection of nodes that match the criteria in the directive. The XPath statement is essentially an address to one or more nodes in an XML document. The XPath is relative to the current node or fully qualified from the root node. For example, the XPath from the root node to our first product in Listing 11-11 is /content/array/Product. XML is case sensitive regardless of the platform the XSL is being processed on.

Once we get directed into the `<xsl:template match="array">` directive, the XSL engine will create an HTML table, add a header row with some labels, and then call another xsl template to format the Product information.

For each Product entry a new table row is added. The directive `<xsl:apply-templates select="Product"/>` returns *all* of the nodes that match that XPath statement (select="Product"). If your XML document contains 1000 products, the returned node list will contain 1000 nodes. The `<xsl:template match="Product">` directive will be called 1000 times and will add 1000 rows into our table created in the `<xsl:template match="array">` directive.

After the product data has been formatted into our HTML table, another directive is called to compute the total value of the products in our shopping cart. Listing 11-13 shows the use of an XSL function to compute and format the value of the shopping cart.

Listing 11-13. *Using XSL Functions*

```
<xsl:template name="total">
    <tr>
        <td colspan="2" align="right">Total:</td>
        <td align="right">
            <xsl:value-of select="format-number(sum(⏎
                Product/Double[1]/value),'$#,###.00')"/>
        </td>
    </tr>
</xsl:template>
```

The sum of all of the products is computed using the xsl:value-of directive with the sum() function. The sum() takes an XPath expression that it evaluates to add the values from. In our case, since this function was originally called from the <array> element level (`<xsl:call-template name="total"/>`) all of our XPath expressions must be relative from that point. The XPath expression Product/Double[1]/value indicates that you would find the value from the first Double element after the Product element.

```
<Product>
     <Double>
            <value>299.0</value>
      </Double>
</Product>
```

Formatting the result of the sum operation is done using another XSL function, `format-number`, which takes a value and a format mask.

This simple example should give you the basics of performing XSL transformations on an XML document. This example generated a simple HTML document, but the transform could just as easily have created any type of text-based document format including WAP, plain text, delimited flat file, etc. There are lots of resources on the Internet that show many examples of XSL transformation. The XSL specification can be found at `http://www.w3.org/TR/xsl/`.

The big question that people ask is: "Why would I want to go through all of this aggravation just to generate HTML from my database when I have WebObjects at my disposal?"

Being able to transform XML into HTML is really useful if you are integrating an external data feed into your application (think RSS syndication), or perhaps you want to output your data in a format suitable for cell phones or other nonstandard delivery channels. Instead of recompiling your WebObjects application every time a new delivery channel is dreamed up, let your WebObjects application dynamically load a different stylesheet and generate your output. While `WOComponents` are very useful, WebObjects is equally adept at creating useful application utilities that can leverage the power of EOF.

Our next step is to extend the functionality of our simple shopping cart by allowing the user to save a copy of their invoice on their computer for later use.

Step 5: PDF Generation

This step will take the output of the previous step and create a different type of output. (Are you starting to get the design pattern? Performing complex tasks in small chunks simplifies the process.) This time we will dynamically create an Adobe PDF formatted document. There are a number of APIs available that can be used to generate a PDF document. A popular open source Java-based API is iText (`http://www.lowagie.com/iText/`); another open source project is Apache's Formatting Objects Processor (FOP) specification.

According to the Apache FOP web site (`http://xml.apache.org/fop/index.html`), FOP is "the world's first print formatter driven by XSL formatting objects (XSL-FO) and the world's first output independent formatter. It is a Java application that reads a formatting object (FO) tree and renders the resulting pages to a specified output. Output formats currently supported include PDF, PCL, PS, SVG, XML (area tree representation), Print, AWT, MIF and TXT. The primary output target is PDF."

The XSL-FO specification is available at `http://www.w3.org/TR/2001/REC-xsl-20011015/`. In order to use FOP, we will need the binary Jar files from the Apache FOP project, available on our classpath for compiling and at runtime. FOP uses some other open source projects for XML parsing, XSL transformation, and the other output formats. The required Jar files are:

- fop.jar
- xerces.jar

- xalan.jar
- batik.jar
- avalon.jar

We will not dive deeply into the XSL-FO stylesheet shown in Listing 11-14, but you should be able to follow its general flow.

Listing 11-14. *XSL-FO Stylesheet*

```
<?xml version="1.0" encoding="UTF-8"?>
<xsl:stylesheet version="1.1" xmlns:xsl="http://www.w3.org/1999/XSL/Transform"
    xmlns:fo="http://www.w3.org/1999/XSL/Format"
    exclude-result-prefixes="fo">
  <xsl:output method="xml" version="1.0" omit-xml-declaration="no" indent="yes"/>
  <!-- ========================= -->
  <!-- root element: content -->
  <!-- ========================= -->
  <xsl:template match="/content">
    <fo:root xmlns:fo="http://www.w3.org/1999/XSL/Format">
      <fo:layout-master-set>
        <fo:simple-page-master master-name="simpleA4" page-height="29.7cm"
            page-width="21cm" margin-top="2cm" margin-bottom="2cm"
            margin-left="2cm" margin-right="2cm">
          <fo:region-body/>
        </fo:simple-page-master>
      </fo:layout-master-set>
      <fo:page-sequence master-reference="simpleA4">
        <fo:flow flow-name="xsl-region-body">
          <fo:block font-size="16pt" font-weight="bold"
             space-after="5mm">Order Form
          </fo:block>
          <fo:block font-size="10pt">
            <fo:table table-layout="fixed">
              <fo:table-column column-width="4cm"/>
              <fo:table-column column-width="5cm"/>
              <fo:table-column column-width="5cm"/>
              <fo:table-body>
                <xsl:apply-templates select="array/Product"/>
                <xsl:call-template name="Total"/>

              </fo:table-body>
            </fo:table>
          </fo:block>
        </fo:flow>
      </fo:page-sequence>
    </fo:root>
```

```
  </xsl:template>
  <!-- ========================= -->
  <!-- child element: Product     -->
  <!-- ========================= -->
  <xsl:template match="Product">
    <fo:table-row>
      <fo:table-cell>
        <fo:block>
          <xsl:value-of select="name"/>
        </fo:block>
      </fo:table-cell>
      <fo:table-cell>
        <fo:block space-after="5mm">
          <xsl:value-of select="spec"/>
        </fo:block>
      </fo:table-cell>
      <fo:table-cell>
        <fo:block>
          <xsl:value-of select="format-number(Double[1]/value,'$#,###.00')"/>
        </fo:block>
      </fo:table-cell>
    </fo:table-row>
  </xsl:template>

  <xsl:template name="Total">
       <fo:table-row>
      <fo:table-cell>
        <fo:block></fo:block>
      </fo:table-cell>
      <fo:table-cell>
        <fo:block font-weight="bold">Total:</fo:block>
      </fo:table-cell>
      <fo:table-cell>
        <fo:block font-weight="bold">
                <xsl:value-of select="format-number(sum(↵
                    array/Product/Double[1]/value),'$#,###.00')"/>
                </fo:block>
      </fo:table-cell>
        </fo:table-row>
  </xsl:template>

</xsl:stylesheet>
```

Again we start with the simplified XML that we generated in Listing 11-11 and use our `XMLSerializer` class to generate the data for our PDF file. The output of our XML-to-PDF transformation is a `byte[]`, We will take that `byte[]` and use it to generate an output that gets sent directly to the user without having to generate a temporary file on our file system. Listing 11-15 shows the source code for our `generatePDF()` method in our `XMLSerializer` class.

Listing 11-15. `XMLSerializer.generatePDF()` *method*

```
public static byte[] generatePDF(String xml, String xslfile) {
    ByteArrayOutputStream out = new ByteArrayOutputStream();
    try {
        Driver driver = new Driver();
        // Setup logging here: driver.setLogger(…
        driver.setRenderer(Driver.RENDER_PDF);

        // Setup the OutputStream for FOP
        driver.setOutputStream(out);

        // Make sure the XSL transformation's result is piped through to FOP
        Result res = new SAXResult(driver.getContentHandler());

        // Setup XML input
        Source src = new StreamSource(new StringReader(xml));

        // Setup Transformer
        WOApplication application = WOApplication.application();
        WOResourceManager resource_manager = application.resourceManager();
        String xsl = new String(resource_manager.bytesForResourceNamed(
            xslfile, null, null));
        Source xsltSrc = new StreamSource(new StringReader(xsl));
        TransformerFactory transformerFactory = TransformerFactory.newInstance();
        Transformer transformer = transformerFactory.newTransformer(xsltSrc);

        // Start the transformation and rendering process
        transformer.transform(src, res);
    } catch (IllegalArgumentException e) {
        // TODO Auto-generated catch block
        e.printStackTrace();
    } catch (TransformerConfigurationException e) {
        // TODO Auto-generated catch block
        e.printStackTrace();
    } catch (TransformerFactoryConfigurationError e) {
        // TODO Auto-generated catch block
        e.printStackTrace();
    } catch (TransformerException e) {
        // TODO Auto-generated catch block
        e.printStackTrace();
    }
    return out.toByteArray();
}
```

The bulk of this code is very similar to the code we used to transform our XML into HTML earlier. The biggest difference is that we need to get the FOP render driver into the mix. The first step is to create the FOP driver and place a reference to the ByteArrayOutputStream that we are going to use for the XSL transformation.

```
Driver driver = new Driver();
driver.setRenderer(Driver.RENDER_PDF);
driver.setOutputStream(out);
Result res = new SAXResult(driver.getContentHandler());
...
```

After the XSL transformation takes place, the resulting XSL-FO document is piped to the FOP driver for rendering into a PDF. The FOP driver reads thru the XSL-FO code and generates the appropriate PDF instructions. The resulting byte[] is returned to our ProductList WOComponent.

Listing 11-16 shows the source code for the WOComponent action used to generate the PDF and return it to the user.

Listing 11-16. *Generate PDF* WOComponent *Action*

```
public WOComponent generatePDF() {
    WOComponent nextPage = pageWithName("ProductList");
    data = new NSData(XMLSerializer.generatePDF(cartXML,
        "cartpdf.xsl"));
    return null;
    }

public void appendToResponse(WOResponse aResponse, WOContext arg1) {
    super.appendToResponse(aResponse, arg1);
    if (data != null) {
        aResponse.disableClientCaching();
        aResponse.removeHeadersForKey("Cache-Control");
        aResponse.removeHeadersForKey("pragma");
        aResponse.setHeader("application/pdf", "content-type");
        aResponse.setHeader("inline; attachment; filename=\"cart2.pdf\"",
            "content-disposition");
        aResponse.setHeader(Integer.toString(data.length()),
            "content-length");
        aResponse.setContent(data);
    }
}
```

The byte[] returned from the XMLSerializer.generatePDF() method is used to create an NSData object that will be returned to the user's browser in the HTTP response. The NSData object is stored as an instance variable on the ProductList class. During the appendToResponse portion of the request—response loop, we intercept the WOResponse from the WOComponent and modify it. We set the MIME type of the response to be application/pdf and specify the file name to be returned to the user. Finally, we replace the content of the response with our

NSData object. When the WOComponent returns to the user, a dialog box will be displayed prompting the user to save the file, as shown in Figure 11-3.

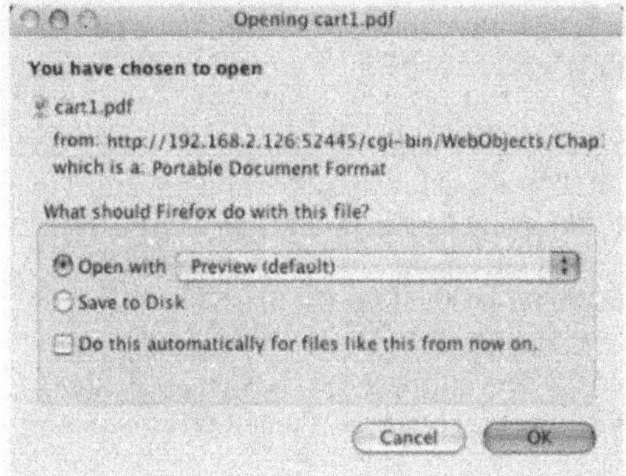

Figure 11-3. *PDF save dialog*

Step 6: Deserialization of XML Back to EO

The final step of our XML adventure will be to take the serialized data and rebuild our EO object. We are going to take the raw serialized data generated from the first step and execute the readObject() method of our Product class. The NSXMLInputStream class ignores the data we added into the original XML stream by using keys in our writeObject() method. Listing 11-17 shows the code used to deserialize our data back into an NSArray.

Listing 11-17. *Deserialize Cart Source Code*

```
public WOComponent deserializeCart() {
    ...
    NSArray results = XMLSerializer.deserializeArray(cartXML);
    ...
}
public static NSArray deserializeArray(String rawxml) {
    NSArray results = null;
    ...
    // Create a stream from the input file.
    ByteArrayInputStream input_stream =
        new ByteArrayInputStream(rawxml.getBytes());
    // Create an XML-input stream.
    NSXMLInputStream xml_stream = new NSXMLInputStream(input_stream);
    // Read the data.
    results = (NSArray)xml_stream.readObject();
    // Close the streams.
    xml_stream.close();
    input_stream.close();
    ...
    return results;
```

The `XMLSerializer.deserializeArray()` takes our raw serialized XML as its input. We then create an input stream and use it to create an `NSXMLInputStream` class. `NSXMLInputStream` does all of the magic of converting the complex serialized XML back into the original `NSArray` of Products. By calling the `readObject()` on the `NSXMLInputStream()`, the XML data is parsed; as each object is created, its `readObject()` method is called to perform any specific initializations required to make the objects usable.

The resulting deserialized array actually contains an `NSArray` of faults instead of Products. Once you access any of the attributes or relationships, the data is retrieved and presented to you. This is convenient if you are storing some state about the last interaction with the system and you want to allow the user to pick up where they left off; the key information can be retrieved and then the latest version of the data can be fetched from the database. If your needs are such that you are moving to a different machine and will not have access to the original database, you will probably need to add the keys during the `writeObject()` method and provide some methods to reload your data during the `readObject()` method called when deserializing the data.

Summary

This chapter introduced the WebObjects developer to some exciting new concepts that open a wide range of possibilities for extending the features and functionality of our WebObjects applications. The XML specification and its supporting technologies are growing very rapidly. Mainstream technologies such as Web Services, RSS syndication, and Web logging ("blogging") are all XML-based technologies. All of the major vendors are providing XML support in their tools. XML is making huge inroads in the EDI marketplace, rapidly replacing older legacy technologies.

The original promise of using XML as the universal data structure has yet to be realized, but great strides are being made across industries in creating standardized XML Schemas to describe complex business processes and interactions. Developing a solid understanding of the foundations of XML processing is essential to remain competitive in the job marketplace. Utilizing XML technology wisely in your applications can add great flexibility and make integration with other applications and technologies much simpler. Go forth and transform your world!

APPENDIX

■ ■ ■

Setting Up the Code

This appendix covers installing and configuring Eclipse, FrontBase, and the code supplied with this book, Practical WebObjects. We assume that you already have WebObjects installed and your web server set up.

Installing FrontBase

The scripts provided to create the database and tables are for FrontBase, which is what we recommend. We also provide an EOJDBCPrototypes entity for OpenBase, but no scripts are provided. As EOF/JDBC is database neutral, you can also make EOJDBCPrototypes entities for other databases if you don't want to use either FrontBase or OpenBase. If you are not using FrontBase, you will have to use your database tools and EOModeler to create the database and tables.

Assuming that you will be using FrontBase, you will need to have FrontBase installed somewhere where your development machine can access it. FrontBase is sufficiently lightweight that it can easily be run on your development machine. If you don't already have FrontBase installed, you can download a free copy from `http://www.frontbase.com/`. If you will be using a FrontBase installation on another machine, you will still need to download and install the WebObjects 5 Plugin for FrontBase.

Installing Eclipse

We will skip any description of Eclipse, as it is covered in Chapter 1. The first thing to do is download Eclipse. We recommend version 2.1.2, as it is more stable than the 3.*x* beta releases. There are versions of WOLips that will work with the 3.*x* versions of Eclipse if you must use that. Eclipse can be downloaded from `http://www.eclipse.org/downloads/index.php`.

NOTE The final version of Eclipse 3.0 will probably be released before you read this. The installation procedure should remain the same, with the exception of the Ant patch (see the following), which should no longer be needed.

Unpack (unzip) the download and copy it somewhere that does not have a space in the path name—C:\Program Files is not a good choice! Either /Developer/Applications or ~/Applications on OS X will work, or something like C:\Programs on Windows.

Launch the Eclipse application to create an initial workspace. There is a readme-eclipse.html file in the readme subdirectory of the Eclipse installation that, among other things, describes how to have Eclipse start up with a different workspace location. This can be useful to keep projects isolated and to keep the code for this book out of your work. The Working Set concept of Eclipse (whereby you can choose to display only a subset of your projects for editing) is another, and easier, way of keeping things organized and manageable.

Stop here, pour a large cup of your favorite beverage, and get to know Eclipse. You will get a lot more out of it if you follow this advice. It is extensive and has some concepts—Perspective and View in particular—that you may find confusing at first. Jumping straight into WOLips is not going to make the transition easier.

The Eclipse Help system has a wealth of information. The first thing to do is to go through the Basic Tutorial in the "Getting Started" section of the *Workbench User Guide*. That will give you an overview of where things are, what they are called, and how the Workbench is laid out. Then pay close attention to the Basic Tutorial in the "Getting Started" section in the *Java Development User Guide*.

TIP Pick up a tip a day in the "Tips and Tricks" section in the *Java Development User Guide*.

Now that you have a clue, make a simple HelloWorld application. Learn how to configure different views, set filters on views, edit and compile code, run the application in normal and debug modes, and use the built-in JUnit unit testing.

A Word on Eclipse Directories

There are some directories under the main Eclipse installation that you should be aware of. The most important one is the plugins directory. Some Eclipse plug-ins get installed manually by being copied into this directory. Eclipse needs to be restarted to see the new plug-in. The other important one is the workspace directory. This is the default place for Eclipse to create new projects. You can launch Eclipse with a `-data` option specifying a different directory. Under the workspace directory is .metadata, which contains logs, preferences, and configuration and other occasionally useful information.

Patching Ant

Eclipse makes extensive use of Ant (`http://ant.apache.org`), a Java-based build tool. Unfortunately, the version that comes with Eclipse has memory leaks. This can result in Eclipse responding slowly, crashing frequently, and in general being unusable. A workaround is available from the same fine folks who brought you WOLips. Before you start really working with Eclipse, you'll want to download and install this patch. Trust us. The patched Ant plug-in is available from `http://objectstyle.org/woproject/compatibilty_matrix.html`.

Installing WOLips

Start Eclipse, pull down the Help menu, and select Software Updates, then Update Manager to open the Install/Update perspective. You can also open this from the Open Perspective option on Window menu. But you already knew that, of course, seeing as how you've already gone on the tour that we recommended and did not just charge ahead. Right?

Right-click (or Ctrl+click) in the Feature Updates pane, and select New, then Site Bookmark. Name the bookmark WOLips and set the URL to `http://www.objectstyle.org/woproject/update/`.

Expand the new WOLips node. In this pane you will see three features: Profiling, Tests, and WOLips. Right now we are only concerned with the WOLips feature, so expand that one as shown in Figure A-1. Select the one with the highest number and click the Install Now button that appears in the Preview pane. You will need to restart Eclipse after installation is complete.

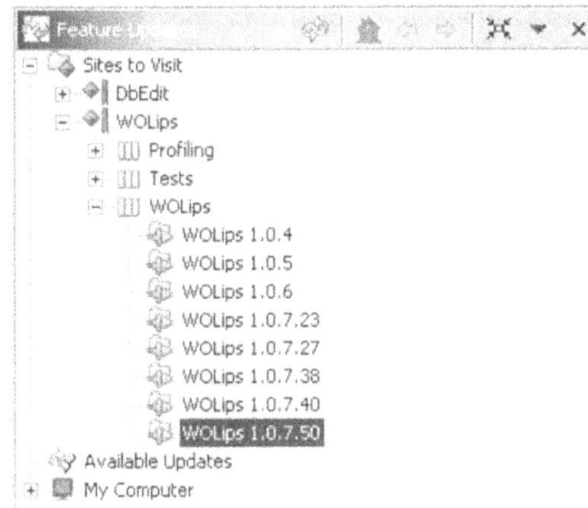

Figure A-1. *The WOLips plug-in with its WOLips feature expanded*

Installing EOGenerator

The code you will download in the next section includes the eos generated by EOGenerator. If you would like to regenerate them, you will need to download and install EOGenerator (`http://www.rubicode.com/Software/EOGenerator/`). Follow the instructions on the web site to install.

Once you have installed it, you'll need to edit each project's build.xml file to properly reference the executable. In each project that generates eos, there will be an Ant target that begins

```
<!-- Generate EOs -->
<target name="generate.eos" depends="setProps">
```

You will need to update the executable path in this target to the location where you have installed the EOGenerator executable. Here is one of the parameters from the PracticalUtilities framework:

```
<exec executable="${wo.wolocalroot}/Developer/Executables/eogenerator">
```

Modify this path to point to the location of your EOGenerator executable. Note that there may be more than one exec parameter, and you will have to change each one.

You will also need to change the referenced model paths (each project that has eos to generate will at least reference the EOPrototypes.eomodel from the EOJDBCPrototypes framework). Look for a parameter that looks like

```
<arg path="${local.framework.dir}/EOJDBCPrototypes.framework/Resources/➥
    EOPrototypes.eomodeld" />
```

As you can see, this assumes that the EOPrototypes eo model is installed in the local framework directory. You can change this to point to the place where you have installed the framework. (The framework doesn't actually have to be installed—just point to the eo model, wherever you have put it.)

Getting Ready to Install the Code

There are several pieces to this and a few steps that need to be followed.

Get the Practical WebObjects File

Download the code the for this book, PracticalWebObjects.tar.gz, from the downloads section of the Apress website at `http://www.apress.com`.

Unpack (with MacSuffit, WinZip, gnutar, etc.) this file into a directory. Remember: don't unpack it anyplace with a space in the path. WebObjects does not like this! We will refer to this as the PracticalWebObjects directory.

Install the Jass4Eclipse Plug-in

This step is optional. All of the code will run without this but you won't get the benefit of Design by Contract. Under the PracticalWebObjects directory you will find a Jass4Eclipse directory that contains Jass4Eclipse_<version>.zip. At present this plug-in needs to be installed manually. Unzip this to the plugins directory under your Eclipse installation. If Eclipse is running, you will need to restart it for this plug-in to be registered.

For more details on this plug-in, see ReadMe.html in the Jass4Eclipse directory. The most recent version of this plug-in can be downloaded from `http://www.global-village.net/jass4eclipse`.

Configuring Eclipse

We have used two classpath variables to make setting up projects easier. One is for JUnit unit testing and the other is for Jass Design by Contract. You will need to define these even if you are not running the unit tests or using Design by Contract.

Select Preferences under the Window menu. Expand the Java node in the tree on the left and select the Classpath Variables node. Click New. The name is JUNIT. The path is to the junit.jar file in the JUnit plug-in installed with Eclipse—for example, C:\Eclipse\plugins\org.junit_3.8.1/junit.jar (). Your New Variable dialogue box should look like Figure A-2.

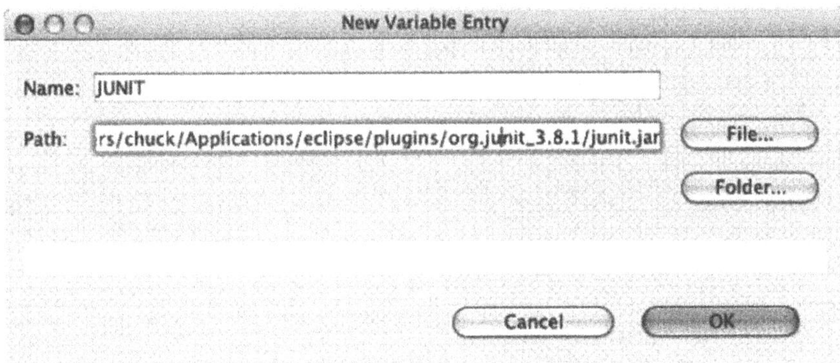

Figure A-2. *The new JUNIT classpath variable*

Create another classpath variable. Name this one JASS. The path is to the jass-rt.jar file in the Jass4Eclipse plug-in installed with Eclipse—for example, C:\Eclipse\plugins\net.globalvillage.eclipse.jassplugin_0.1.0\jass-rt.jar. If you decided not to install Jass4Eclipse, you can define this variable to be anything you like, but it does need to be defined.

You might want to take this opportunity to set other Java-related preferences such as code formatting and import preferences. Poke around a bit and see what is there.

Installing the Practical WebObjects Frameworks

The example applications for each chapter depend on a small set of core frameworks. These need to be imported into Eclipse before the applications. Importing a project into Eclipse makes it available but does not move it into the workspace directory.

Importing the Projects

Select the Import option from the File menu, and then select the Existing Project Into Workspace type. Navigate to where you unpacked the source and select EOJDBCPrototypes, then Finish. The EOJDBCPrototypes project should appear in the Eclipse window under the Navigator or Package Explorer view. If you can't see it, open one of these views.

■ **CAUTION** There is (or was) a bug in the import function of Eclipse that results in an incomplete build when you import a project. Select the newly imported project, open the Projects menu, and select Rebuild Project. Then right-click or Ctrl+click the project and select Refresh.

Repeat the preceding process, importing the PracticalUtilities framework. These two frameworks can be used in your own applications. There is one more project to import at this time, PWOExampleApp; this is a framework of common code used in the example applications in this book. Figure A-3 shows the Navigator view after these projects have been imported.

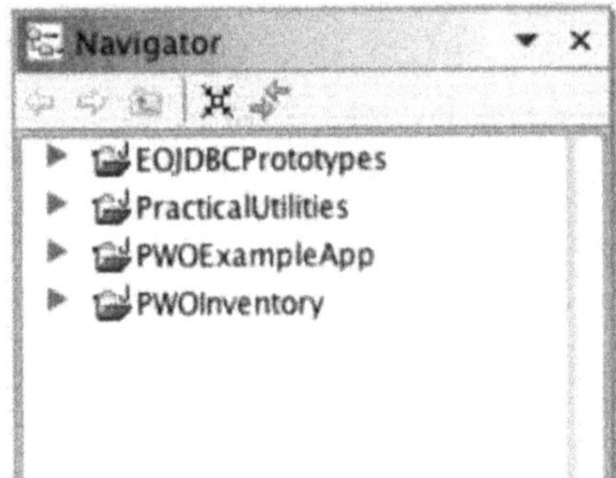

Figure A-3. *Navigator view after importing base Practical WebObjects projects*

Setting up the Database

You should have the database software installed by this point. Now we will create the database, user, and schema. There are Ant tasks in the build.xml file of the PracticalUtilities framework to handle these tasks. Before you run these, you will need to edit the PracticalWebobjects.properties file in the directory where you unpacked the source. Change the sql92 definition to point to the FrontBase sql92 tool.

■ **NOTE** The scripts assume that you have not changed the default FrontBase admin login of `_system` with no password. If you have password-protected this account (a good idea for production!) then you will need to edit the CreatePracticalWebObjectsDB.script and RemovePracticalWebObjectsDB.script files in the DatabaseSetup directory. Also, the scripts create a user and schema named PWUSER. You should use this user when working with the database.

Open the Ant view in Eclipse if it is not already open. Load the build file for the PracticalUtilities framework. Expand the node for this framework and double-click on the `db.create` task (see Figure A-4). When this has finished, double-click on the `db.create.schema` task. The `db.drop` task will remove the database created by `db.create`. Once the PracticalWebObjects database is created and running, you can use the `refresh_database` task to run the `db.drop`, db.create, and db.create.schema tasks together. This can be useful when you want to start from a clean state.

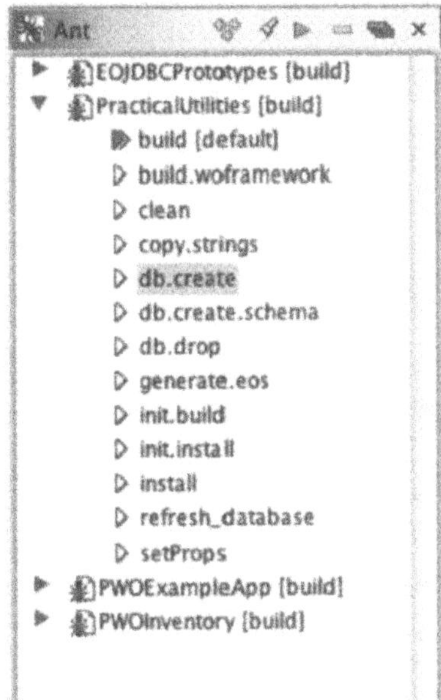

Figure A-4. *The Ant view showing the tasks in the build.xml file of the PracticalUtilities project*

■ **TIP** If the `db.create.schema` task stops with an error about not finding the class `com.frontbase.jdbc.FBJDriver`, this means that the FrontBase JDBC driver was not installed into the JRE that is being used to run Eclipse. This is often a problem on Windows. One solution is to determine which JRE is being used with Eclipse, then find the frontbasejdbc.jar file and copy it into the Java Extensions (jre\lib\ext) directory for that JRE. The other option is to start Eclipse with an explicit indication of which JRE to use by specifying it on the command line: `-vm C:\j2sdk1.4.1_06\jre\bin\javaw.exe`.

Run Unit Tests to Verify Installation

By now everything should be set up to the point where unit tests can be run. We are going to run the unit tests for PracticalUtilities to verify that all is in order before proceeding to import the other projects.

Start by selecting the PracticalUtilities project (in the Navigator or Package Explorer) and then selecting the Run option from the Run menu. Select the JUnit Configuration node and click New. It should be automatically named Practical Utilities for you.

On the Test tab, select the Test Class radio button and use the Search button to select the `com.apress.practicalwo.practicalutilities.tests.AllTests` class (see Figure A-5). We have found that this method is usually less prone to surprises than the All Tests option.

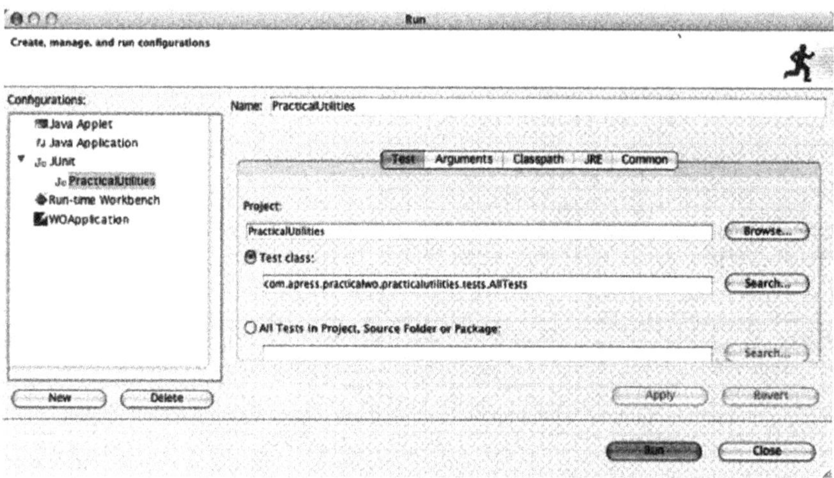

Figure A-5. *Test tab of JUnit launcher for PracticalUtilities framework*

The default working directory for JUnit tests is not suitable for WebObjects, as it prevents proper bundle loading. On the Arguments tab, uncheck Use Default Working Directory at bottom. Click Browse next to Workspace and select PracticalUtilities/PracticalUtilities.framework (see Figure A-6). For an application, you would select the ApplicationName.woa directory.

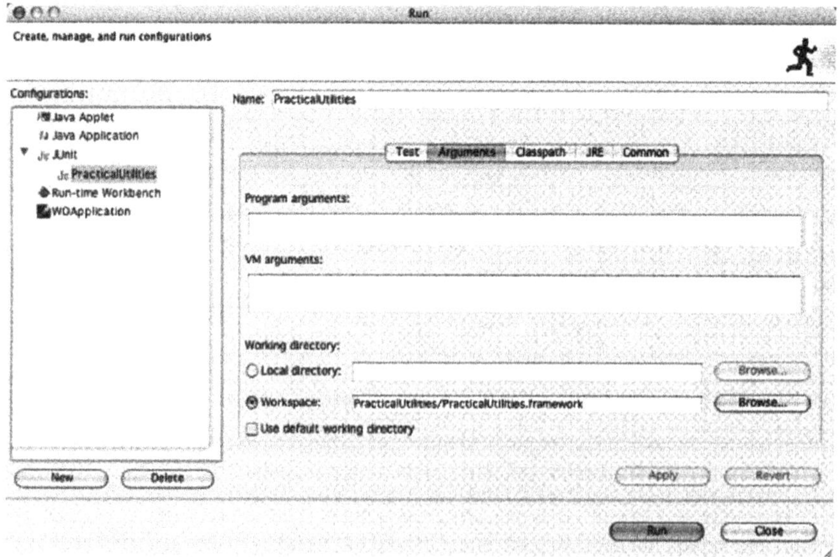

Figure A-6. *The proper working directory for WebObjects frameworks*

Test configuration is now complete. Click Apply, then click Run. All the tests should pass. There will be one message in the console about "Failed to fetch class com.apress.practicalwo .practicalutilities.tests.CooperatingEditingContextTestObject." You should ignore this; it is part of the tests.

If all the tests pass, this shows that the projects are set up correctly and database connectivity is working. If the tests don't pass, there is no point in going further. You will need to look at the failure messages to determine where you have gone wrong.

Setup for Each Chapter

From this point on, importing projects and other setup tasks can be done on a chapter-by-chapter basis as you get to them. With the exception of PWOInventory, you will need to leave the preceding projects open in Eclipse, as they are needed for building.

Chapter 1

There are no applications for this chapter, hence no setup to do.

Chapter 2

There are two projects in this chapter. Import the projects Chap2MutableAttributes and Chap2BigDecimalTest. Chap2MutableAttributes is a WebObjects application while Chap2BigDecimalTest is a single-class Java application.

You will need to configure a standard Java Application launcher for Chap2BigDecimalTest. Start by selecting the Chap2BigDecimalTest project (in the Navigator or Package Explorer) and then selecting the Run option from the Run menu. Select the Java Application node and click New. You will need to change the name from New_configuration to something more recognizable, such as Chap2BigDecimalTest.

Click the Search button to select the main class, `com.apress.practicalwo.ch2.BigDecimalTest`. Then click Apply and then Run at the bottom. The launch configuration will be saved and the application will run. You can rerun it at any time from the Run menu.

You will also need to configure a WOApplication launcher for the Chap2MutableAttributes project. First make sure that the application has been built and that the folder Chap2MutableAttributes.woa is visible in Eclipse. If it is not, right-click or Ctrl+click on the project and select Refresh.

Start by selecting the Chap2MutableAttributes project (in the Navigator or Package Explorer) and then selecting the Run option from the Run menu. Select the WOApplication node and click New. You will need to change the name from New_configuration to something more recognizable, such as Chap2MutableAttributes. Click the Search button and select the main class, `com.apress.practicalwo.ch2.Application`.

There is a bit more configuration that is needed for this particular WOApplication, as it has no UI. Switch to the Arguments tab and add `-DWOAutoOpenInBrowser=false`. Switch to the WO tab and uncheck the `-WOAutoOpenInBrowser true` option. Both of these steps are needed due to a defect in how WOLips sets these: some of the options on the WO tab are for the default value. Unchecking them results in the default value being used—in other words, no change at all!

Go back to the Arguments tab and at the bottom verify that Use Default Working Directory is unchecked and that the Working Directory is set to Chap2MutableAttributes/Chap2MutableAttributes.woa in the Workspace. If it is not, this probably means that it was not already built. You will have to ensure that it gets built and manually change this, or the application will not run properly.

■NOTE By default WOLips creates the .woa and .framework files in a dist directory under the project. We've altered the build files in this book to build directly in the project directory.

Finally, click Apply and then Run at the bottom. The launch configuration will be saved and the application will run briefly and then stop. There is no HTML UI for this application. You can rerun it at any time from the Run menu.

Chapter 3

There is only a single project, Chap3App, that needs to be imported for this chapter. You will need to configure a WOApplication launcher for the Chap3App project. First make sure that the application has been built and that the folder Chap3App.woa is visible in Eclipse. If it is not, right-click or Ctrl+click on the project and select Refresh.

Start by selecting the Chap3App project (in the Navigator or Package Explorer) and then selecting the Run option from the Run menu. Select the WOApplication node and click New. You will need to change the name from New_configuration to something more recognizable, such as Chap3App. Click the Search button and select the main class, `com.apress.practicalwo.ch3.Application`.

Switch to the Arguments tab and at the bottom verify that Use Default Working Directory is unchecked and that the Working Directory is set to Chap3App/Chap3App.woa in the Workspace. If it is not, this probably means that it was not already built. You will have to ensure that it gets built and manually change this, or the application will not run properly.

Finally, click Apply and then Run at the bottom. The launch configuration will be saved and the application will run and open in the browser. You can rerun it at any time from the Run menu.

Chapter 4

This next chapter is much more complicated. One of the sections in this chapter deals with HTTPS/SSL and another with LDAP. You will not only need to be using a web server, but you need to be running a web server configured for HTTPS/SSL. You will also need to have a running LDAP server to test the LDAP functionality.

Configuring Apache with mod_ssl on Windows 2000

Things have gotten better in recent years in regard to installing Apache on Windows. However, it always seems to work out to be painful and not a process that you will be eager to repeat. We'll point you to an outdated How To and wish you the best: `http://raibledesigns.com/tomcat/ssl-howto.html`. Be brave—it can be done!

Configuring Apache with mod_ssl on OS X

Once again the Mac users get off easy. Apache is preinstalled and Apple provides a very straightforward set of instructions for configuring mod_ssl at `http://developer.apple.com/internet/macosx/modssl.html`. We're going to leave it all for you.

CAUTION There is an error in the preceding documentation at the time of this writing. You need to `cd /etc/httpd/ssl.key/` before removing encryption from the `server.key`.

Installing Open LDAP on Windows 2000

Hold on to your hats—this one is fun. This is an older port but it works well and saves you from having to attempt Microsoft's Active Directory stuff. You can download an archive from a link on this page: `http://lucas.bergmans.us/hacks/openldap/`.

When you unpack this, it will create a directory with a name like openldap-2_0_19_no_debug. We suggest renaming it to openldap, and we have used that name to refer to it. We also assume that the full directory path is C:\openldap and leave you to adjust this if you move it someplace else.

Use a text editor to edit the Registry file C:\openldap\cmu-sasl.reg and remove the entries for Kerberos, CRAM, and SCRAM plug-ins and change the directory from C:\\sasl-plugins\\ to C:\\openldap\\. Now double-click the cmu-sasl.reg file to integrate it into the Registry.

The configuration file installed is not suitable to our purposes. Copy the file PracticalWebObjects\CH4\win2k_slapd.conf to C:\openldap\slapd.conf. You will need to edit this file if OpenLDAP is not installed in C:\openldap.

For background details on the changes we made, see *8. Edit the configuration file* at `http://www.openldap.org/doc/admin21/quickstart.html` or `http://www.devshed.com/Server_Side/Administration/LDAP/LDAP2/page4.html`.

The database for LDAP is not created automatically. You will need to manually create a new directory named openldap-ldbm under the C:\openldap directory. If you fail to do this, nothing will work.

Now we are ready to attempt starting the server. Open a command-line window and change to the C:\openladp directory, and start `slapd`. It should look like this:

```
C:\openldap>slapd
starting slapd...
entry is = [c:\openldap\saslANONYMOUS.dll]
entry is = [c:\openldap\saslPLAIN.dll]
```

Assuming that it started OK, we can perform a little verification test. Open a new command-line window, change to the C:\openldap directory, and do a test search to verify that everything is working:

```
C:\openldap>ldapsearch -x -b "" -s base "(objectclass=*)" namingContexts
entry is = [c:\openldap\saslANONYMOUS.dll]
entry is = [c:\openldap\saslPLAIN.dll]
version: 2

#
# filter: (objectclass=*)
# requesting: namingContexts
#
```

```
#
dn:
namingContexts: dc=practicalwebobjects,dc=apress,dc=com

# search result
search: 2
result: 0 Success

# numResponses: 2
# numEntries: 1
```

TIP If you don't want to type these commands, you can copy them from PracticalWebObjects\CH4\LDAPCheatSheet.txt.

We now know that the server is working. We can proceed to load the data for the examples in this chapter. Copy the PracticalWebObjects\CH4\boot.ldif file to C:\openldap. Load this into the LDAP database using the `ldapmodify` command:

```
C:\openldap>ldapmodify -a -x -D ↵
    "cn=Manager,dc=practicalwebobjects,dc=apress,dc=com" -W -f boot.ldif
entry is = [c:\openldap\saslANONYMOUS.dll]
entry is = [c:\openldap\saslPLAIN.dll]
Enter LDAP Password: secret
adding new entry "dc=practicalwebobjects,dc=apress,dc=com"
adding new entry "cn=Manager,dc=practicalwebobjects,dc=apress,dc=com"
```

TIP The password, `secret`, is defined in slapd.conf by `rootpw`.

Check that the addition of boot.ldif was successful by doing a search with `ldapsearch`:

```
C:\openldap>ldapsearch -x -b ↵
    "dc=practicalwebobjects,dc=apress,dc=com" "(objectclass=*)"
entry is = [c:\openldap\saslANONYMOUS.dll]
entry is = [c:\openldap\saslPLAIN.dll]
version: 2

#
# filter: (objectclass=*)
# requesting: ALL
#

# practicalwebobjects, apress, com
```

```
dn: dc=practicalwebobjects,dc=apress,dc=com
objectClass: dcObject
objectClass: organization
o: Practical WebObjects
dc: practicalwebobjects.apress

# Manager, practicalwebobjects, apress, com
dn: cn=Manager,dc=practicalwebobjects,dc=apress,dc=com
objectClass: organizationalRole
cn: Manager

# search result
search: 2
result: 0 Success

# numResponses: 3
# numEntries: 2
```

Now copy the PracticalWebObjects\CH4\users.ldif file to C:\openldap. Add the test users to the LDAP database using the ldapmodify command:

```
C:\openldap>ldapmodify -a -x -D ➥
    "cn=Manager,dc=practicalwebobjects,dc=apress,dc=com" -W -f users.ldif
entry is = [c:\openldap\saslANONYMOUS.dll]
entry is = [c:\openldap\saslPLAIN.dll]
Enter LDAP Password: secret
adding new entry "mail=chill@global-village.net,
dc=practicalwebobjects,dc=apress,dc=com"
adding new entry "mail=sacha@global-village.net,
dc=practicalwebobjects,dc=apress,dc=com"
adding new entry "userid=bobs,dc=practicalwebobjects,
dc=apress,dc=com"
```

Perform a search to verify that they were added:

```
C:\openldap>ldapsearch -x -b ➥
    "dc=practicalwebobjects,dc=apress,dc=com" "(objectclass=inetOrgPerson)"
entry is = [U:\Programs\openldap-2_0_19_debug\saslANONYMOUS.dll]
entry is = [U:\Programs\openldap-2_0_19_debug\saslPLAIN.dll]
version: 2

#
# filter: (objectclass=inetOrgPerson)
# requesting: ALL
#

# chill@global-village.net, practicalwebobjects, apress, com
dn: mail=chill@global-village.net, dc=practicalwebobjects,
```

```
dc=apress,dc=com
objectClass: inetOrgPerson
cn: Chuck
sn: Hill
mail: chill@global-village.net

# sacha@global-village.net, practicalwebobjects, apress, com
dn: mail=sacha@global-village.net, dc=practicalwebobjects,
dc=apress,dc=com
objectClass: inetOrgPerson
cn: Sacha
sn: Mallais
mail: sacha@global-village.net

# bobs, practicalwebobjects, apress, com
dn: userid=bobs,dc=practicalwebobjects,dc=apress,dc=com
uid: bobs
userPassword:: eWVydW5jbGU=
objectClass: inetOrgPerson
cn: Robert
sn: Dinero
mail: bobs@practicalwebobjects.apress.com

# search result
search: 2
result: 0 Success

# numResponses: 4
# numEntries: 3
```

We're done! You can user Ctrl+C to stop `slapd` now, but it will need to be running when you are working with the LDAP code in this chapter.

■ **NOTE** If you are using an older version of WebObjects, you will need to follow the directions at `http://developer.apple.com/documentation/LegacyTechnologies/WebObjects/WebObjects_5.1/PostInstall/EOAdaptors/Installation.html` to allow EOModeler to connect to an LDAP server.

Configuring Open LDAP on OS X

OpenLDAP is part of OS X so there is nothing to install. However, it is configured to work with netinfo, which is not what we want. The LDAP daemon, `slapd`, is normally started with `/System/Library/StartupItems/LDAP/LDAP start` and uses the standard configuration file /etc/openldap/slapd.conf. We will use neither of these so as to not affect the default configuration.

We have included a configuration file that you can use as a base. Copy the file PracticalWebObjects/CH4/slapd.conf to ~/Library/pslapd.conf. You will need to edit this file to set the path for `directory`. If the directory does not exist, you must created it before starting `slapd`. If you fail to do this, nothing will work.

For background details on the changes we made, see *8. Edit the configuration file* at `http://www.openldap.org/doc/admin21/quickstart.html` or `http://www.devshed.com/Server_Side/Administration/LDAP/LDAP2/page4.html`.

Now we are ready to attempt starting the server. Open a terminal window and start `slapd` like this (change the directory after `-f` if you did not place the slapd.conf file in ~/Library):

```
sudo /usr/libexec/slapd  -f ~/Library/slapd.conf
```

The daemon immediately forks and returns to the command line so you will need to use `ps auxww | grep slapd` to see if it started. If it did not, there was a configuration error. You can get an extensive diagnostic dump with this command line:

```
sudo /usr/libexec/slapd  -f ~/Library/slapd.conf -t -d 255
```

TIP If you don't want to type these commands, you can copy them from PracticalWebObjects\CH4\LDAPCheatSheet.txt.

Assuming that it started OK, we can perform a little verification test. Do a test `ldapsearch` to verify that everything is working:

```
[MiniMe:~] chuck% ldapsearch -x -b "" -s base "(objectclass=*)" namingContexts
# extended LDIF
#
# LDAPv3
# base <> with scope base
# filter: (objectclass=*)
# requesting: namingContexts
#

#
dn:
namingContexts: dc=practicalwebobjects,dc=apress,dc=com

# search result
search: 2
result: 0 Success

# numResponses: 2
# numEntries: 1
```

We now know that the server is working. We can proceed to load the data for the examples in this chapter. Use this command to load the basic information into the LDAP database with the `ldapmodify` command:

```
[MiniMe:~] chuck% ldapmodify -a -x -D "cn=Manager,dc=practicalwebobjects, ↵
    dc=apress,dc=com" -W -f /Users/chuck/PracticalWebObjects/CH4/boot.ldif
Enter LDAP Password:
adding new entry "dc=practicalwebobjects,dc=apress,dc=com"
adding new entry "cn=Manager,dc=practicalwebobjects,dc=apress,dc=com"
```

TIP The password, `secret`, is defined in slapd.conf as `rootpw`.

Check that the addition of boot.ldif was successful by performing an `ldapsearch`:

```
[MiniMe:~] chuck% ldapsearch -x -b "dc=practicalwebobjects,dc=apress,dc=com" ↵
    "(objectclass=*)"
# extended LDIF
#
# LDAPv3
# base <dc=practicalwebobjects,dc=apress,dc=com> with scope sub
# filter: (objectclass=*)
# requesting: ALL
#

# practicalwebobjects.apress.com
dn: dc=practicalwebobjects,dc=apress,dc=com
objectClass: dcObject
objectClass: organization
o: Practical WebObjects
dc: practicalwebobjects

# Manager, practicalwebobjects.apress.com
dn: cn=Manager,dc=practicalwebobjects,dc=apress,dc=com
objectClass: organizationalRole
cn: Manager

# search result
search: 2
result: 0 Success

# numResponses: 3
# numEntries: 2
```

Now we will add the users to the LDAP database using `ldapmodify`:

```
[MiniMe:~] chuck% ldapmodify -a -x -D "cn=Manager,dc=practicalwebobjects, ↵
    dc=apress,dc=com" -W -f /Users/chuck/PracticalWebObjects/CH4/users.ldif
Enter LDAP Password:
adding new entry "mail=chill@global-village.net, dc=practicalwebobjects,
dc=apress,dc=com"
adding new entry "mail=sacha@global-village.net, dc=practicalwebobjects,
dc=apress,dc=com"
adding new entry "userid=bobs,dc=practicalwebobjects,
dc=apress,dc=com"
```

Perform a search to verify that they were added:

```
[MiniMe:~] chuck% ldapsearch -x -b "dc=practicalwebobjects,dc=apress,dc=com" ↵
    "(objectclass=inetOrgPerson)"
# extended LDIF
#
# LDAPv3
# base <dc=practicalwebobjects,dc=apress,dc=com> with scope sub
# filter: (objectclass=inetOrgPerson)
# requesting: ALL
#

# chill@global-village.net, practicalwebobjects.apress.com
dn: mail=chill@global-village.net,dc=practicalwebobjects,dc=apress,dc=com
objectClass: inetOrgPerson
cn: Chuck
sn: Hill
mail: chill@global-village.net

# sacha@global-village.net, practicalwebobjects.apress.com
dn: mail=sacha@global-village.net,dc=practicalwebobjects,dc=apress,dc=com
objectClass: inetOrgPerson
cn: Sacha
sn: Mallais
mail: sacha@global-village.net

# search result
search: 2
result: 0 Success

# numResponses: 3
# numEntries: 2
```

We're done! You can use `kill` to stop `slapd` now, but it will need to be running when you are working with the LDAP code in this chapter.

Classpath Variable for the Java Cryptography Extension

The first thing you will need to do is define a classpath variable for the Java Cryptography Extension (JCE) (see Figure A-7). Select Preferences under the Window menu. Expand the Java node in the tree on the left and select the Classpath Variables node. Click New. The name is JCE. The path is to the jce.jar file in the library directory of the JRE you are using—for example, C:\j2sdk1.4.1_06\jre\lib\jce.jar.

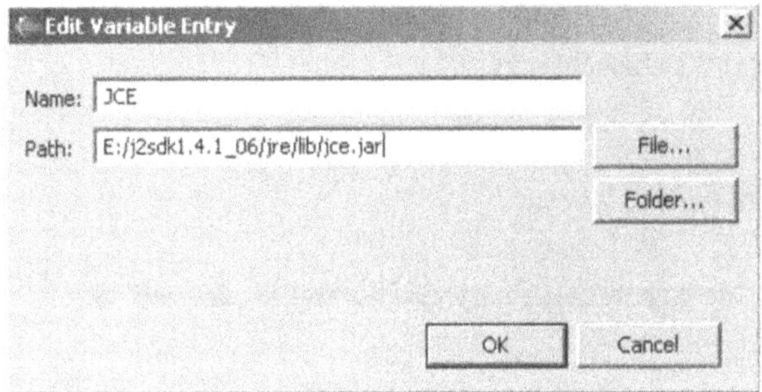

Figure A-7. *The JCE classpath variable*

■ **TIP** If you are using an older version of WebObjects with the 1.3.1 JDK you will need to download and install the Java Cryptography Extension (JCE). See the chapter text for details on where to get this. Point the JCE classpath variable to the jce1_2_2.jar file—for example, C:\Sun\jce1.2.2\lib\jce1_2_2.jar. You can also point to the one in the JRE/lib/ext (/Library/Java/Extensions on OS X) directory.

Importing and Configuring the Application

There is only a single project, Chap4App, that needs to be imported for this chapter. You will need to configure a WOApplication launcher for the Chap4App project. First make sure that the application has been built and that the folder Chap4App.woa is visible in Eclipse. If it is not, right-click or Ctrl+click on the project and select Refresh.

Start by selecting the Chap4App project (in the Navigator or Package Explorer) and then selecting the Run option from the Run menu. Select the WOApplication node and click New. You will need to change the name from New_configuration to something more recognizable, such as Chap4App. Click the Search button and select the main class, `com.apress.practicalwo.ch4app.Application`.

Switch to the Arguments tab and at the bottom verify that Use Default Working Directory is unchecked and that the Working Directory is set to Chap4App/Chap4App.woa in the Workspace. If it is not, this probably means that it was not already built. You will have to ensure that it gets built and manually change this, or the application will not run properly.

On the Arguments tab, add these Program arguments:

```
-DWODirectConnectEnabled=false -DWOAdaptorURL=http://host/cgi-bin/WebOjbects
```

Change `host` in the URL to your local machine name. This needs to match what is configured for the `ServerName` in Apache. Setting the adaptor URL here ensures that WO generates consistently formed URLs.

Switch to the WO tab and uncheck the `-WODirectConnectEnabled true` and `-WOAdaptorURL http://127.0.0.1/cgi-bin/WebObjects` options.

Finally, click Apply and then Run at the bottom. The launch configuration will be saved and the application will run and open in the browser. You can rerun it at any time from the Run menu. You will also need to make sure that your LDAP server is running if you want to test LDAP authentication.

Chapter 5

There is only a single project, Chap5App, that needs to be imported for this chapter. You will need to configure a WOApplication launcher for the Chap5App project. First make sure that the application has been built and that the folder Chap5App.woa is visible in Eclipse. If it is not, right-click or Ctrl+click on the project and select Refresh.

Start by selecting the Chap5App project (in the Navigator or Package Explorer) and then selecting the Run option from the Run menu. Select the WOApplication node and click New. You will need to change the name from New_configuration to something more recognizable, such as Chap5App. Click the Search button and select the main class, `com.apress.practicalwo.ch5.Application`.

Switch to the Arguments tab and at the bottom verify that Use Default Working Directory is unchecked and that the Working Directory is set to Chap5App/Chap5App.woa in the Workspace. If it is not, this probably means that it was not already built. You will have to ensure that it gets built and manually change this, or the application will not run properly.

Finally, click Apply and then Run at the bottom. The launch configuration will be saved and the application will run and open in the browser. You can rerun it at any time from the Run menu.

Chapter 6

There is only a single project, Chap6App, that needs to be imported for this chapter. You will need to configure a WOApplication launcher for the Chap6App project. First make sure that the application has been built and that the folder Chap6App.woa is visible in Eclipse. If it is not, right-click or Ctrl+click on the project and select Refresh.

Start by selecting the Chap6App project (in the Navigator or Package Explorer) and then selecting the Run option from the Run menu. Select the WOApplication node and click New. You will need to change the name from New_configuration to something more recognizable, such as Chap6App. Click the Search button and select the main class, `com.apress.practicalwo.ch6.Application`.

Switch to the Arguments tab and at the bottom verify that Use Default Working Directory is unchecked and that the Working Directory is set to Chap6App/Chap6App.woa in the Workspace. If it is not, this probably means that it was not already built. You will have to ensure that it gets built and manually change this, or the application will not run properly.

Finally, click Apply and then Run at the bottom. The launch configuration will be saved and the application will run and open in the browser. You can rerun it at any time from the Run menu.

Chapter 7

There is only a single project, Chap7App, that needs to be imported for this chapter. You will need to configure a WOApplication launcher for the Chap7App project. First make sure that the application has been built and that the folder Chap7App.woa is visible in Eclipse. If it is not, right-click or Ctrl+click on the project and select Refresh.

Start by selecting the Chap7App project (in the Navigator or Package Explorer) and then selecting the Run option from the Run menu. Select the WOApplication node and click New. You will need to change the name from New_configuration to something more recognizable, such as Chap7App. Click the Search button and select the main class, `com.apress.practicalwo.ch7.Application`.

Switch to the Arguments tab and at the bottom verify that Use Default Working Directory is unchecked and that the Working Directory is set to Chap7App/Chap7App.woa in the Workspace. If it is not, this probably means that it was not already built. You will have to ensure that it gets built and manually change this, or the application will not run properly.

Finally, click Apply and then Run at the bottom. The launch configuration will be saved and the application will run and open in the browser. You can rerun it at any time from the Run menu.

Chapter 8

There are no applications for this chapter, hence no setup to do.

Chapter 9

There are no applications for this chapter, hence no setup to do.

Chapter 10

The project for this chapter requires a servlet API library in order to compile. This Jar file is not included with the downloadable code for the book. It is part of the Tomcat download that you will also need to run the code in this chapter. Once you have downloaded and installed Tomcat, copy the file

```
common/lib/servlet-api.jar
```

(this directory is under the Tomcat installation) to

```
PracticalWebObjects\CH10\Chap10Example\jars
```

There is only a single project, Chap10Example, that needs to be imported for this chapter. First make sure that the application has been built and that the folder Chap10Example.woa is visible in Eclipse. If it is not, right-click or Ctrl+click on the project and select Refresh. There is no need to configure a WOApplication launcher for the Chap10Example project, as it is deployed in Tomcat. The chapter text covers the Tomcat deployment process in detail.

Chapter 11

The project for this chapter requires an XSL transformation file that is included in the WebObjects installation. This file is not included with the downloadable code for the book. You will need to copy it into the project, as it is needed at runtime. On OS X, XML serialization information is found at

```
/Documentation/Developer/WebObjects/XML_Serialization/
```

On Windows, the location is

```
C:\Apple\Documentation\Developer\WebObjects\XML_Serialization
```

Copy the file

```
projects/Transforming/Transformation/SimpleTransformation.xsl
```

into the directory

```
PracticalWebObjects\CH11\Chap11Example\
```

The project for this chapter also requires several Java libraries in order to compile and run. These Jar files are not included with the downloadable code for the book. You will need to download them yourself. The versions we have used are from the Formatting Objects Processor (FOP) distribution. They might not be the most recent version of each, but they do work.

Download the FOP binary distribution from `http://www.apache.org/dyn/closer.cgi/xml/fop`. Unzip this into a directory. You will then need to copy several Jars from the unzipped FOP distribution into the example application and rename them.

Copy and rename lib\avalon-framework-<*version*>.jar to

```
PracticalWebObjects\CH11\Chap11Example\jars\avalon-framework.jar
```

Copy lib\batik.jar to

```
PracticalWebObjects\CH11\Chap11Example\jars\batik.jar
```

Copy build\fop.jar to

```
PracticalWebObjects\CH11\Chap11Example\jars\fop.jar
```

Copy and rename lib\xalan-<version>.jar to

```
PracticalWebObjects\CH11\Chap11Example\jars\xalan.jar
```

Copy and rename lib\xercesImpl-<version>.jar to

```
PracticalWebObjects\CH11\Chap11Example\jars\xercesImpl.jar
```

Copy lib\xml-apis.jar to

```
PracticalWebObjects\CH11\Chap11Example\jars\xml-apis.jar
```

There is only a single project, Chap11Example, that needs to be imported for this chapter. You will need to configure a WOApplication launcher for the Chap11Example project. First make sure that the application has been built and that the folder Chap11Example.woa is visible in Eclipse. If it is not, right-click or Ctrl+click on the project and select Refresh.

Start by selecting the Chap11Example project (in the Navigator or Package Explorer) and then selecting the Run option from the Run menu. Select the WOApplication node and click New. You will need to change the name from New_configuration to something more recognizable, such as Chap11Example. Click the Search button and select the main class, `com.apress.practicalwo.chap11.Application`.

Switch to the Arguments tab and at the bottom verify that Use Default Working Directory is unchecked and that the Working Directory is set to Chap11Example/Chap11Example.woa in the Workspace. If it is not, this probably means that it was not already built. You will have to ensure that it gets built and manually change this, or the application will not run properly.

Finally, click Apply and then Run at the bottom. The launch configuration will be saved and the application will run and open in the browser. You can rerun it at any time from the Run menu.

Index

D

X

GPSR Compliance
The European Union's (EU) General Product Safety Regulation (GPSR) is a set of rules that requires consumer products to be safe and our obligations to ensure this.

If you have any concerns about our products, you can contact us on

ProductSafety@springernature.com

In case Publisher is established outside the EU, the EU authorized representative is:

Springer Nature Customer Service Center GmbH
Europaplatz 3
69115 Heidelberg, Germany

www.ingramcontent.com/pod-product-compliance
Ingram Content Group UK Ltd.
Pitfield, Milton Keynes, MK11 3LW, UK
UKHW051126260726
13967UKWH00010B/2888

* 9 7 8 1 4 3 0 2 5 2 3 9 9 *